FOOD, ENERGY, AND SOCIETY
REVISED EDITION

FOOD, ENERGY, AND SOCIETY
REVISED EDITION

David Pimentel and Marcia Pimentel, Editors

UNIVERSITY PRESS OF COLORADO

Published by the University Press of Colorado
P. O. Box 849
Niwot, Colorado 80544
(303) 530-5337

First published by Edward Arnold (Publishers) Ltd., London.

The University Press of Colorado is a cooperative publishing enterprise supported, in part, by Adams State College, Colorado State University, Fort Lewis College, Mesa State College, Metropolitan State College of Denver, University of Colorado, University of Northern Colorado, University of Southern Colorado, and Western State College of Colorado.

Library of Congress Cataloging-in-Publication Data

Pimentel, David, 1925-
    Food, energy, and society / David Pimentel and Marcia Pimentel,
  editors. — Rev. ed.
      p. cm.
  Includes bibliographical references and index.
  ISBN 0-87081-386-2 (cloth : perm. paper)
    1. Food supply. 2. Power resources. 3. Agriculture—Energy
consumption. I. Pimentel, Marcia. II. Title.
  HD9000.6.P55 1996
  338.1'9—dc20   96-9956
                                           CIP

This book was set in Caslon and AG Old Face.

The paper used in this publication meets the minimum requirements of the American National Standard for Information Sciences—Permanence of Paper for Printed Library Materials. ANSI Z39.48–1948
∞

10 9 8 7 6 5 4 3 2 1

CONTENTS

FIGURES

TABLES

PREFACE

Humans use energy from many sources to grow food, provide shelter, maintain health, and improve their lifestyle. Both the energy source—be it the sun, animal power, or fossil fuels—and its relative abundance influence human activities. As societal groupings have changed, so has energy use. Early humans who hunted and gathered their food in the wild depended primarily on their own energies. Although much of the world's population today relies on fossil fuels, many people in developing countries continue to use animal power, human power, firewood, and crop residues for energy.

In the twentieth century, ample fossil energy supplies have enabled humans to provide food and services for the ever-increasing global population, with a quarter of a million people added each day. The present population of nearly 6 billion is projected to double in just 45 years. With this forecast, pressure on food and fuel intensifies.

From 1 to 2 billion people are malnourished, and 2 billion exist in poverty (the largest number in history), signaling a serious food problem now and for the future. Since 1980 food production, especially grain production, has been declining per capita because population numbers are increasing *geometrically* while food production is increasing *linearly*. If these trends continue, it will be impossible for food production to keep up with population growth.

In the 15 years since the first edition of *Food, Energy, and Society*, world energy supplies, especially fossil fuels, have dwindled as their use has escalated. Supplies of the other major resources required for human life—fertile land, water, and biological diversity—also have come under growing threats. Indeed, the very integrity of the earth's natural environmental resources is threatened. In the face of these changes, this second edition has been expanded to include discussions of the interdependencies among food, land, water, and energy.

Fertile land, perhaps the most basic resource for agricultural production, is being eroded away by wind and water at an alarming rate. During the past 40 years, almost one-third of the arable land worldwide has been lost to erosion. On a per capita basis, land resources must be divided among increased numbers of people not only for food production but also for housing, industry, and roadways.

Water is another essential resource for food production. It takes about 1500 liters of water to produce 1 kg of corn and other grains. One ha of corn will transpire more than 5 million liters of water during the growing season of 3 to 4 months. Worldwide shortages of fresh water are becoming more evident and are beginning to curtail agriculture in some regions. Per capita irrigation of cropland has been declining since 1978, and this trend is expected to continue.

Per capita use of fossil energy is declining worldwide. The U.S. Department of Energy projects that by the year 2020 the United States will be importing 100 percent of its oil, as opposed to the 50 percent imported today. Adequate food production is highly dependent on oil and natural gas to power machines and to produce fertilizers and pesticides. What energy alternatives will be available when oil and gas supplies are close to exhaustion?

In the year 2040, when the world population has reached about 12 billion, what technologies will have been developed to meet the tremendous food demand? What technologies exist or can be developed to increase the number of fish in the oceans, double the amount of arable land in the world, double the supply of fresh water, or pollinate vast quantities of food crops?

These analyses of major resources, we hope, will guide planning and implementation of policies both for individuals and for nations as they face the inevitable dilemma—how can everyone be fed, given the limited and declining resources of our environment?

Two major problems must be addressed. First, and perhaps most difficult, the nations of the world must develop a plan to reduce the global population from nearly 6 billion to about 2 billion. If humans do not control their numbers, nature will. Second, we must sustain our life-supporting resources of land, water, energy, plants, and animals to ensure sustainable agriculture and forestry for future generations.

This second edition represents the cooperative efforts of many people. With sincere appreciation, we acknowledge the assistance of our students, who helped to collect and evaluate data and co-authored some of the chapters. Their efforts, interest, and enthusiasm added a great deal to these studies. Our special thanks to Sandra Bukkens and Tony Greiner for their devoted editorial assistance. Last, but not least, to our many colleagues who have taken their valuable time to suggest ways our manuscripts could be strengthened—a hearty thank you.

FOOD, ENERGY, AND SOCIETY
REVISED EDITION

1

ENERGY AND SOCIETY

David Pimentel and Marcia Pimentel

Adequate food, water, and shelter are basic to human survival. Closely linked to these life essentials is an adequate energy supply, for humans have always used energy to obtain food, water, shelter, and protection from parasites and predators. Over the centuries people have employed energy from many sources. First they depended on their own energy and natural energy from sunlight; later they relied on fire, draft-animal power, and water and wind power. Still later they invented engines fueled by wood, coal, petroleum, and, more recently, nuclear energy. Humans have used these various energy resources to modify and manipulate land, water, plants, and animals to fulfill their survivial needs. Finding, controlling, and using energy has enabled humans to progress from an unsettled, primitive life style to a more settled and sophisticated lifestyle. Alone of all the animals, humans can think creatively and develop advanced technologies.

The attainment of security and stability depends on the expenditure of energy. For example, humans expend energy to control disease; to obtain, purify, and store water; to produce pesticides; to produce antibiotics and other drugs; and to implement public health measures. All of these have enhanced the quality of human life.

Security and stability also entail the protection of one person from another and one group of people and their resources from encroachment by rivals. Social harmony depends not only on the rules established by governments but also on the effectiveness of societal forces used to enforce the laws. Governments, police, and military forces all expend enormous amounts of energy. In the so-called civilized society of nations of the world today, governments, police, and military forces use more energy than farmers use to produce food on the farm for the population being governed.

The availability of increasing energy supplies enabled humans to develop a societal structure more complex than that of the early hunter-gatherers. The present pattern of energy use contrasts sharply with that of the distant past, when finding adequate food dominated people's daily activities. White (1943) proposed that humans evolved in the following three major stages: 1) "savagery"—hunter-gatherers living on wild foods; 2) "barbarianism"—early agriculture and pastoral societies; and 3) "civilization"—development of engines and intensive use of fossil energy to produce food and necessities.

Each step signified major changes in both the type of energy supplies and their use by humans. In fact, White felt people would have remained on the "level of savagery indefinitely if [they] had not learned to augment the amount of energy under [their] control." The total quantity of energy controlled by humans grew to include a surplus above the amount needed for their basic needs.

Development of Societies and Energy

Hunter-gathering societies were small, rarely having more than 500 individuals (Service, 1962; Lee and DeVore, 1976), and simple (Bews, 1973). Because securing food and shelter consumed so much time and energy, other activities scarcely existed. With the development of agriculture, more dependable supplies of food, fiber resources, and surplus energy became available. Concurrently, a greater incentive for increased productivity and a greater interdependence among people evolved in human societies. As the stability of the food supply increased, societies that had once been seminomadic, following their food supply, gained in security and permanence.

In early agricultural societies food production still dominated human activities, and as a result the range of social interactions remained relatively narrow. Then the introduction of draft-animal power into agricultural production decreased human power expenditure and increased free personal time (see Chapters 7 and 10). People gained the freedom to participate in various activities, and social systems became more complex. Over time water and wind emerged as excellent energy resources. Instead of using draft animals that required energy for feed and care, people used waterwheels and windmills. With this change, humans had more power at their disposal and at a lower cost (calculated as human energy input) than in the past. In this way the amount of surplus energy available to society was greatly increased.

The use of water and wind power and the subsequent reduction of dependence on animal power fostered the development of trade and transport between societal groups. Improved communications expanded the exchange of resources and ideas between groups. Technical advances spread more easily than ever before. Further developments in science and technology resulted in the invention of sailing ships, which enhanced communication, transportation, and trade. With these changes human activities diversified, and specialized disciplines such as farming, sailing, trading, and industry developed.

The invention of the steam engine was a highly significant milestone in energy use, for it signaled the beginning of the use of fossil fuels as energy sources. Later engines used coal and oil as fuels, providing humans with immense power to control their environment and to change the total economic, political, and social structure of society (Cook, 1976). Along with these changes came greater stability, even greater specialization of work, longer life spans, and improved diets.

Energy from Fire

Since the earliest human societies, energy from fire has played a dominant role in survival. Although primitive people feared fire, they learned to control and constructively use its energy about half a million years ago. Fire enabled hunter-gatherers to ward off large animal predators and helped them clear vegetation, which provided further protection. Campfires also provided warmth in cold weather.

In addition, fires made it possible to cook foods, often making them better tasting, easier to eat, and easier to digest. Perhaps more important, cooking reduced the danger of illness from parasites and disease microbes that often contaminate raw foods. Heating also destroys some microbes responsible for food spoilage, so fire could be used to dry and preserve surplus foods for later consumption. This advance helped stabilize the availability of food supplies long after the time of harvest.

When primitive agriculture was developing, about 10,000 years ago, people set fires to clear trees and shrubs from the cropland and grazing areas. This simple procedure also helped eliminate weeds that competed with the crops. Furthermore, the ashes added nutrients to the soil and enhanced crop productivity. After cultivating crops on a certain plot for a few years, early farmers abandoned the land and cultivated other plots fertile enough to support crop growth. This form of early agriculture is termed "slash and burn" agriculture.

Wood from trees and shrubs served as the principal source of fuel for fires, although some grasses and other vegetation were also burned. When there was a relatively small human population, ample supplies of renewable energy in the form of wood were available. Today, with 5.5 billion people on earth, firewood and other forms of biomass are in short supply in most parts of the world.

Energy and the Structure of Societies

Early hunter-gatherer soceieities had minimal structure. A chief or group of elders usually led the camp or village. Most of these leaders had to hunt and gather along with the other members because the surpluses of food and other vital resources were seldom sufficient to support a full-time chief or village council.

The development of agriculture changed work patterns. Early farmers could reap 3 to 10 kg of grain from each 1 kg of seed planted. Part of this food/energy surplus was returned to the community and provided support for nonfarmers such as chieftains, village councils, medicine men, priests, and warriors. In return, the nonfarmers provided leadership and security for the farming population, thus enabling it to continue to increase food/energy yields and provide ever larger surpluses.

With improved technology and favorable conditions, agriculture produced consistent surpluses of the basic necessities, and population groups grew in size. These groups concentrated in towns and cities, and human tasks specialized further. Specialists such as masons, carpenters, blacksmiths, merchants, traders, and sailors developed their skills and became more efficient in their use of time and energy. The goods and services they provided brought about an improved quality of life, a higher standard of living, and, for most societies, increased stability.

Ancient Egypt is an outstanding example of an early society that not only possessed environmental resources favorable to agriculture but also developed effective agricultural technology (Cottrell, 1955). The Nile's yearly floods deposited nutrient-rich silt on the adjacent farmland and kept it productive. The river was also a reliable source of water for irrigation. Additionally, the warm Egyptian climate was highly favorable for crop production. This productive agricultural system supported the 95 percent of the Egyptian population that was directly involved in agriculture (Figure 1.1) and provided enough surplus food to sustain the 5 percent of the population who did no work in agriculture (Cottrell, 1955).

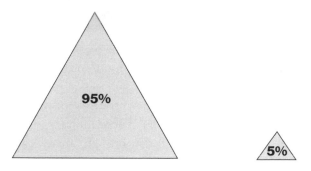

1.1   During the age of the Pharaohs and pyramid projects, ancient Egypt had a population of 3 million. About 95 percent of society was involved in agriculture. The surplus energy of about 5 percent was utilized for the Pharaohs and the construction of the great pyramids.

Relatively little food energy was needed to support the small ruling class. Furthermore, Egypt's naturally isolated location provided protection from invasion, so the society did not have to expend large amounts of energy to maintain a military class. As a result, the Pharaohs could and did use the 5 percent of the population not involved in agriculture as slave laborers to build pyramids and stock them with goods and materials for a life that, Egyptians believed, would come after life on earth.

During this early period the Egyptian population remained relatively constant because of rulers' demands for slaves. As soon as surplus men were mature enough for work they were assigned to pyramid construction and literally worked to death during a few years of slave labor. When they died, they were replaced with new surplus labor. This system was sustained without jeopardizing the fundamental agricultural system that involved the efforts of almost all the Egyptian people.

During the age of the Pharaohs, which spanned the years from 2780 to 1625 B.C. (Fakhry, 1969), Egypt had a population of about 3 million, much less than the 55 million of today. A 5 percent food/energy surplus from about 3 million people is not much; on a per capita basis, this ranges from 100 to 150 kcal per day (Cottrell, 1955), or the equivalent of 10 to 15 kg of surplus wheat per person per year. Based on 3 million people, this totals 30 to 45 million kg of surplus wheat per year.

The construction of the Cheops pyramid over a 20-year span used an amount of energy equal to the surplus energy produced in the lifetime of about 3 million Egyptian people (Cottrell, 1955). During the construction period the pyramid work force was about 100,000 slaves per year. Assuming that each slave received 300 to 400 kg of grain per year, the total cost would be 30 to 40 million kg of grain, or the entire food/energy surplus produced by the Egyptian agricultural community.

Later in its history, Egypt used surplus resources to support large military forces and conquer some of its neighbors. These military operations not only secured additional land and food but also brought many conquered people back to Egypt to be slaves. But the vast deserts over which the Egyptian forces had to travel and transport supplies naturally limited the military operations. Ever-increasing quantities of energy had to be expended simply to protect the supply routes and transport military provisions.

At other times, when the population became large relative to the land and the agricultural resources, agricultural surpluses were not available in Egypt. In these relatively overpopulated conditions and with shortages instead of surpluses, the Egyptian society was just able to maintain itself. Sometimes civil strife and social problems developed. These conditions often led to a decline in population because these unstable societies were unproductive in agriculture or any other essential activity.

Thus, Egypt's early history provides a prime example of the role that energy, as measured by food surpluses, played in the structure and activities of a society. Although the structures of today's societies are far more complex than that of ancient Egypt, energy availability and use continue to be major factors in the standard of living.

Food as a Focal Point of Societies

In natural communities, the entire structure and function of the population revolves around food as an energy source (Elton, 1927). This situation is also true of human societies. Primitive societies used food as the medium of exchange long before money was used. They traded surpluses of crops and in this way not only improved their own diets but also had the opportunity to interact with other groups.

The populations of all species are influenced by the relation between food supplies and demand. As with human societies, stability has advantages for a biotic community's survival and therefore is an important evolutionary trend (Pimentel, 1961, 1988). Evolved balance in supply-demand economies of

1.2   Drawing of a cow and several small horses in the painted cave of Lascaux, France.

natural populations contributes to the relative stability that is observed in these dynamic community systems.

The major reason food and energy are considered critical resources for all natural communities, including humans, is that living plants can convert relatively limited amounts of solar energy—only about 0.1 percent of the sunlight reaching the earth—into biomass. Before fossil fuels were discovered and used, humans shared with other animals that portion of the sun's energy captured by plants and subsequently converted to food/energy.

In prehistoric times, humans acknowledged the importance of food in their lives, as revealed in the many pictures of animals and food plants they painted in caves and on tools (Figure 1.2). Egyptian artwork pictures various food crops and livestock, and grains and other food items were customarily buried with the dead. The Mayan civilization of Central America depended on corn (maize) as its staple food and produced numerous sculptures and paintings of corn. Many religious and cultural groups celebrated successful harvests with ceremony and pageantry.

Use of Energy in Food Systems

One measure of the relative importance of food in society as a whole is the amount of energy and labor devoted to producing it. In prehistoric times, about 95 percent of the total energy expended by the family was used for food.

This included hunting and gathering, transporting the food back to camp, and preparing it for consumption.

Even today in some developing countries, the energy expended on food systems represents from 60 to 80 percent of the total energy expended (RSAS, 1975). By contrast, in many developed countries the proportion of energy devoted to food production ranges from 15 to 30 percent, and little of this is human energy. For example, in the United States and United Kingdom, the amount of energy expended in food production represents about 17 percent of the total energy used (Leach, 1976; Pimentel, 1980). As in the developing countries, this percentage includes energy used for production, processing, packaging, distribution, and preparation of food.

Although the United States spends but 17 percent of its total energy on food, the overall quantity of energy it uses is several times that used in the less complex societies of developing countries (Figure 1.3). The United States expends three times as much energy per capita for food production than do developing countries, for all energy-consuming activities including food production. This comparison emphasizes once again the energy-intensive lifestyle that has developed in such countries as the United States, following the ready availability and low cost of fossil-fuel energy resources.

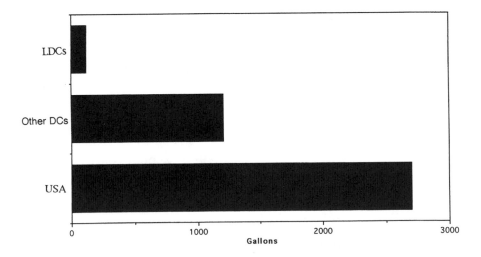

1.3   Energy consumption rates per capita per year in gallons of oil equivalents in the United States, other developed countries (DCs), and less developed countries (LDCs). (1 gallon = 3.78 liters.)

2
ENERGY AND POWER
David Pimentel and Marcia Pimentel

Energy and Work

Energy is defined as the capacity to do work. Although energy is found in many forms (Table 2.1), all forms have the capacity to do work. Light energy coming from the sun is the most important and universal type of energy, supporting all life on earth. Plants have the capacity to capture, or "fix," light energy and convert it into chemical energy, which is used by the plants themselves and the animals that feed on them. Many human activities, most prominently agriculture and forestry, rely on solar energy. Solar energy is also fundamental to wind power, hydroelectric power, and other types of energy systems.

Radio, radar, micro, and television waves use electrical energy. The lifting or moving of objects by man or machine is a form of mechanical energy. Another form of energy—heat generated by the burning of wood, coal, oil, or gas—is used for cooking and to drive engines. Magnetic energy, which is produced from the interaction of positively and negatively charged matter, can be used to do work. Sound waves, another form of energy, are used in communications and other activities. A more recently discovered form of energy is nuclear energy, which is released from the bound atomic particles in, for instance, uranium. Humans have employed nuclear energy not only to create devastating bombs but also to produce electricity.

Laws of Thermodynamics

The use or flow of energy is governed by the two laws of thermodynamics. *The first law of thermodynamics states that energy may be transformed from one*

Table 2.1   Some examples of energy conversion and energy-converting devices

To	From Mechanical	From Thermal	From Acoustical	From Chemical	From Electrical	From Light

Mechanical	Oar
	Sail
	Jack
	Bicycle
		Steam engine	Barograph
			Ear
				Muscle contraction
				Bomb
				Jet engine
					Electric motor
					Piezo-electric
					  crystal
						Photoelectric
						  door opener

Thermal	Friction Brake Heat pump	Radiator	Sound absorber	Food Fuel	Resistor Spark plug	Solar cooker Greenhouse effect
Acoustical	Bell Violin Wind-up phonograph	Flame tube	Megaphone	Explosion	Telephone receiver Loudspeaker Thunder	

Chemical	Impact detonation
	  of nitroglycerine
		Endothermic
		  chemical
		  reactions
				Growth and
				  metabolism
					Electrolysis	Photosynthesis
						Photochemical
						  reactions

Electrical	Dynamo Piezo-electric crystal	Thermopile	Induction microphone	Battery Fuel cell	Transformer Magnetism	Solar cell
Light	Friction (sparks)	Thermolumi- nescence		Bioluminescence	Light bulb	Fluorescence

Source: After Steinhart and Steinhart, 1974a.

type into another (Table 2.1) *but can never be created or destroyed.* For example, light energy can be transformed into heat energy or into plant-food energy (chemical energy). In the process of this transformation, no energy is lost or destroyed; only its form is changed.

The second law of thermodynamics states that no transformation of energy will occur unless energy is degraded from a concentrated form to a more dispersed form. In the real world all energy transformations take place in open systems, because processes necessarily interact with their environment over finite time periods. *Thus, according to the second law, in the real world no transformation is 100 percent efficient.*

The second law states the existence of a spontaneous "direction" for energy transformations. For example, if a hot object is placed next to a cool object, heat will flow from the hot object to the cool one but never in the reverse direction. Because no transformation is 100 percent efficient, the temperature of the cool object will rise, but not enough to account for all the energy that is transferred from the hot object. In the transfer some energy is dispersed into the environment. Consider the example of a cup of boiling water mixed with a cup of cold water. The temperature of the resulting mixture is slightly lower than would be calculated by measuring the energy lost by the boiling water. The cold water is much warmer than it was initially, but because some of the heat energy is lost to the environment, it will not be as hot as the average of the two initial temperatures.

All biological systems, including crops, follow the second law of thermodynamics when solar energy (a high-energy form) is converted into chemical energy. Plants utilize this chemical energy in the process of building their own tissue. Some of the energy being changed from light to chemical energy is lost as heat that dissipates into the surrounding environment.

Measures of Energy and Power

The basic unit of energy, following the International System (SI) of units, is the joule (J), but many other units of energy are used, such as the calorie, Btu (British thermal unit), quad, kWh (kilowatt hour), TOE (metric tons of oil equivalent), and TCE (metric tons of coal equivalent). Both the calorie and Btu, which are probably the most frequently used units, are based on measurements of heat energy. A calorie, or gram-calorie, is the amount of heat that is needed to raise 1 g of water 1°C at 15°C. The Btu is the amount of heat needed to raise 1 pound of water 1°F. Note that heat measurements are related not to the direct ability to do work but to the capacity to raise the temperature of matter or to change the state (solid, liquid, gas) of matter.

Conversion factors for energy units are listed in Table 2.2. Note that the kilocalorie (kcal), or kilogram-calorie, equals 1000 calories, or gram-calories. The large Calorie, used in the field of nutrition, equals 1 kcal, or 1000 (small) calories.

Table 2.2   Energy conversion factors

Unit	Equivalents
1 kilojoule (kJ)	1000 joules (J)
1 kilocalorie (kcal)	1000 calories (cal); 4.184 kJ; 4184 J
1 British thermal unit (Btu)	0.252 kcal; 1.054 kJ; 1054 J
1 quad	1015 Btu; 0.252 × 1015 kcal; 1.054 × 1018 J
1 kilowatt hour (kWh)	3413 Btu; 860 kcal; 3.6 MJ
1 horsepower hour (HPh)	0.746 kWh; 2546 Btu; 642 kcal; 2.69 MJ
1 ton of coal equivalent (TCE)	7 × 106 kcal; 29.31 GJ
1 ton of oil equivalent (TOE)	107 kcal; 41.87 GJ

Note: Kilo (k) = 10^3; mega (M) = 10^6; giga (G) = 10^9; tera (T) = 10^{12}; peta (P) = 10^{15}.

Measurements of energy do not take into account the time required for the conversion process. Work, however, requires the expenditure or use of energy at a certain rate. The term "power" expresses the rate at which work is done and/or energy is expended. The basic unit of power is the Watt (W), which equals 1 joule/second, 14.3 kcal/minute, or 3.41 Btu/hour. Another unit of power commonly used is the horsepower (HP); 1 HP equals 746 W or 2542 Btu/hour.

When the power level, or rate at which work is done, is multiplied by the time the work requires, we obtain the total flow of energy. For instance, the maximum work capacity or power level that a horse can sustain for a 10-hour working day is 1 HP. The power level of a person is about one-tenth of 1 HP; therefore, a person working a 10-hour day produces an energy equivalent of only 1 HPh (horsepower hour), 2.7 MJ (megajoules), or 0.75 kWh. Put another way, one horse can accomplish the same amount of work as ten people in one hour. Horsepower and oxpower were some of the first substitutes for human power and contributed to improving the quality of human life. Certainly people tilling the soil in early agriculture were more productive when they used oxen and horses.

The tremendous effect of technological development on human activities can be appreciated by comparing manpower to the mechanical power of a tractor fueled with gasoline. One gallon (3.79 liters) of gasoline contains about 38,000 kcal of potential energy. When this gallon of gasoline fuels a mechanical engine, which is about 20 percent efficient in converting heat energy into mechanical energy, an equivalent of 8.8 kWh of work can be achieved. Hence, a single gallon of gasoline produces more power than a horse working at maximum capacity for 10 hours (7.5 kWh). Further, 1 gallon of gasoline produces the equivalent of almost 3 weeks of human work at a rate of 0.1 HP, or 0.075 kW, for 40 hours a week.

Biological Solar Energy Conversion in Agriculture

The survival of humans in their ecosystem depends upon the efficiency of green plants as energy converters. The plants convert sunlight into food energy for themselves and other organisms. The total foundation of life rests on plants' unique capacity to change radiated solar energy into stored chemical energy that is biologically useful for humans and other animals.

The amount of solar energy reaching 1 ha each day in the temperate region ranges from 15 to 40 million kcal. Over a year's time the total solar energy received per hectare (ha) ranges from 1.1 to 1.8×10^{10} kcal, with 1.4×10^{10} kcal as a reliable average. This is equivalent to the energy potential of nearly 452,000 gallons (1.7 million liters) of gasoline per year per ha. This sounds like a large quantity of energy, and indeed it is when considered as a unit. But each square millimeter (mm) receives only 0.0038 kcal per day, only enough to raise the temperature of 3.8 milliliters (ml) of water 1°C.

Green plants are able to capture only a small percentage (0.1 percent) of the sunlight reaching the earth (Whittaker and Likens, 1975; ERAB, 1981). Annually, the total light energy fixed by green plants in ecosystems is estimated to be about 400×10^{15} kcal, divided equally between terrestrial and ocean ecosystems (Pimentel et al., 1978). Note that although terrestrial systems cover only about a third of the earth, the plants in these systems fix about half of the total light energy captured.

When only the temperate zone is considered, estimates are that only 0.07 percent of the 1.4×10^{10} kcal of sunlight per ha is fixed in terrestrial ecosystems (Reifsnyder and Lull, 1965). Thus, the net energy fixed by plants in the temperate zone averages about 10 million kcal/ha per year. Expressed as dry weight of plant material, this amounts to an average yield of 2400 kg/ha per year, ranging from near zero in some rock and desert areas to 10,000 kg/ha in some swamps and marshes (Whittaker and Likens, 1975).

In agricultural ecosystems, an estimated 15 million kcal of solar energy (net production) is fixed per ha per crop season. Even so, this amounts to only about 0.1 percent of the total solar energy reaching each ha during the year and equals about 3500 kg/ha of dry biomass. The amount of biomass varies with the crop and ranges from 200 kg/ha for low-production crops under arid conditions to 15,000 kg/ha for corn and sugarcane. An average agricultural ecosystem produces an annual biomass per ha slightly greater than that in natural ecosystems. This is not surprising, as crop plants are grown on the most fertile soils and are usually provided with ample moisture and essential nutrients. Under optimal conditions, during sunny days in midsummer and when the plants are nearing maturity, crops such as corn and sugarcane capture as much as 5 percent of the sunlight energy reaching them. However, the harvested plant material is only about 0.1 percent because over much of the year, including winter, there is no plant growth.

A significant quantity of captured energy is, of course, utilized by the plant itself. For example, a soybean plant uses about 25 percent of the energy it collects for its own respiration and maintenance. About 5 percent of the energy is diverted to provide food for the nitrogen-fixing bacteria that are symbionts with the soybean plant. Another 10 percent is lost to insect pests and pathogens that feed on the plant. Thus, the net yield in beans plus vegetation is about 60 percent of the energy collected by the plant.

Most plants divert significant proportions—from 5 to 50 percent—of the energy they collect into their fruits and seeds, illustrating the high priority plants give to reproduction (Harper, 1977).

Humans have used breeding techniques to reallocate energy in plants and improve crop yields. For example, one of the factors contributing to the increased yields in new breeds of corn has been the change in energy allocation within the plant. In particular, the new breeds produce smaller tassels and less pollen, and the energy saved is reallocated to the production of corn grain. With corn plants, growing as densely as they do under normal cropping conditions, the smaller tassel and less abundant pollen are satisfactory for the production of corn seed.

Renewable Biological Energy Versus Fossil Fuel Energy

By the sixteenth century, England and France were running out of firewood, their most important source of renewable biomass (Nef, 1977). Humans used wood to cook and prepare foods and to heat the homes of the expanding population. They also used it to produce charcoal for the developing metal industry and to provide lumber for the growing shipbuilding and construction industries. Because of wood shortages, London and Paris were forced to turn to soft coal as a substitute fuel (Cook, 1976). Because soft coal is noxious when burned, wood remained the preferred fuel, and those who could afford its high price continued to burn wood. During the eighteenth century, coal was used primarily for heating; its use as a source of energy to replace human and horse power did not occur until the nineteenth century.

Coal was used extensively, however, to fuel pumps in mining operations. As mines were dug deeper, water began seeping into the mines and caused serious flooding problems. The mine operators used windmills, hand pumps, and windlasses to remove water, but with poor results. Then, in 1698, Thomas Savery invented the first steam-powered pump to remove water from the mines. This pump, however, proved dangerous to operate and was never fully adopted. About 10 years later, Thomas Newcomen designed a much-improved steam-powered pump that was extensively employed in the mines. Thereafter coal could be mined more efficiently, and a good supply was ready to replace the declining supply of firewood. It was not until nearly 100 years later that James Watt designed a truly efficient steam engine and pump. When the Watt pump was finally operational, it rapidly replaced the Newcomen steam pump.

The Watt steam engine and the internal combustion engine, developed in 1876, brought dramatic changes in energy consumption. These new fossil fuel–powered engines quickly replaced the less efficient wood-powered steam engines, the horse, and even human power. Production of goods increased, expenditure of energy increased, and each subsequent decade witnessed a further increase in the use of nonrenewable fuel resources.

In the United States from 1700 to 1800, wood was the primary source of fuel. As late as 1850, more than 91 percent of the energy used in the United States came from wood burning (EOP, 1977). The supply of wood was sufficient in the eighteenth and early nineteenth centuries, for two reasons. Not only was the population about 23 million people, or less than 9 percent the present level, but these early settlers consumed only about one-fifth the amount of energy consumed today. Furthermore, American forests had been harvested for only a relatively short period of time compared to European forests. Even so, as early as 1850 firewood was in short supply in the Northeast, especially for larger cities such as New York and Boston, because of the rapid clearing of forestland for agricultural production and the relatively heavy demand for firewood. The problem was worsened by the difficulty and high costs of transporting the bulky and heavy wood over increasingly long distances to the cities.

Obviously, forests cannot meet the high energy needs of today's large U.S. population. At present, fossil fuels account for 92.5 percent of the total fuel consumption in the United States. Of this, oil represents 40 percent, natural gas 28 percent, coal 26 percent, and nuclear fuels 6 percent. Firewood accounts for only 4 percent and hydroelectric energy the remaining 3.5 percent of the total fuel. Fossil fuel consumption today is the highest it has ever been. Annual consumption for the world stands at about 319 quads (80.4×10^{15} kcal) and is increasing every year (IEA, 1991). The United States alone consumes 25 percent of all the fossil energy used in the world annually, amounting to 79 quads (19.9×10^{15} kcal) (IEA, 1991).

The epoch of fossil fuel use has been but a short interval in the more than 1 million years of human existence on earth (Figure 2.1). The era of reliance on fossil fuels will be but a small "blip" in history—about 400 years, or at most 0.1 percent of the time humans have been on earth. Because fossil fuels

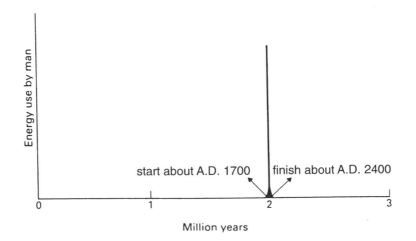

2.1   The epoch of the use of fossil fuels in the history of man on earth.

are nonrenewable resources, they eventually will be exhausted. Oil and gas supplies will be the first fossil fuels to run out. According to the best estimates, 30 to 50 years of these resources remain (Matare, 1989; Worldwatch Institute, 1992a). The United States has only 10 to 20 years of oil reserves remaining, based on current use rates (DOE, 1991a). U.S. oil imports now amount to 54 percent of the country's total use, and this share is expected to increase to about 70 percent by the turn of the century. Most the European countries, Japan, and several other countries in the world import *all* of their oil, which places a strain on their economies.

The world's coal reserves are greater than those of oil and gas because the latter fuels have been more extensively used than coal. There is still an estimated 100-year supply of coal in the world (Hubbert, 1972; Matare, 1989; Worldwatch, 1992a). However, continued heavy use of fossil fuels may cause grave problems relating to global climate change (Schneider, 1989). In addition, the burning of fossil fuels results in major air pollution problems, and coal mining, especially strip mining, damages the environment, destroying vast areas of land valued for food and forest production and wildlife. On average, strip mining is safer for miners, is more economical, and requires less energy than deep underground mining, and it is 80 to 90 percent effective in recovering coal, whereas deep mining is only 50 percent effective. In deep mining small coal seams cannot be economically mined because of the danger of cave-ins.

Coal production requires less energy than oil drilling both in extraction and transportation. About 20 percent of the potential energy in oil is expended to extract and refine it (Cervinka, 1980), resulting in a yield of about 80 percent at point of use. By comparison, coal has a yield of about 92 percent (Cook, 1976). This means that about 108 kg of coal must be mined to produce the equivalent of 100 kg of coal energy, compared with 120 kg of oil pumped for 100 kg of oil energy.

Coal reserves are scattered throughout the world. Western Europe has about 5 percent of the total, the United States about 20 percent. Russia is extremely well endowed, with nearly 56 percent of the estimated coal reserves.

Adjusting from oil and gas to coal will require many changes in lifestyle and industrial production methods. The world is indeed fortunate to have coal reserves as a backup energy resource until renewable energy technologies are developed to supply a portion of the world's energy needs.

3

SOLAR ENERGY IN NATURAL AND MANAGED ECOSYSTEMS

David Pimentel and Marcia Pimentel

Natural ecosystems, of which humans are a part, are fundamentally a network of solar energy and mineral flows. Green plants capture solar energy and convert it into chemical energy for use by themselves and the remainder of the biological system using the elements of carbon, hydrogen, oxygen, nitrogen, phosphorus, potassium, calcium, magnesium, and others. The food supplied by plants in the ecosystem is basic to the survival of all animals, including humans. It is the foundation of the entire life system. Some of the solar energy plants convert into stored chemical energy is passed on to herbivores and parasitic microbes. The success of agriculture and forestry is measured by the amount of solar energy captured as biomass in crops and forests. The biomass yield depends on the manipulation of these plants—which need fertile soil, water, and a favorable climate—using human, animal, and fossil fuel power for tilling, planting, weed control, harvesting, and various other activities.

In this chapter we focus on solar energy as a fundamental resource for the functioning of both natural and managed ecosystems. Also considered are the limitations of solar energy and the land area of the terrestrial ecosystems in the United States.

Natural Ecosystems

The solar energy reaching a ha of land in temperate North America averages about 14 billion kcal per year (Reifsnyder and Lull, 1965). This is the equivalent of the energy contained in about 1.4 million liters (370,000 gal) of oil, or the energy used by 148 Americans for 1 year. However, most plants in the temperate zone of the United States do not grow during the winter months, achieving most of their growth during a relatively short 4-month summer. During this period nearly 7 billion kcal—about half of the year's sunlight energy—reach each ha of land.

Consider now how the solar energy is converted into biomass by vegetation. The total area in the United States, including lakes and rivers, is 1049 million ha. The total biomass produced annually is 3223 million tons, or a little more than 3 tons/ha (Table 3.1). If we assume 4200 kcal per kilogram of biomass, then the total energy captured is 12.6 million kcal/ha per year, or slightly less than 0.1 percent of the total sunlight energy reaching each ha.

Table 3.1   Total annual plant biomass production in the United States

Location	Area (million ha)	Biomass (dry tons/ha)	Total biomass (dry Mt)[a]
Terrestrial			
Farmland			
Cropland	135	6	810
Cropland idle	21	4	84
Cropland in pasture	36	4	144
Grassland in pasture	183	3	549
Forest and woodland	45	4	180
Farmsteads, roads	11	0.1	1
Other			
Grazing land	117	2	234
Forest land	202	4	808
Other land, urban, marshes, desert	167	0.1	17
SUBTOTAL	917	—	2,827
Aquatic			
Lakes and rivers	132	3	396
TOTAL	1,049	—	3,223

Note: [a]Mt = million metric tons.
Source: After Pimentel et al., 1978.

Although in the tropics there are no winters, there are dry periods during which little plant biomass is produced. Thus, biomass productivity in the tropics, on average, is quite similar to that of temperate regions. In the tropics, the prime limiting factor is moisture, whereas in the temperate United States temperature is the prime limiting factor.

In natural ecosystems, the approximately 3 tons/ha/yr of biomass available limits the number of consumers and the number of links in the food chain. Usually only about 10 percent of the energy is passed on from one consumer level to the next. Therefore, rarely do links in the food chain number more than 4 or 5. This explains why some large predators, such as tigers, must range over hundreds of ha to find adequate amounts of food. Thus, energy, along with moisture and nutrients (nitrogen, phosphorous, potassium, etc.), is a major limiting factor for natural ecosystems.

Plants in the United States fix about 13.5×10^{15} kcal of solar energy per year (Figure 3.1), which is significantly less than the current annual fossil energy consumption of about 20×10^{15} kcal. Indeed, Americans burn about 40 percent more fossil energy than the total solar energy captured by all the plant biomass in the United States each year (Figure 3.1). These figures illustrate that humans' use of fossil energy is far out of balance with the energy naturally available and renewable in their ecosystem. In addition, fossil energy has made drastic changes in the U.S. ecosystem, including the removal of forests and natural prairies.

About 70 percent of the total energy fixed in the terrestrial United States is produced on agricultural lands, the remainder from plants growing on nonagricultural lands (Table 3.1). Any analysis of the effectiveness of biological solar energy conversion in nature and managed ecosystems must consider agricultural and forestry production. About 70 percent of the U.S. land area is used for food and forest production (Table 3.1). Each year the total amount of solar energy harvested annually in the form of agricultural crops and forestry products is about 6.9×10^{15} kcal (5.8×10^{15} kcal net energy). This represents about 30 percent of the fossil energy consumption in the United States. Pasture and other forage crops account for about 66 percent of the harvested energy, whereas food crops total 16 percent and forest products 18 percent.

The 6.9×10^{15} kcal of biological energy harvested in the form of agricultural and forestry products has several significant implications. First, about half of all the solar energy fixed by plants in the United States is harvested and used by humans and livestock, whereas the other half is used within the natural ecosystem. Thus, the energy produced in both agriculture/forestry and the natural ecosystem is vital to the functioning of the human economy and sustains the health of the natural environment. This conclusion suggests that Americans are making maximal use of the land to produce biomass for food

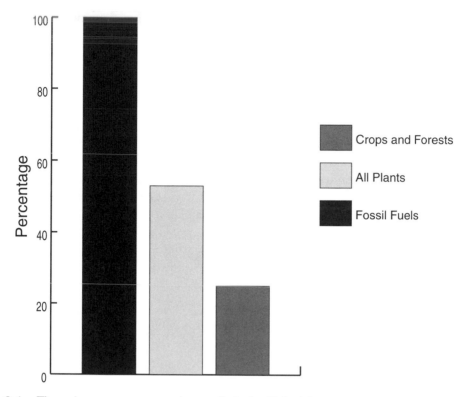

3.1   The solar energy captured annually in the United States compared with fossil energy consumption and the amount of solar energy harvested as crop and forest products.

and forest products and that their natural ecosystem also requires a large amount of biomass to maintain it. Furthermore, the use of biomass as fuel must be limited, because food and forest biomass support the diverse needs and activities of human society.

Forest Ecosystems

Net primary production in U.S. forests is about 4 tons/ha/yr (Table 3.1). This yield is slightly more than the average net primary production for all the ecosystems in the nation. It includes leaves and small twigs, so the net harvest of biomass wood is, optimistically, about 2 tons/ha, which provides about 8.4 million kcal of energy when burned to produce heat energy. Each American consumes the equivalent of 81 million kcal in fossil fuel annually, or the energy produced from about 10 ha of forest.

Agricultural Ecosystems

Annual net primary production in U.S. agricultural ecosystems is about 5 tons/ha (Table 3.1). This figure is higher than the overall average yield of biomass per ha because crops are grown under favorable conditions regarding moisture, soil nutrients, and soil quality. For example, corn grown under favorable conditions will produce 7 tons/ha of corn grain, plus an additional 7 tons/ha of stover. Converted into heat energy, this totals about 60×10^{15} kcal per ha. This represents about 0.5 percent of the solar energy reaching 1 ha during the year, a relatively high rate of conversion for crops and natural vegetation. Most crops have about a 0.2 percent level of conversion.

In summary, the terrestrial ecosystem is extremely important to the survival of humans because more than 99 percent of their food and 100 percent of their forest products comes from terrestrial plants that capture solar energy. In addition, the terrestrial ecosystem, in capturing solar energy, helps maintain the natural ecosystem and a quality environment.

4

ECOLOGICAL SYSTEMS, NATURAL RESOURCES, AND FOOD SUPPLIES

David Pimentel

All basic human needs, including food, energy, shelter, and protection from disease, are fulfilled using the resources found in the ecosystem. Throughout history, humans learned to modify natural ecosystems to better meet their basic needs and desires. Over time, humans have altered ever larger amounts of the environment and used ever more resources.

Human intelligence and technology have developed rapidly, enabling humans to manipulate the ecosystem more successfully than any other animal species. This advantage has given humans power to control and destroy other species. And now, with nuclear weapons, humans have the power to destroy themselves and many other species.

Humans are but one of many species on earth; they form an integral part of the planet's ecosystems. They cannot function in isolation. Furthermore, their numbers cannot grow exponentially forever, because shortages of food, energy, and space will limit the size of the human population eventually, as has occurred for many other species in the past.

In this chapter, the intrinsic dynamics of natural ecosystems—involving land, water, atmosphere, energy, plants, and animals—are examined. The components' interaction and their relationship to agricultural productivity are discussed.

The Structure and Function of Ecosystems

An ecosystem is a network of energy and mineral flows in which the major functional components are populations of plants, animals, and microbes. These organisms perform different specialized functions in the system.

All self-sufficient ecosystems consist of producers (plants), consumers (animals and microbes), and reducers, or decomposers (animals and microbes) (see Figure 4.1). Plants collect solar energy and convert it into chemical energy via photosynthesis. They use this energy for growth, maintenance, and reproduction. In turn, plants serve as the primary energy source for all other living organisms in the ecosystem. Animals and microbes consume plants and other animals, and decomposers break down dead plants and animals and thus recycle chemical elements (carbon, hydrogen, oxygen, nitrogen, phosphorus, potassium, calcium, etc.). Through this process, the elements in the biological system are conserved and reused. Therefore, the components of the ecosystem are all interconnected and interdependent, but plants are the basic foundation of the system.

The exact number of species needed for a particular self-sufficient ecosystem depends upon many physical and chemical factors, including temperature, moisture, and the particular species present. We cannot predict how many and what kinds of species are necessary for the different feeding levels

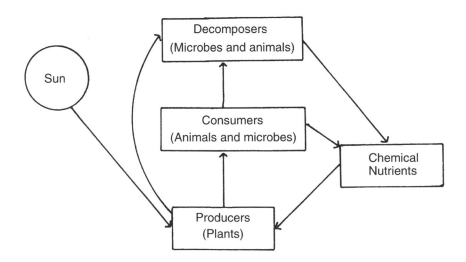

4.1   Structure cf living systems.

in the ecosystem. For a given ecosystem, species numbers may range from hundreds to thousands (Andrewartha and Birch, 1954).

In the United States, approximately 500,000 species of plants and animals are vital to the well-being of the natural environment (Pimentel et al., 1992a). No one knows how many of these species can be eliminated before the quality of the ecosystem will be diminished. Therefore, human societies must exercise great care to avoid causing a reduction in biodiversity. A delicate balance in the natural food system has evolved in each community, and, although there is some redundancy, the linkages in the trophic structure are basic to the system's functioning.

Elton (1927) pointed out that the "whole structure and activities of the community are dependent upon questions of food supply." Plants are nurtured by the sun and by the essential chemicals they obtain from the atmosphere, soil, and water. The remainder of the species in the ecosystem depend on living or dead plants and animals. About half of all species obtain their resources directly from living hosts (Pimentel, 1968; Price, 1975). Sugarcane, for example, supports 1645 parasitic insect species worldwide (Strong et al., 1977) and at least 100 parasitic and disease microbial species (Martin et al., 1961) worldwide. Oaks in the United States support over 500 known insect species and close to 1000 different species (Packard, 1890; de Mesa, 1928; Opler, 1974). One of the major insect herbivores of oaks in the Northeast is the gypsy moth, which in turn has about 100 parasitic and predaceous species feeding on it (Nichols, 1961; Campbell and Podgwaite, 1971; Podgwaite and Campbell, 1972; Campbell, 1974; Leonard, 1974). Clearly, parasitism and dependence on living food resources constitute a dominant way of life in natural ecosystems.

But a host population can support only a limited population of herbivores before it dies or is so damaged that it no longer can provide food for its parasites. An individual host utilizes most of its energy resources for its own growth, maintenance, and reproduction. For example, on average plants use 38 to 71 percent of their energy resources for respiration; poikilotherms, about 50 percent; and homeotherms, 62 to 75 percent (McNeil and Lawton, 1970; Odum, 1971; Humphreys, 1979). In general, less than 10 percent of the host's resources are passed on to herbivores and other parasitic species (Slobodkin, 1960; Phillipson, 1966; Odum, 1978; Pimentel, 1988). A recent survey of 92 herbivores feeding in nature showed that they consumed only 7 percent of the plant host's biomass (Pimentel, 1988). Because hosts utilize most of their energy resources for themselves and their progeny, even a relatively small amount of herbivore/parasite feeding pressure influences the abundance and distribution of hosts. Therefore, from an ecological perspective, host conservation is vital for herbivore/parasite survival.

Many theories exist on how plants survive the attack of herbivore/parasite populations. It is my view that herbivore/parasite populations and plant populations coevolve and function interdependently to balance the supply and demand of food. I have proposed that parasites and hosts are dynamic participants in this economy and that control of herbivore/parasite populations generally changes from density-dependent competition and patchiness to the density-dependent genetic feedback and natural enemy (parasite feeding on parasite) controls (Pimentel, 1988). I also postulate that herbivore and parasite numbers are often controlled by a feedback evolutionary mechanism interdependent with the other density-dependent controls. Feedback evolution limits herbivore/parasite feeding pressure on the host population to some level of "harvestable" energy and conserves the host primarily by individual selection. Most of the host's resources are necessary for growth, maintenance, and reproduction, leaving a relatively small portion of host resources as harvestable energy. This hypothesis suggests one reason why trees and other plants generally remain green and lush and why herbivores and other parasites are relatively sparse in biomass, especially related to their food hosts.

To achieve a balanced economy in parasite-host systems, either individual hosts evolve defense mechanisms or herbivore/parasite populations evolve to moderate exploitation of their host population (Pimentel, 1961; Levin and Pimentel, 1981). The amount of resources consumed by herbivores/parasites is often limited to less than 10 percent of the host's total resources (Pimentel, 1988). Hosts' defenses include nutritional, chemical, and physical resistance and combinations of these factors (Pimentel, 1968; Whittaker and Feeny, 1970; Levin, 1976; Segal et al., 1980; Berryman, 1982; Coley et al., 1985; Rhoades, 1985). If herbivore numbers are limited by parasites and predators, then the herbivores probably exert little or no selective pressure on the plant host (Hairston et al., 1960; Lawton and McNeill, 1979; Price et al., 1980; Schultz, 1983a, b).

Evolutionary feedback may exert density-dependent control over herbivore/parasite populations. Thus, when herbivore numbers are abundant and the feeding pressure on the plant host is relatively intense, selection in the plant population will favor allelic frequencies and defenses in the plant population that reduce herbivore rates of increase and, eventually, herbivore numbers. When slugs and snails, for example, feed heavily on bird's-foot trefoil, the proportion of its resistant alleles and level of cyanogenesis increase (Jones, 1966, 1979). This increase tends to reduce feeding pressure on the trefoil.

This relationship can be illustrated further. For simplicity, assume that at one locus in the host there are two alleles, A and A'. The rate of increase of the parasite on a susceptible-type host with AA is greater than 1, whereas on a resistant-type host with A'A' defenses the rate of increase is less than 1. Thus, through selection on a proportion of the two alleles in the host population, herbivore or parasite numbers will increase or decrease until eventually some equilibrium ratio is approached (Pimentel, 1961). When the herbivore population exerts heavy feeding pressure and there is intense selection on the plant host, the frequency of resistant A' allele will increase in the plant host population. Natural selection acting on the plant host favors the retention of a sufficient proportion of the A'-defense allele (Levin, 1976; Pimentel et al., 1975a). Then herbivore numbers and feeding pressure will decline. The host population probably can never develop 100 percent–effective defensive mechanisms against all herbivores because the production and maintenance of these mechanisms must, at some point, become too costly (McKey, 1974; Cates, 1975; Krischik and Denno, 1983; Rhoades, 1985; Rosenthal, 1986). At the point when herbivore numbers have declined to a suitably low level, the host will no longer benefit from spending energy to increase its level of resistance to its predators.

Evolution of Living Systems

Since the first organisms appeared on earth several billion years ago, many basic trends in the evolution of living systems have been apparent. First, the living system has become more complex, with an ever-growing number of species. Although the total number of species present on earth at any one time has grown, more than 99 percent of all species have become extinct and have been replaced in time with new species better adapted to the developing ecosystem (Allee et al., 1949).

Clearly, the growing number of species has increased the complexity of the existing living system and raised the total volume of living biomass or protoplasm on earth. The growth in living biomass has made it possible to capture more energy that flows through the living system. At the same time, more resources from the environment are being utilized and are flowing through the living system. Thus, the total size and complexity of the living system has increased its capacity to convert more and more energy and mineral resources into itself. This, increased capacity, in turn, appears to have increased the stability of the living system, making it less susceptible to major fluctuations in the physical and chemical environment.

Additional stability in the ecosystem has evolved via genetic feedback between the parasites and their food hosts. Because the activities of parasites (including herbivores and predators) and hosts are interdependent, stability is essential to their survival. Parasites cannot increase their harvest of food from the host species population indefinitely without eventually destroying their food host and, therefore, themselves. This is not to imply that group selection and self-limitation are dominant activities in natural systems. Hosts under selective pressure may evolve various defense mechanisms to protect themselves from exploitation by parasites (Pimentel, 1988). This evolution takes place primarily by individual selection. Evolution in parasite-host systems, together with complexity in general in the ecosystem, leads to increased stability, and has survival value for natural living systems.

Biogeochemical Cycles

Several chemical elements, including carbon, hydrogen, oxygen, phosphorus, potassium, and calcium, are essential to the functioning of living organisms and therefore of ecological systems. Various biogeochemical cycles have evolved to ensure that plants, animals, and microbes have suitable amounts of these vital elements. Biogeochemical cycles both conserve the vital elements and keep them in circulation in the ecosystem. Indeed, the mortality of living organisms keeps the vital elements in circulation, enabling the system to evolve and adapt to new and changing environments. These biogeochemical cycles are themselves a product of evolution in the living system. If the living system had not evolved a way of keeping vital chemicals in circulation and conserving them, it would have become extinct long ago.

Every organism, whether a single cell, a tree, or a human, requires nitrogen for its vital structure, function, and reproduction. Although the atmosphere is the major nitrogen reservoir, plants cannot use atmospheric nitrogen directly. It must be converted into nitrates, which is often accomplished by nitrogen-fixing bacteria and algae (Figure 4.2). Some of these bacteria have a

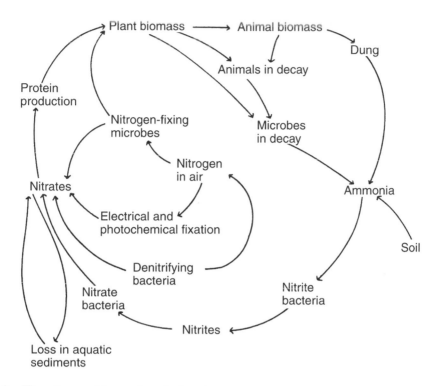

4.2   The nitrogen biogeochemical cycle.

symbiotic relationship with certain plants, such as legumes. These plants develop nodules and other structures on their roots to protect and feed the bacteria. Some plants, for example, provide the associated bacteria with carbohydrates and other nutrients. In turn, the bacteria fix nitrogen for their own and the legume plant's use. In addition, free-living bacteria such as *Azotobacter* and blue-green algae such as *Anabaena* fix atmospheric nitrogen for their own use. When these bacteria and algae die and are decomposed by other bacteria or algae, their nitrogen is released for use by other plants.

The decay of plants, animals, and microbes also recycles nitrogen, but in the form of ammonia (Figure 4.2). Microbes carry out most decomposition of protoplasm. The ammonia released by decomposition of the organic matter is in turn converted by bacteria into nitrates, available for use by plants. Some additional nitrates are produced by electrical storms (Figure 4.2), and some ammonia becomes available to the biological system from volcanic action and igneous rocks.

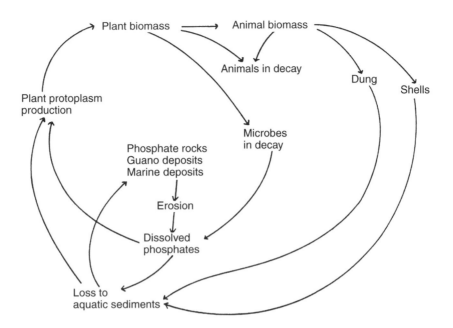

4.3   The phosphorus biogeochemical cycle.

Phosphorus, another essential chemical element, is recycled by the decomposition of plants, animals, and microbes (Figure 4.3). Additional phosphorus comes from soil and aquatic systems. At the same time, some phosphorus is continually lost to the aquatic system, especially the marine system, when it is deposited in sediments. Like nitrogen and phosphorus, all other essential elements depend on the functioning living system for recycling. Sometimes particular organisms serve special roles in recycling the vital elements. Thus, the living system conserves and recycles the essential elements in the biological system.

Aquatic Ecosystems

Water covers approximately 73 percent of the earth, but the aquatic life system accounts for only 43 percent of the total biomass produced annually (Odum, 1978; Pimentel and Hall, 1989). The prime reason for its low productivity is a shortage of nutrients, and the second is lack of sunlight penetration into the aquatic system. However, some shallow aquatic systems with ample nutrients are extremely productive, yielding up to 20 tons/ha of plant biomass.

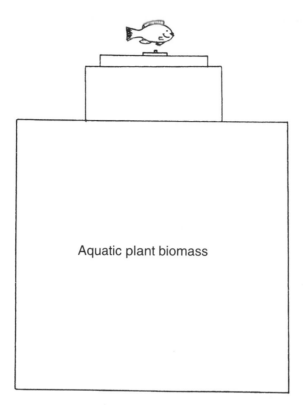

4.4 Trophic pyramid in an aquatic ecosystem indicating the small quantity of fish that might be harvested from the relatively large quantity of aquatic plant biomass.

Although aquatic systems may be productive in terms of plant biomass, the production of fish biomass is quite low. Primary producers (phytoplankton) must often pass through 3 to 5 trophic levels before the biomass is harvested as fish (Figure 4.4). Because only about 10 percent of the energy generally moves from one level to the next, little fish biomass is produced at the top of the food chain. For example, even with 20 tons/ha of plant biomass, the fish harvest is estimated to be only 0.2 kg/ha.

Humans harvest less than 1 percent of their total food from the aquatic system because of its low productivity. Thus, it is doubtful that the aquatic system is capable of providing more human food in the future. In fact, a future *decrease* is likely because of overfishing and pollution.

Terrestrial Ecosystems

Land covers only 27 percent of the earth, yet this small terrestrial system produces an estimated 57 percent of the earth's total biomass (Odum, 1978; Pimentel and Hall, 1989). Forest and agricultural lands account for about 90 percent of total biomass production. More than 99 percent of human food comes from the terrestrial system and less than 1 percent from the aquatic system (Pimentel et al., 1993a).

Solar energy powers the ecosystem. During a year the solar energy reaching 1 ha in temperate North America averages about 14 billion kcal (Reifsnyder and Lull, 1965). Nearly half of this, or 7 billion kcal, comes during the 4-month summer growing season. Under favorable conditions of moisture and soil nutrients, the annual production of natural plant biomass in North America averages about 2400 kg/ha (dry) per year (Pimentel et al., 1978).

The productivity of the terrestrial system depends upon the quality of soil, availability of water, energy, favorable climate, and amount and diversity of biological resources present. Agricultural productivity is affected by the same basic factors that influence the productivity of these natural systems.

Agricultural Ecosystems

To obtain food, humans manipulate natural ecosystems. In altering the natural system to produce vegetation and/or animal types (livestock) different from those typical of the natural systems, a certain amount of energy input is necessary. In principle, the greater the change required in the natural system to produce crops and livestock, the greater the energy and labor that must be expended.

This same principle applies in reverse. That is, the more closely the agricultural system resembles the original natural ecosystem, the fewer the inputs of energy and other factors required. Equally important, the closer the agricultural system is to the natural ecosystem, the more sustainable it is, because less environmental degradation takes place in the less intensively managed systems.

The productivity of agricultural plants is limited by the same factors that limit natural plants—sunlight, water, nutrients, temperature, and animal/plant pests. The agriculturalist seeks to maximize the availability of favorable environmental factors for the crop plants while minimizing the impacts of pests.

Water

Water, followed by nutrients, is the principal limiting factor for terrestrial plant productivity, including agriculture. The United States invests about half of its fossil energy input in agricultural production into supplying irrigation water (20 percent) and fertilizer nutrients (30 percent) (Pimentel and Wen Dazhong, 1990). Agricultural practices that help to conserve water and soil nutrients not only contribute to crop productivity but also reduce the costly fossil energy inputs in the system (Pimentel et al., 1987). Water and soil nutrients can best be conserved by controlling soil erosion and water runoff. These steps also maximize the amount of soil organic matter present, which helps maintain nutrients, water, tilth, and the buffering capacity of the soil. All of these characteristics, combined with ample water and soil nutrients, help keep the agroecosystem productive.

As in natural ecosystems, the goal in agriculture should be to conserve nutrients and water for optimal production while maintaining the stability of the system. In agriculture, this would mean recycling manure, crop residues, and other wastes.

Nutrients

After water, soil nutrients (nitrogen, phosphorus, potassium, and calcium) are the most important factors limiting crop productivity. Valuable nutrient resources available for recycling include crop residues and livestock manure. Crop residues total about 430 million tons/yr. This amount of crop residue contains about 4.3 million tons of nitrogen, 0.4 million tons of phosphorus, 4.0 million tons of potassium, and 2.6 million tons of calcium. The total amount of livestock manure produced annually in the United States is about 1 billion tons. This manure contains about 0.25 percent nitrogen, 0.06 percent phosphorus, and 0.02 percent potassium (Troeh and Thompson, 1993). These quantities of nutrients in both the residues and manure are significantly greater than the quantities of commercial fertilizer applied annually in the United States, which contain 11 million tons of nitrogen, 5 million tons of phosphorus, and 6 million tons of potassium (USDA, 1991a). Except for the extremely small amount of crop residues that are harvested annually, most of the crop residues are recycled on U.S. agricultural land. However, estimates are that only 0.5 million tons of the total nitrogen in the manure are recoverable and usable with present technology. Some of the difficulty is due to the uneven distribution of livestock and crop areas. From 30 to 90 percent of the nitrogen is often lost through ammonia volatilization when manure is left on the surface of croplands and pasturelands (Vanderholm, 1975). However, less than 5 percent of the nitrogen is lost as ammonia when the manure is plowed under immediately.

The major cause of soil-nutrient loss in the United States is soil erosion (Pimentel et al., 1995). Average soil erosion rates are 13 tons/ha/yr (USDA, 1994). A ton of rich agricultural soil contains about 4 kg of nitrogen, 1 kg of phosphorus, 20 kg of potassium, and 10 kg of calcium (Alexander, 1977; Greenland and Hayes, 1981). For nitrogen alone, 20 tons of soil contains 80 kg/ha, which is almost half of the average of 155 kg/ha of nitrogen fertilizer that is applied to U.S. corn (USDA, 1993).

Soil erosion selectively removes different components from the soil. Eroded material usually contains 1.3 to 5 times more organic matter than the remaining soil (Barrows and Kilmer, 1963; Allison, 1973). Soil organic matter is extremely important to the productivity of the land because it helps retain water in the soil and improves soil structure and cation-exchange capacity. In addition, organic matter is the major source of nutrients needed by plants (Volk and Loeppert, 1982). About 95 percent of the nitrogen in the surface soil is stored in the organic matter.

U.S. farmers apply 15 million tons of nitrogen as commercial fertilizer annually, with a total value of $5 billion. Microbes fix about 14 million tons of nitrogen in the United States annually (Delwiche, 1970). This nitrogen has an economic value of nearly $5 billion today.

The harvest of the corn crop itself removes from 25 to 50 percent of the total nitrogen applied. Some nitrogen (15 to 25 percent) is lost by volatilization and 10 to 50 percent by leaching (Schroder, 1985).

Pest Controls

In seeking to achieve pest control, agriculturalists would do well to mimic the natural system. They can do so by maintaining the genetic resistance of crops to pests such as insects, plant pathogens, and weeds; encouraging pests' natural enemies; employing crop rotation and other crop diversity patterns; and utilizing natural forage and trees where appropriate (Pimentel, 1991a). For example, the spotted alfalfa aphid is kept under biological control through the introduction of natural enemies and using alfalfa varieties naturally resistant to the aphid (PSAC, 1965).

Crop rotation can be highly effective in pest control, as demonstrated with the control of the corn rootworm complex (Pimentel, 1977a). In addition to aiding in insect control, crop rotation may also help reduce disease and weed problems.

In the United States, most plant pathogens are controlled through plant host resistance. It is estimated that nearly 100 percent of all crops planted in the nation contain some degree of enhanced resistance to pests (Pimentel, 1991a). Farmers can also prevent disease by planting disease-free propagated material and by using other cultural methods that eliminate the source of the innoculum.

Most weed control is accomplished through mechanical tillage, rotation, and various polycultural means (Pimentel, 1991a). Options for weed control are generally fewer than options for insect and plant pathogen control.

Agricultural Ecosystem Stability

A relatively stable natural ecosystem increases the stability of the human food supply. Over time, humans have enhanced agricultural stability by selecting crops and livestock that are best adapted to particular environments. In addition, they have used increased energy inputs to enhance or control various aspects of the agricultural environment. For example, natural nutrient limitations have been offset by the addition of fertilizers, water shortages overcome by irrigation, and pest attacks controlled by pesticides and various cultural and biological controls.

Species Diversity

Wild plants and animals are the original sources of genetic material used for breeding resistance to pests and improving other crop and livestock features that contribute to increased yields.

Unfortunately, because of the conversion of extensive natural ecosystems into agricultural land, thousands of species are being lost each year (Ehrlich and Ehrlich, 1990; Wilson, 1988a). The most rapid loss of biological diversity is occurring in tropical forests and savannas, the same regions where most crop and livestock species originated. This loss has alarming implications for future production of human food, important medicines, and other products that are obtained from biological resources.

Crop Yields

On rich agricultural soils with ample water and fertilizers, the average biomass production for several major crops is about 15 tons/ha. However, under relatively poor agricultural conditions, biomass yields may range from only 0.5 to 1 tons/ha. Forests on good soils, with ample water and nutrients, and at the proper growth stage may reach a yield of 15 tons/ha. However, on average the yield of forests is about 3 tons/ha.

Under favorable atmospheric conditions and with the addition of nitrogen, phosphorus, potassium, and calcium fertilizers, hybrid corn, one of our most productive crops, will yield annually about 15,000 kg/ha of biomass (dry) or 7500 kg/ha of grain. Wheat production in North America averages about 7000 kg of biomass/ha, or about 3000 kg/ha of grain. Both of these yields are much higher than the yield of natural vegetation. However, many agricultural crops are less productive than either corn or wheat, and overall average crop biomass production is probably close to that of natural vegetation.

To convert corn biomass to heat energy, the 15,000 kg/ha yield is multiplied by 4500 kcal/kg, yielding 67.5 million kcal/ha. This represents only 0.5 percent of the total solar energy reaching 1 ha during the year. The percentage of solar energy harvested as wheat biomass is 0.2 percent. Natural vegetation, producing about 2400 kg/ha, converts about 0.1 percent of solar energy into biomass. This 0.1 percent is the average conversion for all natural vegetation in North America and is about the average for U.S. agriculture (Pimentel et al., 1978).

From the total of 15,000 kg/ha of corn biomass, as mentioned above, humans are able to harvest approximately half, or 7500 kg/ha, as food. This is obviously much more than hunter-gatherers were able to harvest per hectare from the natural environment. Natural ecosystems yield only about 2400 kg/ha of plant biomass, only a small portion of which would be converted into animal and microbe biomass.

Annual Versus Perennial Crops

Most crops cultivated in the world are tropical annuals. The fact that most human societies probably originated in the tropics may explain in part why so many crop and livestock species originated there. Originally, annuals were a practical choice for crops, because pest problems, particularly weeds, could be minimized and the land could be cleared of all vegetation by burning and digging. This gave newly planted crops a head start on weeds and other potential pests (Pimentel, 1977a).

At present, 90 percent of the world's food supply comes from only 15 species of crop plants and 8 species of livestock (Pimentel et al., 1986a). This is a very narrow base, especially considering that there are about 10 million species of plants and animals in the world today (Ehrlich and Wilson, 1991; Myers, 1983).

The human food supply would be enhanced if it could rely on more perennial crops, especially grains (Pimentel et al., 1986a). Because grain crops supply approximately 80 percent of the total food produced worldwide, the development of perennial grain crops would add stability to the food supply and the agricultural ecosystem. A perennial crop is one that might have to be replanted only once every 5 years.

The advantages of perennial grain crops in particular are manifold. First, the soil would not have to be tilled each year. Annual soil tillage requires enormous amounts of fossil, draft animal, and human energy. The energy required to till 1 ha ranges from 200,000 kcal for hand tillage to nearly 600,000 kcal for a small tractor. Further, decreasing tilling would conserve soil and water resources, yielding additional energy savings. Erosion and runoff occur primarily when the soil is tilled and exposed to rain and wind. Vegetative cover is the principal way to protect soil and water resources (Pimentel et al., 1995), so a perennial grain crop would be valuable in decreasing erosion in world agriculture.

At present there are no commercial perennial grain crops, and their development will depend in part on genetic engineering, which in turn depends on maintaining biological diversity. Nature provides the genes that humans use to develop new crop and livestock types. New genetic materials will also be important for use in food processing and the development of new drugs and medicines. Unfortunately, scientists have not had time to investigate the full potential of the world's natural biological resources.

Clearly, much can be learned from natural systems about maintaining the productivity and sustainability of agricultural systems. If the agricultural production system could be designed to more closely resemble natural ecological systems, it would require fewer energy inputs and be more productive and sustainable.

Food Needs for Future Generations

The degradation of agricultural land, forests, and other biological resources greatly affects their productivity. Today the productivity of these resources is being maintained in large measure by the increased input of fossil energy for fertilizers, pesticides, and irrigation. Thus, it will be a challenge to meet the food needs of the rapidly expanding human population. Food production in all countries—especially in the developing nations, where the population growth rates are high and the generation times short—must increase at a greater rate than ever before.

A study by the National Academy of Sciences (1977) targeted 8 food sources for increase: rice, wheat, corn, sugar, cattle, sorghum, millet, and cassava. These foods provide from 70 to 90 percent of all the calories and 66 to 90 percent of the protein consumed in developing countries. The NAS report recommended that developing countries increase food production by 3 to 4 percent per year until the year 2000. Is this realistic when the annual rate of increase in food production has been only 2.5 percent in recent years (NAS, 1977)?

Growing food grain exports in the early 1970s encouraged the United States and other developed countries to expand their production (Webb and Jacobsen, 1982). Because of these encouraging trends, many U.S. farmers purchased more land and invested heavily in new machinery. However, a few years later the situation turned around: OPEC increased oil prices, making it necessary for developing countries to spend their limited funds for imported oil instead of imported food. This change depressed the agricultural markets in most of the developed nations, a situation that continues to date.

Concerning the quantity of food that will have to be produced in the future to meet the food demand of a rapidly growing population, D. Bauman (1982, personal communication) predicted that "an amount of food equal to all the food produced so far in the history of mankind will have to be produced in the next 40 years" to fulfill human food needs. This projection further confirms the staggering impact of the rapidly growing world population on food and natural resources.

Even if individual dietary patterns are modified to include less animal products and more plant foods such as grain, food production must be greatly increased. The message is clear: more food—much more—will have to be grown to sustain the rapidly growing human population of the future.

Requirements for Solving Food Problems

To increase food supplies for current and future populations, humans must protect the environment, develop new technologies, and limit human population growth.

Safeguarding the Environment

The environmental resources for food production, including land, water, energy, forests, and other biological resources, must be protected if food production is to continue to grow. Over the past 4 decades, humans have allowed environmental resources to degrade rapidly. As noted, we have been offsetting this degradation with fertilizers, irrigation, and other massive inputs—all based on fossil energy. Thus, we have been substituting a nonrenewable resource for a renewable resource. Clearly, this has been a dangerous, if not a disastrous, policy.

Science and Technology

Recent decades have witnessed many exciting and productive technological advances that have increased food supplies. For example, advances in plant genetics for some major crops have raised the "harvest index." In addition, agricultural chemicals, pesticides, and fertilizers have helped increase yields of food and fiber crops per ha. Improved processing methods have enabled the food supply to be safely extended beyond harvest time, and the growing transportation network has moved more food from production sites to far-distant markets. In the industrialized nations, the result has been a more abundant, more nutritious, and safer food supply. People living in developing nations, however, have not been as fortunate, although enhanced breeds such as high-yielding rice have benefited millions in the Far East (Baum, 1986).

The new genetic engineering technology offers further promise of raising crop and livestock production and improving the use of some major resources. This will be especially true if, for example, we can develop rice, wheat, corn, and other cereal grain crops that will fix nitrogen, as legumes do. Of the essential nutrients, nitrogen fertilizer requires the largest fossil energy input. Thus, developing cereal grains that fix nitrogen will be a major breakthrough. However, conservative estimates of when this breakthrough will be achieved range from 20 to 30 years in the future.

Some of the other promised benefits of genetic engineering, such as plants that grow with little or no water, are without scientific basis. Even if many of the promises of biotechnology are forthcoming, it is essential that quality soil, water, and biological resources are maintained.

Biotechnology and other new technologies undoubtedly will help conserve energy resources and facilitate increased food production. Sufficient, reliable energy resources will have to be developed to replace most of the fossil fuels now being rapidly depleted. These new sources likely will be more costly than fossil fuels in terms of dollars and the environment. Solar, fission, perhaps fusion, and wind energy will become more viable in the future than they are today. But if we rely solely on new technological advances, we face major problems if the "lottery" of science does not pay off. These developments may not materialize as rapidly as needed to meet future needs. One has only to observe the plight of millions of people in Calcutta and Mexico City to recognize that science and technology have done little to improve their lives during recent decades. Per capita food supply (grains) has been declining for the past 15 years. Clearly, technology has not been able to keep food supplies increasing as rapidly as world population.

Population

Thus far, only factors affecting food production have been considered. But production is only one side of the food equation. The other is the demand, or rate of consumption. This is determined by the size of the human population. Ultimately, the size of the world population will determine the need for food. When human numbers exceed the capacity of the world to sustain them, then a rapid deterioration of human existence will follow. As it does with all forms of life, nature ultimately will control human numbers.

Strategies for increasing food production substantially over present levels and decreasing population growth must be developed now. Both parts of the food equation must be brought into balance if future generations are to have an adequate food supply and live in a world that supports a reasonably acceptable standard of living.

5

MANIPULATING ECOSYSTEMS FOR AGRICULTURE

David Pimentel and Marcia Pimentel

Ecosystems

An ecosystem is a network of energy and mineral flows in which the major functional components are populations of plants, animals, and microbes. These organisms live and perform different specialized functions in the system: plants are generally producers; animals, consumers; and microorganisms, decomposers. In each role, organisms carry out two basic tasks: 1) fixing and utilizing solar energy; and 2) conserving and recycling mineral resources (Figure 5.1).

The collection of solar energy needed to power the entire ecosystem depends directly on plants. Plants themselves depend on solar energy to meet their own energy needs. Of the total energy collected, they use about 25 percent for respiration, 35 percent for building and maintaining structure, and 35 percent for reproduction (Figure 5.2). Plants also produce a small surplus of energy that is used by consumers. Some animals and microorganisms feed directly upon the plant population, but others obtain their energy by feeding on first-order consumers. A relatively small amount of energy—between 5 and 10 percent—moves from one level to the next in the food chain (Pimentel, 1988).

When plants or the animals that feed on them die, decomposers obtain their share of the energy originally fixed by the plant population. Decomposer populations consist mainly of bacteria, fungi, protozoa, arthropods, and earthworms. Some invertebrate populations feed directly on the decaying organic matter, whereas others, such as dipteran larvae, feed on decomposer microorganisms.

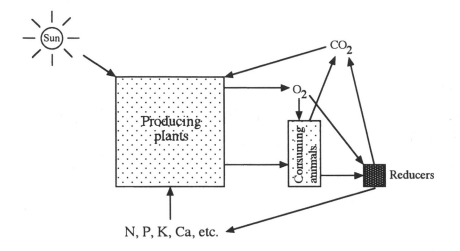

5.1   Producing plant-fixed solar energy which is consumed by animals, and which are in turn consumed by the reducers. The quantity of energy transferred is schematically diagrammed. Recycling of some of the mineral resources is illustrated.

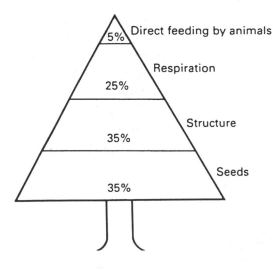

5.2   Of the solar energy fixed by crop plants, about 25 percent is used for respiration, 35 percent for building and maintaining the plant structure, and 35 percent for reproduction (seeds). The energy removed by direct feeding is estimated to be about 5 percent.

Decomposers are essential in the ecosystem because they help conserve mineral resources and cycle these essential elements back into the system for reuse. If the decomposers were unable to recycle the vital elements, the collection and conversion of energy into plant biomass would be limited and eventually cease. A shortage of any one essential element—nitrogen, phosphorus, potassium, calcium, sulfur—can limit or prevent the normal function of the entire ecosystem (Figure 5.1).

A given ecosystem comprises several thousand species of plants, animals, and microorganisms. The actual number of species in the ecosystem network depends on its boundaries and its physical environment. The interactions among and between organisms of the system help regulate and stabilize energy and mineral flows within complex ecosystems. Further, different ecosystems are interdependent; that is, energy and minerals frequently flow from one ecosystem to another.

Agriculture and the Natural Ecosystem

Neither humans, their crops, nor their livestock can exist independently from species in the natural ecosystem. A relatively small number of species—about 15 major crops and 8 major livestock types—are agriculturally produced in the world. By comparison, an estimated 500,000 species of wild plants, animals, and microbes exist in the United States alone. A majority of these wild species are necessary for maintenance of the life system. At present, no one knows how many of the 500,000 species in the U.S. ecosystem can be reduced or eliminated before human life is jeopardized. Therefore, existing biological diversity should be preserved and treasured. Environmental degradation caused by chemical pollutants, construction, deforestation, and other factors should be prevented.

Terrestrial and aquatic plants, including agricultural and forestry plants, not only convert sunlight into biomass energy but also remove carbon dioxide from the atmosphere, a benefit in the prevention of global warming and climate change. Plants also renew the oxygen supply and help clean the atmosphere of chemical pollutants.

Oxygen and ozone prevent a large percentage of the sun's ultraviolet light from reaching the earth and thereby protect plants and animals from injury and death. No terrestrial life could exist on our planet without the ozone shield. A small increase in the amount of ultraviolet light reaching the earth could have serious environmental effects, such as increased genetic mutations.

The excessive release of chlorofluorocarbons (CFCs) into the atmosphere has significantly reduced the ozone layer, allowing more ultraviolet light to reach the earth and increasing the incidence of cancer and eye problems. Nitrogen fertilizers also damage the ozone layer when they volatilize (Schneider, 1989).

Many species in the natural ecosystem play a vital role in the breakdown of wastes produced by humans, agriculture, and wild species. Americans produce about 120 million tons of organic waste annually, and their livestock produce another 1.6 billion tons. Clearly, humans would be buried in wastes were it not for the efficient decomposing organisms of the natural ecosystem. Bacteria, fungi, protozoa, arthropods, and earthworms all help degrade wastes. These decomposing organisms also recycle essential minerals for reuse by all members of the ecosystem.

Some organisms, such as earthworms, arthropods, and microbes, improve soil structure and help create new soil by decomposing organic wastes. For example, it is estimated that earthworms bring to the surface 2.5 to 63 tons of soil castings per hectare per year (Burges and Raw, 1967). Ants may carry an additional 10 tons to the surface (Kevan, 1962).

Other species make possible the pollination of domestic and natural plants to ensure fruit and seed production. In the United States, honeybees and wild bees pollinate crops valued at about $30 billion each year (Robinson et al., 1989). Bees and other animals are also vital in the pollination of natural vegetation.

The total number of honeybee colonies in New York state is estimated to be 125,000, with about 10,000 bees per colony. Wild bees, however, pollinate more than half of the blossoms and are vital to the success of seed and fruit production. An individual honeybee may visit 1000 blossoms on a bright sunny day, making about 10 trips and visiting about 100 blossoms on each trip. In New York state more than 2.5×1012 blossoms may be pollinated in a single day by honeybees and wild bees combined.

Biomass

Overall, humans and their agricultural system represent but a small percentage of the earth's total biomass. Human biomass in the United States averages about 19 kg/ha; U.S. livestock averages 78 kg/ha, outweighing the human population by more than 4 times.

Crops in the United States contribute slightly more than 20 percent of the total plant biomass produced annually. If all U.S. crops, pastures, and commercial forests were combined, the total would represent about 50 percent of the total vegetation biomass produced (Pimentel et al., 1978). Microbes are also important contributors. In rich productive soil, fungi and bacteria populations may total 4000 to 5000 kg/ha (wet).

Certain natural animal populations are abundant in favorable habitats. For example, earthworm populations may weigh up to 1500 kg/ha, and arthropod populations may weigh about 1000 kg/ha. Therefore, compared on a weight basis with humans and their livestock, the natural biota in the ecosystem significantly dominate in biomass.

Manipulating Agroecosystems

One of the earliest views of the relationship of humans to their ecosystem is found in Genesis 1:28, which says: "Be fruitful, and multiply, and replenish the earth, and subdue it." The implication seems clear that humans, by employing their energies, should overcome nature. The verse was prophetic; humans have been "fruitful" and are well on their way overpopulating the earth, threatening the very environment they depend on.

But it was more than mere population numbers that helped humans to subdue nature. The development of tools and machines, coupled with the discovery of new sources of power, especially those based on fossil energy, has enabled humans to exert tremendous control over the environment. As Forbes (1968) pointed out, science and technology are products of the "interaction between man and environment, based on the wide range of real or imagined needs and desires which guided man in his conquest of Nature."

In light of the exponential growth of the human population and of new technologies' ability to alter natural ecosystems, the solemn judgment of Dennis Gabor of the Imperial College of Science and Technology, London, is pertinent: "[E]xponential curves grow to infinity only in mathematics. In the physical world they either turn around and saturate, or they break down catastrophically. It is our duty as thinking men to do our best towards a gentle saturation instead of sustaining exponential growth, though this faces us with very unfamiliar and distasteful problems" (in Forbes, 1968). Evidence of the extensive alteration of the ecosystem by humans, their unrestrained use of energy, land, water, and biological resources, and uncontrolled population growth substantiate Gabor's view.

Human alteration of the natural ecosystem and use of energy to manage agricultural ecosystems directly affect food production. At this point it is helpful to examine the basic characteristics of ecosystems and then, in turn, to see how these characteristics are related to ecosystem management.

As ecosystems mature, or climax, they become more complex and contain a wide variety of plant, animal, and microbe species. Their increased diversity directly contributes to their stability. When natural ecosystems are disturbed, the numbers of species are reduced, and the system becomes relatively simple. After such an alteration, "successional change" begins, and the ecosystem slowly accumulates additional species. Gradually, a new complex and relatively stable ecosystem evolves. As it becomes more complex, an ecosystem captures and circulates increasing quantities of solar energy. More energy must be expended to alter a complex ecosystem than to alter a simple ecosystem. Of course, the quantity of energy needed to alter an ecosystem depends upon the extent of the changes. Clearly, less energy is required to change the numbers of one or two species in the ecosystem than to reduce an entire ecosystem to a pure monoculture of a single species.

For instance, when an ecosystem is altered for hay production, the natural vegetation has to be destroyed; the soil is tilled, limed, and fertilized; and the hay seed is sowed. Large inputs of energy are necessary to make this alteration, whether it is done by human power or by fuel-powered machinery. Changing an ecosystem to a row crop monoculture such as Brussels sprouts or corn requires even larger inputs of energy than changing to hay production. For this kind of modification, not only are energy inputs required to destroy the natural vegetation, but additional energy inputs are needed during the growing season to prevent the invasion of weeds and other pests.

Weeds, early successional plant species in nature, will quickly invade a newly planted Brussels sprout or corn field. The invading weeds must be uprooted, buried, or chemically destroyed, requiring energy expenditures. In spite of the technology available today, it is impossible to exterminate all weeds completely. Even if it were technically possible, it would be economically and energetically impractical. In addition to weeds, insect pests and plant pathogens may invade the crop monoculture. The control of these pests, whether accomplished by cultural, environmental, or chemical methods, requires substantial energy input.

In summary, natural ecosystems possess certain patterns of species interaction and development. Altering or changing the species structure of an ecosystem, especially converting it to a monoculture, requires relatively large energy expenditures. The amount of energy invested depends on the crop, growing season, and other aspects of the environment.

Interdependency of Factors in Crop Production

In the management and manipulation of agroecosystems, land, water, labor, and energy can be substituted for one another, within limits. The possibility of substituting any one of these factors for another provides some flexibility in the utilization and management of these resources.

In certain areas, for example, crops on 1 ha of high-quality land will yield as much as those grown on 2 ha of poorer-quality land. However, the application of fertilizers and other energy inputs, including labor, may improve the poorer-quality land to make it as productive as the high-quality land. Thus, land quality, as one factor in crop production, is dependent on available supplies of water, labor, and energy.

The impact of soil quality on crop yields and energy use is well illustrated by the environmental problem of soil erosion. In fertile agricultural land, topsoil depth usually averages 18 to 20 cm. Each 2.5 cm of topsoil lost from the land results in an average yield reduction of 250 kg/ha of corn, 161 kg/ha of wheat, 168 kg/ha of oats, or 175 kg/ha of soybeans (Pimentel et al., 1976). Although the reduced productivity of the eroded land can be offset by the use of more fertilizer and other inputs, all these interventions require considerable energy expenditures. About one-third of the topsoil from U.S. agricultural land already has been lost. An estimated 46 liters/ha of fossil energy are expended in the form of fertilizers and other inputs just to maintain the productivity of the eroded land.

More important than the loss of soil depth is the loss of water, nutrients, organic matter, and soil biota due to erosion. These losses may reduce crop yields from 15 to 30 percent during the growing season (Follett and Stewart, 1985).

Availability of water often influences the energy inputs and the amount of land needed for desired crop production. With ample moisture and heavy fertilizer use, crop plants can be grown densely, and high yields result. With limited moisture, however, fewer crop plants can be grown per hectare, less fertilizer can be applied, and crop yields decline.

In some regions, such as the wheat-growing section of the state of Washington, lack of moisture requires farmers to let fields lie fallow for a season before being replanted. During the fallow year the land collects and stores sufficient moisture to support a wheat crop the next year. In such an area, overall wheat production is low compared with locations where there is ample moisture.

Irrigation is a common method of making arid land more productive. Unfortunately, pumping and applying the water over large areas requires enormous energy inputs. Therefore, water supply must be considered another interdependent factor in crop production, along with energy, land, and labor.

Labor is the final element in the agricultural equation. Human power can be substituted for machinery power in crop production, though sometimes with little or no effect on yield. For example, a large portion of the agricultural work in India, Africa, Asia, Oceania, Latin America, and other developing countries is performed by human labor. By contrast, in the United States, Europe, and other developed countries, agriculture is heavily mechanized (Figure 5.3). Note that high crop yields are achieved in Taiwan and the United Arab Republic with minimal tractor power.

Energy, Labor, and a Standard of Living

All operations required in agriculture can be carried out by human power. However, producing crops by hand requires about 1200 hours/ha, and each person can manage only 1 ha during the growing season. Under such production conditions, only the bare minimum of essential human needs can be attained; the amount of the surplus (the crop yield not needed to feed the farmer's family) is extremely small. Only the surplus can be traded for other goods and services. For this reason, the standard of living achieved in most societies powered by human labor is relatively low compared with that possible when mechanization and large inputs of fossil fuel are used.

The definition of "standard of living" is based on the availability of goods and services, including food, clothing, housing, transportation, and health care. However, an ample supply of these things cannot and should not be equated with a high quality of life.

Fossil energy can replace large amounts of human labor, and the availability of relatively cheap supplies of fossil energy is a major reason the United States and other developed nations enjoy a high standard of living. For example, a gallon (3.79 liters) of gasoline sells for slightly more than $1.00 in the United States. Based on a minimum wage of $4.25 per hour, this gallon could be purchased with slightly more than 15 minutes of work. However, that gallon of gasoline in an engine will produce the equivalent of 97

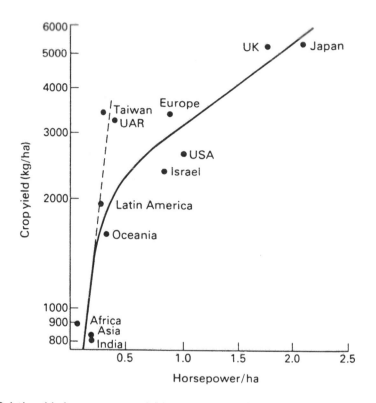

5.3 Relationship between crop yields per hectare of cereals, pulses, oil-seeds, sugar crops, potatoes, cassava, onions, and tomatoes, on one hand, and horsepower per hectare, on the other, in various countries and regions (Asia excludes China) (after Blaxter, 1978).

hours of manpower. Thus, 1 hour of labor at $4.25 would purchase the fossil fuel equivalent of about 375 hours of manpower.

The relative cost of gasoline and human labor affect the price of food. If fossil energy is cheap relative to the price of food, then fossil energy use in food production is an excellent investment. In the United States today, 1000 kcal of sweet corn in a can sells for about $1.00, whereas 1000 kcal of gasoline sells for only about $0.03. Hence, 1 kcal of sweet corn is worth 33 times more than 1 kcal of gasoline energy.

The relationship of energy expenditure and standard of living also can be clarified by comparing production of corn by labor-intensive and energy-intensive systems. In Mexico, for instance, about 1144 hours of human labor are required to produce 1 ha of corn by hand (Lewis, 1951). In the United States, under an energy-intensive system, only 10 hours of labor are expended per hectare. In the midwestern United States, 1 farmer can manage up to 100 ha of corn with the help of large fossil fuel inputs and mechanized equipment. The same farmer producing corn by hand could manage 1.5 ha at most. Assuming the same profit per hectare for each farmer, it is clear that the farmer managing 100 ha will be able to support a higher standard of living.

Liberal supplies of fossil energy have helped humans to manipulate eco-systems more effectively and efficiently for food production than ever before, and this has contributed directly to improving the standard of living in many parts of the world.

6

HUNTER-GATHERERS AND EARLY AGRICULTURE

David Pimentel and Marcia Pimentel

Before the development of agriculture and formal crop culture, wild plants and animals in the natural ecosystem were humans' only food. How much wild plant and animal biomass is available for food, and how much land do hunter-gatherers need to meet their food needs?

The total annual production of plant biomass in the temperate region averages about 2400 kg (dry) per hectare. Under favorable conditions this quantity of plant biomass might support an animal and microbe biomass of about 200 kg/ha (dry) per year. The proportions of the total 200 kg that comprise microbes, earthworms, arthropods, mammals, birds, and other animals are indicated in Figure 6.1.

Let us assume that a hunter-gatherer required 2500 kcal per day to meet his or her energy needs. By harvesting 0.1 percent of the available animal biomass from 40 ha, he or she would be able to consume 88 kcal per day (32,000 kcal per year) in the form of animal protein. The remaining 2412 kcal per day (880,500 kcal per year) of needed food energy would come from other sources, including seeds, nuts, fruits, roots, and other plant foods. Assuming that 1 kg of digestible plant material yields 3000 kcal, the hunter-gatherer would have to harvest about 300 kg of plant material from the 40 ha (7.5 kg/ha per year) to meet calorie needs. Although obtaining this amount of plant material suitable for food might not be possible in a heavily wooded habitat, it likely would be possible on land containing a mixture of wood, shrubs, and herbs, as well as a productive stream.

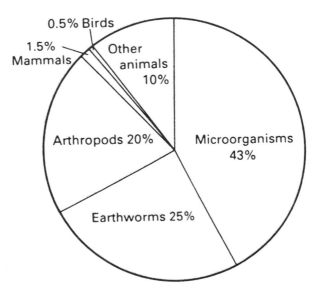

6.1   The proportion of the total biomass of 200 kg (dry) present in 1 ha that is made up of total animals and microorganisms biomass present in 1 ha.

If the plant food gathered contained an average of 5 percent protein, then a total of 12.2 kg of protein could be harvested per year, or about 34 g of plant protein per day. Combining the 34 g of plant protein and the 22 g of animal protein, the hunter-gatherer's diet would include a total of 56 g of protein per day under optimal conditions. The remaining calories would come from plant carbohydrates. Note that the consumption of fat was omitted from these calculations. Fats yielding 9 kcal/g would add substantially more calories to the daily intake. Except for animal flesh and such plant foods as nuts, the fat content of this diet would undoubtedly be lower than that of most diets consumed in the world today. Based on the preceding calculations, a family of five would require an estimated 200 ha of habitat from which to gather animal and plant food.

This estimate is based on an ideal ecosystem, one containing those wild plants and animals that are most suitable for human consumption. Researchers report that, in fact, modern-day hunter-gatherers need much more than 40 ha per person. For instance, Clark and Haswell (1970) estimate that at least 150 ha of favorable habitat per person are needed to secure an adequate food supply. In a moderately favorable habitat, these scientists estimate, 250 ha per person would be required. These estimates are 4 to 6 times greater than those in the model presented earlier.

In marginal environments, such as the cold northwestern Canadian region, each person needs about 14,000 ha to harvest about 912,500 kcal of food energy per year (Clark and Haswell, 1970). The land area may range as high as 50,000 ha per person in subarctic lands, and in these cold regions meat and animal products are the predominant foods in the diet. In fact, animal flesh and fat may constitute up to two-thirds of the food calories consumed.

Plant productivity in such marginal habitats may average only 10 to 200 kg/ha per year (Whittaker and Likens, 1975), and animal production may average only 1 to 4 kg/ha per year. The annual yield of meat for humans may average from 5 to 10 g/ha of protein.

Assuming that two-thirds of human calorie intake in such a habitat comes from animal matter, humans could easily consume 102 g of animal protein per day to meet their needs. The plant products consumed might add another 4 g, bringing the total protein intake per day to about 106 g. This is a high-protein diet, but it is not out of the range of population groups that eat high-protein diets today. For example, in the United States the average per capita protein consumption is about 106 g per day (USDA, 1990). To bring calorie intake up to the 2500 kcal level, animal fat intake would be higher than in the current U.S. diet, which averages more than 40 percent of calories from fat.

Hunters and Gatherers of Food

Hunter-gatherers probably expend 60 to 80 percent of their energy intake in securing food. In fact, obtaining food and collecting firewood for its preparation usually dominate the activities of these societies.

Because so much human energy is expended in searching for, collecting, and transporting food, let us consider the energy required by humans for these various activities. The energy expended is above that used for daily basal metabolism, which is about 45 kcal per hour, or 1080 kcal per day (Pyke, 1970). Walking at a rate of about 4 km (2.5 miles) per hour uses an average of 180 kcal per hour (Table 6.1). If the individual carries a load weighing from 9 to 23 kg while walking, the energy expended nearly doubles, to about 340 kcal per hour. Running at 11 to 13 km (7 to 8 miles) per hour uses 800 to 1000 kcal per hour. If the hunter-gatherer has to walk or run several km in pursuit of food, the energy expended in food procurement can be relatively large.

Table 6.1   Energy requirements for various activities (kcal/h)

Light work	kcal/ha	Moderate work	kcal/h
Sitting	19	Shoemaking	80–115
Writing	20	Sweeping	85–110
Standing relaxed	20	Dusting	110
Typing	16–40	Washing	125–215
Typing quickly	55	Charring	80–160
Sewing	30–90	Metal working	120–140
Dressing & undressing	33	Carpentering	150–190
Drawing	40–50	House painting	145–160
Lithography	40–50	Walking	130–240
Violin playing	40–50		
Tailoring	50–85		
Washing dishes	60		
Ironing	60		
Book binding	45–90		

Hard work	kcal/ha	Very hard work	kcal/h
Polishing	175	Stonemasonry	350
Joiner work	195	Sawing wood	420
Blacksmithing	275–350	Coal mining (average for shift)	800–1,000
Riveting	275	Running	800–1,000
Marching	280–400	Climbing	400–900
Cycling	180–600	Walking very quickly	570
Rowing	120–600	Rowing very quickly	1,240
Swimming	200–700	Running very quickly	1,240
		Walking upstairs	1,000

Source: From Pyke, 1970.

Some hunter-gatherer communities exist at a density of 1 person per 15,800 to 31,600 ha (Sahlins, 1972). If only two-thirds of such a population actively hunts and gathers, then each person must search up to 47,900 ha (185 square miles) per year for food. The remaining third of the population, consisting of young children and elderly, usually does little or no hunting and gathering.

If hunter-gatherers were to search 47,900 ha for food, covering 58 meter-wide swaths, then they would have to travel 8316 km/yr to cover the entire area. This would require that a person walk 4 km per hour for 40 hours per week for 52 weeks per year. Obviously, this pace would test the endurance of the most hardy individual; early hunter-gatherers could not work at such a rate, nor can their present-day counterparts.

Hunter-gatherers do not have to search the total area for food. Because they know their territory well, they know approximately where to find food, greatly reducing the distances they have to travel in search of food. However, distant food locations, even if known, would require a long trip. For example, a journey from one side to the other of the hypothetical 47,900 ha area would cover about 22 km. A round trip across this area would require an expenditure of about 1980 kcal.

The !Kung bushmen, who presently inhabit the Dobe area of Botswana, Africa, illustrate the energy economy of a hunter-gatherer society (Lee, 1969; Lee and DeVore, 1976). The population studied consisted of 248 individuals and occupied an area of 2850 km². Each person required 10.4 km2, or 1040 ha, for support. Note that this is much less land than the hunter-gatherers studied by Sahlins occupied—only 3 percent as much.

The habitat in which the !Kung bushmen live is relatively arid, with an annual rainfall of only 150 to 250 mm per year (Lee, 1969; Lee and DeVore, 1976; Marshall, 1976). Permanent watering holes, existing only in locations where the underlying limestone strata have been exposed, provide the only reliable supply of water. During the rainy season, water is also readily available at temporary water holes. A critical decision facing the bushmen is where to locate their camps. The location must allow them easily to obtain both food and water. Because water is the major limiting factor, the bushmen usually camp within easy reach of a reliable water source.

The food gathered by the bushmen consists, by weight, of 33 percent mongongo nuts, 37 percent meat, and 30 percent miscellaneous plant foods (Lee, 1969; Marshall, 1976). The nuts yield 1200 kcal/day, meat 768 kcal/day, and other plant foods 172 kcal/day, totaling a daily energy intake of 2140 kcal. This means that mongongo nuts contribute most (56 percent) of the daily calorie intake of the !Kung bushmen (Figure 6.2).

As one might expect, the bushmen prefer to collect the desirable foods that are closest to a water supply. They occupy a camp for a period of weeks and literally eat their way out of it. For example, they often camp in the nut forests and "exhaust the nuts within a 1.6 km (1 mile) radius during the first

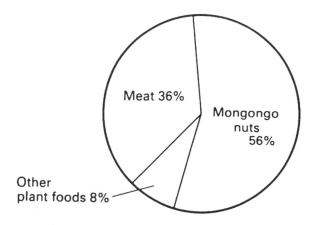

6.2   The percentage of various food types that make up the daily diet of the !Kung bushmen (Lee, 1969).

week of occupation, within a 3.2 km radius the second week, and within a 4.8 km radius the third week" (Lee, 1969).

The energy cost of obtaining mongongo nuts increases with their distance from camp. The cost curve rises gradually as the distance increases from 3 to 19 km (Figure 6.3). After 19 km, however, the cost curve rises sharply, because the gatherer must make a 2-day round trip. An overnight hike requires the gatherer to carry water and heavier loads during the entire trip.

An alternative to making longer food-gathering trips is to eat less desirable foods that can be found closer to the water holes. During the dry season, when there are fewer water holes, the bushmen use both strategies to maintain their food supplies. During these stress periods, "the older, less mobile members of camp stay close to home and collect the less desirable foods while the younger, more active members make the longer trips to the nut forests" (Lee, 1969).

During the rainy season, when there are many temporary pools of water, camps are located so that both nuts and water are relatively close. During these ideal periods, the gatherers seldom travel more than 9.7 km (6 miles) round-trip to collect nuts. The total average energy expenditure for a day that includes nut collecting is about 2680 kcal. This energy expenditure can be broken down by activity, as shown in Table 6.2.

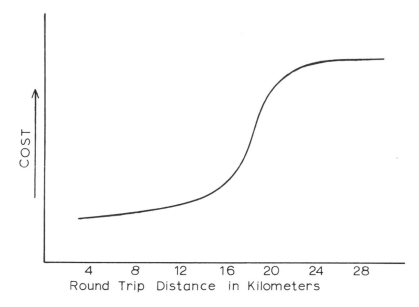

6.3   The energy cost of obtaining mongongo nuts at different distances (after Lee, 1969)

Table 6.2   Input/output analysis of !Kung bushmen gathering mongongo nuts at a distance of 4.8 km from their camp

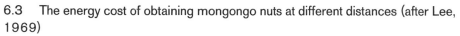

		Hours	**kcal**
Inputs			
Travel to location of nuts		1.2	270
Collecting nuts		3	675
Return trip to camp carrying 12.5 kg nuts		1.2	462
	SUBTOTAL		1,407
Sleep		10.5	473
Other activities		8	800
	TOTAL	24	2,680
Outputs			
Shelled nuts, 1.75 kg			10,500
OUTPUT/INPUT RATIO			3.9:1

Source: Based on Lee, 1969.

The energy expended to collect nuts gathered at an average distance of 4.8 km and the energy return from nut food can be calculated from the data of Lee (1969). Walking at 4 km per hour, it takes about 1.2 hours to reach the location of the nuts. Walking expends about 180 kcal per hour (Table 6.1), and basal metabolism requires 45 kcal per hour, for a total of 225 kcal per hour. Over 1.2 hours, the total energy expended is 270 kcal. Collecting nuts for an estimated 3 hours at 225 kcal per hour burns an estimated 675 kcal.

The return trip to camp at a distance of 4.8 km also takes about 1.2 hours. However, carrying a 12.5 kg load of nuts while walking requires more calories— an estimated 385 kcal per hour (340 kcal + 45 kcal basal metabolism)—than walking unencumbered does. For 1.2 hours, this activity requires 462 kcal.

The bushmen rest and sleep 10.5 hours per day, consuming 473 kcal (the basal rate). Postulate that other light activities are carried on for 8 hours per day at 100 kcal per hour (55 kcal + 45 kcal basal metabolism), or 800 kcal total. This brings the total energy expenditure per day to 2680 kcal.

The 12.5 kg load of nuts contains about 2500 nuts, from which about 1.75 kg of nut meat is extracted for consumption. This volume of nut meat yields about 10,500 kcal.

With 2680 kcal expended to obtain 10,500 kcal of nuts, the basic output/ input ratio is 3.9:1. Using similar assumptions but with the nuts 9.6 km distant, the output/input ratio declines only slightly, to 3.3: 1 (Table 6.3).

Table 6.3   Input/output analysis of !Kung bushmen gathering mongongo nuts at a distance of 9.6 km from their camp

		Hours	kcal
Inputs			
Travel to location of nuts		2.4	540
Collecting nuts		3	675
Return trip to camp carrying 12.5 kg of nuts		2.4	924
	SUBTOTAL		2,139
Sleep		10.5	473
Other activities		8	600
	TOTAL	24	3,212
Outputs			
Nuts shelled, 1.75 kg			10,500
OUTPUT/INPUT RATIO			3.3:1

Source: Based on Lee, 1969.

These output/input ratios are based on data showing that women collect an average of 2.2 days per week (range 1.2 to 3.2 days) and obtain 23,100 kcal in nuts per week. This amount provides sufficient food calories for the gatherer (14,296) as well as a surplus of about 38 percent. The surplus is needed to help feed the children and elderly dependents who make up the third of the population that does not gather food.

If hunters and gatherers have to work an average of 2.2 days per week to obtain food, that leaves approximately 4.8 days for other activities. These include gathering firewood, moving, constructing shelters and clothing, caring for children, and enjoying leisure time (Lee, 1969; Marshall, 1976). Observations indicate that bushmen value their leisure and enjoy dancing, visiting other camps, and engaging in other social activities.

Early Agriculture

Although we have no written account of the evolution of agriculture, we can logically reconstruct what might have happened. No doubt early agriculture evolved slowly from less structured societies of food gatherers. We know that gatherers brought fruits, nuts, vegetables, and seeds, including grains, back to camp for consumption. As expected, some seeds were dropped on the soil in the clearing of the camp and had the opportunity to grow there. Upon returning to the same campsite some time later, the hunter-gatherers discovered a concentration of grains, vegetables, fruits, and/or nuts. Some of the more observant people probably associated seeds with plants and began to plant seeds themselves. The relative ease of harvesting such crops as opposed to randomly gathering food in nature would encourage more plantings. The trend toward food cultivation is thought to have been slow, with the percentage of the food supply produced from gardens gradually increasing over time.

One important step in the emergence of agriculture was the deliberate removal of existing natural vegetation, including shrubs and trees, which would interfere and compete with crop growth. Burning was the easiest and most common means of clearing the land. Thorough burning not only completely destroyed weeds but also added nutrients to the soil. Following burning, the plots were generally clear except for a few large trees and charred stumps.

Early farmers planted crops by poking holes in the soil with digging sticks and dropping the seeds into the holes. Placing seeds in the cleared ground speeded their germination and subsequent growth so they could compete more successfully with other vegetation. After being planted, the early crops were given little or no care. A few months or even a year later, the farmers might return to harvest their crop, or what was left of it. Mammals, birds, insects, and disease organisms shared in the harvest, and weed competition reduced yields. Many of these same pest species still reduce crop yields today.

The next step in the development of agriculture was to expand the crop plantings sufficiently to produce most of the food supply. With time, the camps became relatively permanent because an ample food supply existed nearby; men and women no longer had to travel to find food. Living close to the plantings allowed a group to claim ownership and to protect the plantings from other humans as well as from mammals, birds, and other pests.

Early plots were planted and harvested for about 2 years, then abandoned because production declined as nutrients in the soil became depleted and other problems (such as pest outbreaks) developed. Interestingly, this "cut/burn," or "swidden," type of agriculture is still practiced today in many parts of the world (Ruthenberg, 1971). Swidden agriculture requires that farmed land lie fallow for 10 to 20 years before it can be cleared again and farmed. During the long fallow period, the soil gradually accumulates the nutrients needed for successful crop production.

Swidden agriculture can cause severe soil-erosion problems, especially when practiced on slopes in large hectarages. Erosion, of course, is a major global problem with all crop production systems, but the damage is intensified when hilly cropland is left without vegetation (Pimentel, 1993). Also, if crop residues are harvested and burned, the soil is left unprotected and susceptible to erosion. Thus, there is reason to discourage the burning of crop residues.

A study of a primitive agricultural society in New Guinea provides many insights into the energy inputs and outputs of a swidden-type agricultural system (Rappaport, 1968; 1971). New Guinea has a tropical mountainous ecosystem with about 3910 mm of rainfall per year. The relatively steep slopes and heavy rainfall combine to make soil erosion a problem. These primitive agriculturalists, however, practice soil conservation by employing several of the conservation techniques previously mentioned.

When the New Guinea community was studied, the village numbered 204 inhabitants and occupied about 830 ha. Only about 364 ha of this land was suitable for cultivation. The village annually planted about 19 ha of crops, but because some crops required 2 years before they could be harvested, about

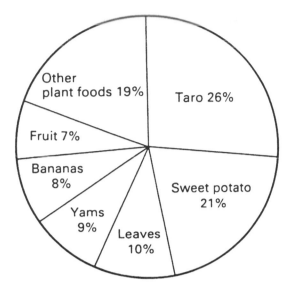

Other plant foods 19%

Taro 26%

Fruit 7%

Bananas 8%

Sweet potato 21%

Yams 9%

Leaves 10%

6.4   Percentage of the plant materials consumed by the villagers in New Guinea.

37 ha were cultivated at any one time. As a result, nearly 90 percent of the village croplands lay fallow each year.

The villagers' food was almost entirely (99 percent) of plant origin. The primary plants consumed (by weight) were taro, sweet potato, fruit, leaves, yams, and bananas (Figure 6.4). The animal protein came primarily from pigs raised by the villagers, who also hunted and ate marsupials, snakes, lizards, birds, and insect grubs.

The adult person's diet averaged about 2400 kcal per day and contained about 35 g of protein, mostly of plant origin (Rappaport, 1968). This protein intake is low by current Food and Agriculture Organization (FAO) standards, which recommend a daily intake of about 40 g of protein per day for an adult living under these conditions.

As expected, food production in swidden agriculture is labor intensive. The New Guinea villagers worked an estimated 1869 hours per hectare per year in crop production (Rappaport, 1968; 1971). About 42 percent of the labor input went into weeding, 15 percent into clearing trees and brush (Table 6.4). Another substantial labor input was for transporting the harvest from the garden plots to people's homes. This activity required about 277 hours but was often viewed as a pleasure because the villagers took pride in harvesting their crops.

The total energy input to raise 1 ha of crops under the New Guinea agricultural system was about 739,160 kcal (Table 6.4). The crop yield averaged about 11.4 million kcal/ha, resulting in an output/input ratio of 15.4: 1 (Rappaport, 1968; 1971).

If we assume an average daily per capita consumption of 2400 kcal, an individual would consume about 876,000 kcal per year. Hence, a 1-ha plot would provide sufficient food energy for 13 persons, and the 37 ha usually cultivated by the villagers would provide more than enough food for the inhabitants. However, the villagers consumed only 55 percent of the energy value of their crops and fed about 45 percent to their pigs. When this is taken into account, the ratio of people to land decreases; only 5.5 persons are sustained per hectare planted.

Table 6.4   Output/input analysis of New Guinea swidden agriculture for 1 ha of mixed crops that included sweet potato, taro, cassava, yam, and banana

	Hours/ha	kcal/h	kcal/ha
Inputs			
Clearing underbrush	175	400	70,000
Clearing trees	68	400	27,200
Fencing garden	84	500	42,000
Weeding and burning	78	300	23,400
Placing soil retainers	44	400	17,600
Planting and all weeding	742	300	222,600
Other maintenance	137	400	54,800
Harvesting	277	300	83,100
Cartage	264	400	145,600
SUBTOTAL	1,869		686,300
Axe, machete (0.8 kg)[a]			16,860
Seeds, etc. (10 kg)[a]			36,000
TOTAL			739,160
Outputs			
Crop yield			11,384,462
OUTPUT/INPUT RATIO			15.4:1

Note: [a]Estimated as additional inputs.
Source: After Rappaport, 1968 and 1971.

Rappaport (1971) reported that each pig required a total of 4.5 million kcal of feed over a 10-year period. If we assume that about 65 kcal of feed are required to produce 1 kcal of pork (Pimentel et al., 1975b), the return from 4.5 million kcal of feed would be 69,230 kcal of pork. This represents only a 1.5 percent return on the food energy fed to the pigs.

From the 11.4 million kcal/ha harvested, as noted, 45 percent (5.1 million kcal/ha) was fed to the pigs. Jf 65 kcal were required to produce 1 kcal of pork, the yield would be only 78,461 kcal/ha. This 78,461 kcal, added to the 6.3 million kcal consumed directly by humans, provides a total yield of food energy of 6.4 million kcal/ha.

Rappaport (1968; 1971) mentions one advantage to pork production: Keeping pigs was a practical way to store some of the excess food during productive years. When crop harvests were poor, the villagers slaughtered some of the pigs to provide needed food.

Table 6.5   Energy inputs in corn production in Mexico using swidden agriculture

	Hours/ha	kcal/h	kcal/ha
Inputs			
Clearing with machete and axe	320	400	128,000
Fencing with poles	96	400	38,400
Burning	64	300	19,200
Seeding	96	300	38,400
Reseeding	32	300	9,600
Weeding	240	300	72,000
Transporting corn	80	400	3,200
Shelling corn	120	300	36,000
SUBTOTAL	1,144		344,800
Rest	1,430		64,350
Other activities	858		85,800
Axe and hoe (0.8 kg)[a]			16,860
Seeds, etc. (10.4 kg)[a]			36,600
TOTAL			548,410
Outputs			
Crop yield	1,944 kg		6,901,200
OUTPUT/INPUT RATIO			12.6:1

Note: [a]Estimated as additional inputs.
Source: After Lewis, 1951.

Another study of swidden-type agriculture was conducted in a village in the Tepoztlan region of Mexico (Lewis, 1951). The manpower input for raising the staple food—corn—was 1144 hours/ha, compared with 1869 hours in New Guinea (Table 6.5).

Calculations for total energy output/input for this system are listed in Table 6.5. Basic activities directly related to corn production involved an expenditure of 344,800 kcal, with 64,350 kcal expended during rest and 85,800 kcal spent for miscellaneous activities. When the energy costs of the axe, hoe, and seeds are added, the total energy input to raise 1 ha of corn was 548,410 kcal. With a crop yield of 6.8 million kcal, the resulting output/input ratio was 12.6:1. This output/input ratio was only slightly lower than the New Guinea swidden agricultural system, which had a ratio of 15.4:1.

Thus, even primitive societies vary in the energy efficiencies of their methods of securing or producing food. The early hunter-gatherers were probably much like the !Kung bushmen of today, who have an average output/input ratio of about 4:1 under ideal conditions. Somewhat more organized agricultural production systems like those of the villagers in New Guinea and Mexico have more favorable energy ratios of 12 to 15:1. In addition, less land per person is necessary in those systems where increased crop culture is practiced.

7

EARLY LIVESTOCK SYSTEMS AND ANIMAL POWER

David Pimentel and Marcia Pimentel

Throughout history, humans have depended upon animals for food, power, and companionship. Humans have worshipped animals such as the tiger, leopard, and lion. Even today, animals seem to symbolize a special power; one can purchase a Jaguar, Eagle, or Ram automobile. The major role of animals, however, has been to provide food and to supply power to help humans cultivate their crops, build their shelters, and transport their supplies.

All available evidence tends to confirm that humans are omnivores. Humans have the capacity to consume not only a wide variety of plant materials but also animal flesh and milk. The relative proportion of plant to animal food consumed varies with cultural habits, availability of food, and personal preference.

Early Animal Herding

Early civilizations depended upon both animal husbandry and crop culture to supplement hunting and the gathering of wild foods. The first animals kept by humans as a source of food were chickens, ducks, pigs, rabbits, sheep, goats, cattle, camels, donkeys, and llamas. These animals provided meat, fat, milk, and blood for energy and protein and supplied other major nutrients.

Animal husbandry probably began when a hunter carried his prey's young back to camp. There, fed and protected, the animals thrived and could be killed when humans needed additional food. Later on, some of the captive animals were tamed and allowed to reproduce. Eventually, the numbers in captivity were sufficient not only to provide immediate food but also to breed, thus ensuring a continuing, stable food supply.

Herding was more efficient and dependable than hunting because it greatly reduced the time and energy humans spent in pursuit of animal foods. Further, the work involved in herding was easily done by weaker members of the group, thus freeing more able individuals to do other tasks necessary to the survival of the community.

In addition, maintaining herds of sheep, goats, cattle, and camels was a dependable way to store surplus food produced during highly successful crop years. Rather than wasting the surplus, the people could feed it to their animals. In periods of poor environmental conditions, when crop yields were low, the livestock were an available food supply.

The stabilization of the food supply through animal husbandry was even more helpful to those humans who lived in marginal habitats. In severely wet, dry, cold, or mountainous environments, crop production is difficult, unpredictable, and sometimes nearly impossible. Moreover, the tolerant grasses and other types of forage that grow well in many of these habitats are not suitable food for humans. However, these plants are suitable food for livestock, which convert them into meat, milk, and blood that humans can utilize.

The herding carried out by the Dodo tribe of northeast Uganda illustrates the advantages of husbanding livestock in marginal habitats (Deshler, 1965). During the Deshler study, the Dodo tribe numbered about 20,000 and herded about 75,000 head of Zebu cattle over an area of about 780,000 ha, or approximately 10 ha per head of cattle. The human population density was low, about 1 per 39 ha, making the ratio of cattle to people about 3.75:1. Based on a biomass comparison, the cattle outweighed the human population by more than 18 to 1.

The habitat in which the Dodos live is bleak, consisting primarily of thorn scrub and perennial grasses and having an average rainfall of between 450 and 620 mm per year. In addition to herding, the Dodos cultivate sorghum, which has ample yields during good rainfall years. However, low rainfall years also are common in that part of Uganda, making sorghum an unreliable food resource. When the sorghum harvest is poor, the cattle provide the needed food in the form of milk, blood, and meat. In addition, cattle are traded for money, which is used to purchase sorghum when local supplies are inadequate.

The 75,000 cattle yield an estimated 2.5 billion kcal in milk, 2.3 billion kcal in meat, and 630 million kcal in blood annually (Pimentel et al., 1975b; Westoby et al., 1979). To produce this total of 5.43 billion kcal of food energy, the Dodos feed the cattle no grain, only pasture forage that is unsuitable for human consumption. Forage consumption is estimated at 8 kg per animal per day (Pimentel et al., 1975b; Westoby et al., 1979).

The Dodos use little or no fossil fuel in managing this livestock, and work is done by human power. With the Dodo population estimated at 20,000, and assuming that 40 percent of the males work 56 hours per week and 40 percent of the females work 7 hours per week in herding, (totaling 26.2 million hours), the estimate is that 34 human hours per hectare of grazing land per year are invested in managing this livestock population. The annual yield in animal protein is 0.7 kg/ha annually.

The energy input is calculated to be 250 kcal per working hour. Assuming that male herders work 8 hours per day with an expenditure of 250 kcal per hour, rest 10 hours at 45 kcal per hour, and spend 6 hours at other activities at 100 kcal per hour, the daily energy input per herder is 3050 kcal. With an estimated 8000 male herders caring for the cattle, this totals 24.4 million kcal per day, or 8.9 billion kcal per year. The females average only 1 hour of herding work per day, spending most of their time caring for the sorghum plots (Deshler, 1965). When the annual female input in herding (730 million kcal) is added to the male input, the total comes to 9.6 billion kcal per year.

With 5.4 billion kcal of animal protein produced and an energy input of 9.6 billion kcal, the output/input ratio is only 0.54:1, or about 2 calories of input per 1 calorie output. Based on the animal protein produced, the Dodo could not maintain themselves only on livestock. However, as mentioned, sorghum is a staple food of the Dodo. Thus, livestock protein is used to supplement the sorghum raised and/or purchased.

The Dodo tribe illustrates the important role livestock can play in providing food for humans. First, the livestock effectively convert forage growing in the marginal habitat into food suitable for humans. Second, the herds serve as stored food resources. Third, the cattle can be traded for sorghum grain during years of inadequate rainfall and poor crop yields.

Animal Power as an Energy Source

For most of the time that humans have inhabited the earth, their prime source of power has been their own muscle power. They moved about on foot, carried their own goods, tilled their own land, planted, cultivated, and harvested crops through their own labor, ground cereals by hand, hunted animals with arrows and spears, and protected themselves from animal predators and human attackers.

Early additional sources of power included human slaves and domesticated animals. The hunting/gathering societies were helped when an extra food gatherer or hunter could join in the task of securing food. Likewise, the labor intensiveness of primitive agriculture increased both the need for and the usefulness of slave and animal labor.

In hunting, 1 or 2 persons could guide wild game to a concealed hunter, and an additional hunter could help in the exhausting task of tracking and killing the wounded prey. Usually the killing of large animals required the efforts of several hunters. Even after the kill, considerable energy was expended in transporting the carcass back to camp, often a long distance away. Thus, additional manpower was a distinct asset both during a hunt and after a successful kill.

The slave or extra hunter, of course, would have to be fed. However, two hunters could kill more than twice as much game as a single hunter could kill alone. In this way, additional labor provided a greater return in energy than the energy input required for its maintenance.

Along with slaves, animals slowly emerged as an additional source of power for humans. Young animals captured in the wild could be tamed and later used to transport goods and people. At first these animals were probably used to carry collected food or animal carcasses back to camp. In addition, nomadic groups used animals to move their belongings to new campsites.

Over time, many kinds of animals have served as beasts of burden. The earliest records of such use show that donkeys served humans in Egypt about 3000 B.C. (Leonard, 1973) and later in Mesopotamia about 1800 B.C. (Zeuner, 1963). Agriculture was already an important activity of these societies, and animals were used to transport the harvest from the field to the village. Gradually, aided by this improved mode of transportation, trade between villages developed.

As early as 2500 B.C., cattle, including oxen and water buffalo, were used to transport people and goods and to draw plows (Leonard, 1973). The use of animal power to cultivate the soil was an immense breakthrough in agricultural production. Tremendous quantities of energy and about 400 hours of heavy labor were expended when humans worked alone to turn 1 ha of soil for planting. With 1 hour of ox power substituting for 3 to 5 hours of human power, the time and energy requirement was drastically reduced.

The use of horses followed and was a significant improvement over oxen because horses move faster. Best estimates are that horses first inhabited Asia but were probably not domesticated until 3000 B.C. (Lee, 1955). As with oxen, horses were first used to transport goods and people and later to help humans till their fields. Other animals that have been used to carry humans and their goods include camels, llamas, goats, and even dogs.

About 3000 B.C. the invention of the wheel made possible a tremendous increase in the efficiency of transportation (Lee, 1955). The wheel doubled the load of goods that could be transported per unit of energy. The surplus energy was then available for use in other ways and undoubtedly helped humans improve their standard of living.

In addition, the wheel led to improved efficiency in other food-related processes, such as grinding cereals. Grinding grain by hand was slow and tedious. Animals powered the early grinding wheels, but later humans found ways to harness wind and water for power. Of course, wind and water power were significantly more efficient than animal power because they did not require food for maintenance.

Although wind and water power are more efficient than either animal or human power for grinding grain, there are many tasks for which human power is the most efficient energy source. This can be illustrated by analyzing the energy inputs in tilling soil and applying herbicides. A person using a heavy hoe to till 1 ha of soil for planting needs about 400 hours, or 40 work days of 10 hours each, to complete the task (Lewis, 1951). If we assume that the individual expends 400 kcal per hour for this heavy work, this amounts to 4000 kcal expended per 10-hour day (though.it is doubtful that a person could maintain a 400 kcal/hour pace for 10 hours). Additional energy is required to maintain the worker for the other 14 hours each day. If we assume the worker rests for 10 hours at 45 kcal per hour and spends the other 4 hours involved in miscellaneous light activities requiring an average of 100 kcal per hour, the total energy expenditure for 1 person tilling the soil is 4850 kcal per day. When this daily energy expenditure is multiplied by 40 days of work, the total energy input is about 194,000 kcal (Table 7.1). An added 6000 kcal input is required for the construction and maintenance of the heavy hoe. Thus, the total energy input to till 1 ha by human labor alone is about 200,000 kcal.

Oxen, small hand tractors, and 50 HP tractors all require a greater total energy expenditure to till the same hectare of land. However, it should be noted that all these other power systems can complete the tilling task in far less time than a human can. For example, 2 oxen take only 65 hours but expend almost 50 percent more energy than a human tiller does (Table 7.1). The oxen must be fed and need a person to guide them as they work. Likewise, 6 HP and 50 HP tractors take much less time—25 and 4 hours, respectively—to till 1 ha than humans. But they use far more energy than either humans or oxen because of the large input of petroleum needed to run the engines.

Considering the current prices of fuel, hay, and labor in all countries, it is generally more economical to till the soil with either machinery or oxen than with human labor alone. If prices of fuels rise, machinery may no longer be quite the energy bargain it is today.

Tilling the soil is an extremely heavy task for both humans and tractors. To keep the relative efficiencies of human labor and tractors in perspective, it is helpful to compare energy inputs involved in applying herbicides. A person takes about 3 hours to hand-spray 1 ha with herbicide, expending an estimated 300 kcal per hour, plus nonworking inputs, for a total of 1455 kcal. Adding 8 kcal for the construction and maintenance of the hand-sprayer brings the total input for the spraying task to 1463 kcal (Table 7.2).

The 50 HP tractor using a power-driven sprayer requires only 0.7 hours to spray 1 ha. The gasoline input is estimated at 3 liters, or 30,327 kcal of energy, and the human labor input for 0.7 hour is assumed to be 340 kcal. An added 21,463 kcal of energy is expended for the construction and maintenance of both tractor and sprayer. Thus, the total energy input for tractor-spraying is about 52,130 kcal, or about 37 times more than for hand-spraying (Table 7.2). Obviously, using a 50 HP tractor for this task is energy intensive; in fact, the tractor is too highly powered for such light work. The tractor and sprayer weigh 5 to 6 tons, and a large input of energy is needed to move these weights over the field.

Table 7.1   Comparison of energy inputs for tilling 1 ha of soil by human power, oxen, 6-HP tractor, and 50-HP tractor

Tilling unit	Required hours	Machinery input (kcal)	Petroleum input (kcal)	Human power input (kcal)	Oxen power input (kcal)	Total input (kcal)
Human power	400	6,000	0	194,000	–	200,000
Oxen (pair)	65	6,000	0	31,525	260,000[a]	297,525
6-HP tractor	25	191,631	237,562[b]	12,125	–	441,318
50-HP tractor	4	245,288	306,303[c]	1,940	–	553,531

Notes: [a]Each ox is assumed to consume 20,000 kcal of feed per day.
[b]An estimated 23.5 liters of gasoline used.
[c]An estimated 30.3 liters of gasoline used.
Source: Pimentel and Pimentel, 1979.

Table 7.2   Comparison of energy inputs for spraying herbicide on 1 ha by human power and 50-HP tractor

Spraying unit	Required hours	Machinery input (kcal)	Petroleum input (kcal)	Human power input (kcal)	Total input (kcal)
Human power	3.0	8	0	1,455	1,463
50-HP tractor	0.7	21,463	30,327[a]	340	52,130

Note: [a]An estimated 3 liters of gasoline used.
Source: Pimentel and Pimentel, 1979.

When only the dollar cost is considered, applying herbicide by hand would be more economical than employing a tractor. Thus, in a country where farm wages might be as low as $0.50 per hour, applying herbicide by hand would cost an estimated $1.60, whereas using a tractor would cost an estimated $2.30 (Figure 7.1). Hand-spraying becomes increasingly expensive as the hourly wage for labor increases.

In these comparisons, nothing has been said about the type of energy used, and this is a vital factor to consider. Humans need food, the tractor depends on petroleum, and the ox consumes forage, a plant product that humans cannot use for food. In many regions, forage is a free energy source. Forage growing along paths, waterways, and similar areas that do not compete with croplands can be fed to the oxen or other draft animals. Also, straw left after the harvest of rice or similar grain crops can be fed to animals. Hence, the energy cost of maintaining an ox might be minimal to the small farmer. Draft animals have additional advantages because they provide milk and meat as well as power. With animal protein foods at a premium in some developing countries, this supply of milk and meat has great nutritional value.

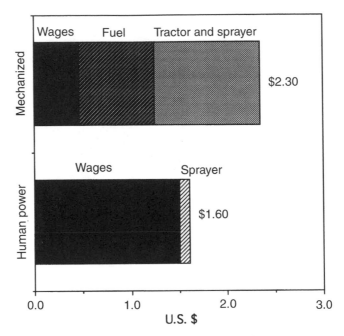

7.1   Economic costs of applying herbicide in a developing country.

Many nations have replaced draft animals with tractors and other machinery. For example, when the United States was first settled in 1620, human power was the prime power source for work, but by 1776 an estimated 70 percent of the power was supplied by animals and only 20 percent by humans (Cook, 1976). By 1850 animal power had declined to 53 percent and manpower to 13 percent (Cook, 1976) (Figure 7.2). By 1950, about 100 years later, animal and human power had declined to only about 1 percent, and fossil-fuel-powered engines provided 95 percent of the power. Thus, a dramatic change with far-reaching consequences has taken place, as humans continue to consume ever-increasing quantities of nonrenewable fossil fuels.

Animal Food-Consumption Patterns

Throughout history animals, either hunted or husbanded, have been valued by humans for food. Even so, the majority of humankind has had to depend primarily on plant materials for energy and other nutrients. Even today most of the world's people live on about 2500 kcal per day and obtain most of their food energy and protein from grains and legumes (Worldwatch Institute, 1992a).

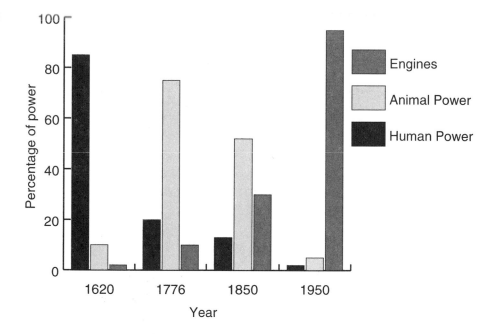

7.2   The percentage of power provided by human power, animal power, and engines during various periods in U.S. history. (Sources: 1620, estimated; 1776, 1850, and 1950, from Cook, 1976.)

Historical examples are numerous. One of the unique human diets on record was consumed in Ireland during the nineteenth century. At this time the Irish people relied primarily on potatoes for both calories and protein, consuming about 4.5 kg of potatoes and half a liter of milk each day (Connell, 1950). These two foods provided about 3852 kcal and 64 g of protein per day, of which 45 g were from the potatoes.

Or recall the diet of the New Guinea villagers studied by Rappaport (1968), who consumed primarily plant foods (Figure 6.4). About 99 percent of their calories came from plant material. A study of 12 rural villages in southern India showed that individuals consumed, on average, between 210 and 330 g of rice and wheat, 140 ml of milk, and 40 g of pulses and beans per day (Tandon et al., 1972). This diet provided about 1500 kcal and 48 g of protein per day, with the major share of both calories and protein coming from plants.

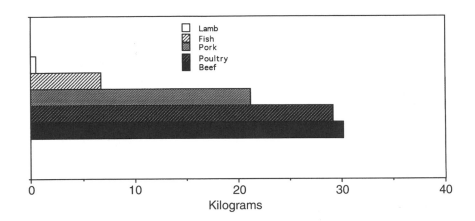

7.3 Annual meat consumption per person in the United States (USDA, 1991b).

In Central America, laborers commonly consume about 500 g of corn per day (E. Villager, ICAIITI, personal communication, 1975). Along with the corn they eat about 100 g of black beans per day, and together these staples provide about 2118 kcal and 68 g of protein daily. The corn and beans complement each other in providing the essential amino acids that humans need. Additional food energy is obtained from other plant and animal products.

A sharp contrast to all these examples is found in the United States, where the daily protein intake is 105 g, of which 71 g is animal protein (Putnam and Allshouse, 1991). U.S. per capita animal and animal protein consumption is among the highest in the world, although similar consumption patterns appear in many highly industrialized nations in Europe (FAO, 1991a). In 1991 annual U.S. per capita meat consumption was 88 kg (Putnam and Allshouse, 1991). Beef is the meat eaten in the largest quantity (Figure 7.3). In addition, annual per capita food consumption includes 14 kg of eggs and about 258 kg of milk and dairy products (Putnam and Allshouse, 1991).

Although mammals and mammal products, such as milk and cheese, dominate the animal products consumed by humans, a great variety of other animal material is also eaten, including many kinds of birds and their eggs, ranging all the way from large ostrich eggs to tiny birds such as the English sparrow. Often the small birds, plucked of feathers and cooked on skewers, are eaten whole, bones and all (Laycock, 1986). Eggs are eaten in a variety of ways: raw, cooked, incubated, preserved, and pickled. Some uniquely prepared eggs are the Chinese, or "century" eggs and the Philippine *balut*. Century eggs are preserved in lime, coated with clay, and buried for long periods of time. As the name implies, century eggs will keep for many years. After the preservation, the white portion of the egg has become black and gelatinous, the yolk a dark green to black color. Balut, a Philippine delicacy, is a duck egg that has been fertilized and incubated for about 17 days. On day 21 a young duckling normally would hatch from the egg, so at day 17 a fairly well-developed young duckling is present within the shell. The egg is boiled and eaten hot or cold.

Fresh and saltwater fish and their eggs are also favorite foods when supplies are easily accessible and ample. Fish are prepared in many different ways—raw, salted, smoked, dried, boiled, baked, broiled, and by combinations of these processes.

People in many parts of the world eat arthropods, such as shrimp, crayfish, lobster, and their close relatives, the insects. In Europe and the United States, shrimp, crayfish, and lobster are some of the most highly valued and highly priced foods, yet their small insect relatives are considered unacceptable. In fact, the U.S. government has established various regulations to ensure that insects and insect parts are kept to a minimum in food. The small herbivorous insects present in U.S. foods despite the regulations include aphids, thrips, and dipterans. Some large insects are intentionally used as food, include grubs, locusts, and grasshoppers (Pimentel et al., 1993b).

Lizards, snakes, snails, and frogs are also eaten by many people. In fact, some cultures consider frogs and snails a delicacy. Lizards and snakes are also eaten and are reported to be excellent food.

Nutritional Quality of Protein Foods

One of the important considerations in evaluating the relative value of plant and animal protein sources is their nutritional content. A broad comparison shows, for instance, that one cup of cooked dried beans (190 g) is quite similar to an 85 g serving of cooked ground beef in the amounts of protein, iron, and important B vitamins. Further, the beans contain no fat, no cholesterol, and no vitamin B_{12}.

Although these foods contain similar amounts of protein, the nutritional quality of the protein differs in terms of both the kind and amounts of "nutritionally essential" amino acids. Animal proteins contain the 8 essential amino acids in optimum amounts and in forms utilizable by humans for protein synthesis. For this reason, animal proteins are considered high-quality proteins.

By comparison, plant proteins contain lesser amounts of some of the essential amino acids and are judged to be lower in nutritional quality than animal sources. In addition, some plant proteins are deficient in one or more essential amino acids. For example, cereal grains as a group are relatively low in lysine, whereas legumes, such as dried beans and peas, are relatively low in methionine but have ample amounts of lysine. Fortunately, it is possible to combine plant proteins to complement the amino-acid deficiencies. Thus, when cereal and legume proteins are eaten together, the combined amino-acid supply is of better quality than that provided by either food eaten alone.

More attention and thought must be given to planning a diet that is either limited in or entirely devoid of animal protein. According to Register and Sonneburg (1973), variety is of prime importance in achieving a nutritionally balanced diet under such constraints. Further, because B_{12}, an essential vitamin, is not found in plant foods, this must be taken as a supplement. The diets of nutritionally vulnerable individuals, such as infants, growing children, and pregnant women often require additional supplements when a strict plant food regime is undertaken. Individuals in these categories often find it difficult to consume the quantity of plant material necessary to provide such essential nutrients as calcium and iron.

Another advantage of animal products over plant products as food for humans, especially children, is the greater concentration of food energy per unit of weight compared with plant material. For example, to obtain 375 kcal of food energy from sweet corn one has to consume 455 g, whereas one can derive the same amount of food energy (375 kcal) from only 140 g of beef. Thus, beef has more than 3 times as much food energy per unit of weight as sweet corn.

8

ENERGY USE IN LIVESTOCK PRODUCTION

David Pimentel and Marcia Pimentel

Production Systems

The amount of energy expended in livestock production systems depends not only on the animal and its reproductive system but also on the type of feed. Animals vary in the efficiency with which they convert plant energy and protein into animal protein. In addition, they vary in their ability to utilize different plant foods.

On a worldwide basis, about 34 percent (44 million tons) of the protein consumed by humans is animal protein (Table 8.1). Best estimates indicate that more than 60 percent of this livestock protein comes from animals fed grasses and forages that cannot be utilized by humans. The remainder comes from livestock fed plant and animal protein that *is* suitable food for humans. These livestock consume 50 million tons of plant and animal protein suitable for humans, yielding an estimated 41 million tons of livestock protein. This means that 1.2 kg of dry plant protein suitable for human consumption is converted into only 1 kg of animal protein. Obviously, the conversion from plant to animal protein is relatively inefficient when compared with direct consumption of plant proteins by humans.

The United States and other highly industrialized countries with high-calorie/high-animal-protein diets maintain intensive livestock production systems to supply large quantities of animal products. These systems use large amounts of cereal grains that, although useful to animals, are also nutritious human food. In the United States, for example, an estimated 740 kg of grain

Table 8.1   Estimated plant and animal protein produced and consumed by humans and livestock in the U.S. and world in 1991 (in million tons)

Item	United States	World
Total grain protein produced	12.0	107
Fed to livestock	10.0	40
Available to humans	2.0	67
Total legume protein produced	9.2	10
Fed to livestock	9.0	9
Available to humans	0.2	1
Other vegetable protein produced	1.3	19
Fed to livestock	0.1	1
Available to humans	1.2	18
Total livestock protein produced	7.0	44
Fed to livestock	0.6	3
Available to humans	6.4	41
Total fish protein produced	1.2	11
Fed to livestock	0.8	3
Available to humans	0.4	8
Total protein produced	30.7	191
Fed to livestock	20.5	56
Available to humans	10.2	135

Source: FAO Production Yearbook. 1992. Rome: Food and Agricultural Organization of the United Nations.

(excluding exports) is produced per person per year (Putnam and Allshouse, 1991). Of this, humans eat only 77 kg, and the remaining 663 kg are fed to livestock. Thus, U.S. livestock, in addition to consuming forage, eat an estimated 20.5 million tons of plant protein suitable for human consumption. These livestock in turn produce 6.4 million tons of animal protein (Table 8.1). Most plant protein fed to livestock comes from grains (10 million tons) and legumes (9 million tons). On average, for every 1.3 kg of plant and fish protein fed to livestock, 1 kg of animal protein is produced. However, when forage is factored in, the ratio rises to 3 kg of plant protein consumed for every 1 kg of animal protein produced.

Whenever plant protein is cycled through animals to provide high-quality animal protein, the costs of production include not only the plant calories and protein fed to the animals slaughtered for food but also that fed to the breeding herd. More will said about both these costs in the following discussion of the production of various livestock foods.

Chicken Production

Of the animal protein production systems, chicken (broiler) production is one of the most efficient (Pimentel et al., 1980a). About 16 kcal of fossil energy is expended per kcal of chicken protein produced. This ratio is quite similar to the 19:1 ratio for milk protein production (Table 8.2).

Table 8.2   Fossil energy input per animal protein production output for various livestock systems

Animal production system	kcal energy input / kcal protein output
Chicken	16:1
Milk	19:1
Eggs	28:1
Beef	35:1
Range beef	10:1
Pork	68:1
Lamb	188:1
Range lamb	16:1

Source: Pimentel et al., 1980a.

The feed energy efficiency in broiler protein production results from the following factors: 1) the hen produces a large number of offspring (230-plus eggs per year); 2) only 10 weeks are necessary to feed a broiler up to the marketable weight; and 3) broilers make efficient use of their feed. Broilers convert about 2 kg of feed (dry) into 1 kg live weight (Pimentel et al., 1980a).

Milk Production

Milk production is another highly efficient system. Several New York state dairy herds produce about 60 kg of milk protein from about 190 kg of feed protein, a conversion rate of 31 percent. Of the 190 kg of plant protein fed to dairy cattle and replacement cattle, about half is from grains suitable for human consumption, the other half from forage.

The dairy cow is considered relatively efficient in converting feed protein into milk protein because it has a fairly long productive period of 4 to 5 years. The cost of replacement cattle is therefore relatively small; from one-fourth to one-fifth of an animal has to be fed per year for the replacement. By contrast, in beef production both the beef animal and its mother must be fed all year.

Additional considerations in the production of milk are the energy expenditures of tractors, trucks, manure movers, and other equipment. In the

United States, the fossil energy input for feed and animal production requires about 19 kcal per kcal of milk protein produced (Table 8.2). This is similar to the 20:1 ratio reported by Leach (1976) for milk protein production in the United Kingdom.

Egg Production

Next to chickens and milk, eggs are the most efficiently produced type of animal protein. An estimated 27 percent of the plant protein fed to the chickens is converted into egg protein. An important consideration, however, is that 70 percent of the plant protein fed to chickens is suitable for human consumption.

An estimated 28 kcal of energy are required per kcal of egg protein produced (Table 8.2). About 2.6 kg of grain is required per kg of eggs produced (Durning and Brough, 1991). Thus, chickens are relatively efficient converters of both feed and fossil energy into egg protein. A chicken is productive for a year, and a replacement hen requires only 3 to 4 months of feed before it, too, begins egg production.

Grain/Grass Beef Production

In the feedlot system, the protein fed to the beef and breeding stock consists of about 42 percent forage, with the remainder being grain. About 1 kg of animal protein is produced from about 4.8 kg of grain protein feed plus forage (Durning and Brough, 1991). The fossil energy input is about 35 kcal per kcal of beef protein produced. This estimated energy cost for beef production is lower than the ratio of 45:1 reported for production in the United Kingdom (Leach, 1976).

Protein production with beef cattle is especially energy expensive because of the great cost involved in maintaining the breeding herd, which has a low rate of offspring production. For each animal sent to the feedlot for fattening, an additional 1.3 breeding animals must be fed and maintained each year. Although the breeding herd mainly eats forage, this is still a relatively inefficient production system. In addition, beef cattle produce an average of 0.8 offspring per dam per year. Certainly it would be a tremendous breakthrough if beef cattle could be bred to produce an average of 2 offspring per dam per year.

Beef cattle, like dairy cattle, can utilize forage for feed. It is possible to produce beef by feeding livestock nothing but forage from pasture and rangeland. The meat produced is somewhat tougher and leaner, but is often considered tastier, than meat from grain-fed feedlot beef. However, more time is required to fatten the beef animal to desirable market weight through grazing than in a feedlot.

Range Beef Production

A major advantage of husbanding beef animals is that they can convert forage grasses and shrubs that are unsuitable for human consumption into animal protein. For example, the excellent pastureland in Texas produces 2.2 kg/ha of beef protein per year. Average-quality grasslands have lower yields ranging from 0.2 to 0.5 kg/ha/yr.

In the Texas example, range beef consume an estimated 1.4 million kcal of feed energy to produce the 2.2 kg of beef protein (Pimentel et al., 1975b). This amounts to about 164 kcal of feed energy consumed for every kcal of beef protein produced. Range cattle have to move about and harvest their own feed. Under feedlot conditions, the feed is brought to the animals. Additionally, there are differences in the kind of feed provided (grain versus forage).

A major advantage of rangeland over feedlot production is that range beef require a substantially smaller fossil energy input—10 kcal per kcal of range beef protein produced, as opposed to 35 kcal per kcal of feedlot beef protein. The fossil energy input primarily fuels pickup trucks used in herding the beef cattle on the range.

Pork Production

Pork production is less efficient than beef production in converting plant protein into animal protein (Table 8.2). Hogs convert only about 14 percent of the plant protein fed to them into pork protein—that is, only 1 kg of pork protein is produced from 6.9 kg of feed protein (Durning and Brough, 1991).

Although much of the protein fed to hogs is suitable for human consumption, they can be maintained satisfactorily on food wastes, such as table scraps or garbage. They also can eat surplus foods produced from gardens during the growing season. Pastured hogs often will root out and eat vegetation and roots, and they sometimes feed on acorns and other plant foods that are considered marginally suitable for human consumption.

The fossil energy input is calculated to be about 68 kcal feed energy per kcal of pork produced, a high ratio for animal protein production.

One of the major advantages of husbanding hogs, rather than cattle or sheep, is that hogs produce litters ranging from 6 to 10 piglets. This litter size substantially reduces the number of animals in the breeding herd that must be fed and maintained to supply the young that will be reared solely for meat. Maintaining a breeding herd has high costs in both feed and husbandry energy.

Lamb Production

Like beef, sheep can be maintained on rangeland, but they require large land areas for grazing. Range production of lamb in Utah illustrates this need. There, it takes nearly 6 ha and a feed energy input of 753,000 kcal to produce 1 kg of lamb protein (Pimentel et al., 1975b). This amounts to 188 kcal of feed energy per kcal of lamb protein produced. If the value of harvested wool were included in the analysis, this ratio would be reduced.

The fossil energy input to produce lamb protein is small, amounting to only about 16 kcal per kcal of lamb protein produced. As with range beef production, the fossil energy input in lamb production is primarily for fuel for pickup trucks used in herding the sheep.

Sheep production has a slight advantage over beef production because sheep usually produce twins, whereas beef cattle usually produce less than 1 calf per dam per year. Indeed, one breed of sheep produces 5 to 6 offspring per litter. If this characteristic could be bred into all commercial breeds of sheep, the efficiency of lamb protein production would be increased because the size of the breeding flock—and of the energy expenditure needed to maintain it—could be reduced.

Grass-Fed Livestock System

If humans no longer fed grain to livestock and only grazed them on available pastures and forest-ranges, animal production systems would be modified to include primarily dairy cattle, beef, and sheep (Pimentel et al., 1980a). The total amount of animal protein produced under this system would be about 3 million tons, or slightly more than half of the animal protein currently produced (Tables 8.3 and 8.4). The inputs for this system of grass-fed livestock would be reduced as follows: land, 8 percent; labor, 34 percent; and fossil energy, 59 percent. However, this 59 percent energy savings (412 × 10^{12} kcal) represents only about 1 percent of the total fossil energy consumed in the United States each year. In addition, the increase in available land would probably not be as large as 8 percent, because some of the former livestock production lands might be used to grow crops to compensate for the reduced animal component in the human diet.

Table 8.3   Current production of animal protein systems and the required resource inputs of land, labor, and energy

Animal production system	Output per year			Input per year		
	Number (× 10³)	Product (kg × 10⁹)	Protein (kg × 10⁶)	Land (ha × 10⁶)	Labor (h × 10⁶)	Energy (kcal × 10¹²)
Chicken	2,932,711	5.02	465	2.5	18	18.24
Turkey	124,255	1.04	118	0.9	14	6.40
Eggs	64,362,000	3.82	438	4.2	78	31.14
Sheep	7,521	0.74	18	94.5	23	7.05
Dairy	11,151	53.26	1,864	16.3	825	87.22
Pork	68,687	7.49	535	15.3	168	91.51
Beef	46,870[a]	20.07	1,957	288.7	592	171.07
TOTAL			5,395	422.4	1,718	412.63

Note: [a]41,464 cattle and 5,406 calves.
Source: Pimentel et al., 1980a.

Table 8.4   Potential production of animal protein systems (forage only) and the required resource inputs of land, labor, and energy

Animal production system	Output per year			Input per year		
	Number (× 10³)	Product (kg × 10⁹)	Protein (kg × 10⁶)	Land (ha × 10⁶)	Labor (h × 10⁶)	Energy (kcal × 10¹²)
Dairy	8,015	38.47	1,346	11.8	590	38.47
Beef	40,110[a]	15.30	1,486	283.2	514	127.77
Sheep	7,521	0.74	18	94.5	23	4.58
TOTAL			2,850	389.5	1,127	170.82

Note: [a]35,616 cattle and 4,494 calves.
Source: Pimentel et al., 1980a.

The decrease in animal protein production in a grass-only system would result from the loss of poultry and hogs plus the reduction of the beef and dairy systems (Tables 8.3 and 8.4). However, a grass-only system would release for human consumption about 135 million tons of grain currently fed to livestock. This amount would be sufficient to feed approximately 400 million people a vegetarian diet for a year (Pimentel et al., 1980a).

Currently, animal products supply about 71 g of Americans' total daily protein intake of 106 g per day. Therefore, reducing the animal protein intake per capita in half, to 35 grams, would mean a total of 70 grams of protein per day. This intake is still significantly above the recommended daily allowance of 56 grams of protein for the average adult.

Evaluation of Livestock Production Systems

Because of the interdependencies between kinds of plant foods consumed by animals and the availability of fossil fuel, land, and labor, it is difficult to establish a simple ranking of the various livestock production systems discussed.

For example, chicken, milk, and egg production rate as the most efficient converters when only energy and land are considered. Chicken production is also extremely effective in use of labor. When only forage is available, then egg, chicken, and pork production are eliminated, leaving milk, beef, and lamb production as the only viable systems. Of these, milk production is the most efficient, because forage can be used and relatively small amounts of energy, land, and labor are needed for its production.

Turning to a comparison of beef production methods, many factors have to be weighed to determine the relative efficiencies of grain/grass-fed versus grass-fed beef. For instance, feedlot cattle put on weight quickly and thus can be put on the market much sooner than range-fed animals. The short feeding period reduces the handling period. Moreover, consumers prefer feedlot beef because it has more fat marbling and is more tender than beef from range-fed animals. Balanced against these advantages is the future outlook in grain availability and price. If prices rise sufficiently, grass-fed beef may have the advantage. Unfortunately, considerable energy, land, and labor will have to be expended to augment production of range-fed beef (Pimentel et al., 1980a). Although the increased land and labor inputs are evident, the larger energy input may come as a surprise. Energy would have to be expended in the form of fertilizers and herbicides to bring marginal agricultural land into forage production, and sufficient rain would have to fall in the region.

Thus, the future of animal protein production is complicated and not easy to project. Supplies of fossil energy, availability of land, and prices of grain will determine the extent and kind of production systems utilized. Consumer preferences, especially in countries where animal protein foods are highly valued, may have to be compromised as the world population increases and animal production is either reduced or modified.

9

ENERGY USE IN FISH AND AQUACULTURAL PRODUCTION*

David Pimentel, Roland E. Shanks, and Jason C. Rylander

The oceans and other aquatic ecosystems are vital to the sustainability of all life on earth. In particular, these aquatic systems provide food for humans and livestock. Overfishing and pollution of fresh and saltwater habitats threaten aquatic systems' continued productivity.

Worldwide approximately 95 million metric tons of seafood, including fish, crustaceans, and mollusks, are harvested annually (Figure 9.1). About 90 percent of all harvested fish are from the marine habitat, the remaining 10 percent from freshwater habitats. About 28 million tons of fish are fed to livestock, and humans consume an estimated 67 million tons (NOAA, 1991). Nonetheless, fish protein represents less than 5 percent of the total food protein (387 million tons) consumed annually by the world's human population and less than 1 percent of the overall caloric intake (FAO, 1991b).

As with agricultural food production, harvesting fish requires significant quantities of fossil energy (Pimentel, 1980; Scott, 1982; Bardach, 1982, 1991; Billington, 1988; Mitchell and Cleveland, 1993). Because the United States already imports more than half of its oil at a cost of $65 billion/yr (Gibbons and Blair, 1991) and proven U.S. oil reserves are projected to be depleted in 10 to 15 years (Matare, 1989; Flavin and Lenssen, 1990; DOE, 1991a; Gever et al., 1991; Davis, 1991; BP, 1991; Worldwatch Institute, 1992a), this is an appropriate time to analyze the use of energy in fishery production and to determine

---

*This chapter will appear in a forthcoming issue of the *Journal of Agricultural and Environmental Ethics*.

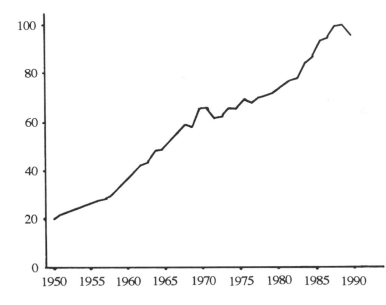

9.1   World fish catch (after WRI, 1992).

which fishery systems are the most energy efficient. Energy shortages and high fuel prices likely will influence future fishery policies and the productive capacity of the industry (Samples, 1983; Mitchell and Cleveland, 1993).

The energy inputs, ecological effects, and relative efficiency of a variety of domestic and international fishery regimes are assessed in this chapter. Also included are effects of different types of vessels and gear on the overall efficiency and sustainability of various fish-catching methods.

Ecological Aspects of Fish Production

Water covers more than 70 percent of the earth, but only about 0.03 percent of the sunlight reaching an aquatic ecosystem is fixed by aquatic plants, primarily phytoplankton (Odum, 1978). This equates to about 4 million kcal/ha per year, or about one-third the energy fixed in terrestrial habitats (Pimentel et al., 1978).

The phytoplankton that collect light energy in oceans and freshwater are eaten by zooplankton. The light energy passes through 4 to 6 six links in the food chain before humans harvest it as fish. Energy is dissipated at each link in the food chain, and the final quantity available to humans is much less than that available at the phytoplankton level.

Assuming that each year the ocean ecosystem collects 4 million kcal/ha of light energy and that there are on average 4 links in the food chain, humans would harvest about 400 kcal/ha per year as fish. Measured in dressed weight of fish, this amounts to only 0.15 kg/ha of harvested fish per year.

If the 115 kg of meat consumed per person per year in the United States were to be supplied by fish from the oceans, and assuming a yield of 0.15 kg/ha of dressed weight (cleaned fish), each person would require nearly 2000 ha of ocean area. Oceans could supply enough fish to meet the needs of only 1.2 billion people.. This estimate assumes that the entire fish yield is suitable for human food and that 40 percent of the catch is edible when cleaned and dressed. Humans actually eat only a few species of fish themselves but feed other fishery products to livestock. Because so many square kilometers of ocean have to be searched for fish, any attempt to increase fish production would be difficult. The farther a vessel must travel from the port, the more energy-intensive the fishing operation.

Overall ecological fishery management will have to be improved, coastal pollution problems solved, and fertilizer nutrient contamination from onshore sources limited if the sea is to remain a viable source of human and livestock food in the future (Bell, 1978; NOAA, 1991).

Energy Efficiency of Fishery Production

The United States ocean fishery industry ranked fifth in the world in 1991 (producing 4.4 million metric tons per year); the former USSR ranked first (NOAA, 1991). The Alaskan region is the largest U.S. producer, contributing about 56 percent of the total production by weight; the Gulf of Mexico region is the next-largest, providing about 17 percent of the total (Table 9.1).

Table 9.1   The total amounts of fishery production in different regions of the United States

Region		Thousand tons	Percentage
Alaska		2,450	56
Pacific Coast and Hawaii		300	7
Great Lakes		20	less than 1
New England		300	7
Mid-Atlantic		90	2
Chesapeake Bay		390	9
South Atlantic		120	3
Gulf		730	17
	TOTAL	4,400	100

Source: NOAA, 1991.

Energy expenditures for fishing vary, depending on the distance traveled to harvest and the type of fishing gear used. For example, fishing vessels from Washington state, located relatively near the Alaskan region, use significantly less fuel than do their Japanese counterparts. Wiviott and Mathews (1975) report that the Washington trawl fleet produced 61.5 kg of fish per liter of fuel, compared with the Japanese production of only 11.4 kg of fish per liter of fuel. They attribute the difference to the fact that the Japanese frequently have to travel long distances for fishing.

Other fishing situations produce different quantities of fish per liter of fuel expended (Table 9.2). For example, Norwegian coastal net fishers produced 13.3 kg of fish per liter of fuel (Bardach, 1982). However, using large factory vessels, they produced only 3.4 kg of fish per liter of fuel. But the Norwegian yield/fuel figure only refers to catching fish, whereas the factory-vessel yield/fuel figure includes both catching and processing.

Table 9.2   Fish production per liter of fuel

Fishing technology	Fish (kg)
Coastal fishing net and longling (northern Norway)	13.3
Longling (Continental Shelf)	7.0
Factory vessels (United States)	3.4

Source: Bardach, 1982.

Another problem in comparing figures for fish produced per liter of fuel is the condition of the fish when weighed. The Norway figure, for example, indicates the weight of fish before processing, but the figure reported for the factory vessel was not qualified and could indicate fish either before or after processing. These issues point to some major problems in assessing the productivity and energy efficiency of the fishery industry. Certainly, the energy inputs for various fisheries differ according to the method of fishing, the type of gear used, the type of vessel used, the level of processing on the vessel, and the geographic region (Schaffer et al., 1989).

Energy Efficiency of Ocean Fisheries

Harvesting ocean fish requires ships and diverse types of gear used to search for, capture, and transport the fish. Both the construction and operation of this equipment consumes energy. Although fishing vessels also require human power, this energy input is not large, especially on today's new, heavily mechanized fishing vessels.

The energy input in several different fishing systems is examined below, with detailed analysis of the fishery in the northeastern United States.

Northeast U.S. Fishery

The location of large fish populations along the continental shelf off the northeastern United States has made this one of the world's most productive fishery regions. Like all food production systems, this fishery cannot operate without energy investments in the form of equipment, fuel, and labor.

Two types of fishing take place in this region: 1) inshore pelagic fishing, which utilizes vessels weighing less than 110 gross registered tons (GRT); and 2) offshore fishing, which employs vessels weighing more than 110 GRT. For the inshore pelagic fishery, an input of only 1.03 kcal of fossil fuel is expended to harvest 1 kcal of fish protein (Rochereau and Pimentel, 1978). The offshore fishery requires an input of 3.9 kcal of fossil energy per kcal of fish protein harvested. Thus, small fishing units are nearly 4 times more efficient than the larger vessels that travel great distances. The inshore fishery's greater efficiency also is due in part to the more productive fish populations of the inshore region. The inshore fish are mainly zooplankton-eating species, and they are about one-third more efficient than the offshore fishes in storing energy per weight of useable biomass (Rochereau and Pimentel, 1978). The offshore fish are primarily carnivorous and are higher up in the food chain than inshore species.

If unused fish are removed from the reported fish yields, the overall efficiency of the Northeastern fishery decreases. The average input/output ratio is 4.1 kcal of fossil energy per kcal of fish protein output (Rochereau and Pimentel, 1978). The inshore fishery expends about 2.2 kcal of fossil energy per kcal of fish protein produced, whereas the offshore fishery requires 9.6 kcal of energy per kcal of fish protein output (Rochereau and Pimentel, 1978).

The U.S. Northeast fishery is is relatively efficient by comparison with other fishery systems. For the U.S. fishery industry as a whole, Hirst (1974) reported, about 27 kcal of fossil energy input are required to harvest 1 kcal of fish protein. Leach (1976) reported about 20 kcal of fossil energy input per kcal of fish protein output in the United Kingdom, and Edwardson (1975) reported that steel trawlers operating from Scotland use about 21 kcal of energy per kcal of fish protein harvested. However, Edwardson also reported that the wooden vessels used for inshore fishing require only 2.1 kcal fossil energy input per kcal of fish protein output. This agrees favorably with the 2.2 kcal fossil energy input for the inshore U.S. fishery (Rochereau and Pimentel, 1978).

A major reason for the high efficiency of the Northeast fishing system is that about 93 percent of the fishing fleet comprises vessels weighing less than 5 GRT (Doeringer et al., 1986). The advantage of using small fishing vessels is illustrated by the following example. Assume an annual yield for the Northeast fishery of 7.6×10^{11} kcal of fish protein and an overall regional fishing capacity of 7 GRT, which is typical of the Northeast fleet. If a fleet of 300-GRT vessels were used instead of the usual small vessels, the input/output ratio would rise from the present 4.1 to about 6.7 kcal fossil energy input per kcal of fish protein harvested (Rochereau and Pimentel, 1978). This represents a 63 percent decline in energy efficiency. All fishing vessels require energy for construction, maintenance, fuel, and onboard processing.

Overall efficiency declines as the size of the fishing vessel increases because a nonlinear relationship exists between vessel size and gross energy requirements (Rochereau and Pimentel, 1978). For example, 22 vessels of 15 GRT have the same capacity as one 330-GRT vessel; yet the smaller vessels are 44 percent more energy efficient in obtaining the same fish yield. In general, larger vessels travel farther to fish and use more energy than smaller vessels. For all vessel types, the energy inputs for operating the vessel are the largest of the three energy inputs (construction/maintenance, fuel, and operations). In smaller vessels (7 to 15 GRT), operating needs significantly dominate energy inputs, whereas in larger vessels the energy expended in construction becomes a major input.

U.S. government policies continue to support the trend toward using larger vessels in the rich Northeast fishery grounds (McGoodwin, 1990; Satchell, 1992), even though such vessels are far less efficient than smaller ones in fossil energy use. Surely this is a questionable policy in view of rising fossil fuel prices and unemployment in the fishing industry (McGoodwin, 1990; Bardach, 1991).

The energy efficiency of the Northeast fishing fleet has been declining steadily since the early 1960s, a decline attributed both to the upsurge of international fishing competition on the Northeast fishing grounds (Bell and Hazleton, 1967; Gulland, 1971, 1974) and to the decline in fish stocks in this

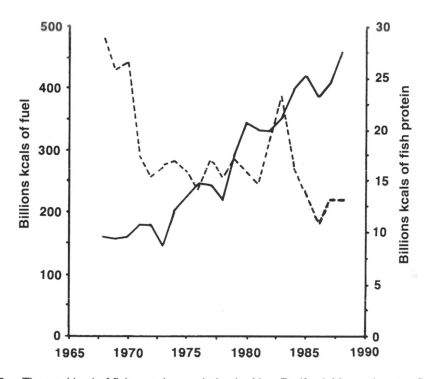

9.2   The total kcal of fish protein caught by the New Bedford, Massachusetts, fleet based on the total amount of fuel used (after Mitchell and Cleveland, 1993). Fish protein (– – –) and Fuel (———).

fishery region (Smith, 1991). Mitchell and Cleveland (1993) document this in their analysis of the New Bedford, Massachusetts, fisheries (Figure 9.2). For instance, in 1966 the ratio of fossil energy to fish protein kcal was 5:1, whereas by 1989 the ratio had dramatically increased to 35:1.

The development of new integrated fishing technologies (i.e., stern-trawling hydraulic systems and electronic detection systems) has increased fishing efficiency but not the energy efficiency of the vessel (Captiva, 1968; DeFever, 1968; FAO, 1972a; Gulland, 1974; Margetts, 1974). From 1960 to 1964, both the total GRT and the total gross energy expenditures for the Northeast fishery increased (Rochereau and Pimentel, 1978). Since 1964 total gross energy expenditures have remained relatively steady, but total GRT has declined sharply. The constancy in total gross energy requirements reflects the replacement of numerous smaller vessels with fewer larger vessels that require more energy both to construct and to operate. Therefore, increasing energy inputs and increasing vessel size have caused a deterioration in the energy efficiency of the Northeast fishery industry.

Another major factor contributing to the deterioration of the Northeast fishery is the continued overfishing of the coastal water zone. That is, the yearly harvests are well above the area's maximum sustainable yield level (NOAA, 1992). Of the 49 fishery stocks monitored in the Northeast, 27 have been identified as overexploited (Table 9.3). Large harvests continue because the fishing system in this region is overcapitalized and requires a high level of exploitation to remain profitable (Bell and Hazleton, 1967; Henry, 1971; Gulland, 1971; FAO, 1972b; USDC, 1974). Many scientists believe there is no extra biological stock available to act as a buffer against heavy overfishing (WRI, 1992; NOAA, 1992).

Table 9.3   The exploitation and status of monitored fishery stocks in the U.S. Northeast

Exploitation status	Number of stocks
Overexploited	27
Fully exploited	9
Underexploited	10
Variable exploitation	2
Protected (closed to exploitation)	10

Source: NOAA, 1992.

As early as the period from 1967 to 1974, the decline in fish protein production and the increase in fossil energy input reduced the investment return of a typical 50-GRT trawler (Rochereau, 1976). Based on the annual operating cost, which reflects the level of seasonal activity, an inverse relationship exists between the return on the investment and the intensity of fishing in the Northeast (Bell and Hazleton, 1967). That is, as the amount of fishing increases, the return in money decreases (Bardach, 1991). Indeed, the Northeast fishery system appears to be approaching the point where the value of the catch will cover only the operating costs; some operations will run in the red. This is beginning to happen, as evidenced by return-on-investment indices. In 1973 the return-on-investment index was more than 5 times lower than in 1968 for a similar level of effort (Rochereau, 1976). The combined effects of overfishing, rising operating costs, and variable earnings account for the economic instability and the gradual deterioration of the Northeast fishing industry.

U.S. Fishery

Rawitscher and Mayer (1977) analyzed energy inputs for several types of sea-food and estimated that from 2 to 192 kcal of energy were expended per kcal of fish protein produced (Table 9.4). As previously stated, the average for all fish produced for the U.S. market was about 27 kcal of fossil energy per kcal of fish protein produced (Hirst, 1974).

Table 9.4   Energy input for production of various fish species in the United States

Seafood type	Fossil energy input / protein output (kcal)
Herring	2:1
Perch, ocean	4:1
Salmon, pink	8:1
Cod	20:1
Tuna	20:1
Haddock	23:1
Halibut	23:1
Salmon, king	40:1
Shrimp	150:1
Lobster	192:1

Source: Calculated from Rawitscher and Mayer, 1977.

The most efficiently harvested fish is herring, with only 2 kcal of fossil energy expended to produce 1 kcal of herring protein (Table 9.4). A common fish such as haddock requires an input of 23 kcal of fossil energy per protein kcal produced. Lobster requires the largest input—192 kcal of fossil energy per kcal of protein produced. This high energy cost is not surprising consider-ing the relative scarcity of lobsters and the extensive fishing effort that goes into harvesting these animals.

Peru

The anchovy fishing grounds off Peru are one of the most productive fisheries in the world (WRI, 1992). Anchovies are consumed fresh, canned, and as fish meal. In particular, Europe and the United States import large amounts of anchovy fish meal for use in poultry and other livestock production systems.

Leach (1976) gathered data on anchovy and fish meal production in Peru and reported that about 2 kcal of fossil fuel are expended to produce 1 kcal of fish protein. This input is nearly twice the 1.03 kcal of fossil energy needed to produce a kcal of inshore fish protein in the Northeast fishery (Rochereau and Pimentel, 1978). In addition, Leach did not include energy inputs for construction of the vessels, equipment, and fishing gear. As the data from the Northeast fishery system indicate, these inputs are substantial and often represent about half of the total energy used in the system (Rochereau and Pimentel, 1978). If these additional energy costs were included in the Peruvian fish production data, the inshore Northeast fishery would be as much as 6 times more efficient than Peruvian anchovy fishing.

Gulf of Mexico and Australia

In comparison with herring, haddock, and anchovies, the production of shrimp in the Gulf of Mexico requires large inputs of energy—about 206 kcal of fossil energy per kcal of shrimp protein produced (Leach, 1976). This ratio is higher than the U.S. average of 150 kcal energy input per kcal of shrimp protein produced (Table 9.4).

Although producing shrimp in the Gulf of Mexico is energy intensive, the investment is profitable at present. Shrimp is considered an extremely choice seafood, and the dollar return is currently high enough to offset the cost of energy expended and other production costs. However, shrimp imported from Asian and South American aquaculture is putting severe economic pressure on the U.S. wild shrimp industry (Coastwatch, 1990; Matherne, 1990).

In the Australian wild shrimp industry, only 22 kcal of fossil energy input are expended to produce 1 kcal of shrimp protein (Leach, 1976). This is significantly less than the U.S. average of 150 kcal and the Gulf of Mexico average of 206 kcal fossil energy input per kcal of shrimp protein harvested.

Malta

The Malta fishing industry reported an input of 25 kcal of fossil energy per kcal of fish protein produced (Leach, 1976). This input/output ratio of 25:1 is similar to the 27:1 reported for the U.S. fishery and the 20:1 for the U.K. fishery (Hirst, 1974; Leach, 1976).

Adriatic

Fish production in the Adriatic region is energy intensive. When small vessels capable of harvesting 50 tons of fish per year were used, the average energy input was about 68 kcal of energy per kcal of fish protein produced (Leach, 1976). However, when large vessels capable of harvesting 150 tons of fish per year were used, the average energy input increased to about 100 kcal of energy per kcal of protein produced.

Marine Fisheries and the Environment

Serious overfishing of the common species already is a serious problem in many parts of the world, and increased pressure on all kinds of fish populations appears to be the worldwide trend (Satchell, 1992; Worldwatch Institute, 1992b). Additional threats to fishery sustainability include: coastal development; loss of coastal wetlands; pollution of bays and estuaries; and bycatch (unintended catch) (Worldwatch Institute, 1992b). Consider that almost 50 percent of the U.S. population now lives within 50 miles of the coastline (Satchell, 1992). Urban development along the coast has infringed on piscatorial breeding grounds and caused massive changes in coastal ecology. For example, Louisiana loses 50 square miles of fish breeding ground each year to development, and only 9 percent remains of California's original 3.5 million acres of wetlands (Satchell, 1992). Although some attempt has been made to protect U.S. wetlands, nearly half of them have been drained and used for agricultural or urban development (Satchell, 1992).

All nations, including the United States, have sought ways to protect their fisheries from foreign exploitation. In 1976 the United States asserted an exclusive claim to the sea's resources within 200 miles of the coast (Sullivan, 1981). The Magnuson Fisheries Conservation and Management Act of 1976 marked the dawning of a new era in fisheries management and eventually decreased the foreign fish catch. Currently, only about 1 percent of the fish landed from U.S. waters are caught under foreign flags (NOAA, 1991).

The Magnuson Act created regional committees to implement management programs. Further, it required that fisheries be managed for optimum sustainable yield (OSY), a new concept that is difficult to define. OSY is intended to combine social, economic, ecological, and biological factors into one standard—an extremely difficult task, to say the least (Weber, 1987).

Along with these legal steps has come the use of larger and more modern ships. Concurrently, the number of harbor facilities, processing plants, and fish-handling systems also has increased. Overcapitalization and overcapacity now plague the U.S. fishery industry (Satchell, 1992).

The 1982 Law of the Sea Convention represented the culmination of a series of unilateral declarations of sovereignty over the oceans in the post–World War II era. However, the United States has never signed this agreement. Although some nations were more concerned about oil and mineral rights than fishing, protection of fish from foreign exploitation was a major concern for many nations.

Management of Fishery Systems

Worldwide, small-scale fishing employs about 100 million people, either directly or in supporting industries (McGoodwin, 1990). Large-scale fishing, by contrast, employs only about 500,000 people. The economic contribution of small-scale fishing is increasing (McGoodwin, 1990; Bardach, 1991).

Small-scale fishing is more effective in other ways. For example, its capital cost per job averages 100 times less than that of large-scale fishing (McGoodwin, 1990; Bardach, 1991). It is less likely to be overcapitalized, which is the major problem with many large-scale fisheries today. Small-scale fishing consumes only about 11 percent of the fuel oil used in commercial fishing, but it produces nearly 5 times as much fish per unit of fuel oil consumed as the large-scale fishing sector (McGoodwin, 1990; Bardach, 1991).

Most experts agree that the best way to halt overfishing and save the troubled fisheries is to ban all fishing in overexploited areas for 5 to 10 years. This step has been taken with the cod fishery in Newfoundland, Canada, which recently shut down for two years (Worldwatch Institute, 1993). Concurrently, all those who depend on the fishery for their livelihood were placed on welfare (Worldwatch Institute, 1993). This approach works for individual nations' fisheries, but it is doubtful that such a ban would prove effective globally.

The Newfoundland approach is drastic, but the situation is critical. Most fishery management policies have two components: conservation (determining the level of harvest that will ensure the sustainability of the fishery) and allocation (determining who fishes). McGoodwin (1990) identifies 7 basic management strategies to achieve sustainability. These include: 1) closing overfished areas for a period of years, as in Newfoundland, to allow the fish populations to come back; 2) establishing closed seasons within each year; 3) establishing aggregate quotas or total allowable catch; 4) restricting gear and technology; 5) using monetary measures such as taxes and subsidies to control fishing; 6) limiting entry in the fishery area; and 7) instituting various forms of property rights over the fishery area.

Gear restrictions and seasonal closings are the traditional methods used to manage fisheries. Many economists dislike these policies because they claim it creates economic inefficiency. However, in certain regions this approach has reduced overfishing and helped maintain the long-term productivity of the fishery (Anderson, 1985). For example, gear restrictions forced New England clam diggers to work only with hand rakes and to harvest only clams above a certain size (Townsend, 1985, 1990; Koppleman and Davies, 1987). As a result, more clam diggers are employed and, more important, the clam population has not been overexploited in New England. These strategies may not be effective in pelagic fisheries unless the number of people fishing in the area is limited as well.

One of the most effective ways to prevent overfishing is to limit access to the fishery. The four major strategies for this are: 1) licensing, which limits the number of fishing boats or fishers per area; 2) allocation of quotas by auction to fishers; 3) implementing restrictive taxes and/or fees that indirectly limit fishing; and 4) establishing a system of catching rights (McGoodwin, 1990; Townsend, 1990; Waters, 1991). A combination of gear restrictions and limited entry has the greatest potential for maintaining the viability of the fishery industry.

With attention and action devoted to preserving the sustainability of fish production, increased quantities of fish could become available for human consumption at decreased energy expense. Certainly, inaction will leave the world fishery in a condition as critical as that now plaguing Newfoundland. Perhaps by more effectively using unexploited fish, implementing sound management of fish populations based on the knowledge of their population ecology, and reducing pollution, the world harvest of fishery products could be improved. However, if the global population doubles in about 47 years, as expected, the percentage of world food calories provided by fish will decline below the present level of less than 1 percent.

Aquaculture

Aquaculture is the farming of fish, shellfish, and other aquatic animals for food (Bardach, 1980). In many regions of the United States, commercial catfish aquaculture is practiced. Catfish is an excellent eating fish, and its popularity has spread throughout the United States.

The largest energy input in catfish aquaculture is the feed. Westoby and Kase (1974) and Mack (1971) reported that catfish required 5.9 tons/ha of feed over the 1.5 years it took them to reach marketable weight of 0.5 kg per fish. The annual catfish yield was 2783 kg/ha (Table 9.5). The total annual fossil energy input for the production of catfish feed is estimated to be 39 million kcal. The other major energy input for this system is 9.5 million kcal/ha per year for production and maintenance of equipment. An additional 4.3 million kcal is expended to pump and circulate the water in the 1-ha pond. The pumping and circulation of water is necessary to remove wastes and protect the fish from diseases, which are a problem when fish are raised in dense populations. A significant environmental problem is the treatment of the wastewater from catfish production. The U.S. Environmental Protection Agency recently adopted new regulations dealing with wastewater from aquacultural systems, and this will increase the cost of production.

Table 9.5   Energy inputs for commercial catfish production in 1 ha ponds in Louisiana

	Quantity/ha	kcal/ha
Inputs		
Labor	120 h	63,250
Equipment	9,500,000 kcal	9,500,000
Pumping	1,667 kWh	4,343,250
Fertilizer and other chemicals	3.3 kg	60,000
Feed	5,925 kg	39,000,000
TOTAL		52,500,500
Outputs		
Catfish yield	2783 kg	
Protein yield[a]	384 kg	1,536,000
Input/Output Ratio		34.2:1

Note: [a]Assuming a dressed weight of 60% and 23% protein content.
Source: After Westoby and Kase, 1974; Mack, 1971.

Producing the yield of about 2783 kg/ha per year of catfish requires an input of 52.5 million kcal of fossil energy. Assuming that dressed weight equals 60 percent of total weight and that protein equals 23 percent of dressed weight, the total production of catfish protein is 384 kg/ha, equivalent to 1.5 million kcal of food energy. Thus, the input/output ratio is about 34 kcal of fossil energy input per kcal of catfish protein produced. This ratio is identical to that of another U.S. catfish production system (Pimentel et al., 1975b) and that of U.S. beef production (Pimentel et al., 1980a).

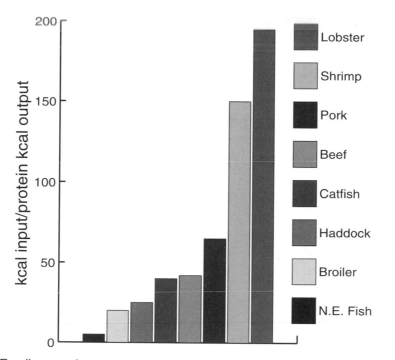

9.3 Fossil energy inputs per protein output for various fisheries and several livestock systems.

Although catfish are cold-blooded and use no energy in heating their bodies, they are not particularly efficient in converting feed into protein. They are much less efficient than chickens but more efficient than hogs, shrimp, and lobster (Figure 9.3).

In addition to the catfish system described in detail above, 5 other aquaculture systems have been analyzed. The first is Malaysian prawn production on Oahu, Hawaii. The fossil energy input per kcal of protein output for this system was about 67:1, or nearly twice that for catfish (Tables 9.5 and 9.6). Prawns, however, have a much higher market value than catfish, and this makes the prawn system profitable.

Oysters were produced through aquaculture on Oahu, Hawaii (Table 9.7). The energy input/output ratio for this system was 89:1, or about one-third higher than that for shrimp production (Table 9.6). The major U.S. oyster-producing regions include Virginia, Maryland, New York, and Connecticut.

Table 9.6   Farm production of Malaysian prawn (*Macrobrachium rosenbergi*) on Oahu, Hawaii

Item	Amount	kcal
Inputs, fixed		
Pond construction	3.5 ha of land	
Tractor grader	27.5 days/year	1,922,291
Pipes	350 m 6 in. pipe 125 psi	36,120
Cement flumes	120 ft² (8 flumes)	238,286
Wooden building	2,000 ft²	217,143
Labor	122 days/year	———
Inputs, annual operating		
Water	130 liters/ha/min	———
Labor; manual/miscellaneous	72 days/year	———
Machinery use:		
Running maintenance	———	———
Harvesting (50 HP tractor)	91 days/year on 3.5 ha	10,102,698
Materials		
Net	4 cm mesh, 135 m × 2 m nylon	7,000
Fertilizer		
Sodium nitrate	14 kg/ha	17,250
Triplesuperphosphate	5 kg/ha	9,000
Feed (chicken mash)	4,500 kg/ha	9,000,000
Larva for planting (seed)	50,000 larva/ton of production	19,333
TOTAL INPUTS		21,569,092
Output		
Live Malaysian prawns[a]	3,000 kg/ha	3,240,000
kcal input / g protein output		328.3:1
kcal input / kcal output		66.6:1
kcal output / labor hour		129.6:1

Note: [a]Edible portion about 45%; caloric content 720 kcal/kg; protein content in prawn flesh 14.6% (65.7 kg protein from 450 kg of prawn that is edible in 1 metric ton).
Source: After Bardach, 1980.

An aquaculture system for lake perch production in Wisconsin proved to be highly energy intensive, with an energy input/output ratio of 189:1 (Table 9.8). It is doubtful that this system will prove economically feasible unless ways are found to reduce energy costs. However, it may become more economical if

Table 9.7   Annual oyster production on land in Oahu, Hawaii

Item	Amount	kcal
Water area under production	0.45 ha	
Inputs, fixed		
Farm construction	2,884,436	
Machinery (tractor, grader, dredger)	5 days	
Labor	26 days	72,200
Pipes and cement flumes	3 level, 30m³, 1,000 m, 6 in. and 4 in. PVC	34,700,000
Plastic trays for oysters	3,400 kg	129,956
Inputs, operating		
Seed oysters	———	———
Labor	1,095 days	———
Electricity, water pumping	10,000 kWh/month	343,560,000
Fertilizer		
triplesuperphosphate	5 kg/day/ha	7,391,250
sodium nitrate	20 kg/day/ha	109,500,000
TOTAL INPUTS		498,237,842
Output		
Oysters[a] (*Grassostrea gigas*)	13,636 kg/ha	5,583,760
kcal input / kcal output		89.2:1
kcal input / g protein ouput		766.5
kcal output / labor hour		619.9

Note: [a]Edible weight (flesh) 45%; 910 kcal/kg oyster flesh; protein content 10.6%.
Source: After Bardach, 1980.

the fish are raised for sport fishing, because sport fish might have a relatively high market value.

In contrast to U.S. perch production, fish polyculture in Israel has proven to be energy efficient (Table 9.9). Producing an array of species, including the common carp, silver carp, tilapia, and mullet, the polyculture system had an energy input/output ratio of 10:1, making it one of the most efficient aquaculture systems for which data are available. The energy advantage of polyculture is mainly due to its fish-herbivore component—that is, having fish types that feed directly on the plants in the system.

Table 9.8   Experimental production of lake perch (*Perca flavescens*) in Wisconsin

Item	Amount	kcal
Inputs, fixed		
Land	2.08 ha (0.2 ha/ton)	———
Containment structures		
Machinery 50 HP	15.3 days	596,277
Pipes, conduits	1,200 m 4 in. PVC, 125 psi	765,217
Buildings	estimated	1,200,000
Water	3,400 m^3/ton	———
Labor	16 days	———
Inputs, operating		
Labor		
Maintenance	250 days	———
Operation	1,095 days/year	———
Harvest (for farm)	95 days	———
Nets, pails, etc.	30 × 1m seine, about 20 kg; dip nets (for farm), 10/20; 1 plastic pail	
Stocking material (fingerlings)	50 kg/ha	4,634,200
Fertilizer	200 kg/ha	3,440
Medication	5 kg/ha	350,000
Feed (40% protein dry pellets)	1,750 kg/ton of fish	5,250,000
Direct energy inputs	2,862 liters fuel oil	32,666,868
Pumping	20,190 kWh	57,803,970
TOTAL INPUTS		103,280,922
Output		
Lake (yellow perch)[a]	per ton	546,000
Protein (19.3%)	115.8 kg protein/ton	891.9
kcal input / kcal output		189.2:1
kcal output / labor hour		181.4

Note: [a]Edible portion 60%; 910 kcal/kg.
Source: After Bardach, 1980)

The energetics of an aquacultural system for sea bass and shrimp in Thailand was calculated from data presented by Pillay (1990) and Shang (1992), respectively. The energy input/output ratios for these high-value

Table 9.9   Pond polyculture in Israel

Item	Amount	kcal
Inputs, fixed		
Pond construction	Moving 3,000 m³ of soil	610,000
Pond inlet (steel pipe)	100 m, 20 cm diameter (4,100 kg)	2,150,000
Pond outlet		
Asbestos-cement pipe	20 m, 35 cm diameter (35 kg)	3,500
Cement base (Monk)	40 kg	3,000
Machinery (used on 100 ha for 10 years)	Jeep, tractors, etc., tank cars (22,800 kg of steel)	705,200
Nets (used on 100 ha for 5 yrs)	200 kg nylon	16,000
Inputs, operating		
Labor	27 days/year	
Machinery operation	Fuel for jeeps, trucks, tractors aerators, pumping	21,744,000
Fertilizer		
liquid ammonia	600 liters (494 kg N_2)	7,200,000
superphosphate	600 kg	1,800,000
Herbicide	About 2 kg	99,000
Feed		
sorghum	4.14 tons	9,108,000
pellets (25% crude protein)	3.38 tons	6,216,000
Seed production	prorated from grow-out figs	15,000
TOTAL INPUTS		49,670,000
Output		
Production total	4,150 kg	4,772,500
Common carp	65.5%	
Silver carp	15.7%	
Tilapia	15.1%	
Mullet	3.7%	
kcal input / kcal output		10.4:1
kcal input / g protein output (unprocessed)		64.7

Source: After Bardach, 1980.

fishery systems were about 65:1 and 70:1, respectively (Tables 9.10 and 9.11). These values are significantly higher than that of the Israeli fish polyculture system and the Louisiana catfish operation (Tables 9.5, 9.9–11).

Table 9.10   Energy inputs and outputs for sea bass production in Thailand

	Quantity/ha	10³ kcal/ha
Inputs		
Labor	80 h	47.4
Ponds and operation	50 × 10⁶ kcal	50,000
Fuel and lubrication	1,890 liters	18,900
Feed	35,000 kg	231,000
TOTAL		299,947.4
Outputs		
Sea bass yield	14,000 kg	———
Protein yield	1,848 kg	4,600
kcal input/kcal output		65.2:1

Source: Calculated from data presented in Pillay, 1990.

Table 9.11   The energy inputs in shrimp production in Thailand

	Quantity/ha	kcal/ha
Inputs[a]		
Labor	70 h	41,475
Electricity and fuel	31,000,000 kcal	31,000,000
Seed	250 kg	125,000
Feed	6,000 kg	24,000,000
Maintenance	14,000,000 kcal	14,000,000
TOTAL		69,500,000
Outputs		
Shrimp yield	2,135 kg	
Protein yield	427 kg	1,067,500
kcal input/kcal output		69.5:1

Note: [a]The inputs were calculated from the economic data of Shang (1992).

In contrast to pond-type aquaculture, marine aquaculture has been tried along the coasts of Norway and Sweden. Atlantic salmon, mass produced in cages, are fed pellets made from fish by-products. These fish pellets represent the consolidation of solar energy fixed by phytoplankton from a sea surface estimated to be 40,000 to 50,000 times larger than the area of the cages housing the salmon (Folke and Kautsky, 1989, 1992). Low-value fish living over vast areas of the sea are harvested and concentrated into pellets to feed the high-value caged salmon. This system requires about 50 kcal of fossil energy per kcal of fish protein produced (Folke and Kautsky, 1989, 1992), a figure that compares extremely well with the energy expenditures of other aquacultural systems.

Norway produces more than 40 tons of salmon each year (Folke and Kautsky, 1992). This highly productive system has many economic advantages, but it creates 2 major environmental problems. The caged Atlantic salmon are not as fit for survival in the open sea as the wild Atlantic salmon, and escaped caged salmon sometimes mate with wild salmon, with a negative impact on the overall population. In addition, the heavy concentration of caged salmon along the Norway coast pollutes some of the fjords with fish wastes (T. Edland, personal communication, Ås, Norway, 1992).

Conclusion

The Northeast fishery system is generally economical both in terms of energy inputs and dollar returns. By contrast, fishery production systems in the northeastern United States and Gulf of Mexico, such as the lobster and shrimp fisheries, are expensive and require extremely high energy inputs. At present the high market value of these species makes them profitable despite the high costs of harvesting, but these costs make it impractical to treat such fish as a common and abundant food source. Some fish production systems, particularly those in some coastal regions, compare favorably to livestock production systems in terms of energy inputs and efficiency, but others require more energy inputs per kcal of protein produced than livestock systems do.

Small-scale fishing systems are generally more energy efficient than large-scale systems. Especially for developing countries, small-scale fishery systems provide a number of benefits, including increased employment and low fuel costs. Large-scale vessels are inefficient, usually requiring government subsidies for their operation (McGoodwin, 1990). In addition, the high costs of large vessels contribute to overcapitalization and overfishing of fishery resources.

Policymakers have at their disposal a wide range of management techniques to improve fishery production in the future. Gear and season restrictions and limited-access regimes seem to have the greatest potential to protect the biotic stability of the world's fisheries, upon which the future of fish as a food source depends. Long-term sustainability must be the first priority of fishery managers and policymakers.

In the near future, overfishing is more likely to cause fish scarcity than are fossil fuel shortages and high energy prices. The causes and seriousness of overfishing and poor management are known. However, at the international and national levels, needed priorities have not been established to deal with the problems. Studies should focus on the breeding habits, population dynamics, and optimal yields of major fish species as well as the effects of pollution on fish habitats to help ensure the sustainability of the major fishery regions. Finding ways to protect wetlands, estuaries, and other aquatic areas will help maintain healthy ecosystems for fish populations.

Concurrently, policymakers need to identify the most efficient type of vessel for each specific region, to encourage development of more energy-effective technologies, and to control harvests. Developing techniques to make effective use of currently unexploited fish will increase the total food harvested from aquatic systems.

However, even if fish production is improved, the rapid growth of the human population will tend to negate the contribution of increased yields. In all probability, the world's fishery industry will not be able to supply more than 1 percent of the world's food energy in the future. It should be emphasized that fish provide high-quality protein, and thus this 1 percent is extremely valuable to society.

10

ENERGY USE IN GRAIN AND LEGUME PRODUCTION

David Pimentel and Marcia Pimentel

Worldwide, plants are extremely important sources of calories, protein, and other major nutrients. Indeed, plant foods provide about three-quarters of the calories and protein consumed by humans. About 73 percent of the plant proteins consumed by humans come from cereal grains, whereas legumes account for about 8 percent (Table 8.1).

Recall that some plant foods are also fed to livestock used for human food. Although some plant foods eaten by livestock, such as grasses and forages, are not suitable for human foods, grains and legumes most certainly are. In the United States about 135 million tons of grains and legumes suitable for human consumption are diverted to livestock (Pimentel et al., 1980a). Almost 90 percent of the plant calories/protein consumed by humans comes from 15 major crops (Harrar, 1961; Mangelsdorf, 1966; Thurston, 1969): rice, wheat, corn, sorghum, millet, rye, barley, cassava, sweet potato, potato, coconut, banana, common bean, soybean, and peanut.

Cereal grains have always been the dominant source of human food, for several reasons. Cereals can be cultured under a wide range of environmental conditions (e.g., soil types, moisture levels, and temperatures), and they yield large quantities of nutrients per unit of land area. In addition, cereals have a relatively low moisture content (13 to 25 percent) at harvest and can be transported more efficiently than potatoes, cassava, and other vegetables, which are about 80 percent water. Cereals' low moisture content facilitates storage for long periods of time with minimal storage facilities. Finally, most cereal grains sustain only minor damage from pests.

The prime disadvantage of cereal grains is that they contain low levels of lysine, an essential amino acid (Burton, 1965; PSAC, 1967). Also, dry cereal grains average only about 9 percent protein, whereas dry legumes average about 20 percent protein. Most legumes are low in the essential amino acid methionine but high in lysine (PSAC, 1967). Therefore, by eating combinations of cereals and legumes, humans can obtain sufficient quantities of the essential amino acids. In fact, grains and legumes have long been staple foods for people in many areas of the world.

Energy Inputs in Grain Production

Corn

The Food and Agriculture Organization (FAO, 1991a) reports that corn is one of the world's major cereal crops. Under favorable environmental conditions, corn is one of the most productive crops per unit area of land. Analysis of energy input and yields must account for the method of corn production: human power, animal power, and full mechanization.

Human power.   In Mexico, a single person with an axe and a hoe can produce corn by hand using swidden or cut/burn agricultural technology (Table 10.1). The total energy input from human labor is 4120 kcal per day (Figure 10.1). Corn production requires about 1140 hours (143 days) of labor, an energy expenditure of 589,160 kcal/ha. When the energy for making the axe and hoe and producing the seed is added, the total energy input comes to about 642,300 kcal/ha. With a corn yield of about 1940 kg/ha, or 6.9 million kcal, the energy output/input ratio is about 11:1 (Table 10.1).

In this system, fossil energy is used only in the production of the axe and hoe. Based on a fossil energy input of 16,570 kcal, the output/input ratio is about 422 kcal of corn produced for each kcal of fossil energy expended.

By comparison, producing corn in Guatemala by human power requires about 1420 hours/ha, nearly 300 hours more than in Mexico (Table 10.2). Moreover, the corn yield is only about 1070 kg/ha, or about half that obtained in Mexico. For these reasons, the output/input ratio is only 5:1, far less efficient than that of Mexico (Table 10.1).

Table 10.1 Energy inputs in corn production in Mexico using only human power

	Quantity/ha	kcal/ha
Inputs		
Labor	1,144 h[a]	589,160
Axe and hoe	16,570 kcal[b]	16,570
Seeds	10.4 kg[b]	36,608
TOTAL		642,338
Outputs		
Corn yield	1944 kg[a]	6,901,200
Protein yield	175 kg	
kcal output/kcal input		10.7:1

Notes: [a]Lewis, 1951.
[b]Estimated.

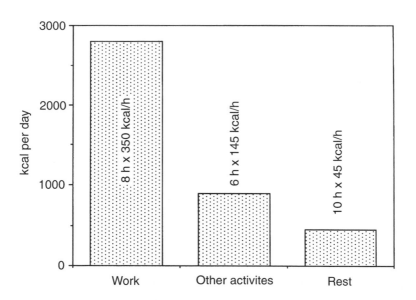

10.1   Total energy expended per adult male in developing countries, in crop-raising activities employing human power only and/or combined with animal power is calculated at 4120 kcal per adult male per day.

Table 10.2   Energy inputs in corn production in Guatemala using only human power

		Quantity/ha	kcal/ha
Inputs			
Labor		1,415 h[a]	728,725
Axe and hoe		16,570 kcal[b]	16,570
Seeds		10.4 kg[b]	36,608
	TOTAL		781,903
Outputs			
Corn yield		1,066 kg[a]	3,784,300
Protein yield		96 kg	
kcal output/kcal input			4.84:1

Notes: [a]Stadelman, 1940.
[b]Estimated.

Corn produced in Nigeria by human power requires only 620 hours of labor per hectare, about half the labor input required in Mexico and Guatemala (Table 10.3). Although Nigerian farmers use a small amount of fertilizer, they produce a corn yield of only about 1000 kg/ha, less than that produced in both Mexico and Guatemala. The output/input ratio, however, is 6:1 because of the relatively low labor input (Table 10.3).

Table 10.3   Energy inputs in corn production in Nigeria using only human power

		Quantity/ha	kcal/ha
Inputs			
Labor		620 h[a]	319,300
Axe and hoe		16,570 kcal[b]	16,570
Nitrogen		11 kg[a]	161,700
Phosphorus		4 kg[a]	12,000
Potassium		6 kg[a]	9,600
Seeds		10.4 kg[b]	36,608
	TOTAL		555,778
Outputs			
Corn yield		1,004 kg[a]	3,564,200
Protein yield		90 kg	
kcal output/kcal input			6.41:1

Notes: [a]Akinwumi, 1971.
[b]Estimated.

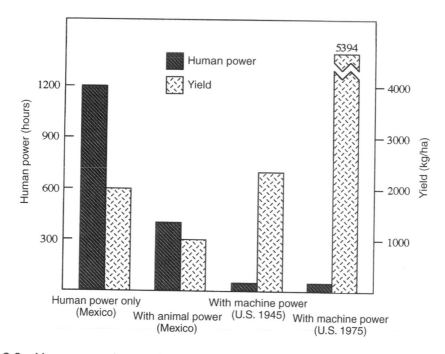

10.2   Human power input and yield per hectare for different corn production systems.

Although the yields of corn produced by hand are significantly lower than yields of corn produced by mechanization in the United States, the reason is not related to the type of power used (Figure 10.2). The lower yields for hand-produced corn can be attributed to the reduced use of fertilizers, lack of hybrid (high-yielding) varieties, poor soil, and prevailing environmental conditions. With the use of suitable fertilizers and more productive varieties of corn, it should be possible to increase crop yields employing only human power.

Draft animal power.   In Mexico, about 200 hours of oxpower are needed to produce 1 ha of corn. Concurrently, the human labor investment is reduced from about 1140 hours to about 380 hours (Table 10.4), a savings of about 760 hours (Tables 10.1 and 10.4). Under these farming conditions, 1 hour of oxpower replaces nearly 4 hours of human power.

Table 10.4   Energy inputs in corn (maize) production in Mexico using oxen

	Quantity/ha	kcal/ha
Inputs		
Labor	383 h[a]	197,245
Ox	198 h[a]	495,000[c]
Machinery	41,400 kcal[b]	41,400
Seeds	10.4 kg[b]	36,608
TOTAL		770,253
Outputs		
Corn yield	941 kg	3,340,550
Protein yield	85 kg	
kcal output/kcal input		4.34:1

Notes: [a]Lewis, 1951.
[b]Estimated.
[c]Assumed 20,000 kcal of forage consumed per day by ox.

An ox produces 0.5 to 0.75 HP. One HP-hour of work equals about 10 human hours of work. Thus, 1 oxpower-hour equals 5 to 7.5 human hours. In Mexico, as noted, 1 oxpower-hour replaces about 4 hours of human power (Tables 10.1 and 10.4), slightly lower than the expected 5 to 7.5 hours.

Assuming that an ox consumes about 20,000 kcal per day in forage and grain (Pimentel, 1974) and that a human consumes 4120 kcal per day at hard work, raising crops with draft animals requires more energy input than raising crops by hand (Tables 10.1 and 10.4). It should be reemphasized, however, that oxen consume mostly forage, which is unsuitable for human consumption.

The total energy input for human/ox corn production is about 770,253 kcal/ha, for an output/input ratio of about 4:1. This low ratio is due to a reduced corn yield, which is less than half (about 940 kg/ha) the yield obtained by human power alone (about 1940 kg/ha) (Table 10.4). One possible reason for this low productivity is that the corn is planted on heavily farmed bottomland. In all probability the fertility of the soil on this bottomland is lower than that in the swidden areas. If leaves and other organic matter were added to the soil each season, the corn yields might equal those of the swidden culture, but additional labor would be needed to gather, transport, and spread this material.

In Guatemala, the use of about 310 hours of oxpower reduces the human labor input almost by half (Table 10.5). Human/ox production requires a greater food energy input (1.2 million kcal) than hand production (781,900 kcal), but the corn yields are the same. Thus, the 3:1 output/input ratio for human/ox production is lower than that for human power alone.

Table 10.5 Energy inputs in corn production in Guatemala using an ox

	Quantity/ha	kcal/ha
Inputs		
Labor	700 h[a]	360,500
Ox	311 h[a]	777,500[c]
Machinery	41,400 kcal[b]	41,400
Seeds	10.4 kg[b]	36,608
TOTAL		1,216,008
Outputs		
Corn yield	1,066 kg[a]	3,784,300
Protein yield	96 kg	
kcal output/kcal input		3.11:1

Notes: [a]Stadelman, 1940.
[b]Estimated.
[c]Assumed 20,000 kcal of forage consumed per day by ox.

When carabao draft animals are used for corn production in the Philippines, the human and animal inputs are similar to those for Mexico (Table 10.6). The corn yield is also similar, even though some fertilizer is used in the Philippines. It is somewhat surprising to find such close similarity in both input and output between two systems located in geographically and culturally different parts of the world.

Machine power. The energetics of mechanized agriculture are distinctly different from those of labor-intensive agriculture. Corn production in the United States is a typical example of machine-driven agriculture. As expected, the total input of human power is dramatically reduced compared to the systems previously discussed, averaging only 10 hours per hectare (Table 10.7). The total energy input per 8-hour day for human labor is calculated to be 3720 kcal/ha (Figure 10.3). Therefore, 10 hours of labor represents a total

Table 10.6   Energy inputs in corn production in the Philippines

	Quantity/ha	kcal/ha
Inputs		
Labor	296 h[a]	152,440
Carabao	182 h[a]	364,325[c]
Machinery	41,400 kcal[b]	41,400
Nitrogen	4 kg[a]	58,800
Phosphorus	1 kg[a]	3,000
Potassium	0.3 kg[a]	480
Seeds	10.4 kg[b]	36,608
Transportation	3,000 kcal	3,000
TOTAL		660,053
Outputs		
Corn yield	941 kg	3,340,550
Protein yield	85 kg	
kcal output/kcal input		5.06:1

Notes: [a]AED, 1960; FAO, 1961; Allan, 1961.
[b]Estimated.
[c]Assumed 20,000 kcal of forage consumed per day by ox.

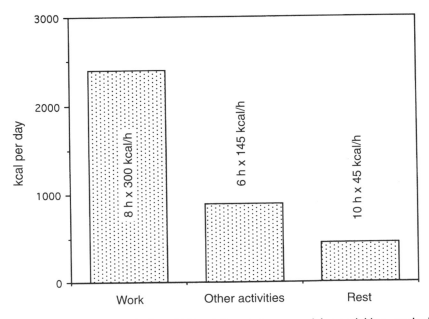

10.3   Total energy expended per U.S. adult male in crop-raising activities employing machinery is calculated at 3720 kcal per day.

Table 10.7   Energy inputs in U.S. corn production

	Quantity/ha	kcal/ha
Inputs		
Labor	10 h	4,650
Machinery	55 kg	1,018,000
Diesel	75 liters	855,000
Gasoline	40 liters	400,000
Nitrogen	152 kg	3,192,000
Phosphorus	75 kg	473,000
Potassium	96 kg	240,000
Limestone	426 kg	134,000
Seeds	21 kg	520,000
Irrigation	660,000 kg	660,000
Insecticides	2 kg	200,000
Herbicides	4 kg	400,000
Drying	660,000 kcal	660,000
Electricity	100,000 kcal	100,000
Transportation	322 kg	89,000
TOTAL		10,535,650
Outputs		
Corn yield	7,500 kg	26,625,000
Protein yield	675 kg	
kcal output/kcal input		2.5:1

Source: After Pimentel and Wen Dazhong, 1990.

energy input of 4650 kcal, substantially less than that expended in any of the agricultural systems previously discussed.

Balanced against this low human power input is the significant increase in fossil energy input needed to run the machines. In the United States in 1990, fossil fuel energy inputs averaged about 10.5 million kcal/ha of corn, the equivalent of about 1050 liters of gasoline. The corn yield is also high, about 7500 kg/ha, or the equivalent of 26 million kcal/ha of energy, resulting in an output/input ratio of about 2.5:1.

Since 1945 total energy inputs in U.S. corn production have increased more than fourfold, resulting in nearly a 30 percent decline in the output/input ratio, from 3.7 to 2.5 (Pimentel and Wen, 1990). During this period fossil fuel has been relatively cheap, so the decline in energy ratios has not reduced the economic benefits received from the high corn yields from intensive production.

The fossil energy inputs into U.S. corn production are primarily from petroleum and natural gas. Nitrogen fertilizer, which requires natural gas for production, represents the largest single input, about 30 percent of the total fossil energy inputs (Table 10.7).

Machinery and fuel together total about 22 percent of the total fossil energy input. About 20 percent of the energy inputs in U.S. corn production are used to reduce human and animal labor inputs, the remaining 80 percent to increase corn productivity.

Wheat

Wheat is the single most important cereal crop grown in the world today. More humans eat wheat than any other cereal grain. Wheat is produced in diverse systems with energy sources ranging from human/animal power to heavy machines. As with corn production, energy inputs and yields vary with each wheat production system and therefore influence ultimate output/input ratios.

For example, wheat farmers in the Uttar Pradesh region of India use human/bullock power (Table 10.8). A total energy input of about 2.8 million kcal/ha is required to attain a wheat yield of 2.7 million kcal/ha of food energy, for an output/input ratio of 0.96:1. Thus, the wheat energy produced is less than the energy expended, and the system appears to create no net gain. However, this output/input ratio may be somewhat misleading, because one of the largest inputs in this production system (2.2 million kcal/ha) is for the 2 bullocks (Table 10.8). Because the bullocks consume primarily grasses and little or no grain, they are in fact a type of food conversion system. The bullocks convert the grass energy into wheat energy through their labor in the wheat fields. If the bullock input is removed from the analysis, then the output/input ratio increases to 5:1, which is a more favorable and realistic representation of this mode of production.

The only fossil energy input in this human/bullock system is that expended for machinery. The ratio of output to fossil energy input is an efficient 65:1 (Table 10.8).

Table 10.8   Energy inputs in wheat production using bullocks in Uttar Pradesh, India

	Quantity/ha	kcal/ha
Inputs		
Labor	615 h[a]	324,413
Bullock (pair)	321 h[a] (each)	2,247,500[c]
Machinery	41,400 kcal[b]	41,400
Manure	Included in labor and bullock	
Irrigation	Included in labor and bullock	
Seeds	65 kg[b]	214,500
TOTAL		2,827,813
Outputs		
Wheat yield	821 kg[a]	2,709,300
Protein yield	99 kg	
kcal output/kcal input		0.96:1

Notes: [a]MFACDCGI, 1966.
[b]Estimated.
[c]Assumed each bullock consumed 20,000 kcal of forage per day.

In contrast with the relatively simple Indian production system, wheat production in the United States requires many more energy inputs (Table 10.9). Large machinery powered by fossil energy replaces animal power and drastically cuts human labor inputs. The machinery and use of fertilizers, though increasing the wheat yield per hectare, also significantly increase the use of fossil fuel energy over that expended in the human/bullock system. Overall, a 2.6 million kcal/ha energy input produces 5.8 million kcal/ha of wheat energy in U.S. production, a 2:1 ratio.

Oats

In the United States, oats are a highly productive grain crop (Table 10.10). In an average year, 2.1 million kcal/ha energy inputs yield 10.9 million kcal of oats. The output/input ratio, therefore, is 5:1, or higher than that for wheat. As with U.S. wheat production, the human labor input per hectare is relatively small, whereas fossil fuel to run machines is one of the major energy inputs.

Table 10.9   Energy inputs in U.S. wheat production in North Dakota

	Quantity/ha	kcal/ha
Inputs		
Labor	4.5 h	2,100
Machinery	19 kg	342,000
Diesel	46 liters	529,000
Gasoline	27 liters	269,000
Nitrogen	46 kg	807,000
Phosphorus	26 kg	78,000
Potassium	7 kg	11,000
Seeds	104 kg	313,000
Insecticides	0.3 kg	26,000
Herbicides	1.74 kg	174,000
Electricity	38,000 kcal	38,000
Transportation	183 kg	47,000
TOTAL		2,633,000
Outputs		
Wheat yield	1,760 kg	5,816,900
Protein yield	247 kg	
kcal output/kcal input		2.2:1

Source: Biggle, 1980.

Table 10.10   Energy inputs in U.S. oats production in Minnesota

	Quantity/ha	kcal/ha
Inputs		
Labor	3.2 h	1,500
Machinery	7.7 kg	139,000
Diesel	30 liters	337,000
Gasoline	20 liters	198,000
Nitrogen	56 kg	824,000
Phosphorus	26 kg	79,000
Potassium	17 kg	27,000
Seeds	108 kg	430,000
Herbicides	0.6 kg	56,000
Transportation	155 kg	40,000
TOTAL		2,129,500

Table 10.10 *(Cont'd)*   Energy inputs in U.S. oats production in Minnesota

	Quantity/ha	kcal/ha
Outputs		
Oat yield	2,870 kg	10,897,500
Protein yield	423 kg	
kcal output/kcal input		5.1:1

Source: Weaver, 1980.

Rice

Rice is the staple food for an estimated 3 billion people, mostly those living in developing countries. This heavy consumption makes an analysis of various techniques used in rice production particularly relevant.

The rice production system used by the Iban tribe of Borneo illustrates cultivation by hand (i.e., using only human power) (Table 10.11). Freeman (1955) reported that the Iban expend a total of 1186 hours of human labor per hectare of rice (Table 10.11). In this swidden production system, farmers cut and burn both virgin and secondary forest growth for subsequent rice cultivation. Energy inputs per hectare of rice total 1 million kcal, with about two-thirds of this total representing human labor and the other one-third representing seeds. The yield is about 2020 kg/ha, or about 7.1 million kcal/ha of food energy. Thus, the output/input ratio is 7.1:1, a relatively high return for the investment.

Table 10.11   Energy inputs in rice production for the Iban of Borneo using only human power

	Quantity/ha	kcal/ha
Inputs		
Labor	1,186 h[a]	625,615
Axe and hoe	16,570 kcal[b]	16,570
Seeds	108 kg[b]	392,040[c]
TOTAL		1,034,225
Outputs		
Rice yield	2,016 kg[a]	7,318,080
Protein yield	141 kg	
kcal output/kcal input		7.08:1

Notes: [a]Freeman, 1955.
[b]Estimated for construction of axe and hoe.
[c]Estimated and direct food energy content of rice used in planting.

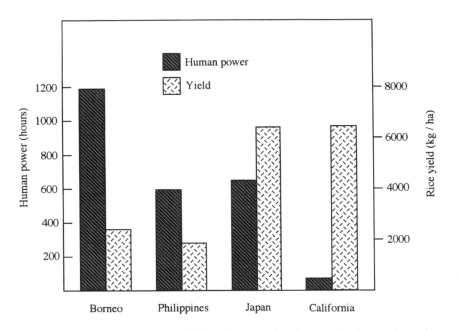

10.4   Human power input and yield per hectare for rice production systems in Borneo (human power only), Philippines (with animal power), Japan (with machine power), and California (with machine power)

As in corn production, yields decline as human labor input increases, except in Japan and China (Figure 10.4). In those countries, high yields of rice can be grown employing human power because appropriate high-yielding varieties, fertilizers, and other technologies are used (Table 10.12).

In the Philippines, both human and animal power are used in rice production (Table 10.13). Total energy inputs of 1.8 million kcal/ha produce 1650 kg/ha of rice, which has the equivalent of 6.0 million kcal of food energy. The resulting output/input ratio is 3:1, about half that of the Iban rice production system. However, like the bullocks used for wheat production in India, the Philippine carabao used in rice production convert grass energy into rice energy. If the energy input for the carabao is removed from the accounting, the output/input ratio rises to 10:1.

As with other grains, the United States uses large inputs of energy, particularly fossil fuel energy, to produce rice (Table 10.14). Based on data from rice production in California, the average yield is 6513 kg/ha (23.6 million kcal), significantly greater than yields from the other systems discussed. However,

Table 10.12   Energy inputs in rice production in Japan

	Quantity/ha	kcal/ha
Inputs		
Labor	640 h[a]	297,600
Machinery	44 kg[b]	860,000
Fuel	90 liters[c]	909,810
Nitrogen	190 kg[b]	2,800,000
Phosphorus	90 kg[b]	300,000
Potassium	88 kg[d]	140,800
Seeds	112 kg[e]	813,120
Irrigation	90 liters[c]	909,810
Insecticides	4 kg[c]	400,000
Herbicides	7 kg[c]	700,000
Electricity	2.6 kWh[c]	7,400
Transportation	300 kg[c]	82,500
TOTAL		8,221,040
Outputs		
Rice yield	6,330 kg[f]	22,977,900
Protein yield	475 kg	
kcal output/ kcal input		2.80:1

Notes: [a]Murugaboopathi et al., 1991.
[b]Hashimoto et al., 1992.
[c]Estimated.
[d]Allan, 1961.
[e]Estimated from Grant and Mullins, 1963.
[f]USDA, 1991b.

the high energy input of 11 million kcal/ha results in a low 2.1:1 output/input ratio. Although most of the energy input is for machinery and fuel, fertilizers account for about 20 percent of the total fossil fuel input. The other inputs are for irrigation, seeds, and drying. The human labor input is only 24 hours/ha, still a relatively high figure for U.S. grain production.

By comparison, rice production in Japan is still relatively labor intensive, requiring about 640 hours/ha of human labor (Table 10.12). Fossil energy inputs are lower in Japan than in the United States, but rice yields in the 2 countries are about the same. As a result, Japanese production methods achieve an output/input ratio of 2.8:1, reflecting a more efficient use of energy than the U.S. system.

Table 10.13   Energy inputs in rice production in the Philippines using carabao

	Quantity/ha	kcal/ha
Inputs		
Labor	576 h[a]	303,840
Equipment	41,424 kcal[b]	41,424[b]
Carabao	272 h[a]	952,000[c]
Nitrogen	5.6 kg[a]	85,008
Seeds	108 kg[a]	399,600[d]
Herbicide	0.6 kg[a]	43,560
TOTAL		1,825,432
Outputs		
Rice yield	1,654 kg[a]	6,004,020[e]
Protein yield	116 kg	
kcal output/kcal input		3.29:1

Notes: [a]De Los Reyes et al., 1965.
[b]Estimated for machinery.
[c]Inputs for carabao were assumed to be similar to that for oxen.
[d]De Los Reyes et al (1965) valued rice seed at 3,700 kcal/kg.
[e]White rice contains 3,630 kcal/kg.
Source: After Pimentel, 1976.

Table 10.14   Energy inputs in U.S. rice production in California

	Quantity/ha	kcal/ha
Inputs		
Labor	24 h	11,000
Machinery	38 kg	742,000
Diesel	225 liters	2,573,000
Gasoline	55 liters	558,000
Nitrogen	132 kg	1,945,000
Phosphorus	56 kg	168,000
Zinc	10 kg	49,000
Seeds	180 kg	722,000
Irrigation	250 cm	2,139,000
Insecticides	0.6 kg	60,000
Herbicides	4 kg	400,000
Copper sulfate	11 kg	56,000
Drying	6,500 kg	1,303,000
Electricity	85,000 kcal	85,000
Transportation	451 kg	116,000
TOTAL		11,017,000

Table 10.14 *(Cont'd)*   Energy inputs in U.S. rice production in California

	Quantity/ha	kcal/ha
Outputs		
Rice yield	6,513 kg	23,642,190
Protein yield	374 kg	
kcal output/kcal input		2.1:1

Source: Rutger and Grant, 1980.

Sorghum

Sorghum is used extensively in Africa for food. The available data indicate that producing sorghum by hand in the Sudan requires less human power than does producing corn by hand in Mexico. Sorghum production in the Sudan requires only 240 hours/ha (Table 10.15), versus about 1140 hours/ha for corn production in Mexico (Table 10.1). Human power is the major energy input, more than half of the total. The hoe represents the system's only fossil energy input, costing only about 16,570 kcal. With a yield of 900 kg/ha, or 3 million kcal/ha, the resulting output/input ratio is 14:1, a relatively high production ratio.

Table 10.15   Energy inputs in sorghum production in the Sudan using primarily human power

	Quantity/ha	kcal/ha
Inputs		
Labor	240 h[a]	126,600
Hoe	16,570 kcal[b]	16,570
Seeds	19 kg[b]	62,700
TOTAL		205,870
Outputs		
Sorghum yield	900 kg[a]	2,970,000
Protein yield	108 kg	
kcal output/kcal input		14.43:1

Notes: [a]BDPA, 1965.
[b]Estimated.

Sorghum production in the United States requires large inputs of energy, mainly fossil energy used in making and running machines and for producing fertilizer (Table 10.16). Thus, although the 3031 kg/ha yield is more than 3 times greater than that of the Sudan, the final output/input ratio of 2:1 is significantly lower.

Table 10.16   Energy inputs per hectare in U.S. sorghum production

	Quantity/ha	kcal/ha
Inputs		
Labor	12 h[a]	5,580
Machinery	31 kg[b]	558,000[b]
Diesel	135 liters[a]	1,540,890
Nitrogen	78 kg[c]	1,146,600
Phosphorus	31 kg[c]	93,000
Potassium	10 kg[d]	16,000
Limestone	30 kg[a]	9,450
Seeds	30 kg[a]	420,000[g]
Irrigation	625,000 kcal[d]	625,000
Insecticides	1 kg[e]	86,910
Herbicides	4.5 kg[e]	449,595
Electricity	380,000 kcal[f]	380,000
Transportation	162 kg	41,634[h]
TOTAL		5,372,659
Outputs		
Sorghum yield	3,031 kg[e]	10,547,880
Protein yield	344 kg	
kcal output/ kcal input		1.96:1

Notes: [a]Estimated.
[b]An estimated 31.4 tons of machinery is used to manage about 100 ha and it is assumed that the machinery depreciates over 10 years.
[c]USDA, 1974.
[d]An estimated 4% of sorghum was irrigated.
[e]Based on USDA, 1975.
[f]Electrical use was assumed to be 380,000 kcal/h.
[g]Heichel, 1980.
[h]162 kg × 257 kcal/kg.

The inputs are lower for sorghum than for corn in the United States (Tables 10.7 and 10.16), but the yield is also considerably lower (3031 kg/ha for sorghum versus 7500 kg/ha for corn). One reason for the lower sorghum yield is that sorghum is produced mainly in dry regions, whereas corn is grown in areas that have moisture conditions more suitable for growing crops.

Energy Inputs in Legume Production

Peas, beans, and lentils, all members of the *Leguminosae* family, are extremely important plant foods, especially in those areas of the world where animal foods are scarce and expensive or where religious or cultural reasons dictate the avoidance of animal flesh as food. Most legumes have a high carbohydrate content of 55 to 60 percent and a high protein content of 20 to 30 percent. The 20 to 30 percent protein content of soybeans is exceptionally high for plants. Legumes are excellent plant sources of iron and thiamine in addition to protein.

Soybeans

Because of its high protein content, the soybean is probably the single most important protein crop in the world. About two-thirds of all soybeans produced are grown in the United States, China, and Brazil. In the United States, relatively little of the soy bean crop is used as human food. Instead, the bean is processed for its valuable oil, and the seed cake and soybean meal are fed to livestock. Soybeans and soy products head the list of U.S. agricultural exports (USDA, 1991b) and therefore are an important factor in the U.S. balance of export/import payments.

In the United States, soybean yields an average in food energy amounting to 7.6 million kcal/ha (Table 10.17). Production inputs total 1.8 million kcal/ha, so the output/input ratio is 4:1. The 2 largest inputs are for herbicides and seeds, the third largest for manufacturing the machinery. Note that the yield of protein is higher for soy beans than for any other legume tabulated.

Legumes need less nitrogen than most other crops. For example, soybeans require only one-tenth the nitrogen input needed for corn (Tables 10.7 and 10.17). Soybeans and other legumes obtain nitrogen from the atmosphere through their symbiotic relationship with microbes in the soil. The nitrogen-fixation process carried on by the microbes uses about 5 percent of the light energy captured by the soybean plants, but it saves on energy used for fertilizer. Supplying 100 kg of commercial nitrogen fertilizer to replace the nitrogen fixed by legumes would necessitate the expenditure of 1.5 million kcal of fossil energy. Overall, it is more economical for plants to provide their own

Table 10.17   Energy inputs in U.S. soybean production

	Quantity/ha	kcal/ha
Inputs		
Labor	10 h[a]	4,650
Machinery	20 kg[b]	360,000[b]
Diesel	7 liters[a]	79,898
Gasoline	5 liters[a]	50,545
Nitrogen	4 kg[a]	58,800
Phosphorus	18 kg[a]	54,000
Potassium	47 kg[a]	75,200
Lime	350 kg[a]	110,250
Seeds	60 kg[a]	480,000[d]
Herbicides	5 kg[a]	499,550
Electricity	10 kWh[a]	28,630
Transportation	100 kg	25,700[e]
TOTAL		1,827,223
Outputs		
Soybean yield	1,882 kg[c]	7,584,460
Protein yield	640 kg	
kcal output/ kcal input		4.15:1

Notes: [a]FEDS data (USDA, 1977).
[b]Estimated.
[c]USDA, 1976a.
[d]Heichel, 1980.
[e]100 kg × 257 kcal/kg.

nitrogen than for humans to make and apply nitrogen fertilizer. The 100 kg of soybean yield that is lost to nitrogen fixation is worth about $9.25, much less than the $58 cost of the 100 kg/ha of nitrogen produced by the plants.

Dry Beans

The energy inputs for production of dry beans are quite similar to those for soybeans (Table 10.18). Average dry bean yields of 1457 kg/ha are lower, however, than the 1880 kg/ha for soybeans, and the output/input ratio is only 1.8:1 for dry beans. In addition, the protein yield is about half that of soybeans.

Table 10.18   Energy inputs in U.S. dry bean production

	Quantity/ha	kcal/ha
Inputs		
Labor	10 h[a]	4,650
Machinery	20 kg[b]	360,000[b]
Diesel	76 liters[b]	867,464
Nitrogen	16 kg[c]	235,200
Phosphorus	18 kg[c]	54,000
Potassium	47 kg[c]	75,200
Lime	350 kg[a]	110,250
Seeds	60 kg[a]	480,000[d]
Insecticides	1 kg[b]	86,910
Herbicides	4 kg[b]	399,640
Electricity	10 kWh[a]	28,630[a]
Transportation	148 kg	38,036[d]
TOTAL		2,739,980
Outputs		
Dry bean yield	1,457 kg[e]	4,953,800
Protein yield	325 kg	
kcal output/ kcal input		1.81:1

Notes: [a]Estimated from soybean data.
[b]Estimated.
[c]Assumed to be similar to U.S. soybean production.
[d]148 kg × 257 kcal/kg.
[e]USDA, 1976.

Cowpeas

Cowpeas are an important food resource in the United States and many other parts of the world. Cowpea production in north-central Nigeria depends primarily on human power (Doering, 1977). The total energy input is 811,800 kcal/ha, with a labor input of 814 hours (419,000 kcal/ha), whereas the yield is 5.2 million kcal/ha (Table 10.19), resulting in an energy output/input ratio of 6.5:1 for this particular cowpea production system.

Table 10.19   Energy inputs in north-central Nigerian cowpea production

		Quantity/ha	kcal/ha
Inputs			
Labor		814 h[a]	419,210
Hoe and other equipment		16,570 kcal[b]	16,570[b]
Insecticides		5.6 liters[b]	319,100[a]
Seeds		16.8 kg[a]	57,000[a]
	TOTAL		811,880
Outputs			
Cowpea yield		1,530 kg[a]	5,247,900[a]
Protein yield		428 kg[a]	
kcal output/kcal input			6.46:1

Notes: [a]Doering, 1977.
[b]Estimated.

Peanuts

Peanuts are an extremely important crop for many people worldwide. In addition to being used for food, they are grown for their valuable oil.

Data on the production of peanuts employing a large input of labor (936 hours) for northeast Thailand have been reported by Doering (1977) (Table 10.20). Total inputs, including the large labor input, total 1.9 million kcal/ha, and the peanut yield is 5.0 million kcal/ha. Thus, the output/input ratio for this peanut production system is 2.6:1 (Table 10.20).

Table 10.20   Energy inputs in northeast Thailand peanut (groundnut) production

		Quantity/ha	kcal/ha
Inputs			
Labor		936 h[a]	585,040
Draft buffalo		0.17 buffalo[a]	1,116,000[a]
Equipment		16,570 kcal[b]	16,570[b]
Insecticides		108,700 kcal[a]	108,700[a]
Nitrogen		2 kg[a]	29,400
Phosphorus		2 kg[a]	6,000
Potassium		2 kg[a]	3,200
Seeds (unshelled)		15 kg[a]	58,500[a]
	TOTAL		1,923,410

Table 10.20 *(Cont'd)*   Energy inputs in northeast Thailand peanut (groundnut) production

	Quantity/ha	kcal/ha
Outputs		
Peanut yield	1,280 kg[a]	4,992,000[a]
Protein yield	218 kg[a]	
kcal output/kcal input		2.60:1

Notes: [a]Doering, 1977.
[b]Estimated.

Peanut production in the United States (Georgia) yields 15.3 million kcal/ha, or about 3 times that in Thailand. However, with the large energy expenditure required, the system achieves an output/input ratio of only 1.4:1 (Table 10.21).

Table 10.21   Energy inputs in peanuts (groundnuts) produced in Georgia, U.S.A.

	Quantity/ha	kcal/ha
Inputs		
Labor	19 h	8,835
Machinery	20 kg	360,000
Gasoline	63 liters	636,867
Diesel	125 liters	1,426,750
Electricity	40,997 kcal	40,997
Nitrogen	33 kg	485,100
Phosphorus	69 kg	207,000
Potassium	112 kg	179,200
Lime	1,362 kg	408,600
Seeds	127 kg	2,286,000
Insecticides	37 kg	3,215,670
Herbicides	16 kg	1,598,560
Transportation	335 kg	86,095
TOTAL		10,947,674
Outputs		
Peanut yield	3,724 kg	15,305,640
Protein yield	320 kg	
kcal output/ kcal input		1.4:1

Source: Pimentel, 1980.

Agricultural Technology

In the future it will be important to find viable ways to increase yields of grains and legumes while keeping the inputs to a minimum.

Yields can be increased through breeding of high-yielding plant varieties such as IR–8, a rice breed developed at the International Rice Research Institute. Yields can also be augmented by the judicious use of fertilizers and pest control. The Green Revolution was built on the use of fossil energy for fertilizers, pesticides, and irrigation.

New varieties of plants should be resistant to naturally occurring pests that all too often reduce yields and necessitate the use of pesticides. Both fertilizers and pesticides cost in fossil energy and dollars, so anything that can be done to reduce these inputs will be a great benefit. Moreover, all parts of the production system that depend on fossil energy will be constrained as supplies of this nonrenewable resource decrease and prices increase.

In the future we must also decide whether we can afford to cycle large quantities of grains through our livestock. The production of animal protein costs not only in terms of energy, labor, and land needed to grow the grains but also in terms of the direct cost of the animal husbandry itself. The conversion of grain protein into animal protein is relatively inefficient and therefore expensive to produce by whatever criteria we set.

11

ENERGY USE IN FRUIT, VEGETABLE, AND FORAGE PRODUCTION

David Pimentel and Marcia Pimentel

Fruits

Fruits, the edible material adhering to the seeds of a plant, are eaten either raw, cooked, or dried. Fruits have a high water content, ranging from about 75 to 90 pecent. Carbohydrates, usually in the form of sugar, are the second-largest constituent, ranging from about 6 to 22 percent. Fruits contain only small amounts of protein and negligible amounts of fats. Citrus fruits, cantaloupes, and strawberries are excellent sources of vitamin C, whereas yellow-orange fruits are considered outstanding sources of beta-carotene, the precursor of vitamin A.

In this section apple and orange production in the United States are analyzed to illustrate energy expenditure and food energy yield in fruit production.

Apples

Apples are an economically valuable crop in many parts of the world. In the United States, petroleum products are used to operate machinery employed in apple orchards, and the inputs for this machinery account for a large percentage of the total energy input (Table 11.1). The next-largest input is for pesticides, which represent nearly 17 percent of the total energy input in apple production.

Table 11.1   Energy inputs in eastern U.S. apple production

	Quantity/ha	kcal/ha
Inputs		
Labor	385 h	179,000
Machinery	88 kg	1,029,000
Diesel	483 liters	5,513,000
Gasoline	1,346 liters	13,607,000
Nitrogen	45 kg	662,000
Phosphorus	114 kg	627,000
Potassium	114 kg	231,000
Limestone	682 kg	1,438,000
Insecticides	47 kg	2,889,000
Herbicides	6 kg	600,000
Fungicides	49 kg	1,361,000
Electricity	57,000 kcal	57,000
Transportation	2,974 kg	787,000
TOTAL		28,980,000
Outputs		
Apple yield	54,743 kg	30,656,080
Protein yield	109 kg	
kcal output/kcal input		1.1:1

Source: Funt, 1980.

The labor input of 385 hours/ha expended in apple production is high compared with those of most other food crops grown in the United States. Most of the labor input occurs during harvesting. The total labor input is calculated to be about 179,000 kcal/ha, which represents only 0.6 percent of the total energy input (29 million kcal/ha) for apple production. The yield in fruit is about 30.6 million kcal/ha, making the output/input ratio is only 1.1:1.

Oranges

Oranges are another valuable fruit in U.S. agriculture. Although oranges and other citrus fruits have more than double the vitamin C content of potatoes, they supply only about half as much vitamin C in the U.S. diet as potatoes do.

The production of oranges requires less energy than apples (Tables 11.1 and 11.2). Specifically, orange production uses less petroleum products and pesticides than apple production. The return in food energy in the form of oranges is 19.8 million kcal/ha, for an output/input ratio of only 1.7:1. Apples, then, are more energy intensive to produce than oranges. From the standpoint of vitamin C content, oranges, with about 50 milligrams (mg) per 100 g, are more valuable than apples, which contain only 3 mg per 100 g.

Table 11.2   Energy inputs in U.S. orange production in Florida

	Quantity/ha	kcal/ha
Inputs		
Labor	210 h	98,000
Machinery	24 kg	432,000
Diesel	90 liters	1,096,000
Gasoline	96 liters	910,000
Nitrogen	225 kg	3,308,000
Phosphorus	116 kg	339,000
Potassium	225 kg	360,000
Limestone	1,288 kg	406,000
Insecticides	5.6 kg	560,000
Herbicides	0.5 kg	50,000
Oil pesticide	66 liters	753,000
Transportation	489 kg	125,000
TOTAL		11,862,000
Outputs		
Orange yield	40,370 kg	19,781,000
Protein yield	404 kg	
kcal output / kcal input		1.7:1

Source: Reitz, 1980.

Vegetables

Vegetables are the various parts of herbaceous plants consumed by humans. For example, cabbage and spinach are plant leaves, carrots and turnips are roots, squash and tomatoes are fruits, peas and corn are seeds, onions are bulbs, and potatoes are tubers.

Vegetables are similar to fruits in that they have high water content (80 to 95 percent) and low fat and, except for beans and peas, low protein content. The carbohydrate content, mainly starch, varies considerably from a high of about 22 percent for lima beans to a low of 2 percent for lettuce. Vegetables generally have a higher mineral and vitamin content than fruits. In particular, dark green leafy vegetables such as spinach are high in vitamin C, beta-carotene, and iron. Also, except for spinach and chard (goosefoot family), these vegetables are excellent sources of calcium. Oxalic acid in spinach may chemically bind some of the calcium, making it insoluble, hence less available to humans. Many vegetables, especially seeds, are reliable sources of thiamine.

This energy analysis covers a broad cross-section of vegetables, including potatoes, spinach, Brussels sprouts, tomatoes, sugar beets, and cassava.

Potato

The white potato is one of the 15 most heavily consumed plant foods in the world today. Even in the United States, where a wide variety of vegetables is available, the potato is the most frequently eaten vegetable. There, about 61 kg of potato are consumed per person per year (USDA, 1993).

Based on data from New York state, the greatest energy input in U.S. potato production is fertilizer, which represents more than one-third of total inputs (Table 11.3). Another one-third of the energy is expended for petroleum and machinery inputs that reduce the human labor input, which averages 35 hours/ha. The total energy input for New York potato production is 16.0 million kcal/ha. The potato yield equals 19.7 million kcal/ha, resulting in an output/input ratio of 1.2:1, slightly lower than the 1.6:1 reported by Leach (1976) for the United Kingdom (Table 11.4). The differences in inputs between New York and U.K. production are considered insignificant.

Although potatoes are only 2 percent protein, the total yield of protein per hectare is substantial, amounting to 722 kg/ha. This a relatively high yield, especially for a food so high in water content.

Table 11.3   Energy inputs in New York state potato production

	Quantity/ha	kcal/ha
Inputs		
Labor	35 h[a]	16,275[d]
Machinery	31 kg[b]	480,000
Diesel	152 liters[c]	1,734,928
Gasoline	272 liters[c]	2,749,648
Nitrogen	205 kg[a]	3,013,500
Phosphorus	348 kg[a]	1,044,000
Potassium	198 kg[a]	316,800
Seeds	1,900 kg[a]	1,088,700[e]
Insecticides	31 kg[a]	2,694,210
Herbicides	18 kg[a]	1,798,380
Fungicides	6 kg[b]	389,460
Electricity	47 kWh[c]	134,561
Transportation	2,249 kg	577,993[f]
TOTAL		16,038,455
Outputs		
Potato yield	34,384 kg[a]	19,702,032
Protein yield	722 kg	
kcal output/kcal input		1.23:1

Notes: [a]Snyder, 1977.
[b]Estimated.
[c]FEA, 1976.
[d]35 h × 465 kcal/h.
[e]1,900 kg × 573 kcal/kg.
[f]2,249 kg × 257 kcal/kg.

Table 11.4   Energy inputs in potato production in the United Kingdom

	Quantity/ha	GJ/ha[a]
Inputs		
Field work		
Fuel for tractors (to harvest)	2.85 GJ	2.85
Fuel for harvester, transport	3.38 GJ	3.38
Tractor depreciation and repairs	1.14 GJ	1.14
Harvester depreciation and repairs	6.70 GJ	6.70
Nitrogen	175 kg	14.0
Phosphorus	175 kg	2.45
Potassium	250 kg	2.25
Sprays	13 kg	1.24
Seed shed fuels (620 MJ/t seed)	1.57 GJ	1.57
Storage (1.65 kWh/net t)	0.57 GJ	0.57
TOTAL		36.15
Outputs		
Potato yield	26,300 kg	56.9
Protein yield	376 kg	
Energy output/energy input		1.57:1

Note: [a]4,186 Joule = 1 kcal.
Source: After Leach, 1976.

Spinach

Spinach, a green leafy vegetable, is eaten raw or cooked. Although it is not a major vegetable throughout the world, it is nutritionally valuable. Like other dark green leafy vegetables, spinach contributes iron, riboflavin, and vitamins A and C to the diet.

The largest energy input in U.S. spinach production is for nitrogen fertilizer, amounting to nearly 50 percent of the total energy input (Table 11.5). The next largest inputs are for fuel and machinery. The overall energy cost is 12.8 million kcal/ha, and the spinach yield is 2.9 million kcal/ha. The output/input ratio is 0.2:1. This negative ratio means that about 5 kcal of fossil energy are required to produce each kcal of spinach.

Table 11.5   Energy inputs in U.S. spinach production

	Quantity/ha	kcal/ha
Inputs		
Labor	56 h[a]	26,040[c]
Machinery	30 kg[b]	480,000
Fuel	297 liters[a]	2,970,000[a]
Nitrogen	470 kg[a]	6,909,000
Phosphorus	354 kg[a]	1,062,000
Potassium	136 kg[a]	217,600
Limestone	454 kg[a]	143,010
Seeds	33.6 kg[a]	135,300[a]
Irrigation	69,500 kcal[a]	69,500[a]
Insecticides	2 kg[a]	173,820
Herbicides	2 kg[a]	199,820
Electricity	300,000 kcal[a]	300,000[a]
Transportation	287 kg	73,759[e]
TOTAL		12,759,849
Outputs		
Spinach yield	11,200 kg[a]	2,912,000
Protein yield	358 kg	
kcal output/kcal input		0.23:1

Notes: [a]Terhune, 1977.
[b]Estimated.
[c]56 h × 465 kcal/h.
[d]1287 kg × 257 kcal/kg.

Tomatoes

Botanically speaking, tomatoes are fruits, but they are included in this section because they are usually consumed as a vegetable. They are eaten in a variety of ways, including raw, cooked, canned, and as juice. They are valued nutritionally for vitamin C (23 mg per 100 g of raw tomato), vitamin A, and iron.

Based on data from California, 58 percent of the energy inputs in tomato production are for fuel and machinery that reduce labor inputs (Table 11.6). The second-largest input is for fertilizers. The total energy input is 16.6 million kcal/ha, and the average tomato yield for California is 9.9 million kcal/ha. This figures result in an output/input ratio of about 0.6:1, or about 2 kcal of energy expended for every kcal of tomato produced.

Because the yield of tomatoes per hectare is so high, the protein yield of 496 kg/ha is excellent, even though tomatoes average only 1 percent protein and have a high water content.

Table 11.6   Energy inputs in California tomato production

	Quantity/ha	kcal/ha
Inputs		
Labor	165 h[a]	76,725[e]
Machinery	30 kg[b]	480,000
Diesel	246 liters[c]	2,807,844
Gasoline	628 liters[c]	6,348,452
Nitrogen	168 kg[d]	2,469,600
Phosphorus	56 kg[d]	168,000
Potassium	96 kg[b]	153,600
Limestone	50 kg[b]	15,750
Seeds	4 kg[b]	20,000[b]
Irrigation	1,010,900 kcal[c]	1,010,900[c]
Insecticides	25 kg[a]	2,172,525
Herbicides	2 kg[a]	199,820
Fungicides	4 kg[b]	259,640
Electricity	200,000 kcal[b]	200,000[b]
Transportation	691 kg	177,587[f]
TOTAL		16,560,443
Outputs		
Tomato yield	49,616 kg[a]	9,923,200
Protein yield	496 kg	
kcal output/kcal input		0.60:1

Notes: [a]Walker and Hunt, 1973.
[b]Estimated.
[c]FEA, 1976.
[d]Cervinka et al., 1974.
[e]165 h × 465 kcal/h.
[f]691 kg × 257 kcal/kg.

Brussels Sprouts

Brussels sprouts are a favorite vegetable in the United Kingdom but are less popular in the United States. Like spinach, they are an excellent source of vitamin A, vitamin C, and iron.

As with most vegetable production, the major energy inputs for Brussels sprout production in the United States are for fuel and machinery, amounting to more than one-third of the total input (Table 11.7). The next major input is for fertilizers. The total energy input for Brussels sprouts production is 8.1 million kcal/ha, and the yield equals about 5.5 million kcal of food energy. Hence, the output/input ratio is 0.7:1. Although Brussels sprouts do not yield as much food energy or protein per hectare as potatoes, they do yield a significant 604 kg/ha of protein. Of the vegetables analyzed here, Brussels sprouts place second to potatoes in calories and protein yield per hectare.

Table 11.7   Energy inputs in U.S. Brussels sprouts production

	Quantity/ha	kcal/ha
Inputs		
Labor	60 h[a]	27,900[c]
Machinery	30 kg[b]	480,000
Fuel	285 liters[a]	2,881,065
Nitrogen	180 kg[a]	2,646,000
Phosphorus	45 kg[a]	135,000
Potassium	40 kg[a]	64,000
Limestone	40 kg[a]	12,600
Seeds	4 kg[a]	16,120[a]
Insecticides	5 kg[a]	434,550
Herbicides	10 kg[a]	999,100
Electricity	300,000 kcal[b]	300,000[b]
Transportation	249 kg	63,993[d]
TOTAL		8,060,328
Outputs		
Brussels sprouts yield	12,320 kg[a]	5,544,000
Protein yield	604 kg	
kcal output/kcal input		0.69:1

Notes: [a]Pimentel, 1976.
[b]Estimated.
[c]60 h × 465 kcal/h.
[d]249 kg × 257 kcal/kg.

Sugar Beets

The sugar beet is another plant that is not generally classed as a vegetable but is included in this section because it is a valuable food commodity in many parts of the world. Both sugar beets and sugarcane contain large quantities of sucrose. Although the sweetener is valued for its energy, it contains no vitamins, minerals, or protein. Sugar beets can be grown in temperate regions, whereas sugarcane can only be produced in tropical or subtropical regions.

Based on data from Leach (1976), about 50 percent of the energy input for sugar beet production in the United Kingdom is for nitrogen fertilizer (Table 11.8). Machinery and fuel constitute the second-largest input. The beet yield averages 35,500 kg/ha and contains about 16.5 percent sugar for processing. For sugar alone, the output/input ratio is about 3.6 :1, making sugar beets one of the more efficient crops analyzed in this section.

Table 11.8   Energy inputs in sugar beet production in the United Kingdom

	Quantity/ha	GJ/ha
Inputs		
Field work		
Tractor fuels (to harvest)	2.50 GJ	2.50
Harvester, transport fuels	2.54 GJ	2.54
Tractor depreciation and repairs	2.00 GJ	2.00
Harvester depreciation and repairs	2.80 GJ	2.80
Nitrogen	160 kg	12.80
Phosphorus	50 kg	0.70
Potassium	150 kg	1.35
Salt	70 kg	0.10
Kainit (17% K_2O)	280 kg	0.43
Sprays	10.9 kg	1.09
Seed (144 MJ/£)	7.5 £	1.08
TOTAL		27.39
Outputs		
Sugar beet yield	35,500 kg	99.1
Energy output/energy input		3.62:1

Note: 4,186 Joule = 1 kcal.
Source: After Leach, 1976.

Cassava

Cassava is an important crop worldwide, especially in Africa and South America. It is one of the highest-producing crops in terms of carbohydrate per hectare but one of the lowest in terms of protein. The low protein content is one of the reasons the crop can grow in soil that is low in nutrients, especially nitrogen.

The data for cassava production are from the Tanga region of Africa. Cassava grown in that region has the efficient output/input ratio of 23:1 (Table 11.9). The root of the cassava shrub is harvested 9 to 12 months after the planting of stem cuttings. Production of this crop requires about 1300 hours of hand labor per hectare. Total energy input is calculated at about 838,300 kcal/ha, and the yield is about 19.2 million kcal/ha. This high energy yield comes mainly from the starch content of cassava. The protein yield, as mentioned, is low, only 58 kg/ha. Furthermore, the quality of cassava protein is considered the lowest of all plant proteins. Given the efficiency of cassava production and the breadth of its consumption in the tropics, it is unfortunate that the quality and quantity of protein is so inadequate.

Table 11.9   Energy inputs in the Tanga region of Africa for cassava production

	Quantity/ha	kcal/ha
Inputs		
Labor	1,284 h[a]	821,760[c]
Hoe	16,500 kcal[b]	16,500[b]
Stem cuttings	none	
TOTAL		838,260
Outputs		
Cassava yield	5,824 kg	19,219,200
Protein yield	58 kg	
kcal output/kcal input		22.93:1

Note: [a]Ruthenberg, 1968.
[b]Estimated.
[c]On a per day basis, the human power energy input is 8 hours of work at 350 kcal/h; 6 hours of other activities at 145 kcal/h; and 10 hours of rest at 45 kcal/h. This totals 4,120 kcal input per person.

Forage Production

Forage production is an essential part of most livestock production systems, especially for ruminant animals. Like all crops, forage requires energy inputs. In general, these crops are not intensively managed because they bring a low monetary return.

Alfalfa, tame hay, and corn silage production are analyzed to estimate typical energy output/input ratios for forage production.

Alfalfa

Alfalfa is not only one of the most productive forages but also one of the most nutritious for livestock. Because it is fairly typical in the United States, data from Ohio were analyzed. The data indicate that the major inputs in U.S. alfalfa production are for fuel and machinery (Table 11.10). Together, these total about 70 percent of total inputs. In contrast to most other crops, alfalfa needs little or no nitrogen fertilizer; like legumes, it is associated with nitrogen-fixing bacteria. Because nitrogen fertilizer is an energy-costly input, this savings helps keep alfalfa production relatively energy efficient.

Table 11.10   Energy inputs in Ohio alfalfa production

	Quantity/ha	kcal/ha
Inputs		
Labor	13 h[a]	6,045[c]
Machinery	20 kg[b]	360,000
Gasoline	129 liters[a]	1,304,061
Nitrogen	7 kg[a]	103,900
Phosphorus	45 kg[a]	135,000
Potassium	59 kg[a]	94,400
Limestone	179 kg[a]	56,385
Seeds	4.5 kg[a]	279,000[d]
Insecticides	0.4 kg[a]	34,764
Herbicides	0.2 kg[a]	19,982
Electricity	26 kWh[a]	74,438
Transportation	132 kg	33,924[e]
TOTAL		2,501,899

Table 11.10 *(Cont'd)*   Energy inputs in Ohio alfalfa production

	Quantity/ha	kcal/ha
Outputs		
Alfalfa yield	6,832 kg[a]	15,440,320
Protein yield	1,127 kg	
kcal output/kcal input		6.17:1

Notes: [a]USDA, 1977.
[a]Estimated.
[c]13 h × 465 kcal/h.
[d]Heichel, 1980.
[e]132 kg × 257 kcal/kg.

The total energy input for alfalfa production is calculated to be 2.5 million kcal/ha. With a yield of about 15.4 million kcal/ha, the output/input ratio is about 6:1.

In addition to a high energy yield, alfalfa provides a high protein yield of about 1100 kg/ha. Alfalfa supplies a major share of the plant protein fed to animals in the United States.

Tame Hay

The major forage feed for cattle, sheep, and other ruminants in the world is tame hay consisting of numerous grass species. Animals are allowed to graze the hay as it grows in the pasture and do the harvesting themselves. Humans mechanically harvest some of the hay, and this production system is analyzed here.

As with alfalfa, two major energy inputs for tame hay production in the United States are for fuel and machinery (Table 11.11). Together these account for about 42 percent of the total energy expended for production. The average yield is estimated to be about 8.6 million kcal/ha in forage feed energy. Balanced against the total energy input of about 1.7 million kcal/ha, the energy output/input ratio is 5:1 for U.S. tame hay production.

Note that the 5:1 ratio for the United States is far better than the 2:1 ratio reported in the United Kingdom (Table 11.12), even though yield in the United Kingdom are more than double those in the United States. The reason is that the nitrogen input used in the United Kingdom is more than 30 times that required in the United States. Another, less intensive hay production system in the United Kingdom yielded a more favorable ratio of 6:1 (Table 11.13).

Table 11.11   Energy inputs in U.S. tame hay production

	Quantity/ha	kcal/ha
Inputs		
Labor	16 h[a]	7,440[d]
Machinery	20 kg[b]	360,000
Fuel	36 liters[c]	363,924
Nitrogen	7 kg[c]	102,900
Phosphorus	8 kg[c]	24,000
Potassium	16 kg[c]	25,600
Limestone	15 kg[b]	4,725
Seeds	30 kg[a]	630,000[e]
Herbicides	1 kg[c]	99,910
Electricity	75,000 kcal[b]	75,000[b]
Transportation	88 kg	22,616[f]
TOTAL		1,716,115
Outputs		
Tame hay yield	5,000 kg[a]	8,578,680
Protein yield	200 kg	
kcal output/kcal input		5.0:1

Notes: [a]Pimentel, 1976.
[b]Estimated.
[c]FEA, 1976.
[d]16 h $\times$ 465 kcal/h.
[e]Heichel, 1980.
[f]88 kg $\times$ 257 kcal/kg.

Table 11.12   Energy inputs for tame hay production for a typical U.K. production system

	Quantity/ha	GJ/ha[a]
Inputs		
Field work, fuels	2.57 GJ	2.57
Field work, machinery	3.53 GJ	3.53
Nitrogen	250 kg	21.62
TOTAL		27.7
Outputs		
Hay yield	10,300 kg	65.5
Energy output/energy input		2.36:1

Note: [a]4,186 Joule = 1 kcal.
Source: After Leach, 1976.

Table 11.13 Energy inputs in tame hay production in an efficient U.K. production system

	Quantity/ha	GJ/ha[a]
Inputs		
Field work, machinery	2.0 GJ	2.0
Nitrogen	80 kg	7.48
TOTAL		9.48
Outputs		
Hay yield	5,600 kg	53.0
Energy output/energy input		5.6:1

Note: [a]4186 Joule = 1 kcal
Source: After Leach, 1976.

Corn Silage

Corn silage consists of mature corn plants that are cut, chopped, and stored in a silo. During storage the chopped corn ferments, and this process helps preserve it. In U.S. production, the total energy input for silage production averages 6.3 million kcal/ha (Table 11.14). Even with 70 percent water content, corn silage produces high yields, averaging 25.3 million kcal/ha. Thus, the output/input ratio for corn silage is 4:1, significantly greater than the 2.5:1 output/input ratio for corn grain.

Vegetarianism and Nonvegetarianism and Energy Inputs

In Chapters 8 through 11, energy inputs for the production of various animal and plant foods have been analyzed. The question then arises as to what the fossil fuel requirements would be for human diets made up of various combinations of animal and plant foods. Do some diets use more fossil energy than others? Humans seldom eat just one or two foods; rather, they make dietary choices from a variety of available foods. Basically, however, eating patterns can be classified as to the type of protein eaten. Nonvegetarian diets include both animal and plant proteins, often, as in the United States, with a predomination of animal protein. In the lacto-ovo diet, eggs, milk, and milk products represent the only animal protein eaten, whereas in the complete vegetarian diet no animal protein is eaten.

The following analysis illustrates some of the differences in fossil fuel requirements of these 3 dietary regimes. The calculations are based on data for various foods produced in the United States. The average daily food intake in

Table 11.14   Energy inputs in New York corn silage production

	Quantity/ha	kcal/ha
Inputs		
Labor	15 h[a]	6,975[d]
Machinery	40 kg[b]	720,000
Diesel	110 liters[c]	1,255,540
Gasoline	105 liters[c]	1,071,554
Nitrogen	116 kg[a]	1,705,200
Phosphorus	66 kg[a]	198,000
Potassium	75 kg[a]	120,000
Limestone	560 kg[a]	176,400
Seeds	19 kg[a]	475,000[e]
Insecticides	2.5 kg[a]	217,275
Herbicides	2.5 kg[a]	249,775
Electricity	12 kWh[c]	34,356
Transportation	211 kg	54,227[f]
TOTAL		6,284,302
Outputs		
Corn silage yield	31,020 kg[a]	25,284,402
Protein yield	393 kg	
kcal output/kcal input		4.02:1

Notes: [a]Snyder, 1976.
[b]Estimated.
[c]FEA, 1976.
[d]15 h × 465 kcal/h.
[e]Heichel, 1980.
[f]211 kg × 257 kcal/kg.

the U.S. is 3600 kcal (Putnam and Allshouse, 1991), so we assumed a constant intake of 3600 kcal/day for all 3 types of diets. The protein intake is over 100 g per day in the nonvegetarian diet and declines to about 80 g in the all-vegetarian diet. Both protein intakes significantly exceed the recommended daily allowance of 56 g/day.

Nearly twice as much fossil energy is expended for the food in a nonvegetarian diet as in the vegetarian diet (Figure 11.1). As expected, the lacto-ovo diet is more energy intensive than the all-vegetarian diet. Based on these sample calculations, the pure vegetarian diet is more economical in terms of fossil energy than either of the other 2 types of diets.

Energy expenditure is not the only factor to be evaluated when dietary choices are made. Decisions are often based on individual preferences and tastes. In addition, there are significant nutritional differences between the pure vegetarian diet and those that include animal products. Pure vegetarian diets lack vitamin B_{12}, an essential nutrient, so this must be taken as a dietary supplement. Further, the quality of protein depends on the combination of foods consumed. When the essential amino acids from a variety of plant food are combined, then the protein quality of a vegetarian diet will be satisfactory. A pure vegetarian diet usually consists of greater volume and bulk than a mixed diet, making it difficult for young children to consume the quantities necessary to meet all nutritional needs. In addition, nutritionally vulnerable people such as infants, rapidly growing adolescents, and pregnant and lactating women may need nutritional supplements of vitamins A and D, calcium, and iron while on a pure vegetarian diet.

When faced with future food options, both in agricultural policy and in personal diet, we must consider the fact that plant food is significantly more energy efficient to produce than a combination of animal and plant food.

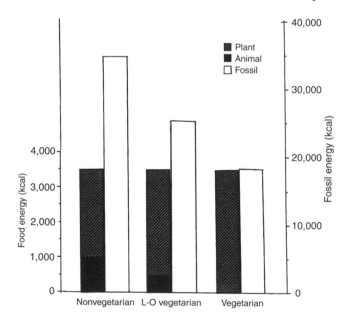

11.1   Daily food energy intake of pure vegetarians, lacto-ovo (L-O) vegetarians, and nonvegetarians and the calculated fossil energy inputs to produce these diets under U.S. conditions.

12

COMPETITION FOR LAND: DEVELOPMENT, FOOD, AND FUEL

David Pimentel and Marcia Pimentel

Projected climatic changes associated with global warming are expected to alter food and fuel biomass production from the land. Although the exact severity of the climatic change and patterns of change are difficult to project, scientists anticipate that some of the best arable land will become less productive (Pimentel et al., 1992b).

These changes are occurring at a time when the rapidly growing world population already is creating significant pressure on supplies of land, food, forest products, and biomass fuel. More than a quarter of a million humans are added to the world population every day—and all require food, water, land, and other basic resources. The fact that the number of malnourished humans is much greater than ever before in history—estimates range from 1 billion (Kates et al., 1989) to 2 billion—adds to the gravity of the present situation. Demographers project that the world population will rise from the present 6 billion to approximately 9.4 billion by 2025 and probably will stabilize at 15 billion by 2100 (PCC, 1989).

Concurrently, supplies of arable land per person are declining. World agriculture has exploited most of the arable land, and as a result millions of hectares of marginal land are being brought into production (Buringh, 1989). Pressure already exists to use land and other resources to alleviate global shortages of food and biomass energy (Hall, 1985; Brown et al., 1986).

Intense soil erosion, deforestation, diminishing water supplies, heavy use of fossil fuels, and pest damage further constrain the production of food, fiber, and forest products (Durning, 1989; Pimentel et al., 1992a). These problems are especially acute in Third World countries, where poverty and malnourishment are growing as a result of explosive population growth and severe environmental degradation, especially on agricultural land. Unstable economies and political conditions exacerbate all these problems (George, 1984).

In this chapter an asssessment is made of the current status of agricultural and forest land, focusing on the interdependence between food and biomass fuel production, which compete for the same basic resource—land. In addition, an analysis is made of the causes and extent of environmental problems associated with food and fuel production and how these problems affect future production.

Land for Food Production

More than 99 percent of the world's food supply comes from the land. Worldwide, about 1.5 billion ha of arable land are cultivated to produce food (Lal and Pierce, 1991). The global supply of arable land is 0.27 ha per capita; in the United States 0.6 ha per capita are cultivated to produce our relatively high animal protein and high calorie diet (Lal and Pierce, 1991). By the year 2025 arable land per capita worldwide will decline to a meager 0.2 ha and to only 0.1 ha by 2100. This estimate assumes there will be no further degradation in the quality of arable land.

During the past 40 years, about 30 percent of the world's arable land has been lost (Pimentel et al., 1995). Current agricultural practices create considerable topsoil erosion. Its severity depends on the particular crops planted, methods of culture and management, topography, rainfall and wind, and other factors (Pimentel et al., 1987; Lal and Pierce, 1991). Worldwide, erosion and its associated problems force the abandonment of 7 (Tolba, 1989) to 15 million (Pimentel, 1993) ha of land each year. This problem is also severe in the United States. For example, Iowa, which has some of the best soil in the world, has lost half of its topsoil after being farmed for about 100 years (Risser, 1981).

To expand current agricultural production, valuable forests are now being cleared to replace degraded fertile land (Pimentel et al., 1986b; Lal and Stewart, 1990; Lal and Pierce, 1991). This practice not only exposes the soil and increases erosion rates but also diminishes needed supplies of forest resources.

Furthermore, much of the land that is not now in crop production is unsuitable for cultivation because it is either too steep, too shallow, or too dry (Bilsborrow, 1987). Thus, only a limited amount of arable land has the potential for future crop production, and this amount cannot be expanded endlessly to meet the basic food needs of the rapidly expanding world population.

Land for Biomass Fuel Production

In addition to land resources devoted to agriculture, much land is used to produce biomass energy, a major source of fuel throughout the world (Pimentel et al., 1986b; Hall and de Groot, 1987; Pimentel et al., 1988). Biomass includes wood products for construction and pulp, corn for ethanol production, fuelwood, crop residues, and dung. High fossil fuel prices coupled with the fuel needs of the rapidly growing population, especially in developing countries, are creating major energy problems in many areas (Timmer et al., 1987; OTA, 1991c).

Forest Harvesting

Worldwide, some 4 billion metric tons of forest resources are harvested each year (FAO, 1983a). About 60 percent of these forest resources are harvested in developing nations, where about 85 percent is burned for cooking and heating (de Montalembert and Clement, 1983). Fuelwood makes up about half (1.3 billion tons) of the 2.8 billion tons of biomass used annually worldwide; the remaining half consists of crop residues (33 percent) and dung (17 percent) (Pimentel et al., 1986b).

Of the original 4.9 billion ha of closed forests in the world in 1950 (Lieth and Whittaker, 1975), only half, or less than 2.0 billion ha, remain. From preagricultural times to the present, temperate closed forests have suffered greater cumulative losses than those in the tropical regions (Repetto and Gillis, 1988). However, the tropical forest areas are being cleared more rapidly than the temperate closed forests. According to Myers (1989), the rate of tropical deforestation increased 60 percent during the 1980s. For example, since 1960 forest areas have been reduced 75 percent in the Ivory Coast and 80 percent in Ghana (Repetto, 1990). Lugo (1988) projects that at least 50 percent of the remaining tropical forests in South America will be cleared for agriculture during the next 20 to 30 years. About half of Africa's forests already have been destroyed, and Thailand has lost a quarter of its forests and continues to lose them (NAS, 1984; J. Krummel, Argonne National Laboratory, 1993, personal communication). Because of environmental degradation and economic policies, nearly 20 million ha of forests are destroyed each year throughout the world (Myers, 1989).

About 80 percent of the cleared forest land is used to provide additional cropland and pastureland for agriculture (Pimentel et al., 1986b). This fact underscores the interdependency of forestry and agriculture. Small farmers are the primary agents of deforestation (Southgate, 1990). Although small-scale fuelwood harvesting seldom causes the disappearance of forests (Leach, 1988), large-scale commercial harvesting of timber can result in vast deforestation (Repetto, 1990).

Biomass Fuel in Developing Countries

Developing countries possess more than two-thirds of the world population, and many of these people are extremely poor (Institute on Hunger and Development, 1990). In some regions—for example, sub-Saharan Africa—from half to three-quarters of the population subsist in abject poverty (Clausen, 1985). Out of necessity, poor people have to rely on biomass in the form of wood, crop residues, and animal dung for energy (Dunkerly and Ramsay, 1983; OTA, 1984; Sanchez-Sierra and Umana-Quesada, 1984; Kotamraju, 1986). Some estimates indicate that the poor in developing nations obtain 90 percent of their energy from these various biomass sources (Chatterji, 1981). For example, in sub-Saharan Africa, about 95 percent of the fuel is from biomass (Leach, 1988), and in the mountain areas of Asia and the Far East crop residues and animal dung represent from 90 to 95 percent of the biomass fuel (Leach, 1988). Biomass provides more than 70 percent of the fuel supply for the rural poor. The poor in developing nations spend from 15 to 40 percent of their income for fuel and/or invest an enormous number of hours in collecting biomass fuel (CSE, 1982; Hall, 1985). Frequently people spend 3 to 5 hours per day in firewood collection, traveling 3 to 10 km to collect their wood (Agarwal, 1986; Soussan, 1988); in some parts of Nepal people walk up to 19 km to obtain firewood (Gilmour and King, 1989). Burning crop residues and dung has a devastating impact on the productivity of the agricultural soils because soils are exposed to erosion, with its associated loss of water and nutrients (Wen and Pimentel, 1984; Pimentel et al., 1986b).

Biomass for Cooking

In rural Third World areas, food is cooked over an open fire or simple cook-stove. Under ideal conditions only 20 to 30 percent of the gross heat energy is transferred to the food, but with damp wood and poor fire management only 5 percent or less of the heat energy is transferred (OTA, 1984). The method of cooking and the type of cooking vessel influence the quantity of heat transferred to foods.

About 2 kcal of firewood are required to cook 1 kcal of food. Thus, based on the amount of food consumed per year, a person in a developing country uses at least 600 kg, or 1 m^3, of dry wood per year for cooking (Foley and Van Buren, 1982; Smith et al., 1983).

By conservative estimates, each person burns from 1200 to 1800 kg of dry wood each year for both cooking and heating (Lemckert and Campos, 1981; de Montalembert and Clement, 1983; Wen Dazhong, Institute of Ecology, Shenyang, China, personal communication, 1984). How much land is required to produce about 1200 kg of wood? In closed, broad-leaved tropical forests the annual increment of stem wood may range from 600 to 3000 kg/ha (dry) but usually falls between 600 and 1200 kg/ha (Lanly, 1982). Growth of branches increases firewood yield by 1000 to 2000 kg/ha. Assuming an annual, sustainable yield of 2000 kg/ha of firewood in tropical forests and an annual firewood need of 1200 kg/person for cooking and heating, each person requires about 0.6 ha of forestland per year. In addition, each person in developing countries needs 0.2 to 1.2 ha of arable land on which to grow basic food supplies using traditional methods (Buringh, 1984). Thus, approximately the same amount of land is needed for firewood as for food production.

Soil Erosion and Land Degradation

With world agricultural efforts focused on augmenting food production, degradation of cropland and pastureland is increasing (Pimentel, 1993). About 80 percent of the earth's land surface suffers from some form of degradation (Pimentel et al., 1995). In many areas the productivity of eroded soils cannot be restored, even with heavy application of fertilizers and other farm inputs (Lal, 1984a; Lal and Pierce, 1991).

The degradation of soil by erosion is of particular concern because soil reformation is extremely slow. Under tropical and temperate agricultural conditions, it takes 200 to 1000 years to form a 2.5-cm depth, or 340 tons/ha, of topsoil (Lal, 1984a, b; Elwell, 1985; Pimentel, 1993). The renewal rate comes to about 1 ton/ha/yr and ranges from 0.3 to 2 ton/ha/yr.

Erosion adversely affects crop productivity by reducing the availability of water to plants, soil nutrients, and organic matter (OTA, 1982). As the fertile topsoil thins, plant rooting depth is restricted. Based on current soil losses and projections for the period from 1975 to 2000, worldwide degradation of arable land is expected to depress food production from 15 to 30 percent (Shah et al., 1985).

A reduction in the amount of water available for plant growth is the most harmful effect of erosion (Follett and Stewart, 1985). Water is lost directly by rapid water runoff. In addition, both water and wind erosion reduce the water-holding capacity of soil by selectively removing organic matter and the fine soil particles (Buntley and Bell, 1976). An investigation of a wide range of soil types showed a strong correlation between effective water infiltration and soil organic matter content (Wischmeier and Mannering, 1965). When soils are degraded by erosion, water infiltration may be reduced as much as 93 percent (Lal, 1976). For example, Elwell (1985) reported that in Zimbabwe runoff of rainfall was 20 to 30 percent greater in eroded areas than in uneroded areas. This pattern of runoff caused water shortages even in years with adequate rainfall.

In most nations, soil loss rates average from 20 to 40 tons/ha/yr, but locally they may range as high as 3600 tons/ha/yr (Pimentel et al., 1987). In the United States, soil erosion occurs 13 times faster than soil formation.

Soil erosion is exacerbated when marginal land is brought into production, when more irrigation is developed, and when forests are cleared (Pimentel, 1993). For example, wind and water erosion, plus salinization and waterlogging from irrigation, cause an annual loss of 7 to 15 million ha of land worldwide (Tolba, 1989). In addition, erosion of arable land results in the yearly conversion of 15 million ha of forestland into cropland, exposing more soil to wind and water erosion. Eighty percent of the forestland destroyed yearly is cleared for agriculture to replace degraded cropland and pastureland (Pimentel et al., 1986b; Myers, 1990). As mentioned, forest removal reduces firewood supplies and forces the poor in developing countries to rely more heavily on crop residues and dung for fuel. Loss of crop residues from the land further intensifies soil erosion and water runoff, and loss of dung prevents the recycling of valuable soil nutrients (Pimentel et al., 1986b).

Worldwide, crop productivity on about 20 million ha is approaching a negative net economic return because the land is severely degraded (Pimentel et al., 1995).

Further contributing to diminished supplies of agricultural land are the vast land acreages continually being lost to urban spread, industrial development, and roadways. For example, in the United States between 1945 and 1975 an area of agricultural land the size of Nebraska was blacktopped with roadways and covered with homes and factories (Pimentel et al., 1976). The nation continues to lose about 525,000 ha/year of land.

Conserving Soil and Protecting Cropland and Pastureland

Vegetative Cover Essential for Soil and Water Conservation

The most effective method of controlling soil erosion and water runoff is to anchor the soil by providing adequate vegetative cover (Pimentel and Krummel, 1987). The removal of vegetation increases water runoff from 10 to more than 100 times over that on vegetated land (Bennett, 1939; Charreau, 1972; Douglas and Goodwin, 1980). In one study, on bare fallow land with a 5 percent slope, the soil erosion rate was 148 tons/ha/yr; however, when 6 tons/ha of rice straw were applied to the land with continuous corn production, the soil loss was reduced to only 0.1 ton/ha/yr (IITA, 1973). Bennett (1939) reported that the erosion rate for corn was 48 tons/ha/yr on land without dung, but application of 36 tons of dung reduced the erosion rate to about 11 tons/ha/yr. Another strategy is the use of no-till culture, which leaves crop residues on the land surface. In Ohio, for instance, soil erosion rates of no-till corn averaged about one-tenth those of conventionally grown corn (Harrold, 1972; Harrold and Edwards, 1974; Mannering and Fenster, 1977; Van Doren et al., 1984). Clearly, practices that remove crop residues, pasture vegetation, dung, and forest cover intensify soil erosion and water runoff.

In addition to controlling erosion and protecting cropland, conservation of crop residues significantly increase crop yields. For example, in Nebraska each ton/ha of crop residues left on the soil surface was found to increase grain and stover production by about 120 and 270 kg/ha, respectively; for corn and soybeans by 90 and 300 kg/ha, respectively (Power and Papendick, 1985). Hence, leaving 5 to 10 tons/ha of crop residues on the surface of the land will greatly reduce soil erosion and increase crop yields 10 to 20 percent. This adds another reason crop residues should not be removed from the land for fuel.

Corn-Agroforestry System Reduces Erosion

Employing an agroforestry system—for example, by combining a fast-growing leguminous tree such as *Leucaena* with a crop such as corn—increases the yield of both food and fuel. In this system half of each plot is planted to corn and half to *Leucaena*, with the corn planted at twice the normal density. After 1 to 2 years, when the *Leucaena* has established itself, the farmer reduces competition between the *Leucaena* and corn by cutting the *Leucaena* to the ground when the corn is planted.

Once established, the *Leucaena* produces about 4500 kg/ha of biomass per year (Rachie, 1983). Of this, 2500 kg of leaves and small twigs can be used as a mulch and worked into the soil to increase biological nitrogen and soil organic matter. This mulch and the rows of small trees protect the soil from erosion and rapid water runoff (Kidd and Pimentel, 1992). The remaining 2000 kg of *Leucaena* biomass are harvested for fuelwood.

In several experiments, the 60 kg/ha of nitrogen added to the soil by the *Leucaena*, plus the reduction of soil erosion from 30 tons/ha/yr to only 1 ton/ha/yr, raised the corn yield from 1000 kg/ha to 2000 kg/ha (Kidd and Pimentel, 1992). The corn/agroforestry system doubled food production, provided a significant amount of fuelwood, and reduced soil erosion.

Conclusion

Worldwide agricultural ecosystems cover about 50 percent, forest ecosystems about 25 percent, and human settlements about 20 percent of the world's land area (Pimentel et al., 1992a). Thus, the present human population is managing approximately 95 percent of the terrestrial environment (Western, 1989). Because of the land lost by degradation and the escalating food needs of people, from 10 to 20 million additional ha of cropland are needed each year for agriculture. At present, most of this new agricultural land comes from cleared forestland. However, the extensive reduction in forestland now occurring throughout the world is reducing the availability of lumber, pulpwood, and fuelwood and reducing the biological diversity that is so important for the vital functioning of the entire ecosystem (Wilson, 1988a).

Most land degradation in the world is occurring because of the excessive removal of biomass for fuel and other purposes. Intense soil erosion is taking place in many parts of the world because of the harvesting and burning of crop residues for cooking and heating (Wen Dazhong and Pimentel, 1984;

Pimentel et al., 1986b; Lal and Stewart, 1990). Crop residues should not be utilized for energy conversion because of the environmental hazards.

Although the best source of biomass energy is from forests, great care must be exercised in harvesting wood resources. Clearly, ecologically sound resource management systems for both agriculture and forestry would help increase the supply of biomass for food and fuel and maintain natural biodiversity.

13

WATER RESOURCES FOR CROP AND BIOMASS PRODUCTION

David Pimentel and Marcia Pimentel

The earth's atmosphere is estimated to contain about 13 km^3 of water. From this renewable source comes all the rain that falls on earth. The 13 km^3 is a relatively small percentage (0.001 percent) of the total amount of water estimated to be in the oceans (1.4 million km^3). The amount of fresh water on the surface of the earth in streams and lakes is estimated to be about 225 km^3. This represents about 3 percent of the total amount of groundwater and soil moisture present on earth.

Few plants send roots deeper than a meter; thus, they cannot reach groundwater resources and must depend on the water in the top layers of soil. This moisture is provided either by rainfall or by water pumped from aquifers.

Groundwater is referred to as "fossil water" because it accumulates deep below the surface and is replenished slowly. In many parts of the world today, the groundwater that has accumulated over millions of years is being mined to offset surface-water deficits that are caused by population growth and expanded agricultural production. Less than 0.1 percent of the stored groundwater mined annually by pumping is replaced (UNEP, 1991). Thus, withdrawal of groundwater exceeds natural water recharge and recycling. For example, in 1978 about 310 × 10^9 liters per day of groundwater was pumped in the United States (USWRC, 1979). In many states, water pumping exceeds replenishment by as much as 80 × 10^9 liters per day, or 25 percent, and in the Texas-Gulf area overdraft was as high as 77 percent (Pimentel et al., 1996).

Water Use by Crops and Forests

Water is the major limiting factor in crop and forest production. Water short-ages severely affect crops at all stages of development by reducing seed germi-nation, seedling emergence, photosynthesis, respiration, leaf number and size, seed number, and seed filling (Jordan, 1983). The photosynthetically active leaf area so essential to crop productivity is the component of growth that is most sensitive to water stress (Jordan, 1983).

Water stress limits the metabolism of nitrogen and other nutrients in crops. In leguminous crops, for instance, nitrogen fixation is much lower in stressed nodules (Pankhurst and Sprent, 1975). Also, water-stressed nonle-gumes show a decreased capacity to utilize soil nitrogen (Hanson and Hitz, 1983). An FAO (1979) study listed several major crops—including corn, wheat, beans, rice, and potatoes—as those most sensitive to water stress; rice and corn suffer the greatest yield losses.

Insufficiency of water reduces crop productivity, but yields increase dra-matically when adequate water is supplied (Figure 13.1). The net primary productivity of natural vegetation increases from about 500 to 1000 g/m^2 when precipitation increases from 250 to 650 mm per year at a constant tem-perature (Lieth and Whittaker, 1975).

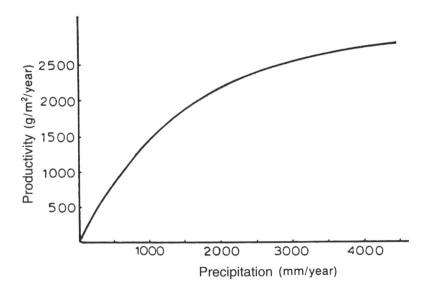

13.1   Net primary activity of natural vegetation related to mean annual precipitation (Siemens and Oschwald, 1978).

All crops require and transpire massive amounts of water. For example, a corn crop that produces 7000 kg/ha of grain will take up and transpire about 4.2 million liters/ha of water during the growing season (Leyton, 1983). Plants play a major role in the hydrological cycle. Of the total precipitation that falls on the conterminous United States, about two-thirds is returned to the atmosphere through evapotranspiration (loss of water from the terrestrial area through transpiration by plants and evaporation from soil and water surfaces). The remaining one-third drains into the oceans.

Although rain falls on most parts of the earth each year, seasonal droughts limit crop yields in many regions. For example, in 1986 the southeastern United States experienced severe water shortages, with the result that little agricultural production and tree growth occurred.

In total, U.S. agriculture uses 600×10^9 liters of water per day (USDA, 1980). About 99 percent is for irrigation, the remainder for livestock. Surface water supplies about 60 percent of the total, and the remainder comes from groundwater (Pimentel et al., 1996). However, even now in some major agricultural regions of the United States as much as 94 percent of the water supply is pumped directly from groundwater.

Irrigation: Benefits and Risks

To sustain crop yields when rainfall is inadequate, farmers use irrigation water. For example, it has been projected that grain sorghum yields under dryland conditions could be raised 67 percent through irrigation (NAS, 1975a). Without sufficient water most new technological inputs in agriculture, such as fertilizers, are relatively ineffective. The yield of grassland in Utah, with limited rainfall, was only 13 kg of forage per kg of nitrogen applied, whereas in the southeastern United States, with ample rainfall, it was 35 kg of forage per kg of nitrogen applied (Beaty et al., 1974). Arid pastures and rangelands are seldom irrigated or heavily fertilized because the economic return on the investment is much too low.

Irrigated crop production requires the movement of enormous amounts of water. Thus, in California it takes 1400 liters of irrigation water to produce 1 kg of corn; 1900 liters for sugar (sugar beets); 4700 liters for rice; and 1700 liters for cotton (Ritschard and Tsao, 1978). Producing 1 kg of grain-fed meat requires from 4200 to 8300 liters when the water input is just for irrigated feed grain production. Unfortunately, approximately 16 percent of the irrigation water does not reach the intended crop; about one-third of this 16 percent is lost by evaporation and the remainder by seepage and percolation during the flow in the irrigation canals (Murray and Reeves, 1977). Thus by some measures irrigation, as is now practiced, wastes water.

Irrigation is costly in terms of both energy and money. Of the 6 percent of total U.S. fossil energy used in agriculture, about one-fifth is expended to move irrigation water (FEA, 1976). In Nebraska, for example, rain-fed corn production uses 630 liters/ha of oil equivalent per season, whereas irrigated corn uses about 1900 liters/ha, or almost 3 times more energy (Pimentel, 1980). Therefore, with adequate rainfall, the same amount of rain-fed corn can be produced with less than one-third the energy input needed for irrigated corn.

Because governments often subsidize irrigation projects, the actual energy cost of irrigation is difficult to figure. Energy costs for building dams and waterways generally are not included in energy assessments. By conservative estimates these costs could add 10 percent to the energy cost of surface irrigation (Roberts and Hagan, 1975). In addition, large quantities of energy are used to lift water over mountain ranges. For example, the surface water moved from the Colorado River Aqueduct to the San Diego River basin requires about 185 liters of oil per 1.2 million liters of water transported over the mountains (Roberts and Hagan, 1977). When the energy cost of such systems is taken into account, the total energy input would be increased from two- to tenfold.

Not only is irrigation costly in terms of depletion of groundwater supplies and fossil energy use, it is also financially draining. Costs differ depending on whether surface or groundwater supplies are used. In the western United States, the cost of surface water for irrigation is about $40 per million liters of water, whereas groundwater costs $140 per million liters (Pimentel et al., 1996). Pumping groundwater from depths of 180 m increases the cost to about $300/ha/yr. Avocado growers in Southern California spend about $2000/ha for irrigation water per year.

This economic pressure is already being felt in some farming regions. For example, in the trans-Pecos region of Texas, because of the increase in irrigation and other production costs, crops such as alfalfa, barley, sorghum, and wheat return less than the break-even price (Patton and Lacewell, 1977). In Arizona, the high price of fossil fuels recently has forced some growers to abandon the production of low-value crops such as alfalfa (Pimentel et al., 1996).

Clearly, as fossil fuel prices escalate, irrigated agriculture will face greater economic difficulties. This occurred in the United States in 1973 when OPEC increased oil prices. The cost to pump irrigation water in the United States jumped from about $550 million/year in 1973 to more than $2.5 billion in 1983, nearly a fivefold increase (Sloggert, 1985). In regions where the groundwater depth was especially great, pumping water became too expensive to allow the profitable production of low-value crops (e.g., forage).

At present, nearly 33 percent of the world's food is produced on irrigated land (Postel, 1989). If food production in developing nations is to double during the next two decades, as recommended by the FAO (1984a), then the total area of irrigated land must be expanded by more than 40 percent, from about 105 million ha to 148 million ha.

Irrigation Affects Soil Quality

Although rainfall and wind erosion on unprotected soils are the prime causes of land degradation, poorly managed irrigation of land with slopes of 2 percent or greater also causes significant erosion.

The major environmental problem associated with irrigation, however, is salinization of the soil. Most often salinization in irrigated areas originates either from a saline, high-water table or from salts present in the irrigation water. Salts originate from dissolution of weathered rocks and soil, enter the irrigation water, and salinize the soil downstream. For example, when irrigation water is withdrawn from the Colorado River in the Grand Valley and later returned to the river, an estimated 18 tons of salt leach from each irrigated hectare of land and return to the river downstream (EPA, 1976). At times during the summer, the Red River flowing through Texas and Oklahoma is more saline than seawater and is therefore unsuitable for irrigation (USWRC, 1979).

When salts accumulate in the root zone of the soil at high enough concentrations, yields decline. The extent of the problem varies according to the salt concentration in the irrigation water, soil type, climate, and crop type. Yield reductions occur when so much salt accumulates in the root zone that the crop plant can no longer extract adequate amounts of water from the soil. When water uptake by the plant is measurably impaired, growth is slowed and yields are reduced. Reactions to salinity vary with the stage of growth of the plant, but they are most severe in young seedlings. When low, uniform levels of salt exist in the soil, the effects of salinization may go unnoticed because the reduction in growth is relatively uniform across the entire field of crops.

Many salinity problems with irrigated crop production are associated with a shallow water table 2 m or less below the soil surface (Kidd and Pimentel, 1992). Salts tend to accumulate in the water and move upward into the crop root zone instead of being flushed into a lower level in the ground. To overcome this problem, farmers have to install drainage pipes throughout the entire irrigated area. This procedure is expensive but vital if the land is to remain productive. With adequate drainage, sufficient water can be applied to leach the salts from the root zone. Without such drainage, applying more water only waterlogs the soil, which is equally disastrous for crop production.

Worldwide, salinization is the single most important factor limiting yields on irrigated lands (Kendall and Pimentel, 1994). Many irrigation systems have failed because they were not designed to control salinity. Currently, irrigated soils in most parts of the world, including India, Pakistan, Egypt, Mexico, Australia, and the United States, face serious salinization problems (WRI, 1992).

Another environmental problem associated with irrigation is the intrusion of saline water into freshwater aquifers. Usually this problem occurs along seacoasts where seawater and fresh water come in contact with one another. Under natural conditions an "interface" usually separates fresh water in the terrestrial aquifer from seawater in the coastal aquifer. When water is pumped from the freshwater aquifer for irrigation or other purposes, the seaward discharge of fresh groundwater is reduced, and the fluid pressure along the interface decreases. This change causes seawater to move landward and upward.

The goal is to maintain the net flow of fresh groundwater toward the sea. With pumping, the interface is moved slightly, but only a minor adjustment takes place, and a new equilibrium results. The wells, however, continue to supply fresh water under these conditions. When carefully designed, the wells simply remove fresh water that formerly seeped into the sea. Overpumping will cause seawater to enter the wells.

Water Conservation

Controlling Water Runoff

When either rainfall or irrigation water runs off soil in large quantities, its usefulness to plant growth is diminished. The best way to control water runoff

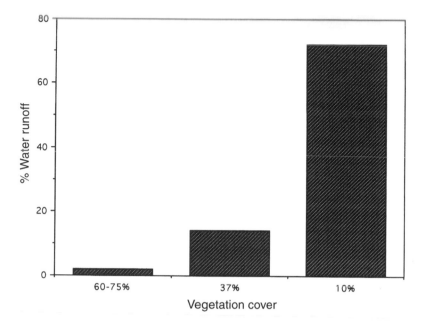

13.2   The effects of vegetation cover on water runoff when rainfall is 61 mm per hour (Shalhevet et al., 1979).

from agriculture is to maintain an adequate vegetation cover on the land. Plant leaves, stems, and other organic matter on the surface of the land all diminish runoff by dissipating the energy in rain and wind before it reaches the soil. Rain then more easily percolates into the soil. Water runoff rates are as much as 10 to 100 time greater on cleared land than on vegetation-covered land (EPA, 1976). Land that retains water is better able to sustain plant growth.

Runoff is particularly intense during heavy rainstorms, as demonstrated during a storm in Utah, when 61 mm of rain fell in 1 hour. Land with 60 to 75 percent vegetation cover experienced surface runoff of only 2 percent, whereas land with only about 10 percent vegetation cover suffered surface runoff of 73 percent (Figure 13.2).

Deforestation and water runoff are of particular concern in tropical areas, where rainfall is often quite severe. In Nigeria water runoff was reported to be only 2.6 mm/ha per year in the early 1980s; when forests were in place, and farmers were making only small, traditional clearings for home gardens (Lal, 1981). However, when the forest area was bulldozed, plowed, and planted,

Table 13.1   Water runoff and soil loss in corn plantings as affected by conservation technology

Technology	Treatment	Water runoff (mm/ha)	Increased loss (mm/ha)	Slope (%)	Reference
Till plant	till plant	120		3.4	Moldenhauer et al., 1971
	conventional	145	25	25	
Chisel plant	chisel plant	11.4		8–12	Romkens et al., 1973
	conventional	45.2	33.8	8–12	
Level terraced	terraced	9.4		2–18	Schuman et al., 1973
	contour planted	81.4	72	2–18	
Mulch	corn stover	0.6		7	Ketcheson and Onderdonk, 1973
	no stover	13	12.4	7	
Mulch	rye cover crop	39		2–4	Klausner et al., 1974
	residue burned	174	135	2–4	
Mulch	manure mulch	90			Musgrave and Neal, 1937
	no manure	131	41		
Disk chisel (no-till)	disk chisel	1		5	Oschwald and Siemans, 1976
	conventional fall plow	29	28	5	
No-till	no-till in sod	37		14	Spomer et al., 1976
	conventional	107	70	14	
No-till	no-till	41		7	Lal, 1984c
	conventional	123	82	7	
Rotation	corn-oats-hay-hay	5.8		7–10	Ketcheson, 1977
	conventional continuous	30.8	25	7–10	
Coulter chisel	coulter-chisel (no-till)	94		1–2	Siemens and Oschwald, 1978
	conventional fall plow	145	51	1–2	
Disk chisel	disk chisel (no-till)	28		5	Lieth and Whittaker, 1975
	conventional fall plow	84	56		

water runoff rates increased to 250 mm/ha per year, or nearly 100 times the rate that occurred in traditional forest plantings.

Although forests are particularly effective in controlling water runoff, good soil quality and water conservation methods in agriculture reduce water runoff significantly. For example, several experimental soil and water conservation techniques saved 100 mm/ha of water per growing season (Table 13.1). Even half of this amount can heavily influence crop productivity. For instance, 50 mm of water applied to corn, spring wheat, and sorghum crops, which normally experience transient drought periods during the growing season, has increased average yields by 15 percent, 25 percent, and 23 percent, respectively (de Wit, 1958; Hanks, 1983; Shalhavet et al., 1979). These calculations assumed that the 50 mm of water lost because of conventional tillage systems would be fully utilized by plants if conservation tillage systems had been used.

Crop Selection

Another method of augmenting crop yields on land where water is a limiting factor is to select crops that grow in arid climates. For instance, sugarcane, bananas, and alfalfa require large amounts of water (800 to 2500 mm/ha) for maximum production (Table 13.2). Next are corn and potato, which need from 500 to 800 mm/ha during the growing season. Some crops with low water requirements (380 to 650 mm/ha) are cabbage and wheat. Some varieties of cowpeas are reported to grow with only 125 to 250 mm/ha of water, although the yield is low (1000 kg/ha) (OTA, 1983). Many investigations are underway to find crops that will grow under relatively arid conditions (Vietmeyer, 1986). Genetic engineering should help reduce the water requirements for some crops, but because water is an essential component of photosynthesis there are physiological limits to how extensively water use can be reduced (Hole, 1981).

Soil Organic Matter

Soil with a high level of organic matter has excellent moisture-holding capacity. The soil's fine structure and the large number of soil organisms associated with organic matter enable rapid water percolation. Some soil surfaces have been reported to have more than 10,000 earthworm holes and channels per m^2 (Hole, 1981; Edwards and Lofty, 1982). These channels greatly improve the infiltration of water into the soil, where it can be used by growing plants.

Table 13.2   Water requirements for selected crops and yields per year

Crop	Crop water requirement (mm)	Yield (tons/ha)
Alfalfa	800–1600	22–28
Banana	1,200–2,200	40–60
Cabbage	380–500	25–35
Groundnut	500–700	3.5–4.5
Maize	500–800	6–9
Potato	500–700	25–35
Rice	450–700	6–8
Sorghum	450–650	3.5–5
Soybean	450–700	2.5–3.5
Sugarcane	1,500–2,500	50–150
Wheat	450–650	4–6

Source: After Hanson and Hitz, 1983.

By contrast, degraded soils with little organic matter and few organisms usually develop crusty surfaces, decreasing water infiltration rates by as much as 93 percent (Lal, 1976). In Zimbabwe, an estimated 20 to 30 percent of the rainfall ran off the cropland, resulting in water shortages even in years with ample rainfall (Elwell, 1985).

Soil types naturally vary in their capacity to hold moisture. For instance, a clay soil may store 5 times more moisture than coarse sand (Table 13.3). However, dense clays are difficult to irrigate because of poor drainage. A sandy loam is the ideal soil for irrigation because it has not only good water-holding capacity but also needed drainage characteristics. Thus, it will store sufficient water during the growing season but will not waterlog (Table 13.3).

Table 13.3   Moisture storage in various soil types

Soil Type	Storage (mm/m)
Clay	200
Silt loam	160
Sandy loam	120
Fine sand	80
Coarse sand	40

Source: P. Riley, Water Resources Use and Conservation (unpublished manuscript).

Improving Irrigation Technology

Given that in many areas crop production necessitates the use of irrigation, steps to enhance water delivery and decrease the deleterious side effects should increase productivity.

One strategy is to genetically engineer crop plants to increase their tolerance to salinity. However, it should be emphasized that although saline-tolerant plants will grow, there will be an obvious cost for plants that grow under stressful conditions (Shannon, 1984)—the yields will be much lower than for crops grown under more favorable conditions. At present, some crops can be grown under relatively high saline soil conditions, including date palm, spinach, garden beet, kale, rape, cotton, and barley grain (OTA, 1983).

Although it is practically impossible to operate an irrigation project without some loss of water, losses can be kept to a minimum through effective management. In areas of sandy loam with good drainage, the goal is to apply just the amount of water needed by the crop and to prevent excess applications. This minimizes seepage and percolation losses. Losses using sprinkler irrigation may be kept as low as 5 percent, whereas flood irrigation often results in the loss of up to 75 percent of the water.

Although trickle (or drip) irrigation delivers the needed amount of water to each individual plant, it requires large amounts of energy and capital equipment. In areas with high lifts, trickle irrigation can save energy, because energy expenditures associated with pumping are much greater than those of installing trickle irrigation systems (Batty and Keller, 1980). Clearly, several possibilities exist to improve irrigation technologies, conserve water and energy (Batty and Keller, 1980; Chen et al., 1976; Stanhill, 1979).

14

CONSERVING BIOLOGICAL DIVERSITY IN AGRICULTURAL/ FORESTRY SYSTEMS

David Pimentel, Ulrich Stachow, David A. Takacs,
Hans W. Brubaker, Amy R. Dumas, John J. Meaney,
John A.S. O'Neil, Douglas E. Onsi, and David B. Corzilius

Maintaining biological diversity is essential, whether for agricultural and forestry production, pharmaceutical research and development, aesthetics, tourism, evolutionary processes, stabilization of ecosystems, biological investigations, or overall environmental quality, or simply because all species have intrinsic worth (Wilson, 1988a; Ehrlich and Wilson, 1991). Although approximately 90 percent of the world's food comes from just 15 plant species and 8 animal species (Wilson, 1988a), several thousand other plant species are used as food by humans (Altieri et al., 1987a).

Furthermore, high agricultural productivity and human health depend on the activity of a diverse natural biota composed of an estimated 10 million species of plants and animals (Wilson, 1988b). The United States is home to an estimated 500,000 species, of which 95 percent are small organisms, such as arthropods and microbes (Knutson, 1989). As many as 1 million species of plants and animals will be exterminated worldwide by the year 2010 (Reid and Miller, 1989). This high rate of extinction is alarming because these organisms may be vital to the functioning of ecological systems that sustain our planet.

Efforts to curb the loss of biodiversity have intensified in recent years, but they have not kept pace with the growing encroachment of human activity.

Many laws (e.g., the National Environmental Policy Act and the Endangered Species Act) still appear to be a patchwork, ad hoc strategy to save species on the brink of extinction. Furthermore, they have primarily focused on a small number of species of large plants and animals, neglecting the small organisms. However, the numerous small organisms, such as insects and fungi, dominate the structure and function of natural ecosystems (Price, 1988). Complementary strategies are needed to protect entire ecosystems to conserve biological diversity.

To date the prime international focus of biological conservation has been on national parks, which only cover approximately 3.2 percent of the earth's land area (Reid and Miller, 1989). It is equally vital to protect the biological diversity of managed agricultural and forest ecosystems and human settlements, which combined cover approximately 95 percent of the terrestrial environment (Western and Pearl, 1989). Even extensive deserts support a few people with domesticated goats and sheep, and tropical rainforests have human inhabitants.

In this chapter we examine patterns of species diversity in natural, agricultural, and forestry ecosystems; the role of biodiversity in maintaining ecosystems; the viability of ecosystems; and the threat to biological diversity. The goal is to identify specific ecological strategies and policies to conserve biological diversity in agricultural and forestry ecosystems.

Biological Diversity

Most knowledge about species diversity concerns large plants and animals such as flowering plants and vertebrates. The extent of the diversity of the smaller plants and animals remains obscure. Estimates of the number of species are listed in Table 14.1.

Arthropods make up approximately 90 percent of all species. Crops and both natural and managed forest ecosystems have abundant arthropod species (Table 14.2). These species contribute a great amount of biomass and great diversity to forest ecosystems (Paoletti, 1988; Paoletti et al., 1989a; Pimentel and Warneke, 1989). For example, the number of arthropod species in temperate and tropical agroecosystems ranges from 232 to 1000 per ha. An Italian study reported an average of 11.0 aboveground arthropod predators per unit sampled in forest ecosystems and 9.8 predators per unit in crop/weed ecosystems (Paoletti et al., 1989a). In another study, Paoletti (1988) found relatively little difference between the number of arthropod species in soil and

Table 14.1   Plant and animal species

Organism	Number of species
Plants	
Vascular plants: dicots, monocots, ferns	260,000
Fungi	47,000
Liverworts and mosses	25,000
Diatoms	17,000
Lichens	16,000
Bacteria	14,000
Animals	
Arthropods	9,000,000
Mollusks	50,000
Protozoa	30,000
Fish	22,000
Helminths	14,000
Annelids	12,000
Nematodes	12,000
Coelenterates	10,000
Birds	9,000
Flatworms	9,000
Reptiles	6,000
Echinoderms	6,000
Sponges	5,000
Mammals	4,500
Moss animals (Bryozoa)	4,000
Amphibians	2,500
Other small animals	1,000
TOTAL	10,000,000

Source: Pimentel et al., 1992c.

litter in an unmanaged forest (232) and the number existing in a managed corn ecosystem (239). Some species occurred in both ecosystems.

Although concern about threats to species diversity tends to focus on impressive species such as whooping cranes and tigers, small organisms such as arthropods and microbes face equal or greater threats (Dourojeanni, 1990). The small organisms often are more specialized and more dependent on certain plant species and habitats than are the large animals, and therefore they are more susceptible than large animals to extinction (Dourojeanni, 1990).

Table 14.2   Arthropod species in various ecosystems

Ecosystem	Location (area)	Arthropod species
Collards	New York (1 ha)	262[a]
Corn and woodland	Italy (1 ha)	200–500
Alfalfa	New York (1 ha)	600[a]
Corn	Hungary (field)	600
Pasture	Britain (1 ha)	1,000
Forest, tropical	Borneo (10 trees)	2,800
Forest, beech	West Germany (forest)	1,500–1,800
Forest, park	Hungary (forest)	4,433–8,847
Forest, tropical	Costa Rica (10,800 ha)	13,000[b]

Notes: [a]Aboveground arthropods.
[b]Insects only.
Source: Pimentel et al., 1992c.

Tropical ecosystems possess prodigious levels of biodiversity. Janzen (University of Pennsylvania, 1989, personal communication) reports that Costa Rica has 15,000 species of butterflies and moths, whereas only 12,000 species exist in the United States, which is 190 times larger than Costa Rica. Yet biodiversity is plentiful in temperate ecosystems, too. Janzen (1981), Southwood et al. (1982), and Wilson (1988a) report that particular kinds of arthropods are more plentiful in temperate than in tropical ecosystems. Biodiversity conservation is not just a project for people in developing nations of the tropics. Much urgent work also needs to be done to prevent large-scale loss of biodiversity in temperate, industrialized nations.

Humans manipulate 70 percent of the temperate and tropical ecosystems to harvest 98 percent of their food and all of their wood products (Vitousek et al., 1986). Approximately 50 percent of the terrestrial area is devoted to agriculture, approximately 20 percent to commercial forests, and another 25 percent to human settlement (Western and Pearl, 1989). Only 5 percent is unmanaged and uninhabited. Most species are located in the land area that is managed for agriculture, forestry, and human settlement (Western and Pearl, 1989). For example, in Germany only 35 to 40 percent of the total of 30,000 species inhabited protected areas; the remaining species lived in human-managed ecosystems (RSU, 1985). Therefore, humans must extend their conservation efforts to include agricultural, forest, and other managed ecosystems.

Preservation of Biological Diversity: Large and Small Organisms

The most magnificent species, the ones that inspire us by their beauty, should continue to receive focus and funding in preservation efforts. But anthropocentric aesthetics should not be the only criteria considered in efforts to conserve global biological diversity. The sheer numbers of insect species suggest that we ought not ignore them. "To a rough approximation and setting aside vertebrate chauvinism," writes Robert May (1988, p. 1446), "all organisms are insects." Insects and other "little things" perform crucial functions that stabilize ecosystems in ways that are scarcely understood (Wilson, 1987).

Elimination or addition of even one species can have profound effects. For example, until recently humans pollinated oil palm trees in Malaysia by hand, an inefficient and expensive way of performing the task. Ten years ago, the government introduced a tiny West African weevil associated with palm pollination. The weevil now accomplishes all pollination of oil palms in Malaysia, with an annual savings of $140 million (Greathead, 1983). In addition, insects are a virtually untapped source of food (DeFoliart, 1989), dyes (Metcalf and Metcalf, 1993), and pharmaceutical products (Eisner, 1990). Various microbes, too, can be more effectively used for nitrogen fixation and waste recycling (Pimentel et al., 1980b).

Functioning, successful ecosystems require a balance among their various organisms. Although the small organisms dominate the structure and function of ecosystems, the large organisms also contribute to balance (Terborgh, 1988). All organisms are useful indicators of the relative health of an ecosystem and its capacity to provide various basic services to humans. Each species has intrinsic value. Earthworms, insects, and fungi are no less fascinating, less threatened, or less worthy of attention and conservation than are the large organisms. Much remains to be learned about the vital role the small organisms play in the functioning and structure of natural systems, and the consequences of eliminating them. Although a few insects, fungi, and other organisms attack humans and their crops, these pests make up less than 1 percent of all species.

Causes of Reduced Species Diversity

Over the past billion years, adaptation and diversification have tended to increase the number of species. However, the proliferation of humans and industrialization have destroyed ecosystems and caused a noticeable decline in species diversity (Wilson, 1988a). Within an order of magnitude, we do not know how many species exist today, nor do we know the number that has disappeared over the past few centuries. However, several sources estimate that at present approximately 150 species per day are being exterminated (Reid and Miller, 1989). The vast majority of species remain undiscovered, and many will never be known because of current extinctions. This observation emphasizes the need for a larger number of systematists and greater support for research to investigate biodiversity (Wilson, 1988b).

The loss of biological diversity results from a wide array of complex factors. Human affluence and the concomitant exploitation of resources; increasing rates of vegetation clearing and habitat destruction; the growth of urban areas; and chemical pollution (e.g., pesticides and acid rain) have the greatest impact on species reduction. These trends are accelerated by the ever-increasing rate of human population growth: a quarter-million people are added each day to the world population of 6 billion (PRB, 1995). Each new person requires food, wood, land, water, fuel, and other resources. In many developing countries, where demand for these resources exceeds supply, the result is increasing human malnutrition and poverty, which contribute to environmental degradation (Brown et al., 1990). However, in developed countries the use of natural resources may be 100 to 600 times more per capita than in developing countries. This excessive consumption directly diminishes biodiversity. Even where progressive laws and land preservation efforts do exist, humans' increasing resource demands undermine progress in biodiversity preservation (Machlis and Tichnell, 1985).

To date, humans have destroyed approximately 44 percent of the world's tropical forests and thereby unbalanced and often reduced much of the biodiversity naturally found (WRI, 1990). Furthermore, in some areas of the developed world, agricultural overproduction is related to species decline and extinction (RSU, 1985). In developing countries, especially where slash-and-burn agriculture is practiced on short rotations, soil nutrients and organic matter are depleted, causing loss of biodiversity in areas of agricultural production (Altieri, 1990). Therefore, the development of sound ecological agricultural production is an essential factor in all conservation. Toxic chemicals added to ecosystems also adversely affect biodiversity. In particular, the 2.5 billion kg per year of synthetic pesticides used worldwide for agriculture, public health, and other purposes damage wild biota of all kinds. Pesticides alone destroy or damage half a million colonies of honeybees annually in the United

States and are equally hazardous to wild bees and other beneficial insects (Pimentel et al., 1992d). Other chemical pollutants released into the air and water by agriculture and other industries result in the extinction of many species (Reid and Miller, 1989).

The introduction of exotic species into new regions of the world has also reduced biodiversity (Wilson, 1988a). Of the more than 1500 insect species that have been introduced into the United States by mistake, approximately 17 percent have become pests, requiring the use of pesticides and increasing damage to wild biota (Sailer, 1983).

National parks and wilderness preserves can serve as havens for threatened species. However, the ability of protected parks to maintain their biological biodiversity depends in large measure on use of the surrounding land and on sociopolitical factors. If the adjacent area is not managed with the objectives of the park in mind, countless species will go extinct. This relationship has clearly been demonstrated by the fate of 62 bird species in an 86-ha woodland in West Java. After several km of surrounding woodland were destroyed, 20 bird species disappeared, 4 almost became extinct, and 5 others suffered noticeable population declines (Diamond et al., 1987). The remaining species appeared to be unaffected. This example highlights the need for regional conservation (Ricklefs, 1987) that incorporates both parks and agriculture/forestry systems. Most U.S. national parks have been protected from mining, logging, and other destabilizing commercial activities. Recently, however, the U.S. government supported mining of oil and other resources in natural reserves, particularly in Alaska. Similar situations exist in other countries, such as Nigeria.

Continued protection of parks and reserves has become increasingly difficult throughout the world because of rapid population growth and the encroachment of human activities. For instance, Kenya's population increases 3.8 percent annually, which means it doubles every 18 years (PRB, 1990). Currently, 7 percent of Kenya's land lies in protected national parks; however, three-quarters of its large rangeland mammals live outside of the parks and within human-managed systems (Western and Pearl, 1989). In addition, an estimated 90 percent of other animal species live outside of the protected parks.

Humans living in or adjacent to national parks often threaten the preservation of biodiversity by hunting, building settlements, and so forth (Browder, 1990; Western and Pearl, 1989). Another typical problem is occurring in

Costa Rica, where, although 25 percent of the land has been designated for protection, ecologically unsound agricultural practices reduce biodiversity anyway (Power, 1989).

Biodiversity and Economic and Environmental Benefits

The domesticated species of agriculture and forestry, which provide the basic food, fiber, and shelter to support human existence, contribute several trillion dollars annually to the world economy. These species depend on most of the estimated 10 million natural (i.e., nondomesticated) species for production and sustainability (Pimentel et al., 1980b). Further, the continued viability and improvement of agriculture and forestry depends on the genetic resources of wild relatives of the cultured species for use in plant breeding to improve crop and forest productivity (Wilson, 1988a).

A diverse group of microbes fix nitrogen from the atmosphere for use by crops and forests. These organisms supply an estimated 14 million tons of nitrogen to U.S. agriculture and, worldwide, an estimated 140 million tons of nitrogen per year.

Cross-pollination is essential to reproduction in many crops and natural vegetation. More than 40 U.S. crops, valued at approximately $30 billion, are absolutely dependent on insect pollination for production (Robinson et al., 1989). Insects also play an important role in pollination of natural vegetation, whereas birds, mammals, and insects are essential in the dispersal of some plant seeds (Reid and Miller, 1989). An estimated $20 billion is spent annually in the world for pesticides. Yet parasites and predators existing in natural ecosystems provide an estimated 5 to 10 times this amount of pest control. Without the existence of natural enemies, pests would cause catastrophic losses in agriculture and forestry, and the costs of chemical pest controls would escalate enormously.

Fish, other wildlife, and plant materials (e.g., blueberries) harvested from the wild have an estimated annual value of $2 billion in the United States (Prescott-Allen and Prescott-Allen, 1986). Natural biota—especially plants, microbes, and invertebrates—serve many essential functions for agriculture, forestry, and other sectors of human society. In addition, these natural biota preserve genetic material for potential agriculture and forestry products. Natural biota, especially arthropods, also serve as food for most species of native fish, many species of birds, and some species of mammals (Janzen, 1987;

Wilson, 1987). Productive agriculture and forestry systems cannot function successfully without the activities of the diversity of natural biota.

Plant and Animal Biomass and Diversity

The data in Table 14.3 indicate that fungi, microbes, and arthropods, along with plants, account for the bulk of the biomass in ecological systems. Fungi alone total approximately 4000 kg/ha, and arthropods contribute approximately 1000 kg/ha. In contrast, mammals and birds contribute only 2 kg/ha and 0.03 kg/ha, respectively.

Table 14.3   Biomass per hectare in a temperate-region pasture

Organism	Biomass/ha (kg fresh weight)
Plants	20,000[c]
Fungi	4,000[a]
Bacteria	3,000[a]
Arthropods	1,000[c]
Annelids	1,320[a]
Protozoa	380[a]
Algae	200[c]
Nematodes	120[c]
Mammals	1.2[b]
Birds	0.3[b]

Notes: [a]Richards, 1974.
[b]Walter, 1985.
[c]Estimated.

Biological diversity in an ecosystem is often related to the amount of living and nonliving organic matter present (Wright, 1983; 1990). Positive correlations have been recorded between biomass production and species abundance (Elton, 1927; Odum, 1978; Sugden and Rands, 1990; M. Giampietro, personal communication, Istituto Nazionale della Nutrizione, Rome, Italy, 1991). Although some ecologists have questioned the universality of this contention (Krebs, 1985), most studies have confirmed the relationship. For example, in New York state, collard biomass in experimental field plots treated with cow manure increased an average of fourfold over biomass in control plots (Pimentel and Warneke, 1989). In the experimental plots with the highest biomass, arthropod species diversity rose 40 percent over that of the control plots. Similarly, in field tests in the former USSR, the species diversity of macrofauna (mostly arthropods) increased 16 percent when manure was added to wheat plots (Bohac and Pokarzhevsky, 1987). Further, in grassland plots in Japan the species diversity of the macrofauna (again, mostly arthropods) more than doubled when manure was added to the land (Kitazawa and Kitazawa, 1980).

In a related study, Ward and Lakhani (1977) reported that the number of arthropod species associated with juniper bushes increased fourfold when the number of bushes increased 100-fold. Elsewhere, a 100-fold increase in plant biomass productivity yielded a 10-fold increase in bird diversity (Wright, 1983; 1990).

Although data for species diversity were not presented, the biomass of arthropods increased by 2 to 7 times per ha as manure was added to either wheat or mangold crops in the United Kingdom (Morris, 1922; Raw, 1967). Also, when manure was added to agricultural land in Hungary, the biomass of soil microbes increased 10-fold (Olah-Zsupos and Helmeczi, 1987). Assuming that biomass is generally correlated with biodiversity, efforts to increase biomass in agricultural and forestry ecosystems can be one important way of preserving the wealth of biodiversity.

Conserving Biological Diversity

Because croplands, forests, and human settlements occupy as much as 95 percent of the terrestrial environment, a large portion of the world's biological diversity coexists in these ecosystems (Western and Pearl, 1989). Therefore, major efforts should be made to conserve the many natural species that now exist in these extensive terrestrial environments. Conservation programs based on ecological principles will help make agricultural and forest production more sustainable and help maintain biological diversity. The following factors favor biodiversity: abundant biomass, diverse plant species, diverse habitats, large territories, stable ecosystems, abundant soil nutrients, high-quality soils, effective biogeochemical cycling, abundant water, and favorable climates (Westman, 1990).

Abundant Biomass and Energy

Except for green plants that capture solar energy to feed themselves and certain bacteria that use inorganic material as an energy source, organisms rely on plant biomass as their energy resource. Crop residues are a vital biomass resource that improves agricultural productivity. Crop residues left on the land for recycling not only protect the soil from erosion and rapid water runoff but also contribute large quantities (2000 to 15,000 kg/ha [dry]) of organic matter and the nutrients contained in the soil. Suggestions that crop residues be harvested for fuel and other purposes have often produced catastrophic consequences. For example, in China and India, the removal of crop residues has proven disastrous for soil quality and fertility, biological diversity, and agricultural productivity (Wen Dazhong, personal communication, Institute of Ecology, Shenyang, China, 1989). Also, sediments from unprotected soils washed into streams and lakes negatively affect aquatic biota and other aspects of the ecosystem.

Furthermore, cover crops such as grasses and legumes are advantageous for agricultural production because they not only reduce soil erosion and compaction and water runoff but also increase soil organic matter (Hartwig, 1987). In addition, cover crops can increase vegetative diversity in crop ecosystems, which in turn benefits overall species diversity (Altieri et al., 1987b). Increased biomass also increases biological diversity by creating shelter and refuge for a variety of species.

Diversity of Plant Species

In the United States, many plant species exist in managed ecosystems. Of the nation's estimated 21,750 plant species, approximately 6000 are crop species, including forages; 708 are commercial trees; and 2000 are weeds.

Increased plant diversity should be encouraged in some managed ecosystems. Multispecies gardens support a diverse group of natural biota and help farmers produce an abundant and wide variety of food. At the same time, farmers benefit from effective use of soil nutrients and reduced water runoff. Examples of such gardens are found in Java, where small farmers successfully cultivate 607 crop species in their gardens, with an overall species diversity comparable to that of deciduous subtropical forests (Dover and Talbot, 1987).

Diversity in forest production is also advantageous. Janzen (1987) reports that a tropical forest that includes some crop production has a larger number of insect species than a primary forest. The mosaic effect apparently increases biological diversity. Other studies (Hanson et al., 1991) show that structural diversity is important in forests to protect biodiversity. This diversity can be maintained with adaptive harvesting strategies that conserve biodiversity.

Intercrops

When leguminous crops such as clover are grown between rows of primary crops such as corn, they serve as an intercrop, or living mulch. Legumes not only fix nitrogen but also enhance plant diversity, conserve soil and water resources, and increase the biomass and animal diversity produced by the ecosystem.

In another system, strips of different crops are grown across the slope of agricultural fields. These strips not only help control soil erosion but also increase the diversity of vegetation and thereby increase the availability of beneficial predators and parasites for biological control. With appropriate combinations of strip crops grown in rotation, various pests can be controlled with smaller amounts of pesticides and in some cases without pesticides. This type of pest control occurs when corn, soybeans, and hay are grown in a strip pattern (Pimentel et al., 1991).

Shelter Belts and Hedgerows

Shelter belts for wind control and hedgerows planted along the edges of cropland and pastureland also increase biological diversity, reduce soil erosion and moisture loss, and increase the biomass present (Elton, 1958). Shelter belts and hedgerows frequently provide refuge for beneficial parasites and predators, which can help control pest insects and weeds and thereby reduce the need for pesticides (Altieri et al., 1987b; Paoletti et al., 1989a). In addition, shelter belts help reduce moisture loss by buffering winds, an especially important benefit in areas of low rainfall, and may reduce irrigation needs (Kedziora et al., 1989).

Biomass and Soil and Water Conservation

High-quality soils that maximize plant productivity and help increase biodiversity have the following characteristics: they are rich in nutrients, have abundant organic matter (2 to 15 percent by weight of soil), store soil moisture (approximately 20 percent by weight), are well drained, are relatively deep (at least 15 cm), and contain abundant biota.

Organic matter not only harbors large numbers of arthropod and microbial species but, equally important, sustains the productivity of the soil by increasing its water-holding capacity, providing a source of nutrients, and improving soil tilth. Because the organic layer is the first to suffer the effects of erosion, its conservation is essential to maximizing biomass productivity and thereby increasing biodiversity. In the temperate zone, soil organic matter in well-managed cropland ranges between 1 and 4 percent, in productive pastures between 4 and 8 percent, and in forests between 6 and 15 percent (RSU, 1985).

All animals and especially plants require water to sustain life. For example, corn producing 14,000 kg/ha of biomass (dry) during the growing season transpires approximately 4.5 million liters/ha of water. Furthermore, a strong correlation exists between precipitation and plant diversity, both between temperate and tropical biomes and within biomes (Gentry, 1982). In general, water increases the productivity of the entire ecosystem and in turn increases the plant diversity in the system.

Many technologies (e.g., crop rotations, strip cropping, contour planting, terracing, ridge planting, and no-till practices) can be used to help conserve soil and water resources. The results of each strategy depend on the particular characteristics of the crop or forest ecosystem (Follett and Stewart, 1985).

Vegetative cover prevents rapid runoff of rainfall and allows water to percolate into the soil. On barren, eroded soils, as much as 90 percent of the water runs off and is lost to the crop plants and forest (Lal, 1984b).

Livestock Manure

The gross amount of fertilizer nutrients present in all the livestock manure produced in the United States is approximately equal to the amount of nutrients applied in commercial fertilizer each year. Estimates are that 5 to 10 times more livestock manure could be effectively recycled for agricultural production. Currently in the United States, only 6 percent of the nutrients in manure is effectively utilized (Safley et al., 1983).

Efficient use of livestock manure would raise the productivity of crops grown on the land, conserve fertilizer nutrients, and thereby decrease expenditures for fertilizers. It also would add valuable biomass to the soil while reducing water and air pollution. All of these factors would tend to stimulate agricultural production, increase soil organic matter, and increase the number of beneficial arthropods in the agroecosystem (Purvis and Curry, 1984).

Habitat Diversity

Increasing the diversity of physical habitats within an ecosystem increases the diversity of associated plants and other organisms (Gentry, 1982). Different birds, arthropods, microbes, and other organisms are associated with different crop and forest ecosystems. Arnold (1983) found only 5 bird species in a crop ecosystem surrounded by more farmland but 8 species when ditch vegetation was present. The number of species increased to 12 when there was a short hedge, to 17 when there was a tall hedge, and to 19 when a strip of woodland was present.

Further, different groups of species are associated with the same crop in different regions (Strong, 1979). For example, worldwide a total of 1905 pest insect species feed on the cocoa plant; however, 80 percent of these species are found in only one tropical region (Strong, 1974).

Agroforestry

Agroforestry, the practice of planting various combinations of food and/or forage crops alongside trees, increases biomass and conserves soil and water resources by preventing erosion. Further, it reduces crop losses to pests because plant diversity is increased (Cromartie, 1991). With all these benefits, agroforestry conserves and in some cases enhances biological diversity (Ewel, 1986; Kidd and Pimentel, 1992).

For example, in tropical Central America, conventional corn plantings produce approximately 10,000 kg/ha of fresh biomass, whereas in an agroforestry system with leguminous trees the corn biomass nearly doubles (Kidd and Pimentel, 1992). At the same time, 22,500 kg/ha of leguminous tree biomass are produced. Thus, in the agroforestry system total biomass increases nearly fivefold over that of the conventional system. In addition, agroforestry significantly conserves soil and water resources, making the agroforestry system more ecologically sustainable and productive than conventional crop production. Combining crops and trees also increases vegetative diversity, which in turn increases species numbers.

Another form of agroforestry combines leguminous trees with pasture grass and livestock production (Kidd and Pimentel, 1992). The trees fix nitrogen, enhancing the total productivity of the system by contributing nitrogen and other nutrients to the pasture system. The trees also serve as a food resource for the livestock, especially during the dry season. As in the former agroforestry system, combining forage crops and trees increases vegetative diversity, which in turn helps conserve biodiversity both in tropical and temperate regions. Trees in agroforestry systems also produce firewood, which helps reduce pressure on natural forests.

Mixed Forests

Mixed forests have a higher rate of biomass production than homogeneous stands of trees (Ewel, 1986). This difference occurs because each tree species has a specific set of nutrient requirements, and the mixed planting of trees makes effective use of the complex mix of nutrients present in the soil. The mixed forest improves biological diversity because different animal and microbe species are associated with different tree species.

Moreover, in commercial forestry, as well as in natural forests, tree diversity increases biomass production by diminishing pest damage (Ewel, 1986). For example, attacks by weevils on white pines and by tussock moths on Douglas firs are significantly more severe in single-species stands than in areas with high tree-species diversity (Metcalf and Metcalf, 1993).

Large-scale clear-cutting of forests reduces biomass and biological diversity. Further, the loss of vegetation results in the rapid loss of nutrients from the soil, which eventually diminishes the productivity of the entire ecosystem. Planting trees along streams and roadways increases biodiversity. Careful, selective cutting of forests, however, helps maintain high biological diversity and a healthy, productive forest ecosystem (Hanson et al., 1991).

Pasture Management

A pasture management strategy that maximizes biomass and prevents overgrazing is most productive and sustainable (Clark et al., 1986). In addition to providing livestock forage and vegetative cover, high pasture productivity prevents soil erosion and rapid water runoff and provides the biomass needed to support other species in the ecosystem. Overgrazing diminishes biomass, especially forage sources for the livestock, curtails livestock production, and reduces biological diversity. For example, 139 microarthropod specimens were collected from litter in 0.5 ha of ungrazed pasture, compared with 36 specimens from 0.5 ha of overgrazed pasture (Petersen et al., 1982).

To prevent overgrazing, the pasture should have the appropriate number of animals per hectare and be grazed on a rotation system. For example, in the northeastern United States grazing pasture for 1 week and resting it for 2 weeks allows sufficient forage and vegetative regrowth.

Stable Ecosystems

Although some moderate environmental flux may be associated with increased biodiversity, extreme fluctuations in the amount of water, wind, temperature, nutrients, and vegetative types adversely affect the biota in all ecosystems. Therefore, management programs for crops and forests should attempt to minimize extreme changes in ecosystems. Hedgerows, forest patches, field verges, ponds, and/or trees serve several purposes. They can buffer an area from extreme microclimate variation, help reduce water loss and erosion, and thereby enhance biological diversity in crop fields and landscapes.

Pesticides and Other Toxic Chemicals

Pesticides severely reduce biological diversity by destroying a wide array of susceptible species in the ecosystem and changing the normal structure and function of the ecosystem. Concern for the negative impacts of pesticides on natural biota and public health has prompted 3 nations (Denmark, Sweden, and the Netherlands), and the province of Ontario to pass legislation to reduce pesticide use by 50 percent (Pimentel et al., 1991).

By employing appropriate biological controls and other agricultural practices, pesticides can be reduced and in some cases eliminated while crop yields are maintained or increased. A wide array of proven nonchemical control methodologies can be substituted for pesticides. These include enhancement of host plant resistance, biological control, crop rotation, short-season cropping, soil and water management, planting of trap crops, fertilizer management, crop density maximimation, planting date alteration, and genetic engineering (Pimentel et al., 1991). Depending on the crop, pest complex, and ecosystem, these controls can be used in various combinations to minimize the use of pesticides and in some cases to eliminate them altogether.

Combined Benefits

If agricultural and forest environments are improved and if biological diversity is conserved on managed ecosystems that adjoin protected national parks, the diversity of park ecosystems will also benefit. Appropriate planting of commercial forests adjoining protected forests provides a helpful transition zone (Reid and Miller, 1989). Such improved environments in managed ecosystems can facilitate species migration between managed and natural ecosystems.

Clearly, increasing biodiversity in agriculture and forestry requires sound ecological practices, which at the same time improve the productivity and sustainability of agriculture. As Altieri (1990) has pointed out, indigenous farming systems often represent the best sources of knowledge on ecologically sustainable agriculture. Government policies must pay attention to such marriage between wild and managed ecosystems to preserve and promote sustainable agriculture and forestry and conserve biological diversity (Kidd and Pimentel, 1992).

Conclusions

The needs and activities of the growing human population are changing natural ecosystems at rapid rates. Millions of species live and carry out vital functions in the biosphere and are essential to society. Yet the importance of most animal and plant species—the small organisms, such as arthropods and fungi, that make up more than 95 percent of all species—is overlooked. Despite being small and inconspicuous, these organisms provide invaluable benefits to agriculture and forestry. During the past decades, conservationists have focused on saving a relatively small number of large animals. Setting aside parks for these species has heightened public awareness and benefited the fight to save these often beautiful creatures. However, future conservation programs should aim to preserve *all* species of organisms and the greater diversity of the environment.

The evidence suggests that more biological diversity exists in croplands, forestlands, and other human-managed ecosystems, which cover approximately 95 percent of the terrestrial environment, than in protected parks, which cover only 3.2 percent. Biological diversity in agricultural/forestry systems can best be conserved by maintaining abundant high levels of biomass/energy and plant and habitat diversity, by conserving soil, water, and biomass resources, and reducing the use of pesticides and similar toxic chemicals in agriculture and forestry. Maintaining biological diversity is essential for productive agriculture and forestry, and ecologically sustainable agriculture and forestry are essential for maintaining biological diversity.

The authors recommend the following policies to enhance the conservation of biological diversity:

• Develop more accurate measures for assessing the value of small and large organisms in protecting the quality of the environment, and work to disseminate basic information concerning the importance of biodiversity to scientists, farmers, foresters, government policymakers, and all citizens.

• Encourage ecologically sound and sustainable management practices in agriculture and forestry.

• Adopt biological controls for pests, and encourage greater use of biological resources for agriculture and forestry systems to replace pesticides, fertilizers, and other chemicals.

• Protect biological diversity to provide a quality environment for everyone and to ensure productive, sustainable agriculture and forestry. Concern should be not for one species or one factor but for the integrated management of the earth's natural resources as a whole.

15

FOOD PROCESSING, PACKAGING, AND PREPARATION

David Pimentel and Marcia Pimentel

Food Processing

Ever since humans first controlled fire, they have used its heat to cook some of their foods. Cooking, either by roasting, baking, steaming, frying, broiling, or boiling, makes many foods more palatable. Indeed, cooking enhances the flavor of foods such as meat; it also improves the flavor and consistency of many cereals and makes their carbohydrate content more digestible. Although not all vegetables are cooked before eating, the heating process, if carefully done, makes them more tender yet preserves their natural colors and flavors. Certainly, cooking enables humans to have a wider variety of food on the dinner table. However, it can cause destruction of vitamin C, thiamine, and solubility losses of valuable minerals, especially if large amounts of water are used.

Heating has an even more important function than merely enhancing palatability characteristics. Heating food to 100°C or higher destroys harmful microbes, parasites, and some toxins that may be natural contaminants of food. *Staphylococcus* and *Salmonella* are destroyed by boiling, whereas *Clostridium botulinum* must be exposed to temperatures of 116°C (attained under pressure) if heat-resistant spores are to be eliminated. Another example is *Trichinella*, a small helminth (parasitic worm) found in uncooked pork. If consumed by humans, the worms migrate to human flesh, causing serious illness. But when pork is cooked to at least 58.5°C, the parasites are killed. Numerous harmful protozoans and worm parasites come from uncooked vegetables and fruits grown in gardens fertilized with human excreta. Although it is logical to associate such problems with primitive agriculture, they remain of concern in areas where organic gardening is not carefully practiced.

Except for grains and sugars, most foods humans eat are perishable. They deteriorate in palatability, spoil, or become unwholesome when stored for long periods. Surplus animal and crop harvests, however, can be saved for future use if appropriate methods of preservation are used. The major ways of preserving foods are canning, freezing, drying, salting, and smoking. With all methods the aim is to kill or restrict the growth of harmful microbes and/or their toxins and to slow or inactivate enzymes that cause undesirable changes in food palatability. For further protection during long periods of storage, preserved food is placed either in sterile metal cans or glass jars or frozen in airtight paper or plastic containers.

In many parts of the world, people continue to raise and preserve a large portion of their own food for use throughout the year, but in the West people rely heavily on fresh and commercially processed foods purchased in nearby supermarkets.

Canning

Ever since Louis Pasteur proved that microbes, invisible to the eye, caused food to putrefy, various methods have been used to kill these harmful organisms. The basic process in canning is to heat the food to boiling or higher under pressure, then pack and completely seal it in sterilized containers. The precise processing temperatures and times are dependent upon the acidity of the particular foodstuffs being processed. Foods with a slightly acidic pH (4.5 and higher) require the high heat of pressure canners to ensure safe processing. Density of the foodstuffs as well as size and shape of container also influence processing times.

The average energy input in commercial canning of vegetables and fruits is about 575 kcal/kg of food (Table 15.1). This figure represents only the energy expended in actual processing by heat and does not include the energy input required for making the container. (Packaging is discussed later in this chapter.) Canning vegetables in the home is much more energy intensive than commercial processing. For example, home-canned beans require 757 kcal/kg (Klippstein, 1979).

Table 15.1   Energy inputs for processing various products

Product	kcal/kg	Remarks
Beet sugar	5,660	Assumed 17% sugar in beets
Cane sugar	3,370	Assumed 20% sugar in cane
Fruit and vegetables (canned)	575	
Fruit and vegetables (frozen)	1,815	
Flour	484	Includes blending of flour
Baked goods	1,485	
Breakfast cereals	15,675	
Meat	1,206	
Milk	354	
Dehydrated foods	3,542	
Fish (frozen)	1,815	
Ice cream	880	
Chocolate	18,591	
Coffee	18,948	Instant coffee
Soft drinks	1,425	Per liter
Wine, brandy, spirits	830	Per liter
Pet food	828	
Ice production	151	

Source: After Casper, 1977.

Freezing

In freezing, many of the desirable qualities of the fresh food are retained for relatively long periods of time. The temperatures employed, −18°C or lower, retard or prevent the growth of harmful microbes. Their growth is also inhibited by lack of water, which is frozen.

Fruits can be frozen dry with added dry sugar or in syrup. Vegetables must be blanched (boiled or steamed a short time) prior to freezing to inactivate plant enzymes that cause deterioration of natural flavors and colors. The energy input for freezing vegetables and fruits is significantly greater than that for canning, averaging 1815 kcal/kg of food frozen versus only 575 kcal/kg for canning (Table 15.1). The canning process requires only heating, whereas freezing may involve brief heating, cooling, and then actual freezing.

Furthermore, canned foods can be stored at room temperature (actually slightly cooler is recommended), whereas frozen food must be kept in freezers at temperatures of −18°C or lower. Maintaining such a low temperature requires about 265 kcal/kg per month of storage (USBC, 1975). The average energy input to store frozen foods in the home freezer is 1060 kcal/kg (Klipp-stein, 1979). Because frozen foods are usually stored about 6 months, this additional energy cost is significant, making the total energy input much greater than that for canning. However, the moisture-resistant plastic and paper containers for frozen foods require less energy to manufacture than the metal cans and glass jars used for canned food.

Salting

Fish, pork, and other meats have been preserved by salting for more than 3000 years (Jensen, 1949). This food-processing method is not employed as widely today in developing countries as it has been in the past, perhaps because other methods make possible the preservation of a wider variety of foods.

Salt (NaCl) preserves fish and meat by dehydrating it and, more impor-tant, by increasing the osmotic pressure to a level that prevents the growth of microbes, insects, and other small organisms. Like sun-drying of foods in warm, sunny climates, salting requires a relatively small input of energy. Usu-ally about 1 kg of salt is added per 4 kg of fish or meat (Hertzberg et al., 1973). The method requires an estimated 23 kcal/kg of fish or meat; addition-ally, 90 kcal of fossil energy is required to produce 1 kg of salt (Rawitscher and Mayer, 1977). Even so, the total energy input for salting is significantly lower than that required for freezing fish or meat.

The salted product can be stored in a cool, dry area or placed in a mois-ture-free container. Before the salted fish or meat can be eaten, it must be soaked and rinsed many times with fresh water to remove the salt. Then the fish or meat is usually cooked, but even after the soaking and the rinsing there is usually a sufficient residue to give the food a noticeably salty taste.

Drying

Reducing the moisture level of grains, meats, legumes, and fruits to 13 per-cent or lower prevents the growth of harmful microbes and lessens chances for infestations by insects and other organisms. Sunlight, an effective source of energy for drying, has been used for centuries and is still used today, especially for such crops as fruits and legumes. It has the distinct advantage of being a continuous, unlimited energy source.

When not accomplished by the slow sun-drying method, drying becomes energy intensive because the removal of water requires large inputs of heat energy. For instance, removing 1 liter of water from grains requires an average energy input of 3600 kcal (Leach, 1976). However, Leach (1976) reports that by using the most efficient technology available it is possible to remove a liter of water from grain with an input of only 1107 kcal/liter.

In investigating the drying of corn in the United States, Pimentel et al. (1973) reported an energy input of 1520 kcal per liter of water removed. Put another way, 1520 kcal are expended to reduce the moisture level of 7.4 kg of field-harvested corn from 26.5 to 13 percent.

The average energy input used to dehydrate foods is 3542 kcal/kg (Table 15.1). Thus, the energy input for drying approximately equals the food energy contained in 1 kg of many typical grains (about 3400 kcal). For potato flakes, the energy input for drying can be as high as 7517 kcal/kg (Singh, 1986).

All these calculated energy inputs for removing moisture from foods are higher than the theoretical values for evaporation. For example, the evaporation of 1 liter of water from an open container theoretically requires as little as 620 kcal of energy (HCP, 1974). However, 2 to 6 times more energy is generally required to dehydrate food because the water in the food is not as accessible as it is in an open dish and must be removed from inside the cells of vegetables, fruits, or meats. In other words, barriers must be overcome in order to remove the water from food, and this requires extra energy.

In freeze-drying, a recently developed technique, the food is first frozen, then dried under extremely low pressure. This makes it possible to attain a moisture content of much lower than 13 percent; the resultant food is exceptionally light and can be stored at room temperature. However, this process is even more energy intensive than regular drying because it requires energy for both freezing and drying.

Smoking

Smoking, like drying, originated in primitive societies yet is still used today. Fish, meats, and grains are the major foods preserved by this method. Smoking preserves food in 2 ways. First, the heat dries or dehydrates the food; second, the various tars, phenols, and other chemicals in the smoke are toxic to microbes and insects. Most of these chemicals are also carcinogenic to humans if consumed in large amounts

In many developing countries, farm families hang grains from the ceiling of the kitchen, where the smoke and heat from the open fire both dry and smoke the stored grain. This simple processing and storage method minimizes insect and microbial growth.

To smoke 1 kg of thin strips of fish, about 1 kg of hardwood (such as hickory) is used. Adding sand to the hardwood chips keeps the fire smoldering during the smoking process. The energy input for smoked fish is estimated to be about 4500 kcal/kg, with all of the energy coming from the wood chips burned.

Various Processed and Prepared Foods

The energy inputs for preserved, processed, and home-prepared foods are substantial. For example, in an analysis of the energy inputs needed to produce a 1-kg loaf of white bread commercially in the United Kingdom, Leach (1976) reported that 77 percent of the 3795 kcal total energy used to produce the bread (including marketing costs) is used in processing, with 13 percent for milling and 64 percent for baking.

In the United States, producing a 1-kg loaf of white bread requires an input of 7345 kcal, substantially greater than that for the United Kingdom. Milling and baking account for only 27 percent of the total energy input, as compared with 77 percent in Leach's analysis (Figure 15.1). Of the 27 percent, 7 percent of the energy is for milling and 20 percent for baking, which is appreciably lower than the input for wheat production, which is 45 percent of the total energy input. Hence, the major energy input for the white bread produced in the United States is expended for wheat grain production, and it would appear that energy inputs for grain production for bread is appreciably lower than in the United States (Figure 15.1).

The energy inputs to produce a 455-g can of sweet corn differ greatly from those expended for a loaf of white bread. The energy for production of the corn itself amounts to little more than 10 percent of the total energy used. (Figure 15.2). Most of the total energy input of 1322 kcal is for processing, in particular for production of the steel can. The heat-processing of the corn requires only 316 kcal, but the production of the can requires about 1006 kcal.

The other large input that must be included in the energy accounting for processed foods is the energy expended by the consumer shopping for the food. In the United States, food shopping usually requires the use of a 1000- to 3000-kg automobile. Based on an allocation of the weight of the corn and other groceries, it takes about 311 kcal—or about three-fourths the amount of energy expended to produce the corn itself—to transport a 455-g can of corn home from the store. Energy expended in home preparation amounts to

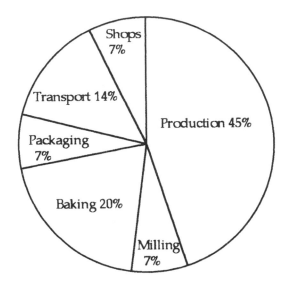

15.1   Percentages of total inputs of (7345 kcal) for the production, milling, baking, transport, and shopping for a 1 kg loaf of bread.

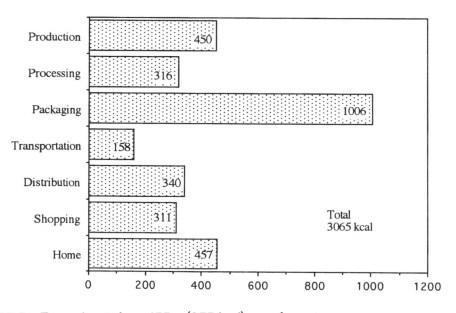

15.2   Energy inputs for a 455 g (375 kcal) can of sweet corn.

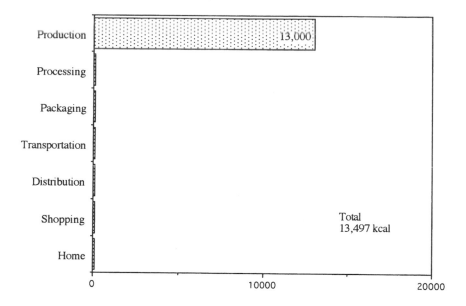

15.3   Energy inputs to supply 140 g of beef (375 kcal) to the table.

457 kcal, or 12 percent of the total, and includes cooking the corn and using an electric dishwasher to clean the pots, pans, plates, and other utensils used.

All the energy inputs for producing, processing, packaging, transporting, and preparing a 455-g can of corn total 3065 kcal (Figure 15.2). Contrast that with the 375 kcal of food energy provided by the corn. Hence, about 9 kcal of fossil energy are necessary to supply 1 kcal of sweet corn food energy at the dinner table.

The pattern of energy inputs for beef differs greatly from that for sweet corn (Figure 15.3). Although 140 g of beef provides about 375 kcal of food energy, about 13,000 kcal of fossil energy are expended just in the production of this amount of beef (Figure 10.3). In other words, beef production requires about 29 times more energy per kcal of food energy produced than does sweet corn. The other energy inputs for beef, including those for processing, transportation, and marketing, are all relatively small compared to the production inputs. The prime reason for the high production input is the large quantities of grain are fed to beef animals in the United States.

Energy accounting of the U.S. food system is complicated by the fact that most of the corn and other cereal grains suitable for human consumption are fed to livestock. Of the estimated 740 kg of grain produced per capita per year in the United States, only about 77 kg are consumed directly by humans (Putnam and Allshouse, 1991).

The energy inputs for processing several other food products are presented in Table 15.1. The relatively large inputs for processing of 1 kg of sugar—3370 kcal for cane sugar and 5660 kcal for beet sugar—are due primarily to the energy used for the removal of water by evaporation, an energy-intensive process. Thus, 1 kg of crystalline sugar, which has a food energy value of 3850 kcal, requires almost that much energy to process the cane.

Breakfast cereals also require much energy to process and prepare—on the average, about 15,675 kcal/kg (Table 15.1). One kg of cereal contains about 3600 kcal of food energy. The energy inputs include those required for grinding, milling, wetting, drying, and baking the cereals. Other technologies, such as extrusion, are sometimes used, and these require additional large inputs of energy.

Both chocolate and coffee concentrates require energy-intensive food-processing techniques, including roasting, grinding, wetting, and drying. Processing of 1 kg of chocolate or coffee requires more than 18,000 kcal/kg (Table 15.1).

The energy inputs for soft-drink processing are high because of the pressurized systems employed to incorporate carbon dioxide (Table 15.1). A total of 1425 kcal are required per liter of soft drink produced. By way of comparison, the processing of milk requires only 354 kcal per liter. A 12-ounce can of diet soda requires about 600 kcal for the soda but 1600 kcal for the aluminum can. Thus, a can of diet soda with 1 kcal of food energy requires a total of 2200 kcal of fossil energy to produce.

Packages for Foods

In general, processed foods must be stored in some type of container. For instance, 455 g of frozen vegetables are usually placed in a small paper box that requires an expenditure of approximately 722 kcal of energy to make (Table 15.2). By contrast, the same quantity (455 g) of a canned vegetable such as corn is placed in a steel can that requires 1006 kcal to make (Table 15.2). The energy input for a glass jar for 455 g of vegetables is 1023 kcal, about the same as that used to produce a steel can (Table 15.2).

Table 15.2   Energy required to produce various food packages

Package	kcal
Wooden berry basket	69
Styrofoam tray (size 6)	215
Moulded paper tray (size 6)	384
Polyethylene pouch (16 oz or 455 g)	559[a]
Steel can, aluminum top (12 oz)	568
Small paper set-up box	722
Steel can, steel top (16 oz)	1,006
Glass jar (16 oz)	1,023
Coca-Cola bottle, nonreturnable (16 oz)	1,471
Aluminum TV dinner container	1,496
Aluminum can, pop-top (12 oz)	1,643
Plastic milk container, disposable (0.5 gallon)	2,159
Coca Cola bottle, returnable (16 oz)	2,451
Polyethylene bottle (1 qt)	2,494
Polypropylene bottle (1 qt)	2,752
Glass milk container, returnable (0.5 gallon)	4,455

[a]Calculated from data of Berry and Makino.
Source: After Berry and Makino, 1974.

Thus, processing 455 g of corn and placing it into a steel can requires an input of about 1270 kcal of energy (Figure 15.2). About 1550 kcal are expended in freezing 455 g of corn and placing it in a cardboard box, and the food must be stored at 0°C or lower, requiring an energy expenditure of about 265 kcal/kg per month.

Although there is little difference between the energy inputs required for the production of steel cans and glass jars, aluminum soft-drink cans require significantly higher energy inputs. A 355-milliliter (ml) steel can for soft drinks requires an input of about 570 kcal; the same size aluminum can requires 1643 kcal, nearly three times as much energy (Table 15.2). A 355-ml aluminum can of soda contains about 150 kcal of food energy in the form of sugar, equivalent to about 10 percent of the energy expended in the production of the aluminum can.

Aluminum food trays commonly used to held frozen TV dinners also require a large energy input. An average tray requires 1500 kcal to make (Table 15.2), often more energy than the food the tray holds (usually 800 to 1000 kcal). In addition, the diverse containers used to display fruits, vegetables, and meats in grocery stores require energy for production. Energy expenditures range from about 70 kcal for wood berry baskets to 380 kcal for molded paper trays (Table 15.2).

Because of increased concern about solid waste, the energy inputs of recycling milk and beverage bottles have been analyzed. A disposable plastic half-gallon milk container requires 2160 kcal for production, whereas a half-gallon glass container requires 4445 kcal (Table 15.2). The returnable glass container must be used at least twice for an energy saving to be realized. Actually, because added energy is expended to collect, transport, sort, and clean the reusable container, it takes about 4 recycles of each glass container to gain an advantage over disposable containers.

Like milk containers, returnable glass beverage bottles require more energy for production than do nonreturnable bottles (Table 15.2). A 16-ounce returnable soft-drink bottle requires about 2450 kcal for production, compared to about 1470 kcal for the same size nonreturnable bottle. Although 2 uses of the returnable bottle would more than offset the production energy input, when the energy costs of collecting, transporting, and cleaning the returnable bottles are factored in, about 4 recycles are necessary to gain an energy advantage. Of course, other considerations, such as the costs and the environmental pollution caused by nonreturnable containers, must be weighed along with energy expenditure before community policies can be decided upon.

Cooking and Preparing Foods

Foods for human consumption are often cooked or reheated in the home, requiring an expenditure of energy. In the United States, an estimated 9000 kcal of fossil energy are used per person per day for home refrigeration, heating of food, dishwashing, and so forth. This averages out to an estimated 4700 kcal/kg of food prepared.

Depending on the food, the fuel used, the material of the cooking containers, the method of preparation, and the stove used, the energy input varies considerably. There appears to be little difference between the total energy expended for baking, boiling, or broiling a similar product, assuming that the exposure of the food to heat is optimal and that the cooking utensils allow for efficient heat transfer to the food itself. In addition to the shape and construction material of the cooking utensils, color also affects the transfer of heat and, therefore, overall cooking efficiency. A shiny aluminum pan reflects much heat and therefore is less efficient than one with a dark, dull surface or one made from glass. Furthermore, the nature of the food itself—fluid, viscous, or dense—will either slow or speed heat transfer and alter the amount of energy used in a particular process. These variables make it difficult to calculate the precise energy expenditure.

When the efficiency of the entire cycle of energy transfer is compared, a gas stove is more efficient than an electric stove. Gas and electricity from coal are used as fuel in residential stoves. Gas is mined, and about 10 percent of its energy potential is lost in production and transport. In transferring its heat energy to a product, it is 37 percent efficient, making overall efficiency of cooking with gas about 33 percent ($100 \times 0.9 \times 0.37$).

The process for electricity is more complicated than for gas. First, mining and transport reduce the energy potential of coal by 8 percent; 92 percent of the initial energy potential of the coal is available at the power plant for generation of electricity. Coal-heat conversion into electricity results in a recovery of 33 percent of the energy potential. The transmission electricity over power lines is 92 percent efficient, and transmission of electric heat to the product is 75 percent efficient. Thus, the overall efficiency of heat to the product is about 21 percent ($100 \times 0.92 \times 0.33 \times 0.92 \times 0.75$).

Less efficient than either electricity or gas is cooking with charcoal or wood over an open hearth, as is often done in developing countries. An open fire is 8 to 10 percent efficient in transmitting heat to the food (Stanford, 1977). However, if the wood fire is carefully tended under the pot, the transfer of energy can be nearly 20 percent, which is nearly as efficient as using a small wood stove, which is from 20 to 25 percent efficient.

The following examples demonstrate the general inefficiency of cooking food over an open wood fire. It takes 600 kcal of heat energy to cook 1 kg of food, so a wood fire, at an efficiency rate of 10 percent for cooking, must produce 6000 kcal of energy. The food itself, if a grain like rice, would contain 3500 kcal of food energy. Hence, nearly twice as much energy would be used to cook the food than the food contains.

In developing nations, cooking uses nearly two-thirds of the total energy expended in the food system, production the remaining one-third (Table 15.3). Almost all of the energy used for cooking in developing countries comes from renewable sources, primarily biomass (wood, crop residues, and dung).

Table 15.3   Model of annual per capita use of energy in the food system of rural populations in developing countries

	Fossil energy (kcal)	Renewable energy (kcal)	Total (kcal)
Production	130,000	490,000	620,000
Processing	15,000	20,000	35,000
Storage	5,000	20,000	25,000
Transport	30,000	20,000	50,000
Preparation	20,000	1,250,000	1,270,000
TOTAL	200,000	1,800,000	2,000,000

Sources: Pimentel, 1974, 1976; Pimentel and Beyer, 1976; RSAS, 1975; Revelle, 1976; and Ernst, 1978.

A significant percentage of wood is converted into charcoal for a cooking fuel. Like wood fires, open charcoal fires are about 10 percent efficient in the transfer of heat energy to food. However, charcoal production is extremely energy-intensive. Although charcoal apparently has a high energy content (7100 kcal/kg), 28,400 kcal of hardwood must be processed to obtain the 7100 kcal of charcoal, a conversion efficency of only 25 percent. Therefore, charcoal heating has an overall energy transfer efficiency of only 2.5 percent (25 percent × 10 percent). Not only is cooking with charcoal an extremely inefficient and costly way to transfer energy, the use of charcoal for fuel depletes forest and firewood supplies (Eckholm, 1976).

16
TRANSPORT OF AGRICULTURAL SUPPLIES AND FOODS

David Pimentel and Marcia Pimentel

Transport is an essential component of all food systems, especially those in industrialized nations such as the United States, which have highly developed industrial complexes and intensive agricultural systems. They grow food crops in specialized regions most conducive to agricultural production (e.g., the corn belt of the United States). Industrial production sites are generally located near population centers and available power sources. Thus, harvested crops have to be transported to the cities and towns where industry is located, and machinery, fertilizers, pesticides, fuel, and other goods used in agricultural production have to be transported from urban areas to farms.

Transportation in the food system is vastly more complex than just shipping food directly from the farm to homes. After being harvested, most food crops have to be processed and packaged, then transported to large wholesale distribution centers. From there, the packaged foods are shipped to retail stores located near population centers, where individuals purchase them and transports them home.

To account for the energy expended in this vast network, the energy inputs in transporting goods to the farm, raw agricultural products to the processors, produce to wholesale–retail markets, and food from the grocery to the home will be analyzed.

Transport of Agricultural Supplies and Goods to the Farm

An estimated 160 million ha of cropland are cultivated annually in the United States (USDA, 1991b). About 50 billion kg of goods and supplies are transported to farms for use in agricultural production each year (USDA, 1991b). On average, then, about 300 kg of goods and supplies must be transported to farms for each ha cultivated.

The energy needed to move goods by truck is estimated at 1.2 kcal/kg/km (Table 16.1). This estimate is based on the fact that trucks require about 0.143 liters of diesel fuel to transport 1 ton 1 km (Thor and Kirkendall, 1982). Moving goods by rail requires an estimated 0.32 kcal/kg/km (Table 16.1), about one-fourth of the energy expended in truck transport (Table 16.1). The energy cost to transport goods by barge is only 0.10 kcal/kg/km, or one-third that of rail transport. As expected, air transport has the highest energy cost, 6.36 kcal/kg/km (Table 16.1), more than 60 times costlier than barge transport.

Table 16.1   Energy needed to transport 1 kg 1 km

Transport system	kcal/kg/km
Barge	0.10[a]
Rail	0.32[a]
Truck	1.20[a]
Air	6.36[b]

Notes: [a]Thor and Kirkendall, 1982.
[b]USBC, 1976.

As noted, 300 kg of goods and supplies are transported to each farm hectare. Available data indicate that 60 percent of the goods are transported by rail, 40 percent by truck, and that the average distance these goods are transported is 1500 km (Smith, 1991). The energy input for the 60 percent of the goods transported by rail is about 86,400 kcal/ha, and the 40 percent transported by truck use 216,000 kcal/ha. Thus, transportation of farm machinery requires a total energy input of 302,400 kcal per hectare cultivated, and 1008 kcal of energy is expended per kilogram of other supplies needed on the farm. Annually, then, an estimated 50×10^{12} kcal is expended annually to transport the 50 million tons of goods and supplies needed on U.S. farms. This energy expenditure is equivalent to 40 million barrels of petroleum each year.

Transport of Food and Fiber Products from the Farm

About 160 million ha of cropland are harvested annually, at an average of 3400 kg/ha. Thus, an estimated 544 million tons of food and fiber products are transported from the farm to various locations for eventual consumption (USDA, 1991b).

About 41 percent of agricultural goods are transported by truck, 40 percent by rail, and 19 percent by barge (Thor and Kirkendall, 1982). The products are transported an average distance of 1000 km (Thor and Kirkendall, 1982). Based on this information, the transport of goods from the farm to cities and towns requires 348×10^{12} kcal of energy per year, or 640 kcal/kg.

Based on experience, families usually shop about 3 times per week. With each person on average consuming 711 kg of food per year, and with 3 people in the average family (Putman and Allhouse, 1991), 13.7 kg of food are transported from the grocery store on each trip. The average round trip to the grocery is estimated to be 7.8 km, or nearly 5 miles. The average automobile today gets about 8.4 km/liter (19.9 miles/gal) (USBC, 1991). Based on these data, it takes about 684 kcal to transport 1 kg of food home from the grocery store. This is slightly more than the amount of energy invested to transport 1 kg of food from the farm to city or town.

17

SOLAR ENERGY PRODUCTION SYSTEMS

D. Pimentel, G. Rodrigues, T. Wang, R. Abrams,
K. Goldberg, H. Staecker, E. Ma, L. Brueckner, L. Trovato,
C. Chow, U. Govindarajulu, and S. Boerke

The United States faces serious energy shortages in the near future. High energy consumption and the ever-increasing U.S. population will force Americans to confront the critical problem of dwindling fossil energy supplies. With only 4.7 percent of the world's population, the United States consumes about 25 percent of the fossil fuel used each year throughout the world. It imports 54 percent of its oil at an annual cost of about $65 billion. American dependence on foreign oil and the high economic cost of current policies (Gibbons and Blair, 1991) have negative effects on national security and the economy.

Fossil fuel reserves are rapidly shrinking. Within a decade or two the United States will be forced to turn to renewable energy to meet some of its energy needs, because proven U.S. oil reserves are projected to be depleted in 10 to 20 years (Hubbert, 1972; Matare, 1989; Flavin and Lenssen, 1990; DOE, 1991a; Gever et al., 1991; Davis, 1991; BP, 1991; van Harmelen and Bakena, 1991; Worldwatch Institute, 1992a; Pimentel et al., 1994a).

Natural gas reserves are expected to last 10 to 20 years, and coal reserves are projected to last about 100 years, based on current use rates and available extraction processes. The rapid depletion of U.S. oil and gas reserves likely will necessitate increased use of coal (Gever et al., 1991). By the year 2020, coal may supply as much as 40 percent of the nation's energy (DOE, 1991a). Based on the projections of increased use and concurrent population growth, the U.S. coal supply could be used up in much less than the projected 100 years (Matare, 1989; DOE, 1991a). Undoubtedly, new mining technologies will make it possible to extract more oil and coal. However, these processes will have ever-greater energy and economic costs. When the energy input needed to power these methods approaches the amount of energy mined, extraction will no longer be energy cost-effective (Hall et al., 1986).

Combustion of fossil fuels, especially coal, significantly increases carbon dioxide concentration in the atmosphere, thereby contributing to global warming. This is considered one of the most serious environmental threats throughout the world because of its potential impact on food production and other aspects of the environment (DOE, 1989; Abrahamson, 1989; Rosen and Glasser, 1992). Concerns about carbon dioxide emissions may discourage widespread dependence on coal use (Schneider, 1989; Rosen and Glasser, 1992) and encourage the development and use of renewable energy technologies.

Even if the rate of increase of per capita fossil energy consumption slows, rapid population growth is expected to speed fossil energy depletion and intensify global warming. In view of this fact, the projected availability of all fossil energy reserves probably has been overestimated. Substantially reducing U.S. fossil fuel consumption through the efficient use of energy and the adoption of solar energy technologies will extend the life of fossil fuel resources, giving researchers more time to develop and improve renewable energy technologies.

Another basic parameter controlling renewable energy supplies is the availability of land. At present more than 99 percent of the world's food supply comes from the land (FAO, 1991b). The domestic harvest of forest resources cannot meet U.S. needs, and the country now imports some of its forest products (USBC, 1992a). With about 75 percent of the total U.S. land area exploited for agriculture and forestry, relatively little land is available for other uses. Population growth will exacerbate the demand for land. Solar energy technologies will compete for land with food and forest production, and conflicts over land use will intensify.

Coal, oil, gas, nuclear, and other mined fuels currently fulfill most of the United States's energy needs, and renewable energy technologies provide only 8 percent (Table 17.1). The use of solar energy, however, is expected to grow. Renewable energy technologies that have the potential to meet future energy supplies include biomass systems; hydroelectric systems; hydrogen fuel; wind power; photovoltaics; solar thermal systems; and passive and active heating and cooling systems.

Table 17.1   Current annual fossil (including nuclear) and solar energy use in the U.S. and world

	U.S.[a]		Percent World[bcd]	
	Quads	Percent	Quads	Percent
Total energy	85.1	100	391.9	100
Fossil energy	78.5	92.3	319.2	81.4
Solar energy	6.6	7.7	72.7	18.6
Hydropower	3.0	3.5	21.2	5.5
Biomass	3.6	4.2	51.5	13.1

Notes: [a]DOE, 1991a.
[b]DOE, 1991b.
[c]UNEP, 1985.
[d]Hall et al., 1993.

Biomass Energy

At present forest biomass energy provides an estimated 4.2 percent, or 3.6 quads, (1 quad = 10^{15} BTU or 1054×10^{15} Joules) of the U.S. energy supply (IEA, 1991) (Table 17.1). Worldwide, and especially in developing countries, biomass energy is more widely used than in the U.S. (Table 17.2). Only forest biomass will be included in this U.S. assessment because it is the most abundant and most concentrated biomass resource (ERAB, 1981; Pimentel et al., 1988).

Table 17.2   Solar energy use by the U.S., world, and developing nations

	U.S.		World		Developing	
	Quads	Percent	Quads	Percent	Quads	Percent
Biomass	3.6	55	51.5	71	45.7	88.2
Fuelwood	3.53	25.8	22.8			
Crop residues	0.07	17.3	15.1			
Dung	0	8.4	7.8			
Hydropower	3.0	45	21.2	29	6.1	11.8
TOTAL	6.6	100	72.7	100	51.8	100

Sources: UNEP, 1985; IEA, 1991; and Hall et al., 1993.

Although in the future most biomass probably will be used for space and water heating, to clarify the comparison with other renewable technologies its conversion into electricity is analyzed here. An average of about 3 tons/ha (dry) of woody biomass can sustainably be harvested per year with small amounts of nutrient fertilizer inputs (Pimentel and Krummel, 1987; Birdsey, 1992). This amount of woody biomass has a gross energy yield of 13.5 million kcal (thermal). The net yield is, however, considerably lower, because about 33 liters/ha of diesel fuel oil is expended for cutting and collecting (Pimentel and Krummel, 1987) and for transportation, assuming an 80 km round trip from processing plant to forest and back (Carl, 1981; Thor and Kirkendall, 1982). The economic benefits of biomass are maximized when the fuel is used close to where it is harvested.

Based on 1 billion kWh (860 kcal = 1 kWh) per year of electrical demand for a city of 100,000 people and using the biomass from a sustainable forest (3 tons/ha) for fuel, about 220,000 ha of forest are required to supply the electricity needs (Table 17.3). Nearly 70 percent of the heat energy produced from burning biomass is lost in the conversion to electricity, similar to losses experienced in coal-fired plants. The area needed by 100,000 people for food production, housing, industry, and roadways is about 211,000 ha of land (USDA, 1991b).

The energy input/output ratio of this system is calculated to be about 1:3 (Table 17.3); that is, about 3 kcal of thermal energy is required to produce 1 kcal of electricity. The cost of producing a kWh of electricity from woody biomass ranges from $0.07 to $0.10 (Table 17.3), which is competitive for electricity production, the cost of which ranges from $0.03 to $0.14 (USBC, 1992a) (Table 17.3). Woody biomass could supply the nation with 5 quads of energy by the year 2050 with the use of at least 75 million ha of land (Table 17.4).

Several factors limit reliance on woody biomass. Wood is a slow-growing resource, even if fast-growing trees are cultivated in a plantation system on prime land (Pimentel and Krummel, 1987), but prime land is essential for food production, making this scenario unrealistic. Furthermore, such intensely managed systems require high fossil fuel inputs for heavy machinery, fertilizers, and pesticides, thereby diminishing the net energy gain.

When natural forests are managed for maximum biomass energy production, loss of vital biodiversity can be expected (DOE, 1979; OECD, 1988; Pimentel et al., 1992a). The conversion of natural forests into plantations leads to soil erosion and water runoff (Cook et al., 1991; Pimentel et al., 1992a); degradation would ultimately reduce the overall productivity of the land (Lal and Stewart, 1990). Despite serious limitations of plantations, biomass production could be increased to some extent using agroforestry technologies designed

Table 17.3 Land resource requirements and structural material and energy inputs for construction of solar and other energy facilities that produce 1 billion kWh/yr of electricity (averaged over 30-year life of unit)

Electrical energy technology[s]	Structural Materials (10³ tons)				Energy inputs (kWh × 10⁶)	Total energy input (kWh ×10⁹)	Energy input/output ratio	Cost per kWh ($)
	Land (ha)	Steel	Concrete	Other Materials				
Hydroelectric	75,000[a]	14.4[b]	155[b]	0.72[b]	0.004[e]	0.021[c]	1:48	.02[d]
Biomass	220,000	0.3[e]	0.2[e]	–	6.7[f]	0.3	1:3	.07–.10[d]
Central receivers	1,100[g]	0.34[g]	11.5[g]	4.2[g]	102.2[g]	0.19	1:10	.10[q]
Solar ponds	5,200[h]	0.3[e]	0.2[e]	Salt+	198[i]	0.248	1:4	.14
Wind power	11,666[p]	18.1[p]	13.0[p]	–	205	0.205	1:5	.06
Photovoltaics	2,700[n]	3[k]	15[k]	1.73[l]	108[m]	0.108	1:9	.30
Passive	>0	–	–	–	–	–	–	.03[r]
Coal	363[o]	0.5[b]	2.0[b]	0.01		0.12	1:8	.03
Nuclear	48[o]	0.3[b]	0.45[b]	0.01		0.20	1:5	.05

Notes: [a]Based on a random sample of 50 U.S. hydropower reservoirs ranging in area from 482 ha to 763,000 ha (FERC, 1984; ICLD, 1988).
[b]Rose and Miller, 1983.
[c]Steel = 21 kWh/kg; concrete = 0.6 kWh/kg; other materials = 21 kWh/kg.
[d]Based on personal communication (10–8–92) with John Irving, Station Superindendent, City of Burlington Electric Light Department (Vermont).
[e]Based on the inputs for a coal-fired plant; for energy inputs, see note c.
[f]Input for harvesting and transport of the biomass to the power plant was calculated to be 27 liters of diesel/ha.
[g]For three 100-MW plants (Vant-Hull, 1992).
[h]Based on 4,000-ha solar pond, plus an additional 1,200 ha for evaporation ponds.
[i]Steel, concrete, salt, plastic, and water = 248 million kWh.
[j]Flavin and Lenssen, 1991.
[k]Voigt, 1984.
[l]Glass (Voigt, 1984) × 21 kWh.
[m]Total energy inputs for steel, concrete, and glass.
[n]Calculated from Hesperia operational statistics in 1989 (EPRI, 1991).
[o]Smil, 1984.
[p]AWEA, 1991.
[q]Gervais, 1986; Williams et al., 1990; Vant-Hull, 1992.
[r]See text.
[s]Ethanol and methanol were not included because of their negative energy balances.

Table 17.4 Current and projected gross annual energy supply from various solar energy technologies based on thermal equivalents

	Current (1992)		Projected (2050)	
	Quads	Million ha	Quads	Million ha
Biomass	3.6	100[c] (50[e])	5	163[c] (75[e])
Hydroelectric	2.9[a]	63[d]	4	87
Solar thermal	>0	>0	6	5
Photovoltaics	>0	>0	8	6
Wind power	0.01[f]	0.5	8[g]	9[h]
Passive solar	0.3[b]	0	6	1
TOTAL	7	164 (114[e])	37	271 (173[e])

Notes:
[a] USBC, 1992.
[b] Flavin, 1985.
[c] This is the equivalent land area required to produce 3.5 tons/ha plus the energy required for harvesting and transport. However, we estimate that 60% of this biomass is coming from forest wastes and residues. Thus, only about 40% of the total land is assumed to be managed for forest biomass energy.
[d] Total area based on an average of 75,000 ha per reservoir area per 1 billion kWh/yr produced (Table 17.3).
[e] See footnote c.
[f] AWEA, 1992.
[g] Ranges from a projected 3–4 quads (DOE, 1992) to 11 quads (DOE, 1990b).
[h] If the potential dual use of the land for agricultural purposes is considered, then it might be possible to reduce the land area by about 95%.

to protect soil quality and to conserve biodiversity. However, the energy and economic costs of this strategy might limit its use (Kidd and Pimentel, 1992).

Although burning biomass produces less pollution (in particular, fewer sulfur dioxide emissions) than the burning of coal, its combustion still releases more than 100 different chemical pollutants into the atmosphere (Alfheim and Ramdahl, 1986; Wright, 1990; Dignon et al., 1991). Wood smoke reportedly contains up to 14 carcinogens, 4 co-carcinogens, 6 toxins that damage cilia, and a number of mucus-coagulating agents (DOE, 1980; Alfheim and Ramdahl, 1986). The pollutants are known to cause bronchitis (Dhar and Pathania, 1991), emphysema, and other illnesses. Of special concern are the relatively high concentrations of potentially carcinogenic polycyclic organic compounds (PAHs—e.g., benzo[a]pyrene) and particulates found in biomass smoke (DOE, 1980, 1981). When biomass is burned continuously in the home for heating, these pollutants can be a threat to human health (DOE, 1981; Lipfert et al., 1988; Dhar and Pathania, 1991). Sulfur and nitrogen oxides (SO_x and NO_x), carbon monoxide (CO), and aldehydes also are released in small but significant quantities and reduce air quality (DOE, 1980, 1981; ERAB, 1981). Because of these pollutants many communities have banned the burning of wood for heating homes (Weston, 1987). In electric generating plants, however, up to 70 percent of these air pollutants can be removed by installing the appropriate air pollution control devices in the combustion system (Clark and Kwasnik, 1986).

Biomass will continue to be a valuable renewable energy resource in the future, but its expansion will be greatly limited because its use causes major environmental problems and conflicts with the needs of sustainable agricultural and forestry production.

Liquid Fuels

Liquid fuels are indispensable to the U.S. economy (DOE, 1991a). Petroleum, which is essential for the transportation sector (Table 17.5) and the chemical industry, supplies about 42 percent of total U.S. energy (DOE, 1990a). Today the United States imports about 54 percent of its petroleum and is projected to import nearly 100 percent within 10 to 20 years (DOE, 1991a). Barring radically improved electric battery technologies, a shift to alternative liquid and gaseous fuels will have to be made.

Table 17.5   Estimated percentages of total annual fossil energy use by sectors in the U.S. and world

Sectors	USA[a]	World[b]
Transportation	26	33
Industry	25	25
Residential	20	15
Food systems	17	15
Commercial	10	10
Military	2	2
TOTAL	100[c]	100

Notes: [a]Total U.S. fossil energy use = 78.5 quads (DOE, 1991a).
[b]Total world fossil energy use = 319.2 quads (UNEP, 1985).
[c]Of total, 34% is used for electricity.

Ethanol

A wide variety of starch and sugar crops (Dobbs et al., 1984), food-processing wastes (Badger and Broder, 1989), and woody materials (Wyman and Hinman, 1990; Lynd, 1990; Lynd et al., 1991) can be used as raw materials for ethanol production. In the United States, corn appears to be the most feasible biomass feedstock in terms of availability and technology (Pimentel, 1991b) (Table 17.6). However, the total fossil energy expended to produce 1 liter of ethanol from corn is 10,200 kcal (Table 17.6), whereas 1 liter of ethanol has an energy value of only 5130 kcal. Thus, using current technologies ethanol production from corn results in a net energy *loss.*

Table 17.6   Inputs per 1,000 liters of ethanol produced from corn.

Inputs	kg	10³ kcal	Dollars
Corn	2,700	3,758[a]	$265[f]
Transport	2,700	325[b]	32
Stain, steel	6[c]	90[c]	20
Steel	12[c]	139[c]	30
Cement	32[c]	60[c]	20
Plant, other	—	186[d]	74[g]
Water	160,000[c]	1,364[c]	25
Electricity	133 kWh[c]	343	13[h]
Fuel	—	3,975[e]	40[i]
Operating, other	—	—	32[j]
TOTAL		10,240	$551

Notes: [a]Pimentel (1991b).
[b]Estimated transport.
[c]Slesser and Lewis (1979).
[d]Doering (1980).
[e]ERAB (1980); NAP (1987).
[f]Bushel of corn = $2.55 (USDA, 1991b).
[g]Portion of capital costs based on $0.40/l (Walls et al., 1989).
[h]NAP (1987).
[i]Using natural gas or fuel oil would raise this price to $0.35/l (NAP, 1987).
[j]Portion of operating costs based on $0.40/l (Walls et al., 1989).
[k]Output: 1,00 liters of ethanol = 5,130,000 kcal.

Almost 40 percent of the fuel is needed to run the distillation process (Table 17.6). This fossil energy input contributes to a negative energy balance and adds to atmospheric pollution. In the production process, special membranes can separate the ethanol from the "beer" produced by fermentation. The most efficient systems rely on distillation to bring the ethanol concentration up to 90 percent, and selective membrane processes can further raise the ethanol concentration to 99.5 percent (Maeda and Kai, 1991). The energy input for this upgrading is about 1280 kcal/liter. Laboratory tests have reduced the total input for producing a liter of ethanol from 10,200 to 6200 kcal, but even then the energy balance remains negative.

About 53 percent of the total cost ($0.55 per liter) of producing ethanol in a large, modern plant is for the corn (Table 17.6). Although the total energy inputs for producing ethanol using corn can be partially offset when dried distiller's grain produced is fed to livestock, the energy budget remains negative.

Any benefits from ethanol production, including the corn by-products, are negated by the environmental pollution caused by ethanol production (Pimentel, 1991b). Intensive corn production in the U.S. causes serious soil erosion and requires the mining of groundwater resources. Another environmental problem occurs during the fermentation process when about 13 liters of sewage effluent is produced for each liter of ethanol produced (Buchler, 1989). Although this pollutant residue can be used for the production of methane in biodigesters (Laluce, 1991; de Bazua et al., 1991), its sheer volume and distribution create major problems.

Although ethanol has been advertised as reducing air pollution when mixed with gasoline or burned alone, this is not the case when the entire production system is considered. Ethanol does release less CO and SO_x than gasoline and diesel fuels. However, NO_x, formaldehydes, other aldehydes, and alcohol, all serious air pollutants, are associated with the burning of ethanol as fuel (Sillman and Samson, 1990). Also, the production and use of ethanol fuel contribute to the increase in atmospheric carbon dioxide because twice as much fossil energy is burned in the production process as is produced as ethanol.

When we factor in the environmental damage caused by corn grown just for ethanol production and the ethics of future food security, the disadvantages of ethanol outweigh the advantages.

Methanol

Methanol, another potential fuel for internal combustion engines (Dovring, 1988; Kohl, 1990), uses various raw materials for production, including natural gas, coal, wood, and municipal solid wastes (Sweeney, 1990). At present the primary source of methanol is natural gas. The major limitation in using any biomass source is the difficulty in amassing the enormous quantities needed by a plant with suitable economies of scale. An efficient methanol plant requires at least 1250 tons of dry biomass per day for processing (ACTI,

1983). Biomass generally is not available in such enormous quantities at acceptable prices (ACTI, 1983).

If methanol from biomass were used to supply the 33 quads of energy now supplied by oil in the United States, between 250 and 430 million ha of land would be needed to supply the raw material. This land area is greater than the area of U.S. cropland now in production, 162 million ha (USDA, 1991b). Furthermore, methanol per unit volume has only half the energy content of gasoline. Although methanol production may be impractical because of the enormous size of the conversion plants (Lawrence, 1990), it is significantly more efficient than ethanol production system based on both energy output and economics (Lawrence, 1990; Sweeney, 1990).

Compared to gasoline and diesel fuel, both methanol and ethanol reduce the amount of carbon monoxide and SO_x pollutants produced. However both contribute other major air pollutants. Air pollutants from these fuels worsen the ozone layer problem because the richer mixtures used in combustion engines increase the emissions of No_x (Sillman and Samson, 1990).

Hydrogen

Gaseous hydrogen, produced by the electrolysis of water, is another alternative to petroleum fuels. Using solar electric technologies for its production, hydrogen has the potential to serve as a renewable gaseous and liquid fuel for transportation vehicles. In addition, it can be used in energy storage and transport systems for electrical solar energy technologies, such as photovoltaics (Winter and Nitsch, 1988; Ogden and Williams, 1989).

The material inputs for hydrogen production are primarily those needed to build a solar electric production facility. Production of 1 billion kWh/yr equivalent of hydrogen a year requires about 337 million liters/yr of water, or about 3370 liters of water per capita, assuming 76 percent electrolysis efficiency (Voigt, 1984). The energy required to produce 1 billion kWh of hydrogen is 1.3 billion kWh of electricity (Voigt, 1984). If photovoltaics (Table 17.3) were used to produce the hydrogen needed, then a total area of 3640 ha would be needed to supply the equivalent of 1 billion kWh/yr of hydrogen fuel. Based on U.S. per capita liquid fuel needs, about 0.15 ha per person (16,300 ft^2) would be needed to produce sufficient liquid hydrogen.

In terms of energy contained, 9.5 kg of hydrogen is equivalent to 25 kg of gasoline (Peschka, 1987). Storing 25 kg of gasoline requires a tank with a mass of 17 kg, whereas the storage of 9.5 kg of hydrogen requires 55 kg

(Peschka, 1987). Part of the reason for this difference is that the volume of hydrogen fuel is about 4 times greater for the same energy content of gasoline (8000 kcal/liter versus 2030 kcal/liter). Although the hydrogen storage vessel is large, hydrogen burns 1.33 times more efficiently than gasoline in automobiles (Bockris and Wass, 1988). In tests, a BMW 745i liquid-hydrogen test vehicle with a 75 kg tank and the energy equivalent of 40 liters (320,000 kcal) of gasoline had a cruising range in traffic of 400 km, or a fuel efficiency of 10 km per liter (Winter, 1986).

At present, commercial hydrogen is more expensive than gasoline. Assuming $0.05 per kWh of electricity from a nuclear power plant during low demand, hydrogen would cost $0.09 per kWh (Bockris and Wass, 1988). This is the equivalent of $0.67 per liter of gasoline. Gasoline sells at the pump in the United States for about $0.30 per liter. However, estimates are that the real cost of burning a liter of gasoline ranges from $1.06 to $1.32 when production, pollution, and other external costs are included (Worldwatch Institute, 1989). Therefore, based on these calculations hydrogen fuel may eventually become competitive.

Some of the oxygen gas produced during the electrolysis of water can be used to offset the cost of hydrogen. Also, the oxygen can be combined with hydrogen in a fuel cell like those used in manned space flights. Present electric-power-generation efficiency averages 33 percent (Rosen and Scott, 1988). Hydrogen fuel cells used in rural and suburban areas as electricity sources could help decentralize the power grid, allowing central power facilities to decrease output, save transmission costs, and make mass-produced, economical energy available to industry.

Gaseous hydrogen can be stored in powdered metal-hydride form that contains 1.9 percent hydrogen (Billings, 1991). The stored hydrogen can power either an internal combustion engine or a fuel cell in a state-of-the-art electric vehicle. Storage of hydrogen in hydride form increases the energy costs but makes its storage safer for vehicle use (Billings, 1991).

Compared with ethanol and methanol, hydrogen requires less land for production using photovoltaics. The environmental impacts of hydrogen are minimal. The minimal negative impacts are all associated with the solar electric technology used in production. Finding enough water for the production of hydrogen may be a problem in the arid regions of the United States, but the amount required is relatively small compared with the demand for irrigation water in agriculture (Pimentel et al., 1994b). Although hydrogen fuel produces emissions of NO_x and hydrogen peroxide pollutants, the amounts are about one-third lower than those produced from gasoline engines (Veziroglu and Barbir, 1992). Based on this comparative analysis, hydrogen fuel has the potential to be a cost-effective alternative to gasoline if the environmental and subsidy costs of gasoline are taken into account.

Hydroelectric Systems

For centuries water has been used to provide power for various systems. In 1988 about 870 billion kWh (3 quads), or 9.5 percent, of the United States's electrical energy was produced by hydroelectric plants (FERC, 1988; USBC, 1992a). Walsh (1983) reported that further development and/or rehabilitation of existing dams could produce an additional 48 billion kWh per year. However, most of the "best candidate" sites already have been fully developed, although some specialists project that U.S. hydropower can be increased by as much as 100 billion kWh if additional sites are found (USBC, 1992a).

Hydroelectric plants require considerable land for their water-storage reservoirs. An analysis of 50 hydroelectric sites in the United States indicated that an average of 75,000 ha of reservoir area are required per 1 billion kWh/yr produced (Table 17.3). However, the ratio of reservoir size to electricity produced varies widely, ranging from 482 ha to 763,000 ha per 1 billion kWh/yr depending upon the hydro head, terrain, and additional uses of the reservoir. The latter include flood control, storage of water for public and irrigation supplies, and/or recreation (Ebel, 1979; FERC, 1984). In the United States the energy input/output ratio of hydroelectricity is calculated to be 1:48 (Table 17.3), for Europe an estimated 1:15 (Winter et al., 1991).

Based on regional estimates of land use and average annual energy generation, about 63 million ha of the 917 million ha of land in the entire United States are covered with reservoirs. To develop the remaining "best candidate" sites and assuming land requirements similar to those of existing dams, an additional 24 million ha of land would be needed for water storage (Table 17.4).

Reservoirs constructed for hydroelectric plants frequently cause major environmental problems. First, the impounded water frequently covers agriculturally productive alluvial bottomland (Mierzwa and Hiemstra, 1981). Reservoirs also accumulate sediments eroded from agricultural lands, thereby reducing the effectiveness of the dam for hydropower and lessening the storage area of the reservoir. Further, dams alter the existing ecosystem, affecting all plant and animal species (Hildebrand, 1979; Szekely, 1982; Flavin, 1985). For example, cold-water fish may be replaced by warm-water species (Ebel, 1979), and fish migration may be (and frequently is) blocked (Hall et al., 1986). However, flow schedules can be altered to ameliorate many of these impacts (Hildebrand, 1979; Szekely, 1982). Within the reservoirs, fluctuating water levels alter shorelines and cause downstream erosion, and physiochemical changes upset aquatic communities (Szluha et al., 1979). Beyond the reservoirs, discharge patterns may adversely reduce downstream water quality and biota, displace people, and increase water evaporation losses (Hildebrand, 1979; Szekely, 1982; Barber, 1993). Because of these diverse problems, there appears to be little potential for greatly expanding hydroelectric power in the future.

Wind Power

For many centuries, wind power, like water power, has provided energy to pump water and run mills and other machines. Since the early 1900s, windmills have been used in the rural United States to generate electricity, a practice that continues today.

Wind turbine technology has made significant advances over the last 10 years. Today, small wind machines with 5 to 40 kW capacity can supply the normal electrical needs of homes and small industries (Twidell, 1987). Medium-size turbines rated 100 kW to 500 kW produce most of the commercially generated wind power in the United States. Large turbines require larger, heavier blades than the medium turbines, and this upsets the ratio between size and weight and lowers efficiency. However, the effectiveness and efficiency of the large wind machines are expected to be improved with the development of lighter but stronger components (Clarke, 1991). Assuming a 35 percent production factor for the turbine, the energy input/output ratio of the system is 1:5 for the material used in the construction of wind machines (Table 17.3).

The availability of sites with sufficient wind (at least 20 km/h) limits the widespread development of "wind farms." Currently, 70 percent of the total wind energy (0.01 quad) produced in the United States is generated in California (AWEA, 1992). However, an estimated 13 percent of the land in the contiguous United States has wind speeds of 22 km/h or higher, which is sufficient to generate about 20 percent of U.S. electricity using current technology

(DOE, 1992). Promising areas for wind development include the Great Plains and coastal regions (Frederick, 1993; Lamarre, 1992; UWIG, 1992).

A serious limitation of this energy resource is the number of wind machines a site can accommodate. For example, Altamont Pass, California, has an average of just 1 turbine per 1.8 ha to allow sufficient spacing to produce maximum power (Smith and Ilyin, 1991). Based on this figure approximately 11,700 ha of land are needed to supply 1 billion kWh/yr (Table 17.3). However, because the turbines themselves only occupy about 2 percent of the area, or about 230 ha, dual land use is possible. For example, current agricultural land has been developed for wind power while the production of cattle, vegetables, and nursery stock continues on the same land (Bodansky, 1993).

Wind energy production does present a few environmental hazards. For example, if the wind turbines stand in or near migratory flyways, birds may fly into the supporting structures and rotating blades (DOE, 1977; Lawrence, 1979; Medsker, 1982; Kaupang, 1983; Estep, 1989; Kellett, 1990; Clarke, 1991). Clarke (1991) suggests that wind farms be located at least 300 m from nature preserves to reduce the risk to birds.

Turbine blades also kill insects but probably have only a minor impact on insect populations, except for some endangered species. However, significant insect accumulation on the blades may reduce turbine efficiency (Smith, 1987; Mukanski and Strauss, 1992).

Wind turbines also create interference with electromagnetic transmission (Hansen, 1980; Stoddard, 1991), and blade noise may be heard up to 1 km away (Kellet, 1990). Fortunately, noise and interference with radio/TV signals can be eliminated by the choice of blade materials and by careful placement of turbines (Kaupang, 1983). In addition, blade noise can be offset by locating a buffer zone between the turbines and human settlements (Rand and Clarke, 1990). New technologies and designs may minimize turbine generator noise.

Under certain circumstances shadow flicker has caused irritation, disorientation, and seizures in humans (Steele, 1991). However, like other environmental impacts, this one can be mitigated through careful site selection away from homes and offices.

Although only a few wind farms supply power to utilities in the United States, widespread expansion may be constrained because local residents feel that wind farms diminish the aesthetics of the area (Smith, 1987; Smith and Ilyin, 1991). Some communities have even passed legislation to prevent wind turbines from being installed in residential areas (Village of Cayuga Heights Ordinance, 1989). Likewise, designation of areas for recreational purposes limits the land available for wind power development.

Photovoltaics

Photovoltaic (PV) cells are expected to provide the nation with a significant portion of its future electrical energy. PV units produce electricity when sunlight excites electrons in the cells. Because the size of the units is flexible and adaptable, PV cells are ideal for use in homes, industries, and utilities.

Before they can be used widely, however, improvements are needed to make PV cells economically competitive. Commercial photovoltaic units that consist of silicon solar cells are about 21 percent efficient in converting sunlight into electricity (Moore, 1992). In order for utility-grid penetration, photovoltaic costs will have to decline to about half the present level of $4.50/wp (peak watt). In addition, their durability, which is now about 20 years, needs to be lengthened and current production costs reduced about fivefold to make them economically feasible. With a major research investment, all of these goals are possible to achieve (DeMeo et al., 1991; Zweibel, 1993).

Currently, production of electricity from PV cells costs about $0.30/kWh, but the price is projected to fall to about $0.10/kWh by the end of the decade and perhaps reach as low as $0.04 by the year 2030, provided the needed improvements are made (Flavin and Lenssen, 1991). In order for PV cells to be truly competitive, the target cost for flat plate concentrator modules would have to be about $0.08/kWh (DeMeo et al., 1991).

Using PV modules with an assumed 7.3 percent efficiency, 1 billion kWh/yr of electricity could be produced on about 2700 ha of land, or about 270 m^2 of land per person (Table 17.3). Based on the present average per capita use of electricity, total U.S. electrical needs theoretically could be met with PV cells on 5.4 million ha, an area smaller than West Virginia. If 21 percent–efficient cells were used, the total area needed would be greatly reduced.

The energy input to construct a PV system delivering 1 billion kWh is calculated to be about 300 kWh/m^2 (OTA, 1978). The energy input/output ratio for production is about 1:9 (Table 17.3).

Locating the photovoltaic cells on the roofs of homes, industries, and other buildings would reduce the need for additional land by about 5 percent (USBC, 1992a) and reduce the costs of energy transmission. However, PV systems require backup with conventional electrical systems because they function only during daylight hours.

PV technology has several environmental advantages over fossil fuel technologies in producing electricity. For example, using present PV technology, carbon dioxide emissions range from 0.17 to 0.25 kg of CO_2 per kWh over the life of a 300-kWp plant (Schaefer and Hagedorn, 1992). If the anticipated technological improvements are achieved, the emissions from construction and maintenance could be reduced. Overall the emissions of SO_x and NO_x associated with the operation and/or construction of a PV plant are negligible (Rogers et al., 1991).

The major environmental problem associated with PV systems is the use of toxic chemicals such as cadmium sulfide and gallium arsenide in their manufacture (Holdren et al., 1980). Because these chemicals persist in the environment for centuries, disposal of inoperative cells could become a major environmental problem. However, the most promising cells in terms of low cost, mass production, and relatively high efficiency are those using silicon, which is environmentally safer than the heavy metals.

Solar Thermal Conversion Systems

Solar thermal energy systems collect the sun's radiant energy and convert it into heat. This heat can be used for household and industrial purposes and can drive a turbine and produce electricity. Systems range from simple (solar ponds) to complex (central receivers). Electricity is selected for analysis to facilitate comparison to the other solar energy technologies.

Solar Ponds

Solar ponds are used to capture solar radiation and store it in concentrated salt at temperatures of nearly 100°C. Natural or man-made ponds can be made into solar ponds through the introduction of a salt-concentration gradient. A typical solar pond contains layers of increasing concentrations of salt. These salt layers prevent natural convection from occurring in the pond and trap heat collected from solar radiation at the bottom, in the brine layer of the pond (Gommend and Grossman, 1988). Then the hot brine stored is piped out to generate electricity. The steam from the hot brine turns freon into a pressurized vapor, which drives a Rankine engine, designed specifically to convert low-grade heat into electricity (Bronicki, 1981). Solar ponds are being used successfully in Israel to generate electricity (Tabor and Doran, 1990).

Approximately 4000 ha of solar ponds (40 ponds of 100 ha) and a set of evaporation ponds covering a combined 1200 ha are needed for the production of 1 billion kWh of electricity, the amount needed by 100,000 people for 1 year (Table 17.3). Therefore, a family of 3 would require about 0.2 ha (22,000 ft^2) of solar ponds for its electricity needs. Although the land area required is relatively large, solar ponds have the capacity to store heat energy for months, thus eliminating the need for backup energy sources from conventional fossil plants. The efficiency of solar ponds in converting solar radiation into heat is estimated to be about 20 percent. Assuming a 30-year life for a solar pond, the construction and operations energy input/output ratio is calculated to be 1:4 (Table 17.3). A 100 ha (1 km^2) solar pond is calculated to produce electricity at a rate of about $0.14 per kWh. According to Folchitto (1991) this cost could be reduced in the future.

In several locations in the United States, solar ponds are now being used successfully to generate heat directly. The heat energy from the pond can be used to produce processed steam for heating at a cost of only $0.02 to $0.04 per kWh (Gommend and Grossman, 1988). Solar ponds are most effectively employed in the U.S. Southwest and Midwest and in Israel (Lin et al., 1982; Tabor and Doran, 1990).

For successful operation, the salt-concentration gradient and appropriate water levels must be maintained. For example, 4000 ha of solar ponds lose about 3 billion liters of water per year in the arid conditions of the Southwest (Tabor and Doran, 1990). In addition, to counteract the water loss and the upward diffusion process of salt in the ponds, the dilute saltwater at the surface of the ponds has to be replaced with fresh water. Likewise, salt has to be added periodically to the heat-storage zone. The evaporation ponds concentrate the brine, which then can be used for salt replacement in the solar ponds (Zangrando and Johnson, 1985).

Some hazards are associated with solar ponds, but most can be prevented with careful management. For instance, it is essential to use plastic liners to make the ponds leakproof and thereby prevent salt contamination of the adjacent soil and groundwater (Maugh, 1982; Dickson and Yates, 1983). Waterfowl and mammals might be attracted to the ponds and be killed by the heat, and burrowing animals must be kept away from the ponds by buried screening (Dickson and Yates, 1983). In addition, the ponds should be fenced to prevent people and other animals from coming into contact with them. Because some toxic chemicals are used to prevent algae growth on the water surface and freon is used in the Rankine engine, methods will have to be devised to safely handle these chemicals (Dickson and Yates, 1983).

Solar Receiver Systems

Other solar thermal technologies that concentrate solar radiation for large-scale energy production include distributed and central receivers. Distributed receiver technologies use rows of parabolic troughs to focus sunlight on a central-pipe receiver that runs above the troughs. Pressurized water and other fluids are heated in the pipe and are used to generate steam to drive a turbo-generator for electricity production or to provide heat energy.

Central receivers have the potential for greater efficiency in electricity production than distributed receivers because they are able to achieve higher energy concentrations and higher turbine inlet temperatures (Winter, 1991). Therefore, central receivers are used in this analysis,although distributed receivers entered the commercial market first because they are less expensive to operate.

Central receiver plants use computer-controlled sun-tracking mirrors, or heliostats, to collect and concentrate sunlight and redirect it toward a receiver located atop a centrally placed tower. In the receiver the solar energy is captured as heat energy by circulating fluids, such as water or molten salts, that are heated under pressure. These fluids either directly or indirectly generate steam, which is then driven through a conventional turbogenerator to yield electricity. The receiver system may also be designed to generate heat for industrial processes.

Central receiver technology requires about 1100 ha of land to produce 1 billion kWh/yr (Table 17.3), assuming peak efficiency and favorable sunlight conditions such as those in the western United States. Proposed systems offer 4 to 6 hours of heat storage and may be constructed to include a backup energy source. The energy input/output ratio is calculated to be 1:10 (Table 17.3). Solar thermal receivers are estimated to produce electricity at about $0.10 per kWh, but this cost could be reduced to more competitive levels in the future (Gervais, 1986; Williams et al., 1990; Vant-Hull, 1992). New technical advances aimed at reducing costs and improving efficiencies include designing stretched-membrane heliostats, volumetric-air ceramic receivers, and improved overall systems (Tracey et al., 1989; Beninga et al., 1991; Grasse, 1991).

Central receiver systems are being tested in Italy, France, Spain, Japan, and at the 10-megawatt (MW) Solar One pilot plant near Barstow, California (Skinrood and Skvarna, 1986). The Barstow plants use distributed receivers to generate almost 300 MW of commercial electricity (Jensen et al., 1989).

The potential environmental impacts of solar thermal receivers include: the accidental or emergency release of toxic chemicals used in the heat-transfer system (Holdren et al., 1980; Baechler and Lee, 1991); bird collisions with heliostats and incineration of both birds and insects that fly into the high-temperature portion of the reflected sunbeams (Medsker, 1982); and burns, retinal damage, and fires if a heliostat did not track properly and focused its high-temperature beam on humans, other animals, or flammable materials (Mihlmester et al., 1980). Flashes of light coming from the heliostats may pose hazards to air and ground traffic (Mihlmester et al., 1980).

Receiver plants will require demineralized water for regularly washing of the mirrored surfaces (Skinrood and Skvarna, 1986; Jensen et al., 1989). Water may be in short supply in the southwestern deserts, considered the best sites for these solar plants. Other potential environmental impacts include microclimate alteration, including reduced temperature, wind speeds, and evapotranspiration beneath the heliostats or collecting troughs. These effects may cause shifts in various plant and animal populations. The albedo in solar collecting fields may be increased from 30 to 56 percent in desert regions (Mihlmester et al., 1980).

The environmental benefits of receiver systems are significant when compared to fossil fuel electrical generation. Such systems cause less acid rain, air pollution, and global warming than fossil plants. Fossil fuel electric utilities account for two-thirds of the sulfur dioxide, one-third of the nitrogen dioxide, and one-third of the carbon dioxide emissions in the United States (Kennedy et al., 1991). Some emissions may be expected during construction of solar plants, but only trace amounts are produced during operation (Spewack, 1988; Kennedy et al., 1991). Externalities of coal-produced electricity cost only $0.01 to $0.02/kWh less than solar-receiver electricity (Baechler and Lee, 1991), but removal of carbon dioxide from coal-plant emissions could raise costs to $0.12/kWh, and a disposal tax on carbon could further raise coal electricity costs to $0.18/kWh (Williams et al., 1990).

Passive Heating and Cooling of Buildings

About 23 percent (18.4 quads) of fossil energy consumed yearly in the United States is used for heating and cooling buildings and for heating water (DOE, 1991a; OTA, 1992b). At present only 0.3 quads of energy are saved through passive and active solar heating and cooling of buildings (Table 17.3). Tremendous potential exists for substantial energy savings through increased energy efficiency and use of solar technologies. Crenshaw and Clark (1982) suggest that conservation measures alone could reduce energy used for space conditioning and water heating in many buildings by 40 percent. Similarly, commercially available cost-effective technologies could reduce energy consumption in buildings as much as 33 percent by the year 2015 (OTA, 1992b). Over the long term, extensive use of solar designs in new buildings coupled with efficiency measures could reduce the fossil fuel energy demand of U.S. buildings by 60 to 80 percent (Brower, 1992).

Diverse solar technologies now are available to improve new building construction and retrofit old structures. Passive solar heating designs make use of the structural elements of a building to collect, store, and distribute heat. The 3 principal types of passive solar heating designs are the direct-gain system, the indirect gain (or "mass-wall") system, and the isolated gain system, which uses solariums or greenhouse units. Natural cooling methods include ventilation, landscaping, attic radiant barriers, wing walls, and daylighting. The most effective solar systems combine solar and conservation technologies—including appropriate building insulation, solar water heaters (active or passive), south-facing windows, construction of a portion of the building underground, heat storage units, roof overhangs—and advanced window technologies, such as low-emissivity coatings, heat-mirror windows, multipane windows, and gas-filled windows (Sheinkopf, 1989). A new system called DESRAD (Dessicant Enhanced Solar Radiation) shows promise as the only passive solar system that both cools and dehumidifies buildings. Engineers at the Florida Solar Energy Center estimate that DESRAD systems could handle 65 to 95 percent of the energy used for summer cooling (Melody, 1991).

Although new and established homes can be fitted with solar heating and cooling systems, installing passive solar systems into the design of a new home is cheapest. Including passive solar systems during new-home construction usually adds less than 10 percent to building costs (Howard and Szoke, 1992); B. Howard (personal communication, 1992) reports that a 3 to 5 percent cost increase is typical. Based on the cost of construction and the reduction in heating costs, we estimate the cost of passive solar systems to be about $0.03 per kWh saved.

Technological improvements are making passive solar technology more effective and less expensive than in the past. For example, current research is focused on the development of "superwindows," which have high insulating values, and on "smart," or "electrochromic," windows that can respond to electrical current, temperature, or incident sunlight to control the admission of light energy (Warner, 1991). Transparent insulation materials (TIMs) enable windows to transmit between 50 and 70 percent of incident solar energy while providing insulating values typical of 25 cm of fiberglass insulation (Chahroudi, 1992). Such materials can be used in a wide range of other solar technologies, including transparent insulated collector-storage walls for house heating and integrated storage collectors for domestic hot water (Wittwer et al., 1991).

Solar water heating is also cost-effective. About 3 percent of all the energy used in the United States is for heating water in homes (DOE, 1991a; OTA, 1992b). Many types of passive and active water heating solar systems are in use throughout the United States, and these systems are becoming increasingly affordable and reliable (Cromer, 1989; Wittwer et al., 1991). The cost of purchasing and installing an active solar water heater ranges from $2500 to $6000 in the northern regions of the nation and $2000 to $4000 in the southern regions (DOE/CE, 1988). Active solar heating technologies are not likely to play a major role in the heating of buildings because they are more expensive per unit of energy saved than passive systems and conservation measures (B. Howard, personal communication, 1992).

Although none of the passive heating and cooling technologies require land, they can cause environmental problems. Some indirect land-use problems may occur, such as the removal of trees, shading, and "sun rights" (Schurr et al., 1979). Glare from solar collectors and glazing could create hazards to automobile drivers, pedestrians, bicyclists, and airline pilots (Schurr et al., 1979). Also, when houses are designed to be extremely energy efficient and airtight, indoor air quality becomes a concern because pollutants may accumulate (NES, 1991). However, well-designed ventilation systems promote a healthful exchange of air while reducing heat loss during the winter and heat gain during the summer (NES, 1991). Barrier and pressurization methods can mitigate levels of radon and keep them at safe levels (Miller and Schmalz, 1990; ASTM, 1992).

Comparing Solar Power to Coal and Nuclear Power

In this section we compare conventional sources of electricity generation—coal and nuclear power—to various future solar energy technologies. At present, coal, oil, gas, nuclear, and other mined fuels provide 92 percent of U.S. energy needs (Table 17.1). Coal and nuclear plants combined produce three-quarters of U.S. electricity (USBC, 1992a).

Energy efficiencies for both coal and nuclear fuels are low because of the thermal law constraint of electric generator designs. Conversion of coal is about 35 percent efficient, nuclear fuels about 33 percent (West and Kreith, 1988). In the future both coal and nuclear power plants may require additional structural materials to meet clean air and safety standards. However, the energy requirements of such modifications are estimated to be small compared with the energy lost because of conversion inefficiencies.

The costs of producing electricity using coal and nuclear energy are $0.03 and $0.05 per kWh, respectively (EIA, 1990). However, the costs of this kind of energy generation are artificially low because external costs, such as damage from acid rain produced from coal and decommissioning costs for nuclear plants, currently are not included. The Clean Air Act and its amendments may raise coal generation costs, whereas the new reactor designs, standardization, and streamlined regulations may reduce nuclear generation costs. Government subsidies for nuclear and coal plants also skew their economies away from solar energy technologies (Wolfson, 1991).

Direct and indirect U.S. subsidies hide the true cost of fossil energy and keep consumers' expenses low, thereby encouraging energy consumption. The energy industry receives a direct subsidy of $424 per household per year (based on an estimated maximum of $36 billion for total federal energy subsidies [ASE, 1993]). In addition, the energy industry does not pay for the environmental and public health costs of fossil energy production and consumption.

The land area required for electrical production of 1 billion kWh/year, including the area for the plant, mining operations, and waste disposal, is estimated at 363 ha for coal and 48 ha for nuclear fuels (Table 17.3). Because coal is a concentrated fuel source, unlike diffuse solar energy, the land requirements are low. However, as the quality of fuel ore declines, land requirements for mining will increase. Efficient reprocessing and the use of breeder reactors may decrease the land area necessary for nuclear power. In any case, the land requirements for fossil fuel– and nuclear-based plants are lower than those for solar energy technologies (Table 17.3).

The occupational and public health risks of both coal and nuclear plants are fairly high, mainly because of the hazards of mining, ore transportation, and subsequent air pollution during the production of electricity. There are 22 times more deaths related to coal than nuclear energy production, basically because 90,000 times more coal than nuclear fuel is needed to generate an equivalent amount of electricity (D. Hammer, personal communication, Cornell University, 1993).

Transition to Solar Energy—Constraints and Opportunities

The supply of and demand for fossil and solar energy; the competition for land on which to produce food, fiber, and lumber; and the rapidly growing number of humans will influence future U.S. choices. The U.S. population doubled during the last 60 years, and the growth rate is now 1.1 percent per year (USBC, 1992b). Based on this rate of increase, the present U.S. population of 260 million will double in 60 years to more than half a billion people. This large population will require more land for homes, businesses, and roads, as well as considerably more cropland and forestland for vital food and forest products. The drain on all energy resources will increase.

Solar energy technologies will compete for land with agriculture and forestry in the United States and worldwide (Tables 17.3 and 17.7). Therefore, land is projected to be a limiting factor in the development of solar energy. Allowing for this constraint, an optimistic projection is that the nearly 7 quads/yr of solar energy currently used in the United States could be increased approximately fivefold to about 37 quads (Pimentel et al., 1984a; Ogden and Williams, 1989). This represents only 43 percent of the 86 quads per year currently consumed in the United States (Tables 17.1 and 17.4). To produce 37 quads with solar technologies will require about 173 million ha, or nearly 20 percent of the U.S. land area. At present this amount of land is available. If land continues to be available, the amounts of solar energy that could be produced by the year 2050 are projected to be: 5 quads from biomass; 4 quads from hydropower; 8 quads from wind power; 6 quads from solar thermal systems; 6 quads from passive and active heating; and 8 quads from photovoltaics (Table 17.4). If the human population continues to grow as projected, some of the presently available land will have to be used to produce food, precluding its use for solar energy.

Table 17.7   Current land uses in major regions of the United States

	Total Area (10⁶ ha)	Area per capita (ha)
Cropland	162	0.63
Pasture	265	1.04
Forest	262	1.02
Special[a]	113	0.44
Other[b]	115	0.45
TOTAL	917	3.58

Notes: [a]Urban areas, roadways, military areas, and recreation areas.
[b]Areas unsuitable for use by agriculture and forestry because they are either too steep, too dry, or too cold.
Source: USDA, 1991b.

In the unlikely event that the U.S. population stabilizes at an estimated optimum of about 200 million (down from today's 256 million) and conservation measures lower per capita energy consumption to about half the present level, then the United States could achieve a secure energy future and a satisfactory standard of living for all its citizens (Pimentel et al., 1994a).

Current subsidies of about $36 billion/year for fossil energy systems encourage wasteful energy use by Americans (ASE, 1993). If energy prices were based on the true cost of production, the price of gasoline would be about $0.70/liter ($2.65/gallon), or similar to that charged in England. Furthermore, each person in England consumes less than half the energy consumed by Americans (Davis, 1991). This fact confirms that it is possible to improve energy efficiency while maintaining a high standard of living. Fossil energy subsidies should be greatly diminished or withdrawn and the monies invested to encourage the development and use of solar energy technologies. This policy will increase the rate of adoption of solar energy technologies in the future and lead to a smooth transition from a fossil to a solar energy economy.

Conclusion

This assessment of solar technologies confirms that solar energy alternatives to fossil fuels have the potential to meet a large portion of future U.S. energy needs, provided that the commitment is made to develop and implement solar energy technologies and to conserve all energy resources. Such policies will also reduce many of the current environmental problems associated with fossil fuel production and use.

If the United States does not commit itself to the transition from fossil to solar energy during the next decade or two, the economy and national security will be adversely affected. A fair balance among energy, land, water, biological resources, and the human population must be reached in order to ensure a reasonable standard of living for all Americans in the future.

18
BIOMASS: FOOD VERSUS FUEL

D. Pimentel, A. F. Warneke, W. S. Teel, K. A. Schwab,
N. J. Simcox, D. M. Ebert, K. D. Baenisch, and M. R. Aaron

Biomass resources (fuelwood, dung, crop residues, ethanol) constitute a major fuel source in the world (Hall et al., 1985; Pimentel et al., 1986b; Hall and de Groot, 1987). Biomass is a prime energy source in developing nations, where it meets about 90 percent of the energy needs of the poor (Chatterji, 1981). Each year 2.5 billion tons of forest resources are harvested for a variety of uses, including fuel, lumber, and pulp (FAO, 1983a). About 60 percent of these resources is harvested in developing nations; of this amount, about 85 percent is burned as fuel (Montalembert and Clement, 1983). Fuelwood makes up about half (1.3 billion tons) of the 2.8 billion tons of biomass consumed annually worldwide; the remaining half consists of crop residues (33 percent) and dung (17 percent) (Pimentel et al., 1986b).

High fossil fuel prices and rapid population growth in developing countries have made it necessary for the people there to rely more on biomass in the form of fuelwood, crop residues, and dung for energy (Dunkerley and Ramsay, 1983; OTA, 1984; Sanchez-Sierra and Umana-Quesada, 1984). Estimates are that the poor in developing nations spend 15 to 40 percent of their income for fuel and devote considerable time and energy to collecting biomass for fuel (CSE, 1982; Hall, 1985).

Biomass Resources

The use of biomass for food and energy in the United States, Brazil, India, and Kenya is compared here. These countries were selected because they represent different economic, social, and environmental conditions.

United States

The United States, with 917 million ha of land and a human population of 256 million (Table 18.1), is the largest of the 4 countries in land area and the second-largest in total population. It has the lowest rate of population growth but the largest per capita GNP (gross national product) (Table 18.1).

Table 18.1   Population, area, and per capita gross national product

Country	Estimated population (10^6)[a]	Annual rate of increase (percent)	Surface area (10^6 km^2)[b]	Density (habitants/ km^2)	GNP[a] ($ per capita)
United States	256	1.1[c]	9.17	28	22,560
Brazil	152	1.5[a]	8.51	18	2,920
India	897	2.1[a]	3.28	273	330
Kenya	28	3.7[a]	0.58	48	340

Notes: [a]PRB, 1993.
[b]UN, 1976.
[c]USBC, 1992b.

Nearly half of the land area in the United States is used for crop production and pastures (Table 18.2). The extensive forested area of 290 million ha provides only about 4 percent of the total energy used in the United States (Tables 18.2 and 18.3). Fossil fuel resources are the major sources of U.S. energy. In per capita use of biomass for fuel, the United States ranks third— just ahead of India (Table 18.2).

Table 18.2   Land distribution by uses and population engaged in agriculture

Country	Total area (10^6 ha)	Cropland (10^6 ha)	Pasture (10^6 ha)	Forests and woods (10^6 ha)	Other land (10^6 ha)	Percentage of laborers in agriculture
United States[b]	917	192	300	290	135	4
Brazil[c]	845	60	184	493	108	31
India[c]	298	170	12	67	49	70
Kenya[c]	57	2.4	38	2.3	14	81

Notes: [a]WRI, 1992.
[b]USDA, 1991b.
[c]WRI, 1984b.

Table 18.3   Consumption of commercial energy (10^{12} kcal)

Country	Solid Fuels[a]	Liquid Fuels[a]	Natural Gas[a]	Hydroelectric and Nuclear[a]	Total	Per capita (10^6 kcal)
United States[a]	4,300	7,775	4,475	1,825	18,375	76.6
Brazil[b]	57	383	19	132	591	4.1
India[b]	439	295	18	104	856	1.1
Kenya	0.8	9.9	0	1.6	12.3	0.6

Notes: [a]DOE, 1983.
[b]UN, 1986.

Wood accounts for about 97 percent of the biomass used as fuel (Tables 18.3–18.7). The second-largest quantity of biomass energy comes from bagasse, the by-product of sugar production. About 172 million tons of biomass are converted for energy use each year, and this quantity could more than double, to about 440 million tons (ERAB, 1981; Pimentel et al., 1994). An increase of this magnitude would conflict with agricultural land needs and probably be detrimental to the environment.

Table 18.4   Tons (10^6 dry) of biomass energy currently used[a]

Country	Firewood	Animal Wastes	Bagasse and crop residues	Food grains, sugars, etc.	Total biomass	Metric tons per capita of biomass
United States[b]	166	1	4[c]	1	172	0.72
	(747)	(5)	(18)	(5)	(774)	
Brazil	102[d]	Negligible	46[e]	10[e]	158	1.1
	(459)		(207)	(45)	(711)	
India	124[f]	38[g]	64[g]	>0	226[f]	0.29
	(558)	(118)	(126)		(855)	
Kenya	20.4[e]	11[e]	1.5[e]	>0	32.9[e]	1.57
	(92)	(50)	(7)		(148)	

Notes: [a]Values in parentheses indicate energy equivalent if dry biomass were incinerated (10^{12} kcal).
[b]ERAB (1981).
[c]Mostly sugar cane bagasse.
[d]UN (1982).
[e]Meade and Chen (1977); FAO (1984b).
[f]UN (1982).
[g]Derived from GI (1979).

Table 18.5   Annual biomass production in the United States, Brazil, India, and Kenya[a]

	United States		Brazil		India		Kenya	
	Land area (10⁶ ha)	Biomass production	Land area (10⁶ ha)	Biomass production	Land area (10⁶ ha)	Biomass production	Land area (10⁶ ha)	Biomass production
Arable land and production crops	192	1,083	75	450	143	858	2.3	13.8
Pasture and grazing land	300	900	164	492	12	36	6.2	18.6
Forests	290	580	568	1,136	46	92	2.4	94.8
Other	135	68	39	20	127	64	46.1	50.7[b]
Total area	917	—	851	—	328	—	57	—
Total biomass	—	2631	—	2098	—	1,050	—	84.2
Total energy fixed (10¹⁵ kcal)	11.8		9.4		4.7		0.38	
Solar fixed energy per capita (10⁶ kcal)	59.2		104		6.0		18.1	
Biomass production (tons/ha)	2.9		2.5		3.2		1.5	

$Notes$: [a]The average biomass yields per hectare were: crops, 6 tons; pastures, 3 tons; forests, 2 tons; and other, 0.5 tons.
[b]Calculated using figures for woody biomass production given by O'Keefe et al. (1984) and assuming an annual nonwoody biomass production of 1 ton/ha in arid grasslands.

Table 18.6 Total annual amount of solar energy harvested in the form of agricultural crops and forestry products (dry)

	United States		Brazil		India		Kenya	
	10^6 metric tons[a]	10^{12} kcal	10^6 metric tons[a]	10^{12} kcal	10^6 metric tons[a]	10^{12} kcal	10^6 metric tons[a]	10^{12} kcal
Corn	194	873	21	95	7.8	35	1.3	6
Wheat	71	320	1.8	8	45	203	0.1	0.5
Rice	6	27	9	41	91	410	0.03	0.1
Soybeans	51	230	16	72	8	4	–	–
Sorghum	22	99	0.3	14	12	54	0.15	0.7
Potatoes	16	72	0.4	18	2.4	11	0.1	0.5
Cassava	–	–	4.2	19	1.2	5	0.15	0.7
Vegetables	6	27	1.8	8	8.8	40	0.02	0.5
Fruits	5	23	4.9	22	3.9	18	0.15	0.7
Nuts	0.8	4	0.1	0.5	0.2	0.9	0.02	0.1
Oil seeds	9	41	2.0	9	18	365	0.13	0.6
Sugar cane	2.5	–	24.1	105	18	81	0.4	1.8
Sugar beets	2	27	–	–	–	–	–	–
Pulses	1	5	2.7	24	13	59	0.25	1.1
Oats	7	32	0.1	0.5	–	–	0.01	0.05
Rye	1	5	<0.1	<0.5	–	–	–	–
Barley	13	59	0.1	0.5	–	–	0.09	0.4
SUBTOTAL	407.3	1,833	88.6	399	229.3	1,032	2.9	13.1
Pasture and others	900[b]	4,050	492[b]	2,214	36[b]	162	19[b]	85
Forest industrial products	100[c]	450	40[d]	180	14[d]	63	0.8[e]	2.3
TOTAL	1,407	6,332	7,590	2,655	274	1,235	22.4	101
TOTAL PER CAPITA (tons)	5.8		4.1		0.3		1.1	
TOTAL PER CAPITA (10^6 kcal)	26.3		18.6		1.6		4.8	

Notes: [a]From data presented by the Food and Agriculture Organization (FAO, 1984b).
[b]From Table 18.5.
[c]USDA (1985).
[d]FAO (1983b).
[e]O'Keefe and Raskin (1985).

Table 18.7   Forest utilization (10^6 tons)

	Potential Sustainable Production[a]	Actual use		
		Industry	Firewood	Total
United States	580	191[b]	166[f]	357
Brazil	1,136	40[c]	102[g]	142
India	92	14[c]	124[d]	138
Kenya	2.5	0.8[e]	19.6[e]	20.4[f]

Notes: [a]Assuming a net productivity of 2 tons/ha.
[b]USDA (1985).
[c]FAO (1983b).
[d]See Table 18.4.
[e]O'Keefe and Raskin (1985).
[f]ERAB (1981).
[g]Bogach (1985).

Brazil

Brazil is the fifth-largest country in the world, with 851 million ha of land. Its population of 152 million is increasing at a rate of 1.5 percent per year (Table 18.1), and its per capita GNP is $2920. At present, 45 percent of its total energy supply comes from fossil fuel and 55 percent from biomass fuel (Tables 18.3 and 18.4). Brazil's total annual biomass production is slightly less than that of the United States and more than that of India and Kenya (Table 18.5). Approximately 23 percent of the biomass produced in Brazil is used for food and fiber (Table 18.6).

Although forests still cover 67 percent of the country (Table 18.2), rapid deforestation is taking place, primarily caused by slash and burn agriculture rather than by commercial logging or cattle production (Myers, 1986a). Much of the tropical rainforest has limited potential as fuel resource because it is located in remote areas and far from consumers. Firewood provides 22 percent of the country's total energy needs (Tables 18.3 and 18.4). Forests not only are important to Brazil as an energy source but also, as in all areas, protect land from soil erosion, reduce flooding, and minimize the silting of rivers, streams, and man-made reservoirs.

After the 1973 oil crisis, Brazil embarked on an ambitious plan to produce ethanol from sugarcane in an effort to reduce its dependence on foreign oil. Currently, Brazil has the largest ethanol system in the world, producing 12 billion liters annually, primarily from sugarcane (Boddey, 1995). The United States produces only 2.4 billion liters of ethanol annually, primarily from corn grain (DOE, 1986). Ethanol supplies approximately 19 percent of Brazil's current biomass energy. However, expansion of the sugarcane crop for ethanol production is associated with a decrease in the per capita production of domestic food crops. From 1974 to 1984 food production decreased 1.9 percent per year, whereas sugarcane production increased 7.8 percent per year (de Melo, 1986). The increasing demand for firewood, construction lumber, and sugarcane, combined with the effects of slash-and-burn agriculture, seem likely to continue to exacerbate problems in agricultural production and the quality of the environment.

India

India's surface area is 36 percent that of the United States, but its population, at 897 million, is more than 3 times greater (Table 18.1). Of the 4 countries, India has the highest population density and the lowest GNP (Table 18.1). Even if India's population growth rate remains at its present rate of 2.1 percent, the country can expect to have more than 1 billion people by the year 2000. A majority of the people live in rural areas and engage in agriculture.

Although India will have to increase food production to keep pace with population growth, it can expand its cropland only by removing forests (Mishra, 1986; Sharma, 1987). The present Indian forest area of about 67 million ha makes up only 23 percent of the country's total land area (Table 18.2). India is losing about 3.4 million ha of forestland each year (World Development Report, 1995), and there is virtually no forest growth left below 2000 m (Myers, 1986b). The principal factor responsible for this deforestation is population pressure imposed by both humans and livestock (Sharma, 1987). Most of India's large livestock population must graze on fallow agricultural land, uncultivated lands, and forest areas because little fodder is produced.

In addition to using biomass resources for food production, India relies heavily on biomass for energy. Biomass resources supply about half of the energy consumed, fossil energy the other half. The Indian household sector utilizes nearly all of the biomass energy consumed (Tables 18.3 and 18.4), primarily for cooking and lighting (Government of India, 1979). The sugar industry uses bagasse to provide heat and steam energy for the manufacture of sugar.

Wood is the primary source of biomass energy, making up 55 percent of all biomass energy consumed, followed by bagasse and crop residues at 28 percent and animal dung at 17 percent (Table 18.4). This pattern of biomass energy use in India resembles the world pattern, which averages about 50 percent wood, 35 percent crop residues, and 15 percent dung. However, India's heavy reliance on firewood is alarming because 45 percent more firewood is being used than its forest area can sustainably provide (Tables 18.5, 18.6; 18.7). It should be noted, however, that not all firewood in India is obtained from forests. Although in total forests are the greatest source of fuelwood (Government of India, 1979), about 22 percent of fuelwood is collected from nonforest land, such as privately owned plantations and woodlots other private property, riverbanks, canals, and roadsides (Government of India, 1979). To meet future food and fuel needs, India will have to utilize more of its biomass resources; however, it is dubious if the land resources can sustain such use. Of the total annual biomass currently produced, India already harvests 25 percent in the form of fuel (Tables 18.4 and 18.5).

Kenya

Kenya occupies 570,000 km² of arid East Africa and has a population of 28 million people that is expanding at a rate of about 3.7 percent per annum (Table 18.1). The per capita GNP in Kenya is $340 (Table 18.1). Of the total land area, 4 percent is in forests and woodland, 4 percent is used for growing crops, and 7 percent is pastureland (Table 18.2). Parks and reserves occupy 4 to 5 percent, and villages and cities occupy 1 percent. The remaining 80 percent of the land comprises semiarid savanna and rangeland.

Although 75 percent of the population lives on 20 percent of the land, resulting in densities of 500 to 1000 people per km² (World Development Report, 1995), only 15 percent live in urban areas. In rural areas, 75 percent of the labor force is engaged in agriculture (Table 18.1). Per capita food production and caloric intake decreased during the 1970s. Thus, the daily per capita food supply was only 90 percent of the minimum requirement of 2340 kcal/person/day necessary for the maintenance of health (Yeager and Miller, 1986). In 1992/93 Kenya imported 569,000 tons of cereals and received another 287,000 tons in aid.

Biomass provides the bulk of Kenya's energy needs (Tables 18.3 and 18.4), with firewood supplying 80 percent of the total annual energy requirements (F. Mugo, Nairobi, Kenya, personal communication, 1995). Most of the wood consumed (about 20 million tons) was removed from arable cropland, grazing land, and urbanlands. Only 27 percent came from forests, yet this amount still exceeded the sustainable yield of the forests by more than 50 percent (O'Keefe and Raskin, 1985). Consumption exceeded yields by 9 million tons, causing depletion of the standing stocks. The yearly rate of deforestation is 1.6 percent, primarily because of expanding agriculture but also because of increased needs for firewood (Molofsky et al., 1986).

In addition to wood, crop residues and dung are used to produce biomass energy. Crop residues, including bagasse, total about 4.2 million tons per year (Table 18.4). All bagasse is used in the sugar-refining process. Of the other crop residues, about 30 percent of the total harvested biomass, including the woody residue from coffee and tea plantations, is used for energy (O'Keefe, 1983).

Of the 12 million tons of dung produced annually in Kenya, an estimated 0.6 million tons are burned. A survey by Hosier (1985) found that rural people burn animal dung when firewood supplies are insufficient, and then only for heating, not for cooking.

Ethanol production using molasses was started at Muhoroni, Kenya (Stuckey and Juma, 1985). (Another plant near Kisumu was discontinued after cost overruns had nearly tripled its initial $60 million cost.) The Muhoroni plant, which has a capacity to produce 64,000 liters of ethanol per day, can produce a liter of ethanol for $0.57, including the cost of molasses, running costs, capital costs, and transportation.

Of the total annual biomass production of 91.3 million tons in Kenya, only 35.2 million tons are produced on arable land, pastureland, and forests, where 80 percent of the population lives (Tables 18.4 and 18.5). Of these 35.2 tons, about 54 percent is used for fuel and 8.2 percent for food (Banwell and Harriss, 1992). Further expansion of Kenyan agriculture and increased consumption of firewood will be necessary through 2000 and thereafter to support Kenya's rapidly growing population.

Biomass Energy Use

Forest and other biomass is produced from solar energy if temperature, soil, water, and biological resources are sufficient for plant growth. In the United States 14.2×10^{15} kcal of solar energy are collected as plant biomass each year (Tables 18.5, 18.6, and 18.7). This amounts to 3.0 tons/ha/yr (Table 18.5). The average yields for Brazil are 2.5 tons/ha, for India 3.2 tons/ha, and for Kenya 1.25 tons/ha. The low yield for Kenya is due to low rainfall (Tables 18.5, 18.6, and 18.7).

How does the amount of solar energy collected annually in biomass compare with fossil energy consumed? The United States uses about 40 percent more fossil energy than all the plant biomass in the United States captures in solar energy. In India, the fossil energy consumed represents about 18.2 percent of the total solar energy captured by plant biomass; in Brazil this percentage is 6.3 percent, and in Kenya only 3.5 percent (derived from Tables 18.3 and 18.5).

Conversion of Biomass to Ethanol, Biogas, and Heat

The utilization of some forms of biomass for fuel requires conversion, which frequently requires significant inputs of energy and may cause environmental as well as social problems. In the following discussion energy inputs, environmental impacts, and social costs are assessed for ethanol, biogas, and heat energy.

Ethanol

The conversion of sugars to ethanol by fermentation is a well-established technology. Yeast carry out the fermentation in an 8- to 12-hour batch process that produces 8 to 10 percent ethanol by volume. The ethanol is then recovered by continuous distillation. Theoretically, each 1 g of sugar or starch should produce 0.51 to 0.57 g of ethanol. In practice, about 90 percent of the theoretical yields are achieved (the yeast population consumes some of the sugar and starch for its maintenance and growth). The yield of ethanol is about 1 liter per 2.7 kg of corn or 14 kg of sugarcane (2.5 kg of sugar) (Table 18.8).

Table 18.8   Inputs per 1,000 liters of ethanol from U.S. sugarcane[a]

Inputs	kg	kcal $\times 10^3$	Dollars
Sugarcane	14,000	1,938[b]	167[b]
Transport of sugarcane	14,000	400[c]	42
Water	125,000[d]	70	20
Stainless steel	3[d]	45	10
Steel	4[d]	46	10
Cement	8[d]	15	5
Bagasse	1,900	7,600	—
Pollution costs	—	—	60
TOTAL		10,114	$ 314

Notes: [a]Outputs: 1,000 liters of ethanol = 5,130,000 kcal.
[b]Table 18.9.
[c]Estimated.
[d]Slesser and Lewis (1979).

Sugarcane production in the United States requires significant dollar and fossil energy inputs (Table 18.9), which represent the major costs in ethanol production. (For details for producing ethanol from U.S. corn, see Chapter 19.) A hectare of U.S. sugarcane yields an average of 88,000 kg and requires 12.2 million kcal of fossil energy and $1059 to produce (Table 18.9).

Table 18.9   Average energy input and output per hectare per year for sugarcane in Louisiana[ab]

	Quantity/ha	10^3 kcal/ha	Dollars/ha
Inputs			
Labor	30 h	21	$ 150
Machinery	72 kg	1,944	119
Gasoline	54 liters	546	15
Diesel	284 liters	3,242	75
Nitrogen (ammonia)	158 kg	3,318	84
Phosphorus (triple)	97 kg	611	49
Potassium (muriate)	149 kg	373	40
Lime	1,120 kg	353	168
Seed	215 kg	802	215
Insecticide	2.5 kg	250	25
Herbicide	6.2 kg	620	62
Transportation	568.9 kg	146	57
TOTAL		12,226	$ 1,059
Outputs			
Sugarcane	88,000 kg	24,618,000	
Sugar yield	6,600 kg		

Notes: [a]Ricaud (1980).
[b]Kcal input/kcal sugar = 2.01.

Once the sugarcane is harvested, 3 additional energy costs are involved in its conversion to ethanol: transport to the plant, the conversion process, and pollution control. These costs in both energy and dollar terms are large for a modern chemical plant with an output of 200 million liters per year (Pimentel, 1991b).

Although the costs of producing ethanol are slightly lower for sugarcane than for corn ($0.31/liter, see Chapter 19), the energetics are similar (Table 18.8). The total energy input to produce 1000 liters of ethanol using sugarcane is 10.1 million kcal, or about double the energy value of the ethanol itself (5.1 million kcal). However, the fermentation/distillation process for ethanol produced from sugarcane has no energy cost because all the required energy is supplied by conversion of the bagasse by-product. However, in this assessment the fuel energy from the bagasse is charged as a cost (Table 18.8) because the bagasse could be used as an organic fertilizer or a fuel source for other processes. For the sugarcane system, sugarcane feedstock represents 53 percent of the cost of producing ethanol; thus, the price of the end product depends on the agricultural production costs.

Production of ethanol in the chemical plant also has major pollution costs (Table 18.8), which add 10 to 15 percent to the overall cost of production. For each 1000 liters of ethanol produced using sugarcane, 160,000 liters of wastewater are produced. This wastewater has a biological oxygen demand (BOD) of 18,000 to 37,000 mg/liter depending on the type of plant (Kuby et al., 1984). (The third supplemental energy input, transportation, is not included in this analysis.)

The foregoing data were based on U.S. sugarcane. Overall costs are slightly lower in Brazil than in the United States (Tables 18.8 and 18.10). The energy inputs for sugarcane production in Brazil are similar to those in the United States (Tables 18.9 and 18.11).

Table 18.10   Inputs per 1,000 liters of ethanol from Brazilian sugarcane[a]

Inputs	kg	10^3 kcal	Dollars
Sugarcane	14,000	1,946[b]	172[b]
Transport of sugarcane	14,000	195	24
Water	125,000	70[c]	20
Stainless steel	3	45[c]	10
Steel	4	46[c]	10
Concrete	8	15[c]	5
Bagasse	1,900	7,600	—
Pollution costs	—	—	60
TOTAL		9,917	$301

Notes: [a]Outputs: 1,000 liters of ethanol = 5,130,000 kcal.
[b]Table 18.11.
[c]Slesser and Lewis (1979).

Table 18.11   Average energy input and output per hectare per year for sugarcane in Brazil[a]

	Quantity/ha	10³ kcal/ha	Dollars/ha[b]
Inputs			
Labor	210 hr[c]	157[d]	120
Machinery	72 kg[e]	1,944	119
Fuel	262 liters[f]	2,635	131
Nitrogen (ammonia)	65 kg[f]	1,364	42
Phosphorus (triple)	52 kg[f]	336	27
Potassium (muriate)	100 kg[f]	250	27
Lime	616 kg[f]	192	92
Seed	215 kg[e]	271[d]	70
Insecticide	0.5 kg[f]	50	5
Herbicide	3 kg[f]	300	30
TOTAL		7,499	$ 663
Output			
Sugarcane	54,000 kg[f]	15,120,000	
Sugar yield	3,672 kg		

Notes: [a]Kcal input/kcal sugar = 2.02.
[b]Calculated based on quantity of inputs.
[c]Calculated from footnote b.
[d]Ghirardi (1983).
[e]Similar to Louisiana (Table 18.9).
[f]da Silva et al. (1978).

About 1.9 million kcal are required to produce 14,000 kg of sugarcane feedstock, which in turn produces 1000 liters of Brazilian ethanol. These figures are similar to the energy inputs required in the United States (Tables 18.8 and 18.10). The total input to produce 1000 liters of ethanol is about 9.9 million kcal, nearly double the yield in ethanol of 5.1 million kcal. About half a liter of imported fossil petroleum equivalent is needed to produce 1 liter of ethanol (Table 18.10). Others have reported that it takes about 1 liter of imported petroleum to produce 1 liter of ethanol (Chapman, 1983; Chapman and Barker, 1987).

Brazilian ethanol costs $0.30/liter to produce (Table 18.10). This figure includes pollution costs of $0.06/liter. With the pollution costs removed, the cost is lowered to $0.24/liter, well within the range of $0.23 to $0.27 reported by others (MME, 1987; Goldemberg, 1987). This $0.30/liter estimate does not factor in the crop subsidy; doing so would add 20 percent to the cost (Nastari, 1983). Sugarcane feedstock accounts for 56 percent of the total production costs. Further, inputs include the costs for controlling pollution. The BOD of wastewater from Brazilian sugarcane-based alcohol plants has an environmental impact about equal to two-thirds of the wastes produced by the total human population in Brazil (Desai et al., 1980).

In the Brazilian ethanol production system 2.6 ha per year of land are needed to fuel one automobile (Tables 18.10 and 18.11). Therefore, if all the automobiles in Brazil were fueled using sugarcane-produced ethanol, a total of 26 million ha of cropland would be needed. This amounts to more than one-third of the total cropland now in production (Table 18.2).

Fuelwood and Other Solid Biomass Fuels

The oldest and simplest use for biomass fuel is cooking and heating. Firewood is the most common form of biomass used. In many environments, wood is readily available and can be easily cut and transported to people's homes. It is easily stored and burns slowly.

Firewood supplies have declined in many parts of the world, creating a need on the part of farmers, governments, development agencies, and many others to promote reforestation to improve the firewood supply (Allen, 1986). Generally, these efforts have been categorized under the titles "social forestry" and "agroforestry" and help increase farmer access to wood supplies outside traditional forest systems.

Social forestry, or community forestry, has received much publicity and has been favored by large donor organizations because they feel large forests have a greater visible impact than numerous scattered, small farm woodlots (Khoshoo, 1987). However, social forest projects have not been successful for many reasons (Allen, 1986; Khoshoo, 1987). First, the people planting and caring for the trees do not have the same interest in these plantings as they usually have in their own trees. They tolerate grazing and other activities, and as a result large portions of these forests have been destroyed. Second, harvesting in such a large area is difficult to control and regulate; people who live close to the forest typically harvest a large share of the wood. Third, many people who depend on the social forests must travel long distances to cut and transport their wood. Together these factors have made social forests much less effective than farm woodlots (Allen, 1986).

Agroforestry is the deliberate management of trees on a given piece of land in association with crops, livestock, or a combination of the two (Teel, 1984). In many situations it has been demonstrated that, although the productivity of a given component may decrease in an agroforestry system, the overall productivity of the entire system increases (Kidd and Pimentel, 1992). Agroforestry should not be regarded as the only strategy for providing energy resources for all the rural poor. It is not appropriate for certain areas, such as the rice-growing regions of India, where population densities of people and animals make the survival of trees nearly impossible. There people have had to use locally available biomass, such as crop residues and dung, as fuel. But dung has value as a fertilizer and in protecting the soil from erosion. The manure and urine of milk cows contains 19.5 percent nitrogen by dry weight (Jewell et al., 1977) and 3.6 million kcal/ton of heat energy (Bailie, 1976). About 195 kg of nitrogen fertilizer is lost for every tonne of dry dung burned. Replacing this nitrogen fertilizer, which has an energy value of 2.87 million kcal/ton, costs $0.53 per kg, or $103/ton. These values do not include the replacement costs for phosphorus, potassium, and calcium, because these are assumed to be recovered from the ash, or the loss to the soil of the organic material in the manure.

Burning crop residues for energy has been proposed. However, many environmental problems are associated with this practice, which involves removing the vegetative covering, a protective layer that significantly decreases soil erosion and water runoff. For example, soil erosion rates may increase 90 percent when crop residues on soil surfaces are reduced from about 6 tons/ha to 0.5 ton/ha (Mannering, 1984). Water runoff rates increase 10 to 100 times when vegetative cover is removed from the land (USDA-ARS and EPA-ORD, 1976). In certain localized land areas that can tolerate some loss of organics without an increase in erosion, crop residues could be an energy source. However, under current agricultural practices in the United States and elsewhere, little or no crop residue should be burned for fuel (ERAB, 1981; Pimentel et al., 1981, 1987).

Burning crop residues is more complicated and costly than burning coal. More work hours are required to tend and stoke the furnace to prevent clogging, control air flow to the chamber, clean the ash, and add small, constant amounts of fuel (Bailie, 1976). Although about 12.5 kg of crops residues equals 1 kg of fuel oil in energy terms, about double the amount of energy is used to obtain the same heat value because of the energy-intensive burning process (OECD, 1984).

Biogas

Biomass material that contains large quantities of water can be effectively converted into usable energy using naturally occurring microbes in an anaerobic digestion system. These systems are presently used with dung and certain plants, such as water hyacinth (though production and harvesting problems are greater with the latter). The system is comparatively simple, utilizing mesophilic bacteria, with an overall construction cost of around $600 (Teel, 1987), or complex systems for 320-cow operations costing $120,000 or more for construction (SF, 1983). The basic principles for both are similar.

On a small dairy or cattle operation, manure is loaded or pumped into a sealed, corrosion-resistant digestion tank and held there for 14 to 28 days at temperatures around 30 to 38°C. In some systems the manure in the tank is constantly stirred to distribute heat and speed the digestion process. During this period the mesophilic bacteria present in the manure break down volatile solids, converting them into methane gas (65 percent) and carbon dioxide (35 percent). Small amounts of hydrogen sulfide may also be produced. These gases are then drawn off through pipes and either burned directly, in the same way as natural gas, or scrubbed to eliminate the H_2S and used to generate electricity. The cost breakdown for one system is listed in Table 18.12.

The amount of biogas produced is determined by the temperature of the system, the manure's volatile solids content, and the efficiency of converting them to biogas. This efficiency varies from 18 percent (Jewell and Morris, 1974) to 95 percent (Jewell et al., 1977). Dairy cows daily produce 85 kg of manure per 1000 kg live weight. The total solids in this manure are 10.6 kg, and of these 8.6 kg are volatile solids. Theoretically, a 100 percent–efficient digester would produce 625 liters of biogas from every 1 kg of volatile solids added (calculated from Stafford, 1983). The digester utilized for the data in Table 18.13 was 28.3 percent efficient, producing 177 liters of biogas/kg of volatile solids added. With this digester 1520 liters of biogas per 1000 kg live weight will be produced each day. If the total heat value of the manure were used in calculating efficiency, then the efficiency rate would be only 5 percent.

Biogas has an energy content of about 5720 kcal/m^3, less than the 8380 kcal/m^3 for pure methane because of the carbon dioxide present. When processed into biogas, 100 tons of manure (wet weight) yields a total of 10.2

Table 18.12   Energy inputs using anaerobic digestion for biogas production from 100 tons wet (13 tons dry) cattle manure[a]

	Quantity	10^3 kcal
Inputs		
Human hours[b]	20 h	—
Electricity	2234 kWh[c]	5,822[d]
Cement foundation[e] (30-yr life)	0.9 kg[c]	2[f]
Steel (gas collector[e] and other equipment with 30-yr life)	35 kg[c]	725[g]
Pumps and motors[h]	0.05 kg[c]	1[g]
Steel truck/tractor[b] for transportation (10-yr life)	10 kg[c]	200[g]
Petroleum for transport[b] (10 km radius)	34 liters[c]	340[i]
TOTAL		7,090
TOTAL OUTPUT		10,200

Notes: [a]The retention time in the digester is 20 days. The unit has the capacity to process 1,825 tons (wet) per year. The yield in biogas from 100 tons of manure (wet) is estimated at 10.2 million kcal. Thus, the net yield is 3.1 million kcal (Pimentel et al., 1978). The energy for heating the digester is cogenerated, coming from the cooling system of the electric generator.
[b]Estimated.
[c]Vergara et al. (unpublished data).
[d]1 kWh = 860 kcal. Based on an energy conversion of fuel to electricity of 33 percent; thus, 1 kWh is equivalent to 2,606 kcal.
[e]The digester was placed underground. Materials used for its construction were concrete and steel. Materials also included a gas storage tank.
[f]1 kg of cement = 2,000 kcal for production and transport (Lewis, 1976).
[g]1 kg of steel = 20,700 kcal for mining, production, and transport (Pimentel et al., 1973).
[h]The design included 3 electrical devices: a motor to drive the agitator in the digester, a compressor to store gas, and a pump to supply hot water.
[i]A liter of fuel is assumed to contain 10,000 kcal. Included in this figure are mining, refining, and transportation costs.
[j]It was assumed that anaerobic digestion of manure takes place at 35°C, with a solids retention time of 20 days. The temperature of the fresh manure is taken as 18°C and the average ambient temperature as 13°C. The manure is assumed to have the following characteristics: production per cow per day, 23.6 kg total; solids, 3.36 kg; biological oxygen demand (BOD), 0.68 kg. The digestion is assumed to transform 83 percent of the biodegradable material into gas. Gas produced is said to be 65 percent methane, and its heat of combustion is 5,720 kcal/m³ at standard conditions.

million kcal; the process itself requires 7.1 million kcal energy, so the net energy yield is 3.1 million kcal (Table 18.12). Much of the energy cost comes from the production of electricity to run the pumps and the stirring system used to reduce the retention time in the digester. The volume of the digester is determined by the amount of manure produced by the animals during the usual retention time. In this example, with a retention time of 14 days, the volume would be slightly more than 75 m³. It is assumed that this added

Table 18.13　Energy inputs for an anaerobic digester for biogas production using 8 tons wet (1 ton dry) cow manure[ab]

	Quantity	kcal
Output from 1 ton biomass (dry) methane gas	143 m³	820,000[c]
Inputs for 1 ton biomass		7,140
Cement foundation (30-yr life)	0.07 kg[d]	140[e]
Steel (30-yr life)	0.33 kg	7,000[f]
Net return/ton dry biomass		812,860

[a]The retention time is 20 days without a means of storing the methane gas (Pimentel, unpublished data).
[b]Efficiency = (812,840 kcal output)/(4.7 × 10⁶ kcal input) × 100 = 17.3 percent. The input is the energy content of manure if burned.
[c]It was assumed that anaerobic digestion of biomass takes place at 35°C with a solids retention time of 20 days. The temperature of the fresh biomass and the average ambient temperature are taken as 21°C. The efficiency of the digester is 25 percent. Gas produced is said to be 65 percent methane, and its heat of combustion is 5,720 kcal/m³.
[d]Vergara et al. (unpublished data).
[e]1 kg of cement = 2,000 kcal for production and transport (Lewis, 1976).
[f]1 kg of steel = 21,000 kcal for mining, production, and transport (Pimentel et al., 1973).

electric energy will be generated from the biogas itself and that the conversion efficiency of this operation is 33 percent. The energy needed to heat the digester is cogenerated by the electric generator via the use of the generator's cooling system. The net energy produced by the digester can be used either to generate electricity for the farm or as a heat source.

When the biogas is not used to produce electricity, the energy data listed in Table 18.12 will change considerably, and other costs will be associated with the changes. The heat requirements were calculated by including the heat losses to the surroundings, the heat associated with the feed and the effluents, and the heat generated by the biological reaction. Processing biogas for use in engines involves significant amounts of added energy for compression and for removal of hydrogen sulfide and water.

Although material costs are lowered if there is no generator or stirring mechanism on the digester, the size of the digester must be increased because the retention time increases. Also, more of the biogas will have to be used to heat during the extended retention time, as much as 610,000 kcal for every 100 tons of wet manure digested (Vergara et al., 1977). In the tropics the overall efficiency of biogas systems is enhanced because the system does not have to be heated.

Dairy cattle are not the only source of manure for biogas systems. They are used as a model because they are more likely to be located in a centralized system, making the process of collecting the manure less time-consuming and energy-intensive than for range-fed steers or even for draft animals. Efficiencies of conversion vary not only from system to system but also from animal to animal (Stafford, 1983). Swine and beef cattle manure appear to yield more gas per kg of volatile solids than dairy cattle manure. Poultry manure is also a good source, but sand and other forms of heavy grit in their dung cause pump maintenance problems.

Manure that exits the digester retains its fertilizer value and has less odor than undigested manure. It can be spread on fields in the usual way and may be easier to pump if a cutter pump is used to break up stray bits of straw or long undigested fibers. Biogas systems can easily be adapted in size according to the scale of the farm operation. However, the pollution problem associated with manure produced in centralized dairy production systems remains.

Biogas for Small Landholders

The costs and benefits of biogas production in a rural area of a developing nation such as Kenya or India are mixed. The capital costs of constructing a simple biogas digester with a capacity to process 8 tons (wet) of manure per 20-day retention period, or 400 kg per day (Table 18.13), are estimated to be $2000 to $2500. Because the unit would have a life of 30 years, the capital cost would be about $80 per year. If rural workers were to construct the generator themselves, material costs might range from $300 to $600. If we assume $400, the capital investment would be only $14 per year for the life of the digester.

A digester this size in India, where the cows are much smaller and produce only 225 to 330 kg manure each per 20 days, would require access to 20 cows. With a conversion rate of 25 percent (Table 18.13) this amount of manure would produce an estimated 2277 m^3 of biogas per year with an energy value of 13.0 million kcal. Assuming $8.38/million kcal, the value of this much energy would be $109. If no charge is incurred for labor and dung, and the capital cost is only $14 per year, the annual net saving is $95.

Although the labor requirement for running the generator described is only 5 to 10 minutes per day, the labor input for collecting and transporting biomass for the generator may be significant. For instance, if the required 400 kg of manure had to be transported an average of 3 km, it would take two laborers a full 8-hour day to collect it, feed it into the digester, and return it to the fields where it could be utilized as a fertilizer. The laborers would have to work for about $0.03 per hour to keep labor costs equal to the value of the gas produced. However, in densely populated areas or with centralized systems, the amount of transport would be minimal.

Although the profitability of small-scale biogas production may be low even without labor costs, digesters have advantages, especially in rural areas. Manure biomass can be processed and fuel energy can be obtained without loss of the valuable nutrients (nitrogen, phosphorus, potassium, and sulfur). Nitrogen and phosphorus are major limiting nutrients in tropical agriculture. The only change in the manure is the breakdown of its fibrous material, making it less effective in controlling soil erosion (Pimentel, 1980). By contrast, when manure is burned directly as a fuel, nitrogen and other valuable nutrients are lost to the atmosphere. The biogas slurry from the U.S. cattle example (146 tons/yr) contains approximately 3.7 tons of nitrogen. This has an energy value of 77 million kcal and, as chemical fertilizer, a market value of $1960 ($0.53/kg) (USDA, 1991). Therefore, producing biogas is more cost effective than burning manure. When the value of the retained nitrogen and the gas output are combined, the return of the system is about $6.42 per hour of work.

Another consideration in assessing the use of biogas production is the possibility of replacing firewood with biogas as an energy resource. The production of 2277 m^3 of biogas (13.0 million kcal) would replace 3 tons of firewood, which has an average energy value of 4500 kcal/kg (NAS, 1980). Because gas is more efficient than wood for cooking (heating), the amount of wood replaced could double. In areas where wood is scarce, biogas could diminish reliance on wood and slow deforestation.

Socioeconomic Factors

Promoters of biomass energy emphasize its benefits to society, the economy, and the environment (Hall et al., 1985; Sourie and Killen, 1986). These include the creation of jobs, increased economic development, reduction in energy cost, debt reduction, and the use of indigenous technology. In this section we attempt to make a detailed analysis of the socioeconomic benefits and costs of the Brazilian alcohol fuels program, which is frequently cited as demonstrating the benefits of biomass energy. In addition, some data are presented on the socioeconomic impact of biomass energy use in the United States.

Brazil

The Brazilian alcohol program, PROALCOOL, is held up as a model of how developing countries can meet their fuel oil needs using renewable biomass resources such as sugarcane. Alcohol production appeared to be an elegant solution to many problems faced by developing countries in the early 1970s. Substituting a homegrown energy resource for costly imported fuel made sense. Sugarcane had been cropped in Brazil since the earliest days of colonization, and Brazilians had conducted research on alcohol production from sugar. Because the concept sounded so sensible and the press coverage was so good, PROALCOOL moved ahead rapidly with little or no criticism.

Analyzing the socioeconomics of Brazilian alcohol production is complicated. Not only must the relationship between the price and elasticity of demand for sugar, alcohol, and gasoline be carefully examined, but this must be done within the context of often rapid inflation and with the limited data provided by the Brazilian government. Although a total analysis is needed, this assessment focuses on the costs of alcohol production in Brazil and the known effects of alcohol production on food prices, food availability, and employment.

By all accounts appearing in the literature, the costs of alcohol production are higher than the price Petrobras charges retailers for alcohol (Ortmaier, 1981). Thus, the Brazilian government must subsidize to make up the difference. Of course, pricing depends on the world prices for sugar and gasoline at any given time. The Ministry of Industry and Commerce published the statement that 56 percent of the cost of alcohol production was assigned to the purchase of sugarcane, resulting in a production cost of $0.33 per liter (Pimentel et al., 1988).

The high cost of production necessitated government subsidies for alcohol producers. According to Nastari (1983), from 1976 to 1980 subsidies reached 61 billion cruzeiros, or about $490 million per year. Alcohol producers increased their gross income by more than 200 percent in this same time period (Nastari, 1983). Although the large subsidies contribute significantly to the Brazilian debt, ethanol production helps the government reduce the amount of foreign exchange expended to import oil. Brazil imports about 39 million liters, or $9 billion worth, of oil annually and has to pay an interest rate of about 4.7 percent per annum on all borrowed money (World Development Report, 1995). Thus, the production of 9.1 liters of ethanol helps reduce the amount of oil imported and, in turn, the level of costly borrowing.

However, 1 liter of ethanol does not equate to 1 liter of imported oil. About 0.5 liter of oil equivalent has to be imported to produce 1 liter of ethanol.

A fundamental economic issue generated by the PROALCOOL program is the relationship among alcohol production and the price and the availability of food. This matter is usually discussed only in terms of the relative proportion of land devoted to energy crops and food crops. The question is particularly complicated in a country such as Brazil, which has abundant cropland and the capacity to provide far more food than its population can consume. Despite the availability of this cropland, 25 percent of Brazil's population is malnourished (Calle and Hall, 1987).

Many factors determine the price and availability of foods, but supply and demand are the primary ones. From 1971 to 1980 an increasing percentage of land was planted to sugarcane and export crops, including soybeans, whereas the percentage of land in food crops remained constant from 1976 to 1980 (Table 18.14). Between 1973 and 1980 black bean production declined by 16 percent, and sweet potato production declined 56 percent (OECD, 1984). From 1976 to 1981, the total area planted for three basic staple crops—maize, rice, and black beans—remained stable at about 1.9 million ha (Pluijm, 1982). During this period the Brazilian population increased by about 15 million people (PRB, 1977), increasing food demand about 12 percent.

Table 18.14   Trends in areas under sugarcane and other crops in Brazil from 1971 to 1980[a]

	1971–1973	1975	1976	1977	1978	1979	1980
Alcohol production (10^6 liters)[b]	654	556	664	1,470	2,491	3,396	3,786
Area under sugarcane (10^3 ha)	1,830	1,969	2,093	2,270	2,391	2,537	2,607
Soybeans (10^3 ha)	2,507	5,824	6,417	7,070	7,782	8,256	8,766
Food crops (10^3 ha)[c]	24,659	25,837	28,036	28,270	26,922	27,542	28,030
Export crops (10^3 ha)[d]	12,951	15,566	14,526	16,730	17,789	18,408	18,949
Total cultivated area (10^6 ha)	37.3	42.0	43.3	45.7	45.5	46.8	47.9

Notes: [a]OECD (1984).
[b]Production from May of the year concerned until April of the following year.
[c]Rice, potatoes, beans, manioc, maize, wheat, bananas, onions.
[d]Cotton, groundnuts, cocao, sissal, coffee.

In Sao Paulo state, where 70 percent of the alcohol is produced, significant changes have taken place in agriculture since the start of the PROAL-COOL program. Sugarcane production increased by 1.1 million ha from 1968/69 to 1982/83, whereas acreage planted in food crops declined by 0.4 million ha during the same period (excluding soybeans that are exported) (Calle and Hall, 1987). About 60 percent of the expansion in sugarcane acreage came from reclaimed pastureland, adversely affecting milk and meat supplies. In this same period, export crop acreage increased by 0.2 million ha, further diminishing acreage used for domestic food crop and milk/meat production (Calle and Hall, 1987).

The stagnant levels of food production in Brazil overall and growing food demand has led to reduced availability and high prices of food (La Rovere, 1985). In 1976 riots broke out in Rio de Janeiro over a shortage of the local staple, black beans, coupled with general political and economic unrest (Goldemberg, 1987). The decline in black bean availability led to the importation of black beans from Chile. The cycle continued, with increases in alcohol production and export crops, accompanied by a decline in per capita output of major staple food crops. At the same time, food prices increased more than the general inflation rate, an occurrence without precedent in Brazil's economic history (La Rovere, 1985).

An additional incentive to produce sugarcane and alcohol was provided by the rapidly escalating value of land located near distilleries. Land prices in Brazil for producing sugarcane rose to about $1500 per ha (Ghirardi, 1983). With the income of the Brazilian laborer estimated to be about $1000 per year, it would take a laborer many years to save sufficient money to purchase even 1 ha of land. Increased land values also encouraged smallholders, who usually grow food crops for domestic consumption, to sell their land to large sugarcane growers, thereby expanding the land area devoted to sugarcane (Pluijm, 1982). Because most distilleries are located close to towns and urban centers, basic food production has moved farther away from food consumers, increasing the energy costs of transport and contributing to higher food prices.

The workplace and wages were also affected by the PROALCOOL program. Landless agricultural workers who live on the periphery of cities accept almost any job they can find, often being trucked to rural areas each day to work in the fields (Desai et al., 1980; Burbach and Flynn, 1980). Thousands of small farmers were transformed into landless laborers during a period in which food production for the domestic market was stable. Small farmers provide the bulk of their own subsistence. The displacement of small subsistence farmers meant food production for domestic consumption would have to increase to enable these workers to eat as they once did. This did not occur. Instead, about 40 percent of the Brazilian labor force now earns a minimum wage of about $100/month, or about $0.63/hour. Basic foods per month for a family cost 3 times this wage (World Tables, 1995).

Another aspect of the food-versus-fuel question is employment. According to Ortmaier (1981) 51 percent of the land converted to sugarcane in 1975 previously had been planted to food crops. Whenever sugarcane production replaced a more labor-intensive crop or a crop providing year-round employment, a net loss of jobs resulted.

Typically, sugarcane/alcohol production work is highly seasonal, resulting in at least 50 percent unemployment among sugar and alcohol workers during the 4-month off-season (OECD, 1984). Only when sugarcane production is accompanied by diversified agricultural production can people find steady work. This is not the usual practice.

Projections concerning the creation of jobs because of the ethanol program were encouraging. The World Bank (1980) reported that 1 new job would be created for each 20,000 liters of alcohol produced and that 172,000 new jobs would be created if alcohol production was increased by about 7 billion liters. A similar trend was suggested by Pereira (1983). OECD (1984) projected that 27,700 jobs would be created if the increased production was from large alcohol plants (production of up to 120,000 liters of alcohol per day). However, other analysts reported that the overall increase in employment was not as great as anticipated, with far fewer jobs created than either the World Bank or the Brazilian government projected (OECD, 1984).

Obviously, the 25 percent of the people who are malnourished (Calle and Hall, 1987) and the 40 percent who are unemployed have not benefited from the Brazilian alcohol program. Their plight contrasts sharply with the 10 percent of the people who own cars and have benefited from low fuel costs of the subsidized ethanol program (Kurian, 1995).

United States

Although biomass production in the United States has certain problems (Pimentel, 1991), it will provide at least one advantage—some increased employment. For example, the direct labor inputs for wood biomass resources are 2 to 30 times greater per million kcal energy produced than for coal (Pimentel et al., 1983a); thus, wages would be lower for workers in biomass production. A wood-fired steam plant requires 2 to 5 times more construction workers and 3 to 7 times more workers per plant. Total employment overall would be expected to increase from 5 to 20 percent depending on the quantities of biomass used and general economy of the nation.

However, a shift to more biomass energy production can be expected to increase occupational hazards in the industry (Morris, 1981). Significantly more occupational injuries and illnesses are associated with biomass production in agriculture and forestry than with either coal (underground mining), oil, or gas recovery operations (OTA, 1980b). Agriculture has the highest rate of injuries—25 percent more injuries per day of work than any other private industry (OTA, 1980b). The total injury rate in logging and other forest industries annually averages about 25 per 100 full-time workers, whereas it is about 11 for bituminous coal miners, who work mostly underground (BLS, 1978, 1979, 1980, 1981). Per kilocalorie output, forest biomass production has 14 times more occupational injuries and illnesses than underground coal mining and 28 times more than oil and gas extraction (BLS, 1978).

Food and lumber products have a higher economic value per kcal in their original form than when converted into either heat, liquid, or gaseous energy (ERAB, 1980, 1981; OTA, 1980b). For example, 1 million kcal of corn grain has a market value of $40, but when converted to heat energy it has a value of only $5. Producing liquid fuels (e.g., ethanol) is also expensive. A liter of ethanol now costs about $0.40 to produce; nearly 65 percent of the cost of production is for the grain itself (Pimentel et al., 1991).

Subsidies help make gasohol competitive with gasoline. Federal and state subsidies may range as high as $0.36 per liter for U.S. ethanol (OTA, 1980b). As a result, when production and subsidies are included, a liter of ethanol costs $0.83, compared with the $0.15 cost of a liter of gasoline at the refinery (Pimentel, 1991). For the equivalent of 1 liter of gasoline (8000 kcal), 1.5 liters of ethanol (5310 kcal/liter) would be needed, with a total value of $1.25.

The real cost to the consumer is greater than the $0.83 needed to produce a liter of ethanol because 50 percent of all grain consumed in the United States is fed to livestock (WRI, 1994). Therefore, shunting corn grain into ethanol will increase the demand for grains, resulting in higher grain prices. Higher grain prices will in turn raise the consumer prices of meat, milk, and eggs (ERAB, 1980).

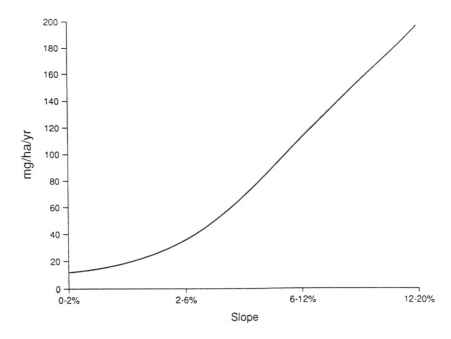

18.1   Increased soil erosion rates (mg/ha/yr) associated with rising land slope percentages.

Environmental Impacts

The removal of biomass from land for energy production increases the effects of wind and water on soil degradation. Erosion and increased water pollution and flooding disrupt many wildlife communities and may adversely affect the health of some human populations.

Soil Erosion Problems in Biomass Systems

It is difficult to derive biomass for energy use from crops such as corn, sugarcane, wheat, and rape grown on sloping land that is unsatisfactory for agriculture (Figure 18.1). High erosion rates for these crops occur even when biomass residues are left on the land (Table 18.15). If these crop residues are harvested for fuel, the erosion rates increase (Pimentel et al., 1981). For example, leaving 6.7 tons/ha of corn residues on land will keep erosion rates at 1 to 1.6 tons/ha when no-till planting is employed. However, if 4 to 5 tons/ha of residues are removed, soil loss increases about 8 times (Table 18.16). This latter erosion rate is about 14 times greater than the soil re-formation rate

Table 18.15   Selected erosion rates in certain geographical regions

Country	Erosion rate (tons/ha/yr)	Comments	Sources
United States	13[a]	Average, all cropland	USDA (1994)
Midwest, deep loess hills (Iowa and Missouri)	35.6[a]	MLRA[b] # 107, 2.2 million ha	Lee (1984)
Southern high plains (Kansas, New Mexico, Oklahoma, and Texas)	51.5[a]	Lee (1984) MLRA[b] # 77, 6.2 million ha	
Brazil	150	Beans grown up and down slope	Silva et al (1985)
	12	Beans grown with agroforestry	
India	25–30	Cultivated land[c]	DST (1980)
	28–31	Cultivated land	Narayana and Babu (1983), CSE (1982)
Deccan black soil region	40–100		
China	43	Average, all cultivated land middle reaches, cultivated rolling loess	Brown and Wolf (1984)
Yellow River Basin	100	Brantas river basin	AAC (1980)
Java	43.4		Brabben (1981)
Belgium	10–25	Central Belgium, agricultural loess soils	Bollinne (1982; in Richter, 1983)
East Germany	13	1,000-year average, cultivated loess soils in one region	Hempel (1951, 1954; in Zachar, 1982)
Ethiopia	20	Simien Mountains, Gondor region	Lamb and Milas (1983)
Madagascar	25–40	Nationwide average	Randrianarijaona (1983); Finn (1983)
Nigeria	14.4	Imo region, includes uncultivated land	Osuji (1984)
El Salvador	19–190	Acelhuate basin, land under basic grains production	Wiggins (1981)
Guatemala	200–3,600	Corn production in mountain region	Arledge (1980)
Thailand	21	Chao River basin	El-Swaify et al. (1982)
Burma	139	Irrawaddy River basin	El-Swaify et al. (1982)
Venezuela and Colombia	18	Orinoco River basin	El-Swaify et al. (1982)

Notes: [a]Indicates combined wind and water erosion, all others are water erosion only.
[b]MLRA: Major Land Resource Area.
[c]Assumes that 60 to 70 percent of the 6 million tons of topsoil lost is from cultivated land.

(Pimentel et al., 1987). The production of forage and hay crops for energy is possible on land with slopes of up to 12 percent, provided that care is taken to maintain a dense stand of vegetation cover and that good management practices are employed in the harvesting of biomass (ERAB, 1981). Unless steps are taken to protect soil, the removal of crop residues from slopes of 2 percent or greater would seriously degrade soil resources.

Table 18.16   Percentage of soil loss from several conservation tillage systems compared with conventional tillage on land with continuous corn culture[a]

	Surface residue after planting				
Tillage system	1.1–2.2 tons/ha	2.2–3.4 tons/ha	3.4–4.5 tons/ha	4.5–6.7 tons/ha	Over 6.7 tons/ha
Till planting (chisel, disk)	89 percent	61 percent	48 percent	33 percent	20 percent
No till	71 percent	48 percent	33 percent	18 percent	8 percent

Note: [a]Continuous corn with conventional tillage on land with a slope of 2 percent or more will suffer about 20 tons/ha/yr soil erosion.
Source: Data from Mannering (1984).

Soil erosion rates of undisturbed forests, with their dense soil cover of leaves, twigs, and other organic material, typically range from less than 0.1 to 0.2 tons/ha/yr (Megahan, 1972, 1975; Dissmeyer, 1976; Patric, 1976; USFS, 1977; Yoho, 1980; Patric et al., 1984). These conditions make most natural forest soils, even those on steep slopes of 70 percent, fairly resistant to erosion and rapid water runoff.

Forests lose significant quantities of water, soil, and nutrients when the trees are cut and harvested. For instance, the surface runoff after a storm from a forested watershed averages 2.7 percent of the precipitation; after forest cutting and/or farming, water runoff rises to 4.5 percent (Dils, 1953). Clear-cutting of trees without harvest and without soil disturbance causes flood damage from high stream flow to occur 10 percent more often than with the normal forest stand (Hewlett, 1979). Replacing natural forest growth with coppice forest regrowth increases annual stream flow about 10 cm above normal (Swank and Douglass, 1977). Nitrogen leached after forest removal may be 6 to 9 times greater than in forests with normal cover (Hornbeck et al., 1973; Patric, 1980).

In any area, harvesting timber and pulpwood greatly increases erosion, because covered land becomes exposed and the clearing process disturbs the soil. Typically, tractor roads and skid trails severely disturb 20 to 30 percent of the soil surface (Megahan, 1975; Froelich, 1978). Harvesting techniques such as highland and skyline disturb 10 to 20 percent, whereas balloon harvesting disturbs only about 6 percent of the land area (Rice et al., 1972; Swanston and Dyrness, 1973). Further, the heavy equipment used compacts the soil, causing increased water runoff.

For example, compaction by tractor skidders harvesting ponderosa pine reduce growth in pine seedlings from 6 to 12 percent over a 16-year period (Froelich, 1979). Water percolation in wheel-rutted soils is significantly reduced for as long as 12 years and in log-skid trails for 8 years (Dickerson, 1976). This creates a long-range problem, because lack of water is the major limiting factor in forest biomass production. Growth of slash pine in Florida over a 5-year period with irrigated treatment is 80 percent greater than in the untreated acreage (Baker, 1973). Depending on slope, soil type, and climate, the effects of soil compaction on tree growth may last from 8 to 16 years (Dickerson, 1976; Froelich, 1979).

Though erosion rates can be as high as 215 tons/ha/yr on severely disturbed slopes, average soil erosion in harvested forests ranges from 2 to 17 tons/ha/yr, with long-term averages between 2 and 4 tons/ha/yr (USFS, 1977; Yoho, 1980; Patric, 1976; McCashion and Rice, 1983). Erosion from conventional logging can last for 20 years, but the most serious erosion ceases in about 5 years, when vegetation cover becomes established (Patric, 1976; McCashion and Rice, 1983). Although erosion caused by forest harvesting is not great compared to that associated with row crop production, its effects can be long-lasting because of the extremely slow rate of soil formation in forest ecosystems. The nutrients lost when topsoil is eroded also affect forest growth. Loosing 3 cm of soil surface reduces biomass production in ponderosa pine, Douglas fir, and lodgepole pine seedlings as much as 5-fold (Klock, 1982).

As the need to produce more biomass for energy becomes critical in countries such as Brazil, more land will have to be placed under cultivation to supply it. If this additional land is taken from food crop acreage, farmers may be forced to clear forests or use poor-quality cropland in an effort to maintain or augment the level of food production to feed the expanding human population. Utilization of poor-quality land for crops only will further intensify soil erosion rates. Often these marginal lands are on slopes, making them highly susceptible to erosion when planted to crops.

Nutrient Losses and Water Pollution Associated with Biomass Energy and Erosion

Rapid water runoff and soil nutrient losses occur when crop residues are harvested and subsequent rainfall erodes soils. Water quickly runs off unprotected soil because raindrops free small soil particles, which in turn clog holes in the soil and further reduce water infiltration (Scott, 1985). For example, conventional corn production causes an average of about 5 cm/ha/yr more water runoff than production employing conservation practices (Pimentel and Krummel, 1987). Harrold et al. (1967) reported that under conventional corn production, erosion reduced soil moisture volume by about 50 percent compared with no-till corn culture. Rapid water runoff not only diminishes the amount of water reaching plant roots, it also carries valuable nutrients, organic matter, and sediments with it. Soil nutrient losses have a major negative effect on soil quality. One ton of fertile agricultural soil contains about 4 kg of nitrogen, 1 kg of phosphorus, and 20 kg of potassium (Buttler, 1986). Based on these soil nutrient values and average U.S. erosion rate of 18 tons/ha/yr, erosion causes an average yearly loss of about 72 kg/ha of nitrogen, 18 kg/ha of phosphorus, and 360 kg/ha of potassium.

When conservation technologies are employed by protecting the soil with residues and vegetation, increased crop yields result because water, nutrients, and soil organic matter are retained. For example, in Texas, yields of cotton grown on the contour and with ample soil protection are 25 percent greater than from cotton grown with the slope (Burnett and Fisher, 1954). Similar results have been reported for corn (12.5 percent) in Missouri (Smith, 1946) and for corn (12 percent), soybeans (13 percent) and wheat (17 percent) in Illinois experiments (Sauer and Case, 1954). On land with a 7 percent slope, yields from cotton grown in rotation increase 30%, and erosion is cut nearly in half (Hendrickson et al., 1963). In Nigeria, yields from no-till corn grown under favorable soil and climatic conditions are 61 percent greater than from corn grown with conventional tillage (Wijewardene and Waidyanatha, 1984). In an experiment comparing tillage practices used on 22 consecutive maize crops grown on highly erodible Nigerian soils, the average grain yields from no-till plots were 20 percent higher than those from conventional plots because of the accumulated effects of erosion-induced degradation of the unprotected soil (Lal, 1983).

When crop residues are removed and burned, significant quantities of nutrients are lost. On average, residues contain about 1 percent nitrogen, 0.2

percent phosphorus, and 1.2 percent potassium (Table 18.17). When burned, the nitrogen volatilizes into the atmosphere, and 70 to 80 percent of the phosphorus and potassium is lost with the particulate matter during the process (Flaim and Urban, 1980). Thus, a relatively small percentage of the nutrients in crop residues would be conserved, even if the ash residue were returned to the cropland.

Table 18.17 Nitrogen, phosphorus, and potassium content of crop residues and firewood

	Nutrient content (percent)		
	Nitrogen	**Phosphorus**	**Potassium**
Corn[a]	1.1	0.2	1.3
Rice[a]	0.6	0.1	1.2
Wheat[a]	0.7	0.1	1.0
Soybean[a]	2.3	0.2	1.0
Sugarcane[a]	1.0	0.3	1.4
Firewood[b]	0.12	0.01	0.06

Notes: [a]Power and Papendick (1985).
[b]Pimentel et al. (1983b).

Air Pollution

The smoke produced when firewood and crop residues are burned for energy contains nitrogen, particulates, and other chemicals, making it a serious pollution hazard. A recent EPA report (1986) indicated that although burning wood provides only about 2 percent of U.S. heating energy, it causes about 15 percent of the air pollution in the United States. Emissions from wood and crop residue burning are a threat to public health because of the highly respirable nature of some of the 100 chemicals the emissions contain (Pimentel et al., 1983a). Of special concern are the relatively high concentrations of potentially carcinogenic polycyclic organic compounds (POMs, e.g., benzo(a)pyrene) and particulates. Sulfur and nitrogen oxides, carbon monoxide, and aldehydes are also released, but usually in smaller quantities (DOE, 1981; Morris, 1981). According to the Department of Energy (1980), wood smoke contains "up to 14 carcinogens, 4 co-carcinogens, and 6 cilia toxic and mucus coagulating agents." Concern is being expressed for people in developing nations who cook indoors, breathing in the smoke released by burning wood, dung, and crop residues.

The concerns of inhaling wood smoke have been particularly great in India, where people commonly cook in inefficient stoves known as *chullahs* without venting the smoke from the house. Wood smoke, as mentioned, contains many dangerous chemicals, including carbon monoxide, which has been associated with poor fetal development and heart disease in Indian women (Sharma, 1987). Sharma (1987) also reported that women are routinely exposed to chemicals and suspended particulate matter levels as much as 10 times higher than safe public health levels.

Air particulates increase when dung is used in addition to or in place of wood as a fuel (CSE, 1985). However, biogas can be a healthier energy option for cooking than dung. In India, 1000 to 1050 million tons (Mt) of wet dung is available from 237 million cattle for recycling into biogas. The 206 Mt/yr of manure slurry provides about 1.4 Mt of nitrogen, 1.3 Mt of phosphate, and 0.9 Mt of potash for the soil (Khoshoo, 1986). As of 1992 approximately 1.4 million biogas plants were operational in India; their use predicted to save 1.2 million tons of wood equivalent each year (Sinha, 1992).

Methanol and ethanol are also proposed as cooking-fuel options. These are liquid fuels, made from wood or crops such as sugarcane and cassava, but the short supply of these crops makes the process expensive (CSE, 1985).

Offsite Environmental Effects from Biomass Harvesting and Erosion

Harvesting biomass and thereby intensifying erosion and water runoff causes several offsite environmental problems. For instance, water runoff in the United States is "delivering approximately 4 billion tons/year of sediment to waterways in the 48 contiguous states" (Pimentel, 1995). About 60 percent of these sediments come from fertile agricultural lands (Highfill and Kimberlin, 1977; Larson et al., 1983). These off-site effects cost an estimated $6 billion annually in the United States (Clark, 1985). Dredging several million cubic meters of sediments from U.S. rivers, harbors, and reservoirs is costly. An estimated 10 to 25 percent of new reservoir storage capacity in the United States is built solely to store sediments (Clark, 1985). These problems are universal. For example, in India the cost associated with low water flows and heavy siltation that have reduced the storage capacity of reservoirs was estimated to be about $427 million per year in 1980 (Myers, 1986b).

Soil sediments, particularly those containing pesticides and fertilizer nutrients, that are carried into rivers, lakes, and reservoirs from agricultural and forest lands adversely affect fish production (USDI, 1982). Sediments interfere with fish spawning, increase predation on fish, and frequently destroy fish food (NAS, 1982). These destructive effects reach into estuarines, coastal fisheries, and coral reefs (Alexander, 1979; Day and Grindley, 1981). In the United States the diverse effects of soil erosion on fish and other wildlife, as well as on water-storage facilities and waterway navigation, are estimated to cost $4.1 billion each year (Clark, 1985).

Conclusion

Reaching a sound balance between biomass-food and biomass-fuel production would bring additional economic benefits, despite the fact that food is given higher priority by society and has higher price values than biomass fuels. When governments subsidize biomass fuel production—as in Brazil and the United States with ethanol programs based on sugarcane and corn grain, respectively—a few producers may make enormous profits. In Brazil, revenues to sugarcane growers increased 200 percent with the ethanol program (Nastari, 1983). However, the heavy subsidization of biomass fuel tends to give higher priority to biomass fuel rather than food. The result is often reduced food production and higher food prices. Food shortages and high food prices have many negative effects for society, including poor child nutrition. The poor commonly suffer the most when food costs rise. Without sound soil and water conservation policies, subsidizing biomass fuel can result in poorer management of important soil, water, and biological resources (ERAB, 1981).

Other societal effects from biomass fuels programs include reducing the standard of living of the labor force, as happened in Brazil (Pluijm, 1982; OECD, 1984). In addition, the occupational risks in the labor force increase when biomass fuels are given priority over fossil fuels (Pimentel et al., 1984b).

19

ETHANOL FUELS: ENERGY, ECONOMICS, AND THE ENVIRONMENT

David Pimentel

Numerous reports have concluded that ethanol production does not provide energy security, is not a renewable energy source, is uneconomical, and causes environmental degradation (ERAB, 1980, 1981; USDA, 1986; Dovring, 1988; Pimentel et al., 1988; Walls et al., 1989; Kane et al., 1989; Sparks Commodities, 1990). Related to these findings, a recent report by the U.S. General Accounting Office (GAO, 1990) analyzed projected tax costs and federal farm program expenditures associated with increased ethanol production. The GAO report concluded that: 1) increasing ethanol production would greatly increase tax-subsidy expenditures; 2) no net federal budget savings would result from increased ethanol production; and 3) the uncertainties about production economics for both ethanol and gasoline precluded any estimate of overall budget impacts (GAO, 1990, p. 25; Pimentel, 1991b). Also, the report indicated that it was not possible to calculate how much higher the subsidies might have to be to encourage expansion of ethanol production.

Clearly, conclusions about the benefits and costs of ethanol production will be incomplete or misleading if only part of the system is assessed. The objective of this chapter is to evaluate *all* the factors that affect ethanol production. These include the direct energy and dollar costs of producing the corn feedstock, as well as the costs of fermentation and distillation. Additional expenses accrue from federal and state subsidies and from environmental degradation caused by the production system. Decisions about the practicality of ethanol production in the United States will effect the nation's energy security, agricultural system, economy, and environment, as well as government and consumer expenditures. Ethical questions involved in converting human food into fuel also deserve serious consideration.

Energy Balance

Ethanol production is energy inefficient, requiring considerably more energy input than is contained in the ethanol produced.

The conversion of corn and some other food/feed crops into ethanol by fermentation is a well-established technology. The yield from a bushel of corn in a large processing plant is about 2.5 gallons of ethanol.

Producing corn for fermentation requires significant energy and dollar inputs under U.S. agricultural systems. Indeed, growing corn is a major energy and dollar cost of producing ethanol (Tables 19.1 and 19.2). Producing an average of 110 bushels (bu) per acre of corn using conventional production technology requires about 137 gallons of gasoline equivalents (Table 19.1) and costs about $280 (USDA, 1989a; Pimentel, 1989). The main energy inputs in corn production are oil, natural gas, and/or other high-grade fuels. Fertilizers and mechanization costs account for about two-thirds of the energy inputs for corn production (Table 19.1). The 2.8 million Btu shown in Table 19.1 for partial irrigation represents a relatively small input. However, when corn is produced under complete irrigation, the energy input for irrigation is more than 3 times higher than the energy inputs used in producing rain-fed corn (Batty and Keller, 1980; Pimentel and Burgess, 1980). About 16 percent of U.S. corn is grown under irrigation (FEA, 1976; USDA, 1989a), as reflected in Table 19.1.

Once corn is harvested, 3 additional energy expenditures contribute to the total costs of the conversion process. These include transport of corn to the ethanol plant, energy expended for capital requirements, and plant operations (Table 19.2).

The average energy and dollar costs for a large (60 to 70 million gallons/year), modern ethanol plant are listed in Table 19.2. The largest energy inputs are for fuel used in corn production and the fermentation/distillation process. The total energy input to produce 1 gallon of ethanol is 131,017 Btu. However, 1 gallon of ethanol has an energy value of only 76,000 Btu. Thus, a net energy loss of 55,017 Btu occurs for each gallon of ethanol produced. Put another way, about 72 percent more energy is required to produce a gallon of ethanol than a gallon of ethanol yields (OTA, 1990; Pimentel, 1991b).

Table 19.1   Energy inputs for corn production in the United States

Inputs	Quantity/Acre[a]	Btu/Acre $\times 10^3$
Labor	4 hr	0
Machinery	50 lb	1,630
Gasoline	4.3 gallon	520
Diesel	8.0 gallon	1,080
Irrigation	2,840 $\times 10^3$ Btu	2,840
Electricity	14 kwh	144
Nitrogen	136 lb	5,107
Phosphorus	67 lb	757
Potassium	86 lb	384
Lime	380 lb	214
Seeds	19 lb	832
Insecticides	1 lb	160
Herbicides	3.6 lb	640
Drying	100 bu	1,970
Transport	280 lb	145
TOTAL		16,423

Note: [a]Corn yield = 110 bu/acre.
Source: Modified after Pimentel and Wen Dazhong, 1990.

About 53 percent of the cost of producing ethanol ($1.94/gallon) in a large plant is for the corn feedstock itself (Table 19.2). This cost is offset in part by the by-products produced, including dry distillers' grains (DDG) that are made from dry milling and can be fed to animals, primarily cattle (NAS, 1981). Wet-milling ethanol plants produce such products as corn gluten meal, gluten feed, and oil. Sales of the by-products offset the costs of ethanol production by an average of $0.50/gallon for dry milling and $0.61/gallon for wet milling (Walls et al., 1989). However, these by-products would most likely decline in price as they saturate the market. Moreover, the protein in ethanol by-products is expensive compared with alternate sources of protein, such as soybeans. The price of protein per pound in DDG for livestock feed ranges between $0.33 and $0.41, whereas soybean protein costs only $0.25 per pound (Glaze et al., 1982; USDA, 1993).

The energy credit for the dry distillers' grain fed to cattle ranges from 11,000 Btu/gallon (ERAB, 1980) to 32,000 Btu/gallon (based on protein value as livestock feed). Thus, the total energy inputs in Table 19.2 for producing ethanol can be partially offset by 11,000 to 32,000 Btu. The resulting

Table 19.2   Inputs per gallon of ethanol

Inputs	Pounds	Btu	Dollars ($)
Corn	22.4	56,720[a]	1.02[f]
Transport	22.4	610[b]	0.12
Stain, Steel	0.05[c]	1,348[c]	0.04
Steel	0.10[c]	2,106[c]	0.04
Cement	0.27[c]	909[c]	0.04
Plant, other	–	2,800[d]	0.28[g]
Water	1,279[c]	1,364[c]	0.08
Electricity	0.5 kWh[c]	5,160	0.05[h]
Fuel	–	60,000[e]	0.15[i]
Operating, other	–	–	0.12[j]
TOTAL		131,017	1.94

Notes: [a]Table 1.
[b]Estimated transport.
[c]Slesser and Lewis, 1979.
[d]Doering, 1980.
[e]ERAB, 1980; NAP, 1987.
[f]Bushel of corn = $2.55 (USDA, 1989a).
[g]Portion of capital costs based on $0.40/gallon (Walls et al., 1989).
[h]NAP, 1987.
[i]Using natural gas or fuel oil would raise this price to $0.35/gallon (NAP, 1987).
[j]Portion of operating costs based on $0.40/gallon (Walls et al., 1989).
[k]Output: 1 gallon of ethanol = 76,000 Btu.

energy input-output comparison, however, is still negative. Even when the energy in by-products is included, the energy output from ethanol production ranges from only 87,000 Btu to 108,000 Btu per gallon, compared with more than 131,000 Btu required for production.

Furthermore, most of the gains from by-products are negated by the environmental pollution costs, estimated to be $0.36/gallon (Pimentel, 1991b). U.S. corn production erodes soil about 18 times faster than it can be re-formed (Lal and Stewart, 1990). In irrigated acreage, groundwater is being mined 25 percent faster than the recharge rate (Pimentel et al., 1996). Thus, corn production rapidly degrades the agricultural environment. The U.S. corn production system is not sustainable for the future unless major changes can be made in the cultivation of this important food/feed crop. From a practical standpoint, corn used for ethanol production is not a renewable resource.

About 1 billion gallons of ethanol are produced in the United States each year (Shapouri et al., 1995). This amount of ethanol provides less than

1 percent of the fuel utilized by U.S. automobiles (USBC, 1994). Therefore, even if ethanol production from corn more than doubled, to 2 billion gallons, ethanol would supply less than 2 percent of U.S. automobile fuel.

When considering the advisability of producing ethanol for automobiles, a vital consideration is the amount of cropland required to grow the corn. The amount of cropland needed to fuel 1 automobile with ethanol for a year is calculated as follows. An average U.S. car travels about 10,000 miles/year and uses about 515 gallons of fuel (USBC, 1989). Although 110 bu/acre of corn yield 275 gallons of ethanol, the equivalent in gasoline energy is only 174 gallons because ethanol has a much lower Btu content than gasoline (76,000 Btu/gallon, versus 120,000 Btu/gallon for gasoline). As shown above, there is a significant net energy loss in producing ethanol. However, even assuming no energy charge for the fermentation and distillation process and charging only for the energy required to produce corn (Tables 19.1 and 19.2), the net fuel energy yield from 1 acre of corn is only 37 gallons (174 minus 137 gallons). To provide the 515 gallon/car/yr, about 14 acres of corn must be grown. In comparison, only 1.5 acres of cropland per year is currently used to feed each American (USDA, 1989a). Therefore, nearly 9 times more cropland would be required to fuel 1 car than is needed to feed 1 American. Assuming a net production of 37 gallons of fuel per acre, nearly 2 billion acres of cropland would be required to provide sufficient corn feedstock to fuel all cars in the United States with ethanol. This amount of acreage totals more than 4 times all the cropland that is actually and potentially available for all crops in the United States (USDA, 1993).

To produce the current figure of 850 million gallons of ethanol, about 3 million acres, or 5 percent, of U.S. corn land is devoted to ethanol (USDA, 1989a). If ethanol production were more than doubled to 2 billion gallons or tripled to 3 billion gallons, then the land required for feedstock would be 7.3 million acres (13 percent) or 10.9 million acres (19 percent), respectively. Possibly this added cropland could be obtained from cropland that is currently idle (USDA, 1989a). However, unused land is usually of marginal quality for crop production (Batie, 1983), and using it would increase both the cost of production and the costs associated with environmental degradation.

Increasing the use of marginal land also increases the susceptibility of the corn crop to climate fluctuations, particularly droughts. For example, during 1988 a drought reduced the corn crop by about 30 percent (USDA, 1989a).

Severe disruptions in corn production occur every 4 to 5 years, raising questions about the wisdom of relying on corn/ethanol to meet U.S. energy needs. When there is a shortage of corn due to a drought, the expected priority for corn would be for use as food and feed, both domestically and as exports.

Ethanol Economics

Ethanol costs substantially more to produce than it is worth in the market, and its production has been sustained by large government subsidies.

The data in Table 19.2 and numerous other studies confirm that the dominant cost (53 percent) in ethanol production is the price of the corn feedstock. In this analysis, a value of $2.55/bu of corn was used (USDA, 1989a). However on average, corn costs more than $3.00/bu to produce when the farmer's fair wage is included (USDA, 1989a; Garst, 1990). The fermentation/distillation costs are relatively small compared with that of the corn feedstock (Table 19.2).

Based on current production technology and recent oil prices, ethanol costs substantially more to produce than it is worth in the market (USBC, 1994). Without subsidies, U.S. ethanol production would be reduced or cease altogether for the simple reason that it is uneconomical (Pimentel et al., 1988). Federal subsidies average $0.60/gallon and state subsidies average $0.19/gallon (EPA, 1990). When a credit of $0.61/gallon is given for byproducts and the pollution costs of $0.36/gallon are subtracted, the total cost of a gallon of ethanol comes to $1.70. Then we account for the relatively low energy content of ethanol (1.5 gallons of ethanol contain as much energy as 1 gallon of gasoline), and the cost rises to $2.55/gallon. Gasoline costs significantly less to produce, about $0.60/gallon.

Federal and state subsidies for ethanol production total about $700 million per year (EPA, 1990). More than doubling ethanol production to 2 billion gallons would require $1.6 billion per year in subsidies. However, corn prices would also rise, and price supports for corn production would decrease. According to GAO (1990) data, more than doubling ethanol production would reduce federal price supports (subsidies) to farmers by about $930 million/year (or less if price supports decline faster or over a longer period of time than the GAO study assumed). Still, the taxpayers would have to pay federal and state subsidies for ethanol totaling about $700 million/year. Moreover, subsidies might have to be increased to encourage the expansion of ethanol production (GAO, 1990). This would be expected, because increased ethanol production will increase the price of the corn feedstock and other raw materials. Also, it should be noted that corn subsidies have declined during recent years and are projected to continue to decline (USDA, 1989a). Therefore, any reduction in price supports would probably not be as large as some models have projected.

Actually, the real costs to consumers would be greater than the conservative estimate of $700 million a year needed to subsidize ethanol production because of increased corn prices. Higher corn prices translate into higher meat, milk, and egg prices (Sparks Commodities, 1990) because about 70 percent of U.S. corn grain is fed to livestock (USDA, 1989a). Doubling ethanol production could be expected to inflate corn prices about 9 percent (GAO, 1990). Therefore consumers, in addition to paying tax dollars for ethanol subsidies, would be paying significantly higher food prices.

Environmental Impacts

Ethanol produced from corn causes environmental degradation from increased soil erosion and aquifer mining, from soil, water, and air pollution, and from increased emissions of global-warming gases.

Ethanol production, including corn cultivation and fermentation/distillation, adversely affects the quality of the environment in many ways. These environmental problems cost the consumer and the nation every year and, most important, diminish the sustainability of U.S. agriculture for the future.

Corn causes serious soil erosion in the United States. About 9 tons/acre of soil are eroded per year by rain and wind in corn production areas. (Follett and Stewart, 1985; NAS, 1989a; Paoletti et al., 1989b; Lal and Pierce, 1991). As mentioned, this rate of soil loss is 18 times faster than the rate of soil reformation (Lal and Stewart, 1990). Replacing even a portion of the nutrients and water lost to soil erosion requires large amounts of fertilizers and water. Troch et al. (1991) report that about $20 billion in fertilizer nutrients are lost in the United States each year.

If the corn ethanol program were to be expanded, more marginal land would have to be put into production. Such land is highly susceptible to soil erosion (Follett and Stewart, 1985), making it less productive than most other cropland. More fossil fuel–based inputs would be required. Overall, corn production on such land would be considerably more costly than corn production on highly productive land.

At present more than 16 percent of the U.S. corn crop is irrigated, which requires enormous amounts of energy for pumping water. About 20 percent of the total energy expended in U.S. agriculture is for irrigation (FEA, 1976). Producing an acre of corn using irrigation requires more than 3 times the energy than producing the same yield under rain-fed conditions (Batty and Keller, 1980; Pimentel and Burgess, 1980). Another major problem associated with irrigation is the overdraft of water from aquifers, which are being mined about 25 percent faster than they can be recharged (Pimentel et al., 1996). The current level of irrigation used on corn is contributing to the water overdraft problem and to other water quality problems, such as the salinization of land and rivers (NAS, 1989b).

In addition to using more fertilizer than any other crop, corn also uses the most insecticides and herbicides in the United States (USDA, 1989a). Substantial amounts of pesticides are washed from the target area and contaminate adjoining terrestrial and aquatic ecosystems (Pimentel and Levitan, 1986). Monitoring for fertilizer and pesticide pollution in U.S. well water and groundwater costs $2 billion per year ($1.2 billion just for pesticides) (Nielsen and Lee, 1987). Other environmental damage caused by pesticides is estimated to cost about $8 billion per year (Pimentel et al., 1992d). Although these may be necessary expenditures for food production, their impact must be considered when assessing the costs of producing alternate fuels.

As expected, major pollution problems also are associated with the production of ethanol in the chemical plant. Each gallon of ethanol produced using corn yields about 160 gallons of wastewater. This wastewater has a biological oxygen demand (BOD) of 18,000 to 37,000 mg/liter depending on the type of plant (Kuby et al., 1984). The cost of processing this sewage is not included in the pollution cost of $0.36/gallon; if included, it adds another $0.06/gallon to the cost (Pimentel et al., 1988).

Ethanol seriously pollutes the air. It does reduce carbon monoxide but increases NO_x, aldehydes, and alcohol pollutants. In addition, the 135,812 Btu of fossil fuels (including coal, oil, and natural gas) burned in corn production and in the ethanol plant release significant amounts of pollutants into the atmosphere. Also, the carbon dioxide emissions released from burning these fossil fuels contribute to global warming (Schneider, 1989). This becomes a very serious concern when coal is used as the fuel for the fermentation/distillation process. Overall pollution and its associated costs will increase if ethanol production is expanded.

Food Versus Fuel Issues

Ethanol produced from corn is not a renewable energy source. Its production adds to the depletion of agricultural resources and raises ethical questions at a time when food supplies must increase to meet the basic needs of the rapidly growing world population.

Burning a human food resource (corn) for fuel, as happens when ethanol is produced, raises important ethical and moral issues. Malnourished people worldwide number 1.6 billion, or about 30 percent of the world population (Kates et al., 1989). This number is larger than ever before in human history and is growing. Coupled with this problem is the escalating rate of human population growth. More than a quarter of a million people are added each day, and each of them requires adequate food.

Present food shortages throughout the world call attention to the importance of continuing U.S. exports of corn and other grains for food. In recent years U.S. corn grain exports have nearly doubled, increasing U.S. export trade by some $5.2 billion per year (USBC, 1989). Increased corn exports improve our balance of payments, and, more important, help feed people who face food shortages. Clearly, using corn for food serves ethical purposes not served by burning corn as ethanol.

Expanding ethanol production could entail diverting valuable cropland from production of corn needed to sustain human life. This would create serious practical and ethical problems. Already, per capita supplies of cropland and freshwater are declining worldwide (including in the United States), and soil erosion, deforestation, and food losses to pests are increasing. All these factors are contributing to food shortages throughout the world (Durning, 1989).

When all factors involved in ethanol production are evaluated, we must conclude that ethanol production from corn is unproductive and raises ethical questions about the use of valuable food resources. Certainly it is a very expensive and energy-inefficient way to produce motor fuel.

20

THE IMPACT OF ENERGY
USE ON THE ENVIRONMENT

D. Pimentel, M. Herdendorf, S. Eisenfeld, L. Olander,
M. Carroquino, C. Corson, J. McDade, Y. Chung, W. Cannon,
J. Roberts, L. Bluman, and J. Gregg

From the beginning, humans have sought control over their environment. The consequences of this long fight against nature have reached a critical stage: Far-reaching environmental degradation is commonplace throughout the world.

Excessive fossil energy use, overpopulation, and consumerism, place limited natural resources under stress and are causing serious environmental and economic problems in the United States and other nations (WRI, 1991; Worldwatch Institute, 1992a). Because the strength and sustainability of the nation's environmental and economic futures are already intertwined, the development of renewable, efficient energy sources has become essential to maintaining the quality of the environment.

Energy Use

The worldwide annual consumption of energy is presently 369 quads (369 × 10^{15} BTU, 390 × 10^{18} joules, or roughly the equivalent of 74 million barrels of oil) each year. Fossil fuels are the major source, supplying 319 quads, or 87 percent, of the total annual energy consumed worldwide (Table 20.1).

The United States, with only 4.7 percent of the global population, consumes about 25 percent of all the fossil fuel consumed in the world each year

Table 20.1   Fossil and solar energy use in the United States and the world

		United States[a]		World[bc]	
		Quads	**Percent**	**Quads**	**Percent**
Fossil energy		78.5	92.3	319.2	86.5
Solar energy		6.6	7.7	49.7	13.5
Hydropower		3.0	3.5	21.2	5.7
Biomass		3.6	4.2	28.5	7.8
	TOTAL	85.1	100	368.9	100

Notes: [a]DOE, 1991a.
[b]DOE, 1991b.
[c]UNEP, 1985.

(DOE, 1991a). The average American uses more than 2700 gallons of oil equivalents each year, or 5 times the amount used by an average world citizen.

The use of fossil fuels within the United States is divided into 6 different sectors. Two of them, the transportation and industry sectors, account for more than half of the total annual fossil fuel consumption in the United States. Within transportation, 19 quads per year (73 percent) are used for highway transportation (DOE, 1991a). This consumption is greater than the entire transportation expenditure for all of Western Europe, Canada, Japan, Australia, and New Zealand combined (IEA, 1989). Industry uses 25 percent of the total fossil fuel consumption in the production of fertilizers, pesticides, paints, and other toxic chemicals (IEA, 1989).

Each year the residential sector of the United States accounts for 20 percent of total U.S. fossil fuel consumption. Of this, more than half is for space heating (DOE, 1988, 1990a). The 2 other major uses are appliances (25 percent) and water heating (18 percent). The food, commercial, and military sectors account for 17, 10, and 2 percent, respectively, of total U.S. fossil fuel consumption.

Consumption of fossil energy for agricultural production is extremely high because intensive agricultural techniques are necessary to offset shortages and degradation of fertile land, water, and biological resources. On U.S. farms, about 3 kcal of fossil energy are needed to produce just 1 kcal of human food. This expenditure is similar for other industrialized nations. The question is, how long can such intensive agriculture be maintained in the industrialized nations, and how long can the rapidly growing use of fossil energy for agriculture and other purposes be sustained in developing nations? Between 1955 and the mid-1980s there was a 100-fold increase in the use of fossil energy for agriculture in China (Wen and Pimentel, 1984). As the world population escalates, how many 100-fold increases in fossil energy use are possible?

Energy Use and Environmental Degradation

Fossil energy has increased humans' ability to control nature and the environment. A rapidly growing world population is constantly increasing its consumption, and this has led to unprecedented environmental degradation. The major environmental consequences are global warming, ozone depletion, severe soil erosion, deforestation, loss of biodiversity, and increased production of solid and chemical wastes that pollute the entire ecosystem. All are related to the high consumption of fossil fuels.

Human Populations

The world population of 6 billion is expected to double by about 2040 (PRB, 1995). Overpopulation already has placed great stress upon the resources needed to support human survival. For example, about 1.6 billion people are malnourished (Kates et al., 1989), and from 1.2 to 2 billion are living in poverty, including the malnourished, people with heavy disease burdens, and those with shortened lives (Pimentel et al., 1996; V. Abernethy, Vanderbilt University, personal communication, 1992).

The United States has 260 million people, most of whom are consuming resources in an unsustainable manner. Land, groundwater, fossil energy, and biological resources are being depleted with no hope of renewal during the next century. The average standard of living for children in the United States declined during the 1980s and is projected to continue to decline (Fuchs and Reklis, 1992) because of wasteful habits and an ever-increasing population. Based on current rates of growth, the U.S. population will double by the year 2055 (USBC, 1992b).

Land

Rapid land degradation and loss caused by erosion and unsuitable agriculture threaten food security (Lal and Pierce, 1991; Pimentel, 1993). Agricultural land degradation can be expected to depress food production between 15 and 30 percent over the next 25-year period unless sound conservation practices are instituted now (Buringh, 1989).

Each year, because of land degradation (primarily erosion), about 15 million ha of new land must be found for agriculture (Pimentel et al., 1992a). About 10 million ha are needed to replace losses caused by land degradation, and an additional 5 million ha must be found to feed the 100 million people added yearly to the world population. This added agricultural land tends to come from the clearing of vast forest areas (Table 20.2). The spread of agriculture accounts for about 80 percent of the deforestation occurring worldwide (Myers, 1990). In turn, soil erosion and water pollution start another cycle of degradation and pollution in the environment.

Table 20.2   Land area (million ha) uses in major regions of the world

Region	Total area	Cropland	Pasture	Forest	Other [a]
Africa	2,965	184	792	688	1,301
North America	2,139	274	368	684	813
South America	1,753	140	468	905	240
Asia	2,679	450	678	541	1,010
Europe	473	140	84	157	92
TOTAL	10,009	1,188	2,390	2,975	3,456
	100 percent	12 percent	24 percent	30 percent	34 percent

Note: [a]Land that is either too dry, too steep, or too cold to use in agriculture and forestry.
Source: Data from (WRI, 1991).

In many cases the mining of fossil fuels threatens protected national parks. Dwindling oil and natural gas reserves have caused many countries to permit fossil fuel mining in nature preserves. In the United States, the possible opening of the Arctic National Wildlife Refuge (ANWR) for oil development is a highly controversial issue. ANWR covers about 18 million acres of northeastern Alaska and includes the native lands of the Athabaskan Indians. Estimates are that about 3.2 billion barrels of oil, plus some natural gas, lie beneath this wilderness (Dentzer, 1991). This amount of fossil energy would provide the U.S. with only 200 days' worth of fuel at current consumption rates. Yet extracting it could destroy significant amounts of habitat for native species and disrupt the Alaskan Indians' way of life—effects that will last far longer than a mere 200 days.

Water

The greatest threat to fresh water supplies is overdraft, or excessive pumping of surface and groundwater resources, to meet the needs of a rapidly growing human population. The rate of U.S. groundwater pumping is 25 percent higher than that of replenishment (Pimentel et al., 1996). Each individual requires nearly 3 liters of fresh water per day for drinking and at least 90 liters per day for cooking, washing, and other domestic needs (Brewster, 1987). Including industrial and agricultural water use, each American consumes about 5200 liters per day (USBC, 1990).

Worldwide, about 87 percent of the fresh water that is pumped is consumed (nonrecoverable) to support agriculture (S. Postel, Worldwatch Institute, personal communication, 1992). In the United States 85 percent is consumed by agriculture (NAS, 1989a), with the remaining 15 percent consumed by the public and industry.

Another major threat to water resources both in the United States and the world is pollution (USBC, 1990). Pollution is a more serious problem in developing countries, where industries frequently dump toxic chemicals into rivers and lakes without treatment (WRI, 1991). Likewise, the dumping of untreated sewage makes water unsafe for human drinking and agriculture. For example, in Latin America, where most urban sewage is dumped directly into rivers and lakes, the fecal-coliform bacterial counts in drinking water are frequently a million times higher than in the United States (WRI, 1991).

Biological Damage

World energy use and activities such as deforestation, urbanization, and pollution are closely linked to the loss of an estimated 150 species per day (Reid and Miller, 1989; Myers, 1992) (Figure 20.1). Natural biota are vital to agriculture, forestry, and the integrity of the environment in general because they help to recycle organic wastes, to degrade chemical pollutants, and to purify water and soil (Pimentel et al., 1992a). Furthermore, biodiversity is a vital reservoir of genetic material for agricultural, forestry, and pharmaceutical products (Wilson, 1988a).

Odum (1971) suggests that if natural diversity sufficient for environmental quality is to be maintained, then about one-third of the terrestrial ecosystem should be kept in natural vegetation. Worldwide only 3.2 percent of the terrestrial environment is in protected parks (Reid and Miller, 1989); humans occupy approximately 95% of the terrestrial ecosystem (Western and Pearl,

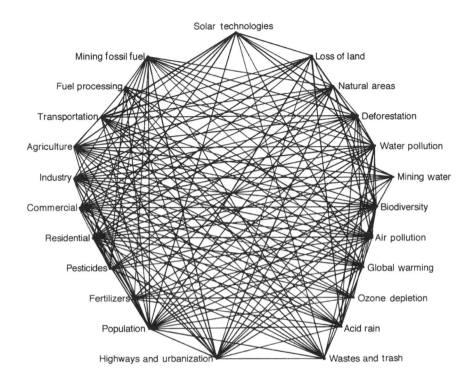

20.1   Energy system impacts on the environment.

1989). The human race cannot survive with only crops and livestock; however, world population growth and consumerism continue to diminish the biodiversity in our ecosystem.

Atmospheric Pollution

Human energy use causes adverse changes in the atmosphere, and damages ultimately are inflicted on terrestrial and aquatic ecosystems. The burning of wood biomass and large quantities of fossil fuels has increased the level of atmospheric carbon dioxide and other gases since the start of the Industrial Revolution, worsening the global warming problem (Schneider, 1989). Fossil fuel burning has by itself added about two-thirds of the more than 175 billion tons of carbon dioxide expelled into the earth's atmosphere (Woodwell et al., 1983). Of this total, approximately two-thirds has been released in the last 35 years, which attests to the the escalating use of fosil fuels and the intensity of the problem (DOE, 1989). The extensive deforestation by burning accounts for the remaining third.

Another serious group of pollutants are volatile compounds known as chlorofluorocarbons (CFCs), which also reduce the ozone layer. This upper atmospheric layer protects all life, including humans, from dangerous ultraviolet (UV) radiation (Kerr, 1992). Destruction of the ozone layer causes increased levels of UV radiation (especially in the Southern Hemisphere), which can lead to skin cancer, cataracts, and reduced immunity to disease.

Many other pollutants are emitted through energy consumption, especially from coal and oil burning. An estimated 7 million tons of particulate matter, 20 million tons of SO_2 , 61 million tons of carbon monoxide, 20 million tons of nitrous oxides, and 20 tons of other pollutants are produced in the U.S. each year from the burning of fossil fuels (USBC, 1990). These pollutants may directly or indirectly result in mortality and morbidity in humans, kill vegetation, degrade ecosystems, and damage buildings and monuments (UCS, 1991).

Known Fossil Energy Resources for the Future

Fossil energy—oil, natural gas, and coal—is a nonrenewable resource that is being rapidly depleted worldwide. At current rates of consumption, U.S. oil and natural gas reserves are projected to last between 10 and 20 years and coal reserves about 100 years (Matare, 1989; Gever et al., 1991; Davis, 1991; BP, 1991; Worldwatch Institute, 1992a).

The fossil energy supply problem is especially critical in the United States because the country is such a heavy user of energy. Oil, the primary energy source, accounts for 40 percent of total annual energy consumption (DOE, 1991a). The nation has only 10 to 20 years of proven and potential supplies of oil (BP, 1994). Based on constant 1967 dollars, the cost to discover a marginal barrel of U.S. oil rose from $0.18 in 1967 to $8.81 in 1982 (K.E.F. Watt, University of California [Davis], personal communication, 1992). This is nearly a 50-fold increase, and costs continue to rise.

In addition to the decline in oil reserves, our country also has a limited supply of natural gas and coal. The Department of Energy (DOE, 1991a) reported that at current usage rates U.S. natural gas reserves will run out in 20 years and U.S. coal reserves in 100 years. The rapid depletion of U.S. oil reserves is expected to result in an increased dependence on coal (Gever et al., 1991). By the year 2010, coal is projected to constitute about 40 percent of

U.S. total energy use (DOE, 1991a). Given these projections and the absence of natural gas in 20 years, our coal supply could be used up much sooner than the predicted 100 years.

Projected Increase in Fossil Fuel Consumption

Despite the rapid decline in U.S. fossil fuel reserves, fossil fuel use is expected to increase to 107 quads per year by the turn of the century (DOE, 1991a). This increase is attributed both to the growing consumption per capita and the expanding U.S. population.

Furthermore, studies by Matare (1989), the Worldwatch Institute (1992a), and British Petroleum (BP, 1994) project that the availability of fossil energy is rapidly declining not only in the United States but worldwide. Per capita fossil energy use is projected to start declining by 2000 and to continue to decrease for the next 100 years while the remaining supply of fossil energy runs out (Figure 20.2).

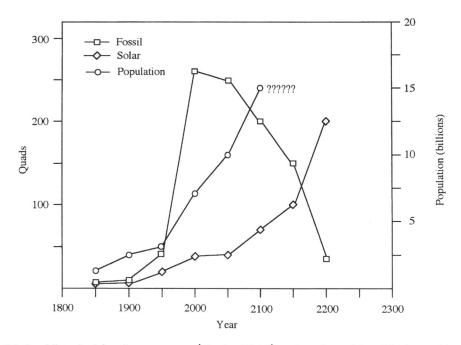

20.2   Historical fossil energy use (Davis, 1991) and projected fossil fuel use; historical solar or renewable energy use (Davis, 1991) and projected solar energy use; historical population growth (Coale, 1974) and current (PRB, 1991) and projected population growth.

These projections raise many questions concerning future energy use and availability. What will happen to fossil energy supplies as the world population continues to grow (Figure 20.2)? The International Institute for Applied Systems Analysis (IIASA, 1981) predicts that, if the world population doubles and developing countries increase their use of fossil energy, then fossil energy use worldwide will increase 2 to 3 times above the 1980 level by the year 2030. Starr et al. (1992) make a similar estimate, projecting that global energy demand will increase about 4 times over present levels by the middle of the next century. This is an unrealistic projection.

Everyone agrees that developing countries should have a greater share of fossil energy resources in the future than they currently do. Assuming that these projections are accurate, the depletion of the world's nonrenewable fossil energy resources will occur much more rapidly than projected in Figure 20.2.

Transition from Fossil to Renewable Energy

Worldwide, solar energy accounts for only 13.5 percent of total energy use (Tables 20.1 and 20.3). The remaining 86.5 percent of the world's energy is based on fossil energy.

Table 20.3   Solar energy use by the United States, world, and developing nations

	United States		World		Developing	
	Quads	Percent	Quads	Percent	Quads	Percent
Biomass	3.6	55	28.5	57	22.5	81.8
Fuelwood	3.53		17.4		11.5	
Crop residues	0.07		8.6		8.5	
Dung	0		2.5		2.5	
Hydropower	3.0	45	21.2	43	5	17.2
TOTAL	6.6	100	49.7	100	27.5	100

Source: Data from (UNEP, 1985; IEA, 1991).

Developing countries use about 27.5 quads of solar energy each year, or nearly one-third of their total consumption of energy (OTA, 1991a). Biomass constitutes about 82 percent of this solar energy, hydropower the remainder. Of the biomass, about 51 percent is firewood, 38 percent is crop residues, and 11 percent is dung (Table 20.3).

In 1850 the United States was 91 percent dependent on biomass wood (Pimentel and Pimentel, 1979). Gradually, fossil energy use increased, until today the U.S. is 92 percent dependent on nonrenewable fossil energy. The remaining 8 percent comes from biomass (4.2 percent) and hydropower (3.5 percent) (Tables 20.1 and 20.3).

During the next decades a transition from fossil energy to renewable energy sources will have to occur in the United States (Figure 20.2). This should be done while fossil energy supplies are still available. Research focusing on how to make solar energy usable for society should receive high priority. Some renewable energy technologies are already available, including solar thermal receivers, photovoltaics, solar ponds, hydropower, and biomass. Also, several technologies have been developed by which biomass is converted into liquid fuel such as methanol and ethanol (ERAB, 1981, 1982). Though these solar energy systems have benefits, evidence also suggests that all solar energy technologies have serious environmental impacts (Holdren et al., 1980; Pimentel et al., 1984a; Pimentel, 1992).

Biomass Energy

Worldwide, some 2.5 billion metric tons of biomass, including forest resources, crop residues, and dung, are harvested each year for energy (Pimentel et al., 1986). As mentioned, biomass currently provides 4.2% of total energy needs in the United States (DOE, 1991a), compared to an average figure of 25 percent in developing countries (Table 20.3).

Reliance on biomass as a direct source of energy is likely to increase in the future, but there are major limitations to expanded use, primarily land availability. For example, about 330,000 ha of sustainable forest area are needed to supply the electrical needs of a city of 100,000 people, which consumes 1 billion kWh of electricity per year (USBC, 1990). This is the largest amount of land area required for any solar energy technology. Approximately 0.1 percent of the total solar energy per hectare can be realized from direct burning of biomass (ERAB, 1981; Loftness, 1984).

The total amount of solar energy captured by U.S. vegetation each year is about 58 quads (ERAB, 1981). The figure for agricultural crops and forest products harvested alone is 28 quads—about half of the energy captured by all the U.S. vegetation. This suggests that the human population is having a major impact on the U.S. environment.

Three quarters of all U.S. land is already in production to provide food and forest resources such as fiber, pulp, and lumber (USDA, 1990). Another

10 percent of the land area is taken up by roadways and urbanization, leaving a relatively small percentage of land available for solar energy development. Most other regions (e.g., Europe and Asia) suffer more serious land shortages than the United States. As populations increase, the need for land to meet demands for increasing food and forest products must necessarily be given priority over land requirements for biomass energy production and other solar technologies. In addition, the removal of biomass for fuel also has severe negative side effects. Removal of vegetation threatens the environment by exposing the soil to erosion, rapid water runoff, and other ecological problems (ERAB, 1981; Darmstadter, 1992).

Energy Efficiency and Conserving Environmental Resources

Transportation

Current U.S. subsidies of $44 billion per year to the energy industry obscure the true cost of energy, encourage energy consumption, and discourage energy conservation (Heede et al., 1985). The elimination of these subsidies and the transfer of the true costs of energy to the consumer would emphasize the need to reduce consumption and could help pay the nation's enormous debt, which is caused mostly by oil imports. With the elimination of energy industry subsidies, the average household would save $523 in taxes (Heede et al., 1985).

Because transportation is the largest consumer of fossil energy in the United States (26 percent), major changes are needed in this sector to reduce fuel use (UCS, 1991). The Union of Concerned Scientists (UCS, 1991) suggests that energy use for transport could be reduced by more than 60 percent. One major step in this direction would be to price gasoline at $4.50/gal, which represents the real cost of its use in motor vehicles—including air pollution, highway construction, traffic regulation, police, and other service costs related to transportation (Worldwatch Institute, 1989). High fuel prices would also reflect the true cost of driving. Currently, "the market and external costs of motor vehicle use that are not reflected in user charges amount to almost $300 billion per year" (MacKenzie et al., 1992, p. 23). Any program for raising fuel prices should take place over a period of time.

The widespread use of small, energy-efficient cars would cut present energy use. Europeans have already taken this step and are able to conduct business and pleasure with small cars. U.S. autos average only 19 mpg

(USBC, 1990); however, present technology could increase this to 45 mpg (Schipper, 1991; OTA, 1991b).

Mass transit is a necessity in the future for efficient, economic transport. At present mass transit represents only 6 percent of public transport in cities (Bleviss and Walzer, 1991). Europeans utilize mass transit 6 times more than Americans (Newman and Kenworthy, 1989). According to the UCS (1991), a single metro rail can carry 17,000 passengers per hour, whereas a single auto lane can transport only 3000 passengers per hour (Marston, 1975). In addition, a change to electric rail travel would reduce hydrocarbon emissions by an estimated 90 percent and nitrous oxides by 50 percent.

At present trains account for 37 percent of inter-city transport of goods in the United States, trucks for 25 percent (UCS, 1991). Trucks not only use 6.4 times more fuel per ton of goods transported than trains but also are heavily subsidized by state and federal taxes (UCS, 1991). Having fewer trucks would make highways safer for automobile drivers. The recent adoption of higher speed limits in the United States will increase the number of accident-related deaths to about 60,000 per year and increase air pollution and the use of fossil energy.

Where feasible, more goods should be transported by ship; ship transport is nearly 10 times more energy efficient than truck transport (Pimentel, 1980).

Industry

Between 1970 and 1983, U.S. industry made an effort to reduce its energy use in production by 30 percent (IEA, 1989). Nevertheless, U.S. industry remains only 60 percent as energy-efficient as Japanese industries (IEA, 1989). A five-fold increase in the cost of energy over today's low, subsidized rates would immediately encourage the efficient use of energy, as it has in Japan, Germany, and other nations. Using a wide variety of known technologies, such as solar energy systems, U.S. industries could improve their energy efficiency by at least 50 percent (Reddy and Goldemberg, 1991).

Food Production

Food production is the fourth-largest consumer of energy in the United States. Agricultural production—including cultivation, planting, fertilizer and pesticide use, and harvesting—accounts for 33 percent of the total energy consumed by the U.S. food system (Pimentel, 1992). Most of the fruits and vegetables produced in California and Florida are transported long distances to the marketplace, requiring large energy expenditures (Pimentel et al., 1975c). Producing fruits and vegetables close to major markets when possible would reduce transport and irrigation energy costs.

Packaging

Packaging requires about 15 percent of the energy used in the U.S. food system (Pimentel and Pimentel, 1979). Evidence suggests that packaging could be reduced by half without any effect on the quality or shelf life of foods. Outright waste of food is responsible for energy waste. For example, studies have shown that about 15 percent of U.S. food, representing a value of about $50 billion/year, is wasted in homes and restaurants (Harrison et al., 1975; Alive, 1988). Reducing this waste would save energy, protect land and water resources, and reduce the garbage transported to landfills.

As much as two-thirds of the metal, glass, and paper now discarded could be reused in various ways (Neal and Schubel, 1987). Much of this material comes from packaging for foods, beverages, and other goods. If industry used recycled materials, it could reduce energy use substantially. This, of course, would require that the public participate in recycling. Consider that in the United States each day 230 and 103 million pounds of steel and aluminum, respectively, are discarded. When aluminum is recycled, about 90 percent of the energy required to produce the same product from virgin materials is saved (OTA, 1989). There has been a marked increase in recycling during the past decade.

Residential and Industrial Buildings

In the home, considerable energy can be saved by switching to more efficient appliances and increasing insulation (OTA, 1992b). Lowe (1991) estimates that the use of energy in residential establishments can be reduced by from 50 to 75 percent through improved appliances, lighting, and heating. For the country as a whole, the cost of conserving energy is 2 to 10 times less than the cost of developing new energy supplies (Kahn, 1986).

In industrialized countries, space heating accounts for 54 percent of energy use in residential buildings (DOE, 1990a). Between 20 and 25 percent more energy is used for heating in U.S. homes than in European homes (Schipper, 1991), but U.S. homes are larger, and more are individual structures than in Europe.

Lighting energy could be reduced by as much as 90 percent without any effect on the home environment or work efficiency (Fickett et al., 1991). Designing or retrofitting buildings to take advantage of passive heating and cooling helps reduce fossil energy use in buildings (Brower, 1990). Commercial establishments and homes can be retrofitted with improved insulation and efficient storm windows.

Energy and Environmental Security

Until the 1960s, the United States generally held the belief that energy and other natural resources were unlimited and that pollution and other environmental problems were of minimal concern. In fact, the impact of human activities, including fossil energy use, was not even considered in energy-use policies until the 1960s (Spurr, 1982).

In the late 1970s, governmental policymakers recognized the seriousness of the growing energy shortage. Intense research and development of alternative energy sources followed. During the remainder of the decade, great strides in conservation and improved efficiency occurred, resulting in savings of $100 billion to the economy (N. Myers, Oxford, personal communication, 1991).

However, during the 1980s the successful conservation policies of the 1970s were almost all abandoned on the assumption that individual initiative would take over where government regulation left off. During the 1980s energy conservation appropriations decreased by more than 96 percent, and funds for the development of renewable energy resources fell by 91 percent (USC, 1991).

Accurate pricing of energy products could catalyze conservation efforts and perhaps even spur research and development of alternative energy sources. However, current prices do not reflect environmental damage and its costs. If the market price of petroleum products for transportation and fossil fuels for electrical generation truly reflected the associated environmental and social costs, oil would cost $4 to $5 per gallon (Worldwatch Institute, 1989). Present U.S. gasoline prices are unrealistically low (from $0.83 to $1.25 a gallon) and do not encourage efficient energy use (UCS, 1991). Indeed, the opposite is true.

Security

U.S. oil production has declined from 400,000 and 500,000 barrels per year for the past 2 decades (USC, 1990). The United States imports 54 percent of its oil (Gibbons and Blair, 1991), and this rate is projected to rise to between 60 and 70 percent by the turn of the century. With only 10 to 20 years' worth of domestic reserves, the United States will enter the twenty-first century captive to a growing oil import bill.

The decline in our own fossil energy supplies and our escalating reliance on imported oil place the United States's energy and economic security, food security, environmental integrity, and overall security in jeopardy (Pendleton, 1991). Most policy analysts agree that a strong economy and military ensure a strong and secure nation. But domestic oil is a finite resource and will be scarce in the very near future. Furthermore, the world oil market is increasingly volatile because of instability in the Middle East and the former Soviet Union. Oil consumption in developing countries is projected to rise by 170 percent by the year 2010, so U.S. oil dependency becomes an ever-worsening policy (Murkowski, 1991).

Excessive oil dependency is an equally inept policy from an economic perspective. The United States spends about $65 billion a year on oil imports (Gibbons and Blair, 1991), plus an additional $50 billion to protect U.S. interests in the Middle East (Rader, 1989). These expenditures further increase the U.S. trade deficit and hinder the entire economy. According to Pate (1991), for every $1 increase per barrel in the price of imported oil, American consumers must spend $3 billion more per year on energy and goods (Pate, 1991). He further noted, "Oil price volatility and increased import reliance have combined to reduce America's productivity and purchasing power."

Thus, our great dependency on foreign oil not only threatens our national security but also balloons our trade deficit and weakens the economic foundation of the nation. The only sure way to remedy these problems is to drastically cut oil use and develop and use renewable and stable energy sources.

Conclusion

Among the major problems facing the United States today are rapid population growth, excessive consumption of fossil energy and other natural resources, economic decline, and serious environmental degradation. Throughout the world the problems are similar to those in the U.S., except that the rate of population growth is much higher and energy consumption per capita is much lower elsewhere than in the United States.

The United States, with only 4.7 percent of the world population, consumes 25 percent of the fossil energy used annually worldwide. Heavy fossil energy consumption is one of the major reasons U.S. oil reserves are estimated to last only 10 to 20 years. Despite this critical situation, current government tax and subsidy policies encourage energy consumption. Worldwide, the energy situation is also critical.

The degradation of land, water, atmospheric, and biological resources now occurring in the United States is directly tied to population size and heavy energy consumption. The problems of global warming, diminishing supplies of groundwater, soil erosion, and loss of biodiversity attest to the seriousness of the present situation.

In addition, the U.S. population is too large to support a sustainable society and environment. The 260 million-plus people in the United States are burning 40 percent more energy from fossil fuels than all the plant biomass in the country captures in solar energy. Clearly, U.S. population and consumption are out of balance with the nation's natural resource supply, particularly if Americans seek a sustainable environment and prosperity for future generations.

The use of energy among the transportation, industry, residential, commercial, and food sectors could be reduced. It is estimated that the United States could reduce its per capita energy use by at least 50 percent through use of alternative energies and improved efficiency (UCS, 1991). Transition to renewable fuels should remain a high priority and should include approaches that consider environmental hazards as well as sustainability for future generations.

21

SUMMING UP: OPTIONS AND SOLUTIONS

David Pimentel and Marcia Pimentel

Tough questions about conservation of natural resources, development of alternative energy resources, desired standards of living, types of diet, and optimum populations size must be answered. All require decisive action.

The foremost question is how humans will be able to provide a nutritionally adequate diet for a world population expected to be more than 6.1 billion by 2000 and 12 billion by about 2040.

Food security for all is dependent on and interrelated with many factors within the vast human social and ecological system. Fundamentally, it depends upon human population numbers and the standard of living those humans desire. Environmental resources such as arable land, water, climate, and fossil energy for fertilizers and irrigation influence the outcome. The food supply is also affected by crop losses to pests, availability of labor, environmental pollution, and the health and lifestyle of the people. Distribution systems and the social organization of families and countries play a role in the solution.

Future Food Needs

For about a million years, the human population growth rate was slow, averaging only about 0.001 percent per year. During that long period of time, the world population numbered less than 10 million (Keyfitz, 1976). Growth in human population numbers began to escalate about 10,000 years ago, when agriculture was first initiated. Rapid population growth, however, only started after the year 1700, when it accelerated to today's rate of 1.7 percent per year, about 1700 times the historical rate of 0.001 percent (NAS, 1975b; Keyfitz, 1976; PRB, 1993). World population now stands at 6 billion and is expanding at a quarter million persons per day. Unless unforeseen factors intervene, it will reach more than 6.1 billion by 2000 (PRB, 1995) and about 12 billion by 2040 or so. Growth is not expected to end until after the year 2100.

The rapid growth in the world population has already resulted in an increased need for food. Estimates are that today from 1 to 2 billion people, or approximately 25 percent of the world population, are seriously malnourished.

Population Health

Rapid growth in the world population coincided with the exponential growth in the use of fossil fuels (Figure 21.1). Some of this energy has been used to promote public health, control disease, and increase food production for the ever-growing world population. The control of typhoid disease, for example, was achieved by improving water purification, which required large energy expenditures (Audy, 1964). The program for eradicating malaria-carrying mosquitoes required the application of DDT and other insecticides. Producing these insecticides used substantial quantities of energy (Audy, 1964).

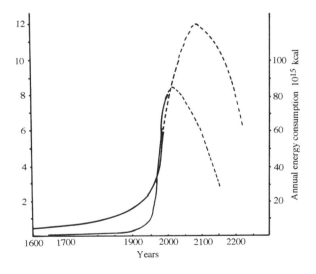

21.1   World population growth and fossil energy use (———) and projected (- - -) future trends for each (Environmental Fund, 1979; Linden, 1980; USBC, 1994; PRB, 1995).

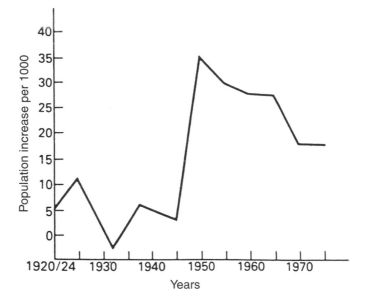

21.2 Population growth rate on Mauritius from 1920 to 1970. From 1920 to 1945 the growth rate was about 5 per 1000. After malaria control, in 1945, the growth rate exploded to about 35 per 1000 and has since very slowly declined. After 25 years the rate of increase is still nearly 4 times the 1920–1945 level (Pimentel and Pimentel, 1979).

Reduction in death rates through effective disease control has been followed by substantial increases in population growth rates. For example, in Sri Lanka (Ceylon), after spraying mosquitoes with DDT, the death rate fell from 20 per 1000 in 1946 to only 14 per 1000 in 1947 (PEP, 1955), and population growth rates concurrently increased. A similar dramatic reduction in death rate occurred after DDT was used on the island of Mauritius, where death rates fell from 27 to 15 per 1000 in 1 year, and population growth rates increased from about 5 to 35 per 1000 (Figure 21.2).

Historical evidence documents many similar occurrences in nations where public health technology improved sanitary practices and medical supplies have significantly reduced death rates (Corsa and Oakley, 1971). The effective control of human diseases, coupled with increased food production, has contributed significantly to rapid population growth (NAS, 1971). Unfortunately, the immediate increase in family size and explosive population increase in cities, towns, and villages all too often overwhelms existing food, education, health, and social systems (NAS, 1971).

The presence of some chronic diseases also increases the need for food. For example, when a person is ill with diarrhea or malaria or is infested with a parasite such as hookworms, anywhere from 5 to 20 percent of the individual's energy intake is expended to offset the illness. With malaria, hookworms, and amoebic dysentery, the parasites removes blood and nutrients and reduces the individual's ability to make effective use of his food.

Food Losses

Significant quantities of our food supply are lost to insects, plant pathogens, weeds, birds, rodents, and other pests. World crop losses due to pest infestation are estimated to be about 40 percent (Pimentel, 1991c). These losses include destruction by insects (15 percent), plant pathogens (12 percent), weeds (12 percent), and mammals and birds (1 percent). Although mammal and bird losses are more severe in the tropics and subtropics than in the temperate regions, they are still low compared to those attributed to insects, pathogens, and weeds.

In addition, available evidence tends to suggest that some Green Revolution technologies have intensified losses to pests (Pradhan, 1971; I. N. Oka, Bogor Food Research Institute, Indonesia, personal communication, 1991). Some of the new high-yielding crop varieties exhibit greater susceptibility to some pests than do traditional varieties. In the past, farmers saved seeds from those individual plants that survived and yielded best under local cultural conditions and planted them in subsequent years. These genotypes were naturally resistant to pest insects and plant pathogens and competitive with weeds. In this way, farmers developed genotypes that grew best in their localities.

The newly developed grain varieties have more genetic uniformity, and this can become a distinct disadvantage when the variety is planted over large areas in a new environment. Such plantings provide an ideal ecological environment in which the plant pathogens can evolve highly destructive genotypes (Frankel, 1971; I. N. Oka, Bogor Food Research Institute, Indonesia, personal communication, 1991). Concurrently, programs have been developed for multiple cropping in an effort to increase food supplies from limited land resources. This type of continuous crop culture has resulted in increased pest outbreaks (Pathak, 1975). Higher crop losses to pest damage mean lower yields and less food.

Not all losses occur during the growing season; substantial postharvest losses occur. These are estimated to range from 10 percent in the United States to a high of 25 percent in many developing countries. The major pests that destroy harvested foods are microbes, insects, and rodents. When postharvest losses are added to preharvest losses, total food losses due to pests rise to an estimated 50 percent. Thus, pests destroy about half of the potential world food supply. We cannot afford a loss of such magnitude when faced with an increasing need for food to feed the growing world population.

Strategies for Meeting Food Needs

Two-thirds of the world's people consume primarily a vegetarian-type diet. These individuals eat about 200 kg of grain products yearly. They consume this grain directly and eat little food of animal origin. In contrast, the remaining one-third of the world's people, including those living in industrial countries such as the United States, consumes about 360 kg of animal food products yearly (Putnam and Allshouse, 1991). To produce this amount of animal food in the United States, about 665 kg of grain per person are raised and then fed to animals (Putnam and Allshouse, 1991).

About 141 million tons of plant and animal protein are produced annually worldwide for human consumption. If evenly divided, this would provide about 64 g of protein per person per day. Of this total amount, animal protein (meat, milk, eggs, etc.) accounts for 34 percent, or about 44 million tons (Table 8.1). Livestock, including poultry, in the United States alone number 6 billion and outweigh the human population by more than 4 times (Pimentel, 1990). Worldwide there are an estimated 20 billion livestock. These animals graze on 3.1 billion ha, or about 24 percent of the world land area (World Resources Institute, 1992).

To increase the production of animal protein, the process must be made more efficient than it has been in the past. This is especially relevant to livestock production. Overgrazing should be prevented and more productive pasture plant species developed and cultured. Applications of limited amounts of livestock manure and perhaps fertilizers would increase forage yields. The annual supply of animal protein could be increased from the present 44 million tons to about 50 million tons by the year 2000. This increase, however, would not be sufficient to maintain the present protein intake of 64 g per person per day for the world population, which in the meantime will also have increased substantially.

Some estimates report that the fishery harvest is about 95 million tons (see Chapter 9). This is probably the maximum yield, considering the serious overfishing problems that already exist. In addition, fish production is energy-intensive; this energy has been and will continue to be a constraint on its expansion.

One way to increase food supplies is for humans to become more vegetarian in their eating habits. Annually, an estimated 40 million tons of grain protein suitable for human consumption are fed to the world's livestock. This represents 34 percent more protein that would be available as food for the world population if it was not cycled through livestock.

If the protein currently fed to livestock were instead fed directly to humans, then more food grains would be available to the world population. Assuming that improved management of livestock pasture and rangeland yielded an additional 25 million tons of livestock protein, then the increases needed in the following crops over a 20-year period would be: cereals, 41 percent; legumes, 20 percent; and other plant proteins, 50 percent. It is doubtful that these increases can be achieved. However, increased yields in plant crop production are more easily achieved than increases in animal production. Nevertheless, just as livestock production is vital to humans today, it will be important to humans in the future. Cattle, sheep, and goats will continue to be of value because they convert grasses and shrubs on pastures and rangeland into food suitable for humans. Without livestock, humans cannot make use of this type of vegetation on marginal lands.

Energy Needs in Food Production

In past decades humans did not have to concern themselves about fossil fuel supplies, because relatively inexpensive and ample supplies were available. Such will not be the case in the twenty-first century. An estimated 17 percent of the fossil energy consumed in the United States is used in the food production system. This 17 percent may seem neither large nor important when considered as a portion of the total U.S. energy expenditure, but compared to that of other nations (especially developing countries) it is extremely large. It amounts to more than twice the total per capita fossil use in Asia and about 4 times that in Africa (Figure 1.3).

The following analysis may help clarify the relationships of fossil fuel supplies to production of food supplies. The total energy used annually in the United States for food production, processing, distribution, and preparation is about 1600 liters of oil per capita per year. Using U.S. agricultural technology to feed the present world population of 6 billion, a high protein/calorie diet for 1 year would require the equivalent of 9000×10^9 liters of fuel annually.

Another way to understand the dependency of food production on fossil energy is to calculate how long it would take to deplete the known world reserve of petroleum if a high protein/calorie diet, produced using U.S. agricultural technologies, were fed to the entire world population. The known world oil reserves have been estimated to be 87×10^{12} liters (Matare, 1989), so if we assume that 75 percent of raw oil can be converted to fuel (Jiler, 1972), this would provide a useable reserve of 66×10^{12} liters of oil. Assuming that oil were the only source of energy for food production and that all known oil reserves were used solely for food production, the reserves would last a mere 7.3 years from today. This estimate is based on a hypothetical stabilized population of 5.5 billion. The reality is that each day an additional quarter million new mouths must be fed.

How then can food supply and energy expenditures be balanced against a growing world population? Even tripling the food supply in the next 40 years would just about meet the basic food needs of the 11 billion people who will inhabit the earth at that time. Doing so would require about a 10-fold increase in the total quantity of energy expended in food production. The large energy input per increment increase in food is needed to overcome the incremental decline in crop yields caused by erosion and pest damage (Figure 21.3).

One practical way to increase food supplies with minimal increase in fossil energy inputs is for the world population as a whole to consume more plant foods. This diet modification would reduce energy expenditures and increase food supplies, because less food suitable for human consumption would be fed to livestock. With livestock, roughly 20 calories of increased energy are needed to obtain 1 calorie of food.

Land Constraints

Feeding a population of more than 6 billion a high protein/calorie diet using U.S. agricultural technology would require large areas of arable land. This will be the case even if only plant production is to be increased. Thus, it is important to know how much arable land now is available for use in agricultural production.

The United States, with a current population of 260 million people, has about 160 million ha planted to crops (USDA, 1991b). This averages out to

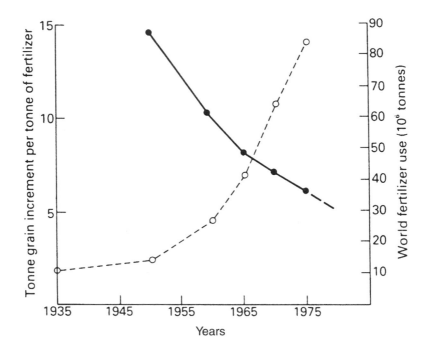

21.3 Declining grain yield increment per fertilizer input (——) (Brown, 1978) and world fertilizer use (– – –) in metric tonnes.

0.6 ha per person. However, the cropland needed per American is only about 0.50, because 20 percent of our present crop yield is exported.

Worldwide, about 1.5 billion ha of arable land now exist for crops. Based on the present population of 6 billion, this averages out to be only 0.25 ha per person. Therefore, if at least 0.50 ha per person is needed to produce a U.S-type diet, there is not sufficient arable land, even with the addition of energy resources and other technology, to feed the rest of the world a U.S.-type diet.

In some regions it may be possible to bring some poor land into production. Best estimates are that cropland resources might be doubled to 3 billion with great cost, using large amounts of energy for fertilizers and other inputs. This increase in cropland would necessitate cutting down most forests and converting some pasturelands to cropland. Both changes would have negative impacts on biodiversity and production of needed forest products. Also, forest removal increases erosion, flooding, and other environmental damage (Pimentel et al., 1992a).

Worldwide, more than 10 million ha of agricultural land are abandoned annually because of serious soil degradation. During the past 40 years, about 30 percent of total world arable land has been abandoned because it was no longer productive. Loss of arable land is increasing because poor farmers worldwide have to burn crop residues and dung as fuel because firewood supplies are declining and fossil fuels are much too costly. It is expected that 750 million ha of cropland will be abandoned by 2050 because of severe degradation. This is extremely bad news; about half of the current arable land now in cultivation will be unsuitable for food production by the middle of the twenty-first century.

Wind and water erosion seriously reduce the productivity of land. In the United States, the rate of soil erosion is estimated at 13 tons/ha annually. The United States has already abandoned an estimated 100 million ha (Pimentel et al., 1995). At least one-third of the topsoil has been eroded from U.S. cropland during more than a century of farming (Handler, 1970). Iowa, which has some of the best soils in the United States, reportedly has lost half its topsoil after little more than 100 years of farming (Risser, 1981).

So far, the reduced productivity of U.S. cropland due to erosion has been offset by increased use of fertilizers, irrigation, and pesticides. The estimate is that about 50 liters of oil equivalents per hectare are expended each year to offset cropland degradation. In developing countries, the rate of soil loss is more than twice that of the U.S., an estimated 30 to 40 tons/ha/yr (Pimentel, 1993). Therefore, based on what we presently know, both the amount of arable land available for crop production and the amounts of extra energy needed to put poor land into production are serious constraints on expansion of crop production.

Water Constraints

Water is the major limiting factor in crop production worldwide because all plants require enormous amounts of water for their growth. For example, a corn crop will transpire about 4.5 million liters of water during the growing season (Leyton, 1983). If this water has to be added by irrigation, approximately 8 million liters of irrigation water must be applied. Another way of assessing water needs is to point out that 1400 liters of water are necessary for the production of 1 kg of corn.

Indeed, agriculture is the major consumer of available water. In the United States, irrigated agriculture consumes (nonrecoverable) about 85 percent of the fresh water that is pumped, and the public and industry consume the remaining 15 percent (NAS, 1989a). Worldwide, agriculture uses about 87 percent of the fresh water pumped (Postel, 1989).

Only about 16 percent of the world's cultivated land is now irrigated (WRI, 1992). In the arid lands, various sectors of the economy have conflicting demands for available water. Agriculture must compete with industry and public use of water, because the economic yields from agriculture per quantity of water used are far less than economic yields from industry. The public always needs water to drink and for other personal uses.

Expansion of irrigation is further limited because it requires large amounts of energy. About 20 million kcal of energy is needed to pump 8 million liters of water from a depth of 30 m and irrigate by sprinkler system (Smerdon, 1974). This is more than 3 times the fossil energy input of 6 million kcal usually expended to produce 1 ha of corn (Pimentel, 1980). In addition, 13 percent more energy is required to maintain the irrigation equipment. These figures do not include the environmental costs of soil salinization or waterlogging often associated with irrigation.

High rainfall and/or the presence of too much water, or rapid water runoff, also cause serious environmental problems. The removal of forests and other vegetation, in particular on slopes, encourages water runoff and often results in serious flood damage to crops and pasture (Beasley, 1972). In fact, environmental damages caused by floodwater, soil sediments, and related watershed damage are estimated to be about $6 billion per year (Clark, 1985).

Climate

Climate has always determined the suitability of land for cultivation of crops. For this reason, changes in temperature and/or rainfall can be expected to influence food production and supplies (Pimentel et al., 1992b). These two considerations must be evaluated on different time scales. Within any given decade, there are likely to occur irregularities in temperature and rainfall patterns that may either improve crop yields or inflict enormous damage to agricultural yields (for example, the drought that occurred in the United States in 1988) (USDA, 1989a). However, long-term changes may have far more serious consequences. In particular, many scientists are concerned about global warming because of the greenhouse effect, which may affect agricultural production (Pimentel et al., 1992b). The sensitivity of crops to temperature change is illustrated with corn. For example, a mere

0.6°C increase in temperature would lengthen the growing season by about 2 weeks and increases crop yields. However, global warming would also reduce the amount of water available for crop production. On balance, global warming would have a negative impact on agriculture.

The changes wrought by irregularities of climate patterns call attention to the interdependency of nations and the importance of cooperative planning. The effects of such irregularities also emphasize the need for the establishment of an international food reserve to offset years in which crop yields in the food-producing regions of the world are unexpectedly low.

Environmental Pollution

Numerous wastes produced by agricultural production are considered pollutants. These include fertilizers; pesticides; livestock manure; exhaust gases from machinery; soil sediments; odors; dust; wastewater; and crop wastes. Pesticide use in the world totals 2.5 million tons, yet insects, plant pathogens, and weeds still destroy about 40 percent of all potential food in the world. However, pesticides are important, for without them food losses would rise to about 55 percent.

Pesticides, however, also cause serious public health and environmental problems. Worldwide, about 3 million human people a year suffer from pesticide poisoning, with about 220,000 fatalities. In the United States there are about 67,000 human pesticide poisonings per year with about 27 fatalities (Litovitz et al., 1990). In addition, there are as many as 10,000 cases of cancer associated with pesticide use (Pimentel et al., 1992d). In addition, fish, honeybees, birds, and natural enemies are killed. The total environmental and health costs of using pesticides are estimated to be more than $8 billion per year (Pimentel et al., 1992d).

On the world scene, pesticide use in agriculture has contaminated water with pesticides and exposed mosquito populations to insecticides. The result has been the development of high levels of resistance to insecticides worldwide and an explosion in the incidence of malaria, which is now difficult to control (NAS, 1991). The various environmental problems associated with pesticides appear to be increasing worldwide (Pimentel et al., 1992d).

The Future

There is no single cause of the growing shortages of food, land, water, and energy or pollution of the environment, nor are there simple solutions. When all the world's resources and assets must be divided among an increasing number of people, each one has a smaller share, until there are insufficient amounts to go around.

At this point it is relevant to reconsider the biological law Malthus proposed: "First, that food is necessary to the existence of man. Secondly, that the passion between the sexes is necessary and will remain nearly in its present state. . . . Assuming then my postula are granted, I say that the power of population is definitely greater than the power of the earth to produce sustenance for man." Malthus may not have been thinking about this aspect, but it is true that food production increases linearly, whereas the human population increases geometrically. Therefore, there is no biophysical way for food production to increase and stay with the growth of the human population. Even if population increase were not geometric, there are limits to the earth's carrying capacity.

Perhaps Bertrand Russell (1961) best expressed the biological law related to population growth when he wrote: "Every living thing is a sort of imperialist seeking to transform as much as possible of its environment into itself and its seed." This law suggests that the human population will increase until food or some other basic need limits its survival and growth.

Although science and technology will help alleviate some of the future shortages, they cannot solve all the problems the world faces today. Science has been unable to solve many of the world's problems during the past 50 years, and with fewer resources that must be shared with more people we have no reason to expect that biophysical limits can be overcome. For example, more, larger, and faster fishing vessels have not increased fish production; on the contrary, it is declining. Likewise, water flowing in the Colorado River now ceases to reach the Sea of Cortes. There is no technology that can double the flow of the Colorado and/or increase rainfall.

We remain optimists, for we see some signs that people are beginning to understand that resources are not unlimited and that a balance must be achieved between the basic needs of the human population and environmental resources, many of which are finite. This is the time to take action.

Above all else humans must control their numbers. This task is probably the most difficult one facing all of us today. If birth rates are to decline on a massive scale, parents must understand that having fewer children is in their own and their children's interest. This understanding can be achieved only if the direct costs of having children are increased and if socially acceptable substitutes for large families are developed. Within each country and each ecological system, difficult social changes must be encouraged in conjunction with policies that augment food supplies and improve health, education, and lifestyle.

What humans choose to do in the coming two decades will determine the kind of world the next generations will live in. Ultimately, it is up to each individual to reduce his or her reproductive rate. Clearly, if humans do not control their numbers, nature will do so through poverty, disease, and starvation.

REFERENCES

AAC. 1980. *Agricultural Almanac of China (Zhonggue Nongye Nianjian)*. Agricultural Press, Beijing.

Abrahamson, D.E. 1989. *The Challenge of Global Warming*. Washington, D.C.: Island Press.

ACTI. 1983. *Alcohol Fuels: Options for Developing Countries*. Edited by A. C. T. Innovation. Washington, D.C.: National Academic Press.

AED. 1960. *Cost of Production of Corn*. Manila: Department of Agriculture and National Resources.

Agarwal, B. 1986. *Cold Hearts and Barren Slopes*. London: Zed Press.

Akinwumi, J. A. 1971. Costs and returns in commercial maize production in the derived savanna belt of Western State, Nigeria. *Bulletin of Rural Economists and Sociologists, Ibadan* 6: 219–251.

Alexander, M. 1977. *Introduction to Soil Microbiology*. 2nd ed. New York: Wiley.

Alexander, W.J.R. 1979. Sedimentation of estuaries: causes, effects and remedies. Fourth (South African) National Oceanography Symposium. Cape Town, July. Council for Scientific and Industrial Research, Pretoria.

Alfheim, I., and T. Ramdahl. 1986. *Mutagenic and Carcinogenic Compounds from Energy Generation*. Final Report No. NP–6752963 (NTIS No. DE 86752963). Oslo, Norway: Center for Industriforkning.

Alive, 1988. *Checking Out Trash*. Division of Nutritional Sciences, Cornell University, Ithaca, NY.

Allan, P. 1961. Fertilizers and food in Asia and the Far East. *Span* 4: 32–35.

Allee, W. C., A. E. Emerson, O. Park, T. Park, and K. P. Schmidt. 1949. *Principles of Animal Ecology*. Philadelphia: Saunders.

Allen, J.A. 1986. Fuelwood policies for Swazi nation land: Farm and community approaches for fuelwood production. M.S. thesis, Cornell University, Ithaca, NY.

Alliance to Save Energy (ASE). 1993. *Federal Energy Subsidies: Energy, Environmental, and Fiscal Impacts*. Washington, D.C.: The Alliance to Save Energy.

Altieri, M.A. 1990. Why study traditional agriculture? In C. R. Carroll, J. H. Vandermeer, and P. M. Rossett (eds.), *Agroecology*, pp. 551–564. McGraw-Hill, New York.

Altieri, M. A., M. K. Anderson, and L. C.Merrick. 1987. Peasant agriculture and the conservation of crop and wild plant resources. *Conservation Biology* 1: 49–58.

Altieri, M. A., F. J. Trujillo, and J. Farrell. 1987. Plant-insect interactions and soil fertility in agroforestry systems: implications for the design of sustainable agroecosystems. In H. L. Gholz (ed.), *Agroforestry: Realities, Possibilities, and Potentials*, pp. 89–108. Dordrecht, Netherlands: Nijhoff.

American Society for Testing Material (ASTM). 1992. Standard guide for radon control options for the design and construction of new low rise residential buildings. In *Annual Book of American Society for Testing Material*, E1465–92, 1117–1123. Philadelphia: ASTM.

American Wind Energy Association (AWEA). 1991. Wind energy comes of age. *Solar Today* 5: 14–16.

———. 1992. *Wind Technology Status Report*. Washington, D.C.: American Wind Energy Association.

Anderson, L. G. 1985. Potential economic benefits from gear restrictions and license limitation in fisheries regulation. *Land Economics* 61: 409–418.

Anderson, L. L. 1972. *Energy Potential from Organic Wastes: A Review of the Quantities and Sources*. Washington, D.C.: Information Circular No. 8549, U.S. Bureau of Mines.

Andrewartha, H. G., and L. C. Birch. 1954. *Distribution and Abundance of Animals*. Chicago: University of Chicago.

Arledge, J. E. 1980. Soil conservation at work: Guatemala's small farmer project. *Journal of Soil and Water Conservation* 35: 187–189.

Arnold, G. W. 1983. The influence of ditch and hedgerow structure, length of hedgerows, and area of woodland and garden on bird numbers on farmland. *Journal of Applied Ecology* 20: 731–750.

Audy, J. R. 1964. *Public Health and Medical Sciences in the Pacific–a Forty-year Review*. Honolulu: Pacific Science Congress, 10th, University Press.

Badger, P. C., and J. C. Broder. 1989. Ethanol production from food processing wastes. *HortScience* 24: 227–232.

Baechler, M. C., and A. D. Lee. 1991. Implications of environmental externalities assessments for solar thermal powerplants. In T. R. Mancini, K. Watanabe, and D. E. Klett (eds.), *Solar Engineering 1991*, pp. 151–158. New York: ASME.

Bailie, R.C. 1976. *Technical and Economic Assessment of Methods for Direct Conversion of Agricultural Residue to Energy*. Morgantown, WV: West Virginia University.

Baker, J. B. 1973. Intensive cultural practices increase growth of juvenile slash pine in Florida Sandhills. *Forest Science* 19: 197–202.

Banwell, P. S., and R. C. Harriss. 1992. Enhancing biomass energy use in Kenya. *Natural Resources Forum* 16 (4): 298–304.

Barber, M. 1993. Why more energy? The hidden cost of Canada's cheap power. *Forests, Trees and People Newsletter* 19: 26–29.

Bardach, J. 1980. Aquaculture. In D. Pimentel (ed.), *Handbook of Energy Utilization in Agriculture*, pp. 431–440. Boca Raton, FL: CRC Press.

———. 1982. Oil, fish, and the sun and the wind. In R. C. May, I. R. Smith, and D. B. Thomson (eds), *Appropriate Technology for Alternative Energy Sources in Fisheries*, pp. 1–6. Manila: International Center for Living Aquatic Resources Management.

———. 1991. Sustainable development of fisheries. In International Ocean Institute (ed.), *Ocean Yearbook 9*, pp. 57–72. Chicago: University of Chicago Press.

Barrows, H. L., and V. J. Kilmer. 1963. Plant nutrient losses from soils by water erosion. *Advances in Agronomy* 15: 303–315.

Bartlett, A.A. 1989. Fusion and the future. *Physics and Society* 18 (3): 11.

Batie, S. 1983. *Soil Erosion: Crisis in America's Cropland?* Washington, D.C.: The Conservation Foundation.

Batty, J. C., and J. Keller. 1980. Energy requirements for irrigation. In D. Pimentel (ed.), *Handbook of Energy Utilization in Agriculture*, pp. 35–44. Boca Raton, FL: CRC Press.

Baum, W. C. 1986. *Partners Against Hunger.* Washington, D.C.: World Bank.

Beaty, E. R., Y. C. Smith, and J. D. Powell. 1974. Responses of Pensacola Bahiagrass to irrigation and time of N. fertilization. *Journal of Range Management* 27 (5): 394–396.

Bell, F. W. 1978. *Food from the Sea: The Economics and Politics of Ocean Fisheries.* Boulder, CO: Westview Press.

Bell, F. W., and J. E. Hazleton. 1967. *Recent Developments and Research in Fisheries Economics.* New York: Oceana Publications.

Beninga, K., R. Davenport, J. Sandubrue, and K. Walcott. 1991. Design and fabrication of a market ready stretched membrane heliostat. In T. R. Mancini, K. Watanabe, and D. E. Klett (eds.), *Solar Engineering 1991*, pp. 229–234. New York: ASME.

Berry, R. S., and H. Makino. 1974. Energy thrift in packaging and marketing. *Technology Review* 76: 1–13, 32–43.

Berryman, A. A. 1982. Population dynamics of bark beetles. In J. B. Mitton and K. B. Sturgeon (eds.), *Bark Beetles in North American Conifers. A System for the Study of Evolutionary Biology*, pp. 264–314. Austin: University of Texas Press.

Bews, J. 1973. *Human Ecology.* New York: Russel and Russel.

Biggle, L.W. 1980. Introduction to energy use in wheat production. In D. Pimentel (ed.), *Handbook of Energy Utilization in Agriculture*, pp. 109–116. Boca Raton, FL: CRC Press.

Billings, R.E. 1991. *Hydrogen Fuel Cell Vehicle*. Houston: American Academy of Science.

Billington, G. 1988. Fuel use control in the fishing industry. In S. G. Fox and J. Huntington (eds.), *World Symposium on Fishing gear and Fishing Vessel Design*, pp. 112–115. St. John's, Canada: Marine Institute.

Bilsborrow, R. E. 1987. Population pressures and agricultural development in developing countries: A conceptual framework and recent evidence. *World Development* 15: 183–203.

Birdsey, R. A. 1992. *Carbon Storage and Accumulation in United States Forest Ecosystems*. General Technical Report WO 59. Washington, D.C.: U. S. Department of Agriculture, Forest Service.

Biswas, A. K. 1984. *Climate and Development*. Dublin: Tycooly International Publishers, Ltd.

Blaxter, K. 1978. What happens to farming when the fossil fuels run out? *Farmer's Weekly*, January 20.

Bleviss, D. L. and Walzer, P., 1991. Energy for motor vehicles. In J. Piel (ed.), *Energy for Planet Earth*, pp. 47–58. New York: W. H. Freeman Co.

Bockris, J. O'M., and J. C. Wass. 1988. About the real economics of massive hydrogen production at 2010 AD. In T. N. Veziroglu and A. N. Protsenko (eds.), *Hydrogen Energy VII*, pp. 101–151. New York: Pergamon Press.

Bodansky, D. 1993. Panel on public affairs workshop on electricity from renewable resources. *Physics and Society* 22 (3): 5–8.

Boddey, R. M. 1995. Biological nitrogen fixation in sugar cane: A key to energetically viable biofuel production. *Critical Reviews in Plant Sciences* 14: 263–279.

Bogach, V. S. 1985. *Wood as Fuel*. New York: Praeger Publishers.

Bohac, J., and A. Pokarzhevsky. 1987. Effect of manure and NPK on soil macrofauna in chernozem soil. In J. Szegi (ed.), *Soil Biology and Conservation of the Biosphere*, pp. 15–19. Proceedings of the 9th International Symposium. Akademiai Kiado, Budapest, Hungary.

Bolline, A. 1982. Etude et prevision de l'erosion des sols limoneux cultives en Moyenne Belgique. These presentee pour l'obtention du grade de Docteur en Sciences Geographiques, Universite de Liege. Cited in Richter, G. 1983.

BP. 1991. *British Petroleum Statistical Review of World Energy*. London: British Petroleum Corporate Communications Services.

———. 1994. *British Petroleum Statistical Review of World Energy*. London: British Petroleum Corporate Communications Services.

Brabben, T. E. 1981. Use of turbidity monitors to assess sediment yield in East Java, Indonesia. In *Erosion and Sediment Transport Measurement,* pp. 105–113. International Association of Hydrology Sciences Publication No. 133.

Brewster, J. A., 1987. *World Resources 1987.* New York: Basic Books, Inc.

Brodrick, A. H. 1949. *Lascaux. A Commentary.* London: Linsay Drumond Ltd.

Bronicki, Y. 1981. Electricity from solar ponds. *Chemtech* 11: 494–498.

Browder, J. O. 1990. Extractive reserves will not save the tropics. *BioScience* 40: 626.

Brower, M. 1992. *Cool Energy. Renewable Solutions to Environmental Problems.* Cambridge, MA: Union of Concerned Scientists.

———. 1990. *Cool Energy. The Renewable Solution to Global Warming.* Cambridge, MA: Union of Concerned Scientists,

Brown, L., A. Durning, C. Flavin, H. French, J. Jacobson, M. Lowe, S. Postel, M. Renner, L. Starke, and J. Young. 1990. *State of the World 1990.* Washington, D.C.: Worldwatch Institute.

Brown, L. R. 1978. *The Global Economic Prospect: New Sources of Economic Stress.* Worldwatch Paper No. 20. Washington, D.C.: Worldwatch Institute.

Brown, L. R., and E. C. Wolf. 1984. *Soil Erosion: Quiet Crisis in the World Economy.* Worldwatch Paper No. 60. Washington, D.C.: Worldwatch Institute.

Buchler, P. M. 1989. The treatment of waste waters from sugar can alcohol production with modified bentonites. *Water Science and Technology* 21: 1845–1847.

Bureau pour le Development de la Production Agricole (BDPA). 1965. *Techniques Rurales en Afrique. Les temps de traux.* Republiques Francaise: Ministere de la Cooperation.

Bureau of Labor Statistics (BLS). 1978. Chartbook on occupational injuries and illnesses in 1976. Report 535. U.S. Department of Labor, Washington, D.C.

———. 1979. Occupational injuries and illnesses in 1977, summary. Report 561. U.S. Department of Labor, Washington, D.C.

———. 1980. Occupational injuries and illnesses in the United States by industry, 1978. Bulletin 2078. U.S. Department of Labor, Washington, D.C.

———. 1981. Occupational injuries and illnesses in the United States by industry, 1979. Summary. Bulletin 2097. U.S. Department of Labor, Washington, D.C.

Burges, A., and F. Raw (eds.). 1967. *Soil Biology.* London: Academic Press.

Buringh, P. 1984. The capacity of the world land area to produce agricultural products. In *Options MÈditerranÈennes, CIHEAM IAMZ–84–1* (Proceedings of the Agroecology Workshop, Zaragoza, Spain, 1984), pp. 15–32. Paris: Centre International de Hautes Etudes Agronomiques Mediterraneennes (CIHEAM).

————. 1989. Availability of agricultural land for crop and livestock production. In D. Pimentel and C. W. Hall (eds.), *Food and Natural Resources*, pp. 69–83. San Diego: Academic Press.

Burnett, E., and E. C. Fisher. 1954. The effect of conservation practices on runoff, available soil moisture and cotton yield. *Proceedings of the Soil Science Society of America* 18: 216–218.

Burton, B. T. 1965. *The Heinz Handbook of Nutrition.* New York: McGraw-Hill.

Buttler, I. 1986. Personal communication. Department of Agronomy, Cornell University, Ithaca, NY.

Calle, F. R., and D. O. Hall. 1987. Brazilian alcohol: food versus fuel. Unpublished manuscript.

Campbell, R. W. 1974. The gypsy moth and its natural enemies. *Forest Service Agriculture Information Bulletin* 381. Washington, D.C.: U.S. Department of Agriculture.

Campbell, R. W., and J. D. Podgwaite. 1971. The disease complex of the gypsy moth. I. Major components. *Journal of Invertebrate Pathology* 28: 101–107.

Captiva, F. J. 1968. Modern U.S. shrimp vessels design, construction, current trends and future developments. In G. DeWitt (ed.), *The Future of the Fishing Industry of the United States*, pp. 141–148. Seattle: University of Washington, Publications in Fisheries, New Series.

Carl, W. H. 1981. *Biomass as an Alternative Fuel.* Washington, D.C.: Government Institute Investigations.

Casper, M. E. 1977. *Energy-saving Techniques for the Food Industry.* Park Ridge, NJ: Noyes Data Corp.

Cates, R. G. 1975. The interface between slugs and wild ginger: Some evolutionary aspects. *Ecology* 56: 391–400.

Centre for Science and Environment (CSE). 1982. *The State of India's Environment 1982. A Citizen's Report.* New Delhi: CSE.

————. 1985. *The State of India's Environment 1984–85. The Second Citizens' Report.* New Delhi: CSE.

Cervinka, V. 1980. Fuel and energy efficiency. In D. Pimentel (ed.), *Handbook of Energy Utilization in Agriculture*, pp. 15–24. Boca Raton, FL: CRC Press.

Cervinka, V., W. J. Chancellor, R. J. Coffelt, R. G. Curley, and J. B. Dobie. 1974. *Energy Requirements for Agriculture in California.* Davis, CA: California Department of Food and Agriculture, University of California.

Chahroudi, D. 1992. Weather panel architecture: a passive solar solution for cloudy climates. *Solar Today* 6: 17–20.

Chapman, D. 1983. *Energy Resources and Energy Corporations.* Ithaca, NY: Cornell University Press.

Chapman, D., and Barker, R. 1987. Resource depletion, agricultural research, and development. Paper prepared for U.S. National Academy of Sciences– Czechoslovak Academy of Sciences Workshop on Agricultural Development and Environmental Research, April 6–16, Ceske Budejovice, Czechoslovakia.

Charreau, C. 1972. Problemes poses par L'utilisation agricole des sols tropicaux par des cultures annuelles. *Agronomie Tropical (France),* 27 : 905–929.

Chatterji, M. 1981. Energy and environment in the developing countries: An overall perspective and plans for action. In M. Chatterji (ed.), *Energy and Environment in Developing Countries,* pp. 3–25. New York: Wiley.

Chen, K. L., R. B. Wesink, and J. W. Wolfe. 1976. A model to predict the total energy requirements and economic costs of irrigation systems. Paper No. 76– 2527. presented at the 1976 Winter Meeting of the American Society of Agricultural Engineers, Chicago, December 14–17.

Clark, C., and M. Haswell. 1970. *The Economics of Subsistence Agriculture.* London: MacMillan.

Clark, D. A., M. G. Lambert, and D. A. Grant. 1986. Influence of fertilizer and grazing management on North Island moist hill country. 5. Animal production. *New Zealand Journal of Agricultural Research* 29: 407–420.

Clark, E. H. II 1985. The off-site costs of soil erosion. *Journal of Soil and Water Conservation* 40: 19–22.

Clark, J. P., and A. F. Kwasnik. 1986. *Boiler Design Criteria for Dry Sorbent SO2 Control with Low-NOX Burners: New Unit Applications.* Final Report No. EPA/ 600/7–86/053 (NTIS No. PB 87–139952). Windsor, CT: Cobustion Engineering, Inc.

Clarke, A. 1991. Wind energy progress and potential. *Energy Policy* 19: 742–755.

Clausen, A. W. 1985. Poverty in the developing countries, 1985. *The Hunger Project Papers.* Atlanta: Martin Luther King Center for Nonviolent Social Change, Hunger Project.

Coale, A. J., 1974. The history of the human population. *Scientific American* (September): 41–51.

Coastwatch. 1990. Shrimping: a fishery in trouble? *Coastwatch* 10: 1–2.

Coley, P. D., J. P. Ryant, and F. S. Chapin. 1985. Resource availability and plant antiherbivore defense. *Science* 230: 895–899.

Connell, K. H. 1950. *The Population of Ireland.* Oxford: Clarendon Press.

Cook, E. 1976. *Man, Energy, Society.* San Francisco: W. H. Freeman.

Cook, J. H., J. Beyea, and K. H. Keeler. 1991. Potential impacts of biomass production in the United States on biological diversity. *Annual Review of Energy* 16: 401–431.

Corsa, L., and D. Oakley. 1971. Consequences of population growth for health services in less developed countries—an initial appraisal. In National Academy of Sciences (ed.), *Rapid Population Growth,* pp. 368–402. Baltimore: Johns Hopkins Press.

Cottrell, F. 1955. *Energy and Society.* Westport, CT: Greenwood Press.

Council on Environmental Quality (CEQ). 1980. *The Global 2000 Report to the President of the U.S. Entering the 21st Century.* New York: Pergamon Press.

Crenshaw, R., and R. E. Clark. 1982. *Optimal Weatherization of Low-Income Housing in the U.S.* Gaithersburg, MD: National Institute for Standards and Technology.

Cromartie, W. J. Jr 1991. The environmental control of insects using crop diversity. In D. Pimentel (ed.), *Handbook of Pest Management in Agriculture,* Vol. I, pp. 183–216. Boca Raton, FL: CRC Press.

Cromer, C. J. 1989. Water heating. In D. A. Andrejko (ed.), *Assessment of Solar Energy Technologies,* pp. 1–3. Boulder, CO: American Solar Energy Society.

da Silva, J. G., G. E. Serra, J. R. Moreira, J. C. Concalves, and J. Goldemberg. 1978. Energy balance for ethyl alcohol production from crops. *Science* 201: 903–906.

Darmstadter, J., 1992. Energy transitions. *Resources* 106: 29–32.

Davis, G. R. 1991. Energy for Planet Earth. In J. Piel (ed.), *Energy for Planet Earth,* pp. 1–10. New York: W. H. Freeman and Co.

Day, J. H., and J. R. Grindley. 1981. The estuarine ecosystem and environmental constraints. In J.H. Day (ed.), *Estuarine Ecology,* pp. 345–372. Rotterdam: A.A. Balkema.

De Los Reyes, B. N., E. V. Quintana, R. D. Torres, O. M. Ela, N. M. Fortuna, and J. M. Marasigan. 1965. A case study of the tractor- and carabao-cultivated lowland rice farms in Laguna, crop year 1962–63. *Phillipine Agriculture* 49: 75–94.

de Bazua, C. D., M. A. Cabrero and H. M. Poggi. 1991. Vinassess biological treatment by anaerobic and aerobic processes: Laboratory and pilot-plant tests. *Bioresource Technology* 35: 87–93.

de Melo, F. H. 1986. Brazil and the CGIAR Centers: A Study of Their Collaboration in Agricultural Research. CGIAR Paper #9. Washington, D.C.: World Bank.

de Mesa, A. 1928. *The Insect Oak-Galls in the Vicinity of Ithaca.* Thesis. Ithaca, NY: Cornell University.

de Montalembert, M. R., and J. Clement. 1983. *Fuelwood Supplies in Developing Countries.* Rome: Food and Agriculture Organization.

de Wit, C. T. 1958. Transportation and crop yields. *Verslag Landbouwkundig Onderzoek* No. 64: 6.

Defever, A. 1968. Modern U.S. tuna vessel construction, design and future trends. In G. DeWitt. (ed.), *The Future of the Fishing Industry of the United States,* pp. 134–140. Seattle: University of Washington, Publications in Fisheries, New Series.

DeFoliart, G. R. 1989. The human use of insects as food and as animal feed. *Bulletin of the Entomological Society of America* 35: 22–35.

Delwiche, C. C. 1970. The nitrogen cycle. *Scientific American* 223: 137–158.

Demeny, P. G., 1986. *Population and the Invisible Hand.* Center for Policy Studies, paper No. 123. New York: Population Council.

DeMeo, E. A., F. R. Goodman, T. M. Peterson, and J. C. Schaefer. 1991. *Solar Photovoltaic Power: A U.S. Electric Utility R&D Perspective.* New York: IEEE Photovoltaic Specialist Conference Proceedings.

Dentzer, S., 1991. The U.S. should decrease its dependence on foreign oil. In C. P. Cozic and M. Polesetsky (eds.), *Energy Alternatives*, pp. 31–34. San Diego: Greenhaven Press.

DOE. 1977. *Environmental Studies Related to the Option of Wind Energy Conversion Systems.* Columbus, OH: Batelle Laboratories, U.S. Department of Energy.

———. 1979. *Environmental Readiness Document: Wood Combustion.* Washington, D.C.: U.S. Department of Energy, ERD.

———. 1980. *Health Effects of Residential Wood Combustion: Survey of Knowledge and Research.* Washington, D.C.: Department of Energy, Technology Assessments Division.

———. 1981. *Wood Combustion: State of Knowledge Survey of Environmental, Health and Safety Aspects.* Report No. DOE/EY/10450–74. Baltimore: Mueller Associates Inc.

———. 1982. *Secretaries Annual Report to Congress.* Published by Office of State and Local Programs, Office of Conservation and Renewable Energy, U.S. Department of Energy, Washington, D.C.

———. 1983. *Energy Projections to the Year 2010.* Office of Policy, Planning, and Analysis, U.S. Department of Energy, Washington, D.C.

———. 1986. Personal communication. Information Office, Alcohol Fuels Program, Department of Energy, Washington, D.C.

———. 1988. *Energy Conservation Indicators 1986.* Energy Information Administration, U.S. Department of Energy, Washington, D.C.

———. 1989. *Report to the Congress of the U.S.: A Compendium of Options for Government Policy to Encourage Private Sector Responses to Potential Climate Changes, Methodological Justification and Generic Policy Instruments.* U.S. Department of Energy, Office of Environment Analysis, Assistant Secretary for Environment, Safety and Health, Washington, D.C.

———. 1990a. *Annual Energy Outlook.* Washington, D.C.: U.S. Department of Energy.

———. 1990b. *The Potential of Renewable Energy.* Golden, CO: SERI, Department of Energy.

———. 1991a. *Annual Energy Outlook with Projections to 2010.* Washington, D.C.: U.S. Department of Energy, Energy Information Administration.

————. 1991b. *1989 International Energy Annual.* Washington, D.C.: U.S. Department of Energy.

————. 1992. *Wind Energy Program Overview.* Golden, CO: National Renewable Energy Laboratory, Department of Energy.

DOE/CE. 1988. *Passive and Active Solar Domestic Hot Water Systems.* 3rd ed. FS–119. Washington, D.C.: U.S. Department of Energy, Conservation and Renewable Energy Inquiry and Referral Service.

Department of Nonconventional Energy Sources (DNES). 1984–85. Annual Report. New Delhi: Government of India.

Department of Science and Technology (DST). 1980. Report of the Committee for Recommending Legislative Measures and Administrative Machinery for Ensuring Environmental Protection. Government of India: DST.

Desai, I. D., G. Tavares, D. de Oliveira, A. Douglas, F.A.M. Duarte, and J.E.D. de Oliveira. 1980. Food habits and nutritional status of agricultural migrant workers in southern Brazil. *American Journal of Clinical Nutrition* 33: 702–714.

Deshler, W. W. 1965. Native cattle keeping in Eastern Africa. In A. Leeds and A. P. Vayda (eds.), *Man, Culture and Animals.* Washington, D.C.: AAAS Publication No. 78.

Dhar, S. N. and A.G.S. Pathania. 1991. Bronchitis due to biomass fuel burning in North India Gujjar lung an extreme effect. *Seminars in Respiratory Medicine* 12: 69–74.

Diamond, J. M., K. D. Bishop and S. Van Balen. 1987. Bird survival in an isolated Javan woodland: island or mirror? *Conservation Biology* 1: 132–142.

————. 1976. Soil compaction after tree-length skidding in northern Mississippi. *Soil Science Society of America Journal* 40: 965–966.

Dickson, Y. L., and B.C. Yates. 1983. *Examination of the Environmental Effects of Salt-Gradient Solar Ponds in the Red River Basin of Texas.* Denton, TX: North Texas State University, Denton Institute of Applied Sciences.

Dignon, J., C. J. E. Atherton, J.E. Penner, and J.J. Walton. 1991. *NOx Pollution from Biomass Burning: A Global Study.* 11th Conference on Fire and Forest Meterology, Missoula, MT: Report No. UCRL-JC–104735 (NTIS-No. DE9101054). Washington, D.C.: U.S. Department of Energy.

Dils, R. E. 1953. Influence of forest cutting and mountain farming on some vegetation, surface soil, and surface runoff characteristics. USDA Forest Station Paper No. 24, Southeast. Forest Experiment Station.

Dissmeyer, G. E. 1976. Erosion and sediment from forest land uses, management practices and disturbances in the southeastern United States. In Proceedings of the Third Federal Interagency Sedimentation Conference, March 22–25, Denver, CO. Sedimentation Committee, Water Resources Council, pp. 1140–141, 148.

Dobbs, T.L., D. Auch, R. Hoffman, W. R. Gibbons, C. A. Westby and W. E. Arnold. 1984. *Alternative Crops for Ethanol Fuel Production: Agronomic, Processing, and Economic Considerations.* Brookings: South Dakota State University.

Doering, O. 1977. The energy balance of food legume production. In R. A. Fazzolare and C. B. Smith (eds.), *Energy Use Management*, pp. 725–732. New York: Pergamon.

———. 1980. Accounting for energy in farm machinery and buildings. In D. Pimentel (ed.), *Handbook of Energy Utilization in Agriculture*, pp. 9–14. Boca Raton, FL: CRC Press.

Doeringer, P.B., P. I. Moss, and D. G. Terkla. 1986. *The New England Fishing Economy: Jobs, Income, and Kinship.* Amherst, MA: University of Massachusetts Press.

Douglas, J. E., and O. C. Goodwin. 1980. Runoff and soil erosion from forest site preparation practices. In *U.S. Forestry and Water Quality: What Course in the 80's?*, pp. 50–74. Washington, D.C.: Proc. Richmond, VA, Water Pollution Control Federation.

Dourojeanni, M. J. 1990. Entomology and biodiversity conservation in Latin America. *American Entomologist* 36(2): 88–93.

Dover, N., and L. Talbot. 1987. *To Feed the Earth: Agroecology for Sustainable Development.* World Resources Institute, Washington, D.C.

Dovring, F. 1988. *Farming for Fuel.* New York: Praeger.

Dunkerley, J., and W. Ramsay. 1983. *Analysis of Energy Prospects and Problems of Developing Countries.* Report to AID Bureau for Program and Policy Coordination. Washington, D.C.: Resources for the Future.

Durning, A. B. 1989. *Poverty and the Environment: Reversing the Downward Spiral.* Worldwatch Paper 92. Washington, D.C.: Worldwatch Institute.

Durning, A. B. and H. B. Brough. 1991. *Taking Stock: Animal Farming and the Environment.* Washington, D.C.: Worldwatch Institute.

Earl, D. E. 1975. *Forest Energy and Economic Development.* Oxford: Clarendon Press.

Ebel, W. 1979. Effects of hydoelectric projects on fish populations. In *Hydropower: A National Energy Resource*, pp. 170–176. Washington, D.C.: The Engineering Foundation, New York.

Eckholm, E. P. 1976. *Losing Ground. Environmental Stress and World Food Prospects.* New York: Norton.

Edwards, C. A., and J. R. Lofty. 1982. Nitrogenous fertilizers and earthworm populations in agricultural soils. *Soil Biology and Biochemistry* 14: 515–521.

Edwardson, W. 1975. *Energy Analysis and the Fishing Industry.* A Report of the Energy Analysis Unit. Glasgow: University of Strathclyde.

Ehrlich, P., and A. Ehrlich. 1990. *The Population Explosion.* New York: Simon and Schuster.

Ehrlich, P. R. and E. O. Wilson. 1991. Biodiversity studies: science and policy. *Science* 253: 758–762.

Eisner, T. 1990. Prospective for nature's chemical riches. *Issues in Science and Technology* 6 (2): 31–34. National Academy of Sciences, Washington, D.C.

El-Swaify, S. A, E. W. Dangler, and C. L. Armstrong. 1982. *Soil Erosion by Water in the Tropics.* Resource Extension Series 024, College of Tropical Agriculture and Human Resources, University of Hawaii, Honolulu.

Electric Power Research Institute (EPRI). 1991. *Photovoltaic system performance assessment for 1989.* EPRI Intermim Report 65–7286. Los Angeles: EPRI.

Elton, C.S. 1927. *Animal Ecology.* London: Sidgwick and Jackson, LTD.

———. 1958. *Ecology of Invasions by Plants and Animals.* London: Methuen.

Energy Information Administration (EIA). 1990. *Electric Plant Cost and Power Production Expenses.* Washington, D.C.: Energy Information Administration.

Energy Research Advisory Board (ERAB). 1980. *Gasohol.* Washington, D.C.: ERAB, U.S. Department of Energy.

———. 1981. *Biomass Energy.* Washington, DC: ERAB, U.S. Department of Energy.

Environmental Fund. 1979. *World Population Estimates.* Washington, D.C.: The Environmental Fund.

Environmental Protection Agency (EPA). 1976. *Evaluating Economic Impacts of Programs for Control of Saline Irrigation Return Flows: A Case Study of the Grand Valley, Colorado.* Denver: EPA.

———. 1986. *National Air Pollutant Emission Estimates, 1940–1984.* Research Triangle Park, NC: EPA, Office of Air Quality Planning and Standards.

———. 1990. *Analysis of the Economic and Environmental Effects of Ethanol as an Automotive Fuel.* Washington, D.C.: EPA.

Ernst, E. 1978. *Fuel Consumption Among Rural Families in Upper Volta.* Upper Volta: Eight World Forestry Congress.

Estep, J. A. 1989. *Avian Mortality at Large Wind Facilities in California: Identification of a Problem.* Sacramento, CA: California Energy Commision.

Ewel, J. J. 1986. Designing agricultural ecosystems for the humid tropics. *Annual Review of Ecology Systematics* 17: 245–271.

Executive Office of the President (EOP). 1977. *The National Energy Plan.* Washington, DC: Executive Office of the President, Energy Policy and Planning.

Fakhry, A. 1969. *The Pyramids.* Chicago: University of Chicago Press.

Federal Energy Administration (FEA). 1976. *Energy and U.S. Agriculture: 1974 Data Base.* Washington, D.C.: U.S. Government Printing Office.

Federal Energy Regulatory Commission (FERC). 1984. *Hydroelectric Power Resources of the United States*. Washington, D.C.: Federal Energy Regulatory Commission.

———. 1988. *Hydroelectric Power Resources of the United States: Developed and Undeveloped*. Washington, D.C.: Federal Energy Regulatory Commission.

Fickett, A. P., C. W. Gellings, and A. B. Lovins. 1991. Efficient use of electricity. In: J Piel (ed.), *Energy for Planet Earth*, pp. 11–24. W. H. Freeman Co., New York.

Finn, D. 1983. Land use and abuse in the East African region. *Ambio* 12: 296–301.

Flaim, S. and D. Urban. 1980. *The Costs of Using Crop Residues in Direct Applications*. SERI TR 353–513. Golden, CO: Solar Energy Research Institute.

Flavin, C. 1985. *Renewable Energy at the Crossroads*. Washington, D.C.: Center for Renewable Resources.

Flavin, C., and N. Lenssen. 1990. *Beyond the Petroleum Age: Designing a Solar Economy*. Washington, D.C.: Worldwatch Institute.

———. 1991. Here comes the sun. In L. Brown (ed.), *State of the World*, pp. 10–18. Washington, D.C.: Worldwatch Institute.

Folchitto, S. 1991. Seawater as salt and water source for solar ponds. *Solar Energy* 46: 343–351.

Foley, G., and A. van Buren. 1982. Energy in transition from rural agriculture. In M. S. Wionczek, G. Foley, and A. van Buren (eds.), *Energy in the Transition from Rural Subsistence*, pp. 1–20. Boulder, CO: Westview Press.

Folke, C., and N. Kautsky. 1989. The role of ecosystems for a sustainable development aquculture. *Ambio* 18: 234–243.

———. 1992. Aquaculture with its environment: prospects for sustainability. *Ocean and Coastal Management* 17: 5–24.

Follett, R. F., L. C. Benz, E. J. Doering, and G. A. Reichman. 1978. Yield response of corn to irrigation on sandy soils. *Agronomy Journal* 70, 823–828.

Food and Agriculture Organization (FAO). 1961. *Production Yearbook 1960*. Rome: Food and Agriculture Organization of the United Nations.

———. 1972a. *FAO Catalogue of Fishing Gear Designs*. London: Fishing News (Books) LTD.

———. 1972b. *Atlas of the Living Resources of the Seas*. Rome: Food and Agriculture Organization of the United Nations, Department of Fisheries.

———. 1979. *Irrigation and Drainage*. FAO Paper No. 33. Rome: Food and Agriculture Organization of the United Nations.

———. 1981. *Agriculture: Toward 2000*. Rome: Food and Agriculture Organization of the United Nations.

———. 1983a. *1981 Production Yearbook of Forest Products*. Rome: Food and Agriculture Organization of the United Nations.

————. 1983b. *Country Tables. Basic Data on the Agricultural Sector.* Rome: Food and Agriculture Organization. Microfiche 833041.

————. 1984a. Land, Food and People. *FAO Economic and Social Development Series 30.* Rome: Food and Agriculture Organization of the United Nations.

————. 1984b. *Production Yearbook, Vol. 38.* Rome: Food and Agriculture Organization.

————. 1991a. *The State of Food and Agriculture.* Rome: Food and Agriculture Organization of the the United Nations.

————. 1991b. *Food Balance Sheets.* Rome: Food and Agriculture Organization of the United Nations.

Forbes, R. J. 1968. *The Conquest of Nature.* New York: Frederick Praeger.

Fornos, W. 1987. *Gaining People, Losing Ground: A Blueprint for Stabilizing World Population.* Washington, D.C.: The Population Institute.

Frankel, O. H. 1971. Genetic dangers in the Green Revolution. *World Agriculture* 19: 9–13.

Frederick, D. J. 1993. *Modern Windmills Blow Fresh Breeze Worldwide.* Washington, D.C.: National Geographic News Service.

Freeman, J. D. 1955. *Iban Agriculture.* London: Her Majesty's Stationer Office.

Froelich, H. A. 1978. Soil compaction from low ground-pressure, torsion-suspension logging vehicles on three forest soils. Forestry Research Laboratory. Research Paper 36, Oregon State University, School of Forestry, Corvallis, OR.

————. 1979. Soil compaction from logging equipment: effects on growth of young ponderosa pine. *Journal of Soil and Water Conservation* 34, 276–278.

Fuchs, V. R., and D. M. Reklis. 1992. America's children: Economic perspectives and policy options. *Science* 255: 41–46.

Funt, R. C. 1980. Energy use in low, medium and high density apple orchards— Eastern U.S. In D. Pimentel (ed.), *Handbook of Energy Utilization in Agriculture,* pp. 235–246. Boca Raton, FL: CRC Press.

Garst, D. 1990. *What Farmers Want.* Washington, D.C.: Talk to the Agri-Business Council.

General Accounting Office (GAO). 1980. *Conduct of DOE's Gasohol Study Group.* GAO/EMD–80–128. Washington, DC: U.S. GAO.

————. 1990. *Alcohol Fuels.* GAO/RCED–90–156. Washington, DC: U.S. GAO.

Gentry, A. H. 1982. Patterns of neotropical plant species diversity. *Evolutionary Biology* 15: 1–80.

George, S. 1984. *Ill Fares the Land. Essays on Food, Hunger and Power.* Washington, D.C.: Institute for Policy Studies.

Gervais, R. L. 1986. Commercialization of solar central receiver technology. In M. Becker (ed.), *Solar Thermal Central Receiver Systems*, pp. 125–135. Berlin: Springer-Verlag.

Gever, J., R. Kaufman, D. Skole, and C. Vorosmarty. 1991. *Beyond Oil*. Niwot, CO: University Press of Colorado.

Ghirardi, A.G. 1983. Alcohol fuels from biomass in Brazil: A comparative assessment of methanol vs. ethanol. Ph.D. Dissertation, University of California, Berkeley.

Giampietro, M., S. Bukkens, and D. Pimentel. 1992. Limits to population size: Three scenarios of energy interaction between human society and ecosystem. *Population and Environment* 14: 109–131.

Gibbons, J. H., and P. D. Blair. 1991. U.S. Energy transition: On getting from here to there. *Physics Today* 44: 22–30.

Gilmour, D.A., and G. C. King. 1989. Management of forests for local use in the hills of Nepal. 1. Changing forest management paradigms. *Journal of World Forest Resource Management* 4: 93–110.

Giriappa, S. 1986. *Rural Energy Crisis*. Bombay: Himalaya Publishing House.

Glaze, D. H., S. E. Miller, and C. S. Thompson. 1982. The demand for distillers dried grains in South Carolina. *Bulletin of South Carolina Agriculture Experimental Station* 642. Clemson, SC: The Station.

Goldemberg, J. 1987. Personal communication. Institute of Physics, University of Sao Paulo, Brazil.

Goldemberg, J., T. B. Johansson, A.K.N. Reddy, and R. H. Williams. 1988. *Energy for a Sustainable World*. New York: John Wiley and Sons.

Gommend, K., and G. Grossman. 1988. Process steam generation by temperature boosting of heat from solar ponds. *Solar Ponds* 41: 81–89.

Government of India. 1979. Report of the Working Group on Energy Policy. New Delhi: Government of India, Planning Commission.

Grant, W.R., and T. Mullins. 1963. Enterprise costs and returns on rice farms in Grant Prairie, Ark. *Arkansas Agricultural Experimental Station Reports Series* 119.

Grasse, W. 1991. PHOEBUS international 30 MWe solar-tower plant. *Solar Energy Materials* 24: 82–94.

Greathead, D. J. 1983. The multi-million dollar weevil that pollinates oil palm. *Antenna (Royal Entomological Society of London)* 7: 105–107.

Greenland, D. J. 1981. Soil management and soil degradation. *Journal of Soil Science* 32: 301–322.

Gulland, J. A. 1971. *The Fish Resources of the Ocean*. London: Fishing News (Books) LTD (for FAO of UN).

———. 1974. *The Management of Marine Fisheries*. Seattle: University of Washington Press.

Hafele, W. 1991. Energy from nuclear power. *Scientific American* (September): 137–144.

Hairston, N. G., F. E. Smith, and L. B. Slobodkin. 1960. Community structure, population control and competition. *American Naturalist* 94: 421–425.

Hall, C.A.S., C. J. Cleveland, and R. L. Kaufmann. 1986. *Energy and Resource Quality: The Ecology of the Economic Process.* New York: Wiley.

Hall, D. O. 1985. Biomass: Fuel versus food, a world problem? In D. O. Hall, N. Myers, and N. S. Margaris (eds.), *Economics of Ecosystems Management,* pp. 207–226. Dordrecht, The Netherlands: Junk Publishers.

Hall, D. O., and P. J. de Groot. 1987. Introduction: The biomass framework. In D. O. Hall and R. P. Overend (Ees.), *Biomass,* pp. 3–24. Chichester: Wiley.

Hall, D. O., F. Rosillo-Calle, R. H. Williams, and J. Woods. 1993. Biomass for energy: Supply prospects. In T. B. Johansson, H. Kelley, A.K.N. Reddy, and R. H. Williams (eds.), *Renewable Energy.* Washington, D.C.: Island Press.

Hall, D. O., N. Myers, and N. S. Margaris (eds.) 1985. *Economics of Ecosystems Management.* Dordrecht, The Netherlands: Junk Publishers.

Hansen, A. C. 1980. *Community Impact of SWECS noise.* Rocky Flats, CO: Rocky Flats Wind Systems Test Center.

Hanson, A. D., and W. D Hitz. 1983. Whole-plant response to water deficits: water deficits and the nitrogen economy. In H. M. Taylor, W. R. Jordan, and T. R. Sinclair (eds.), *Limitations to Efficient Water Use in Crop Production,* pp. 331–344. Madison, WI: American Society of Agronomy, Crop Science Society of America, and Soil Science Society of America.

Hanson, A. J., T. A. Spies, F. J. Swanson, and J. L. Ohmann. 1991. Conserving biodiversity in managed forests. *BioScience* 41: 382–392.

Hardin, G., 1986. Cultural carrying capacity: a biological approach to human problems. *BioScience* 36 : 599–606.

Hardy, R.W.F., P. Filner, and R. H. Hageman. 1975. Nitrogen input. In A.W.A. Brown, T. C. Byerly, M. Gibbs, and A. San Pietro (eds.), *Crop Productivity: Research Imperatives,* pp. 133–176. Proceedings of an international conference at Michigan State University Agricultural Experiment Station, and Charles F. Kettering Foundation.

Harper, J. L. 1977. *Population Biology of Plants.* London: Academic Press.

Harrar, J. G. 1961. Socioeconomic factors that limit needed food production and consumption. *Federation Proceedings* 20: 381–383.

Harrison, G. G., W. L. Rathje, and W. W. Hughes. 1975. Food waste behavior in an urban population. *Journal of Nutritional Education* 7: 13–16.

Harrold, L. L. 1972. *Soil Erosion by Water as Affected by Reduced Tillage Systems.* Columbus, Ohio: Center for Tomorrow.

Harrold, L. L., and W. M. Edwards. 1974. No-tillage system reduces erosion from continuous corn watersheds. *Transactions of American Society of Agricultural Engineering* 17: 414–416.

Harrold, L. L., G. B. Triplett, Jr., and R. E. Youker. 1967. Watershed tests of no-tillage corn. *Journal of Soil and Water Conservation* 22 (3): 98–100.

Hartwig, N. L. 1987. Cropping practices using crownvetch in conservation tillage. In J. F. Power (ed.), *Role of Legumes in Conservation Tillage Systems*, pp. 109–110. Ankeny, IA: Soil Conservation Society of America.

Hashimoto, K., A. M. Heagler, and B. McManus. 1992. A comparison of rice production cost, Japan and southwest Louisiana. *Agricultural Economics and Agribusiness* 106.

HCP. 1974. *Handbook of Chemistry and Physics*. Cleveland: The Chemical Rubber Co.

Heede, R., R. Morgan, and S. Ridley. 1985. *The Hidden Costs of Energy: How Taxpayer's Substitute Energy Development*. Washington, D.C.: Center for Renewable Resources.

Heichel, G. H. 1980. Assessing the fossil energy costs of propagating agricultural crops. In D. Pimentel (ed.), *Handbook of Energy Utilization in Agriculture*, pp. 27–33. Boca Raton, FL: CRC Press.

Hempel, L. 1951. Uber Kartierungsmethoden von Bodenerosion durch Wasser. Neves Arch. Niedersachsen 26, 590–598. In D. Zachar, *Soil Erosion*. Developments in Soil Science 10. Amsterdam: Elsevier Scientific, 1982.

———. 1954. Beispiele von Bodenerosion karten im Niedersächsischen Bergland sowie Bermerkungen uber Ber¸cksightigung der Erosionsschaden bei der Bodenschützung. Neves Arch. Niedersachsen 4–6, 140–143. In D. Zachar, *Soil Erosion*. Developments in Soil Science 10. Amsterdam: Elsevier Scientific, 1982.

Hendrickson, B. H., A. P. Barnett, J. R. Carreker, and W. E. Adams. 1963. Runoff and erosion control studies on Cecil soil in the southern Piedmont. U.S. Department of Agriculture Technical Bulletin No. 1281.

Henry, K. A. 1971. *Atlantic Menhaden (Brevoortia tyrannus) Resource and Fishery—Analysis of Decline*. Technical Report, National Marine Fisheries Service, Seattle, WA.

Hertzberg, R., B. Vaughan, and J. Greene. 1973. *Putting Food By*. Brattleboro, VT: Stephen Green Press.

Hewlett, J. D. 1979. Forest water quality. An experiment in harvesting and regenerating Piedmont forest, Georgia Forest Research Paper, School of Forest Resources, University of Georgia, Athens.

Highfill, R., and L. Kimberlin. 1977. Current soil erosion and sediment control technology for rural and urban lands. In *Proceedings of a National Symposium on Soil Erosion and Sedimentation by Water*, pp. 14–22. Chicago: American Society of Agricultural Engineers.

Hildebrand, S. G. 1979. Potential environmental impacts of hydroelectric development: an overview. In *Hydropower: A National Energy Resource.* Edited by Engineering Foundation Conference: National Energy Resource March 11–16 Easton, MD. 322–329. Washington, D.C.: The Engineering Foundation, New York given with U.S. Army Corps of Engineers, Ft. Belvoir, VA.

Hirst, E. 1974. Food-related energy requirements. *Science* 184: 134–139.

Holdren, C. 1992. Population alarm. *Science* 255: 1358.

Holdren, J. P. 1991. Energy in transition. In J. Piel (ed.), *Energy for Planet Earth.* W. H. Freeman Co., New York, pp. 119–130.

Holdren, J. P., G. Morris, and I. Mintzer. 1980. Environmental aspects of renewable energy. *Annual Review of Energy* 5: 241–291.

Hole, F. D. 1981. Effects of animals on soil. *Geoderma* 25: 75–112.

Hornbeck, J. W., G. E. Likens, R. S. Pierce, and F. H. Bormann. 1973. Strip cutting as a means of protecting site and streamflow quality when clearcutting northern hardwoods. In B. Bernier and C. H. Winget, eds., *Forest Soils and Forest Land Management,* pp. 209–225. Procedures of the Fourth North American Soils Conference. Quebec, Canada: Laval University Press.

Hosier, R. 1985. *Energy Use in Rural Kenya: Household Demand and Rural Transformation.* Beijer Institute, Royal Swedish Academy of Sciences, Scandinavian Institute of African Studies. Energy, Environment and Development in Africa No. 7, OAE. Stockholm, Uppsala.

Howard, B., and S. S. Szoke. 1992. *Advances in Solar Design Tools.* 5th Thermal Envelope Conference, December, 1992. Clearwater, FL: U.S. Department of Energy, ASHRAE.

Hubbert, M. K. 1972. Man's conquest of energy: Its ecological and human consequences. In A. B. Kline (ed.), *The Enviromental and Ecological Forum 1970–1971,* pp. 1–50. Oak Ridge, TN: U.S. Atomic Energy Commission Technical Information Center.

Humphreys, W. F. 1979. Production and respiration in animal populations. *Journal of Animal Ecology* 48: 427–454.

Institute on Hunger and Development. 1990. *Hunger 1990: A Report on the State of World Hunger.* Washington, D.C.: Institute on Hunger and Development.

International Atomic Energy Agency (IAEA). 1991. Senior Expert Symposium on Electricity and the Environment: Key Issues Papers. Helsinki: IAEA.

International Commission on Large Dams (ICLD). 1988. *World Register of Dams.* Paris: International Commission on Large Dams.

International Energy Agency. 1989. *Energy Balances of OECD Countries.* Paris: IEA.

———. 1991. *Energy Statistics of OECD Countries.* Paris: IEA.

International Institute for Applied Systems Analysis (IIASA), 1981. *Energy in a Finite World—A Global Systems Analysis.* Cambridge, MA: Ballinger.

International Institute of Tropical Agriculture (IITA). 1973. *Year report 1973.* Ibadan, Nigeria: IITA.

Janzen, D. H. 1981. The peak in North American ichneumonid species richness lies between 38 and 42° N. *Ecology* 62: 532–537.

———. 1987. Insect diversity of a Costa Rican dry forest: why keep it, and how? *Biology Journal of the Linneaus Society* 30: 343–356.

Jensen, C., H. Price, and D. Kearney. 1989. The SEGS power plants: 1989 performance. In A. H. Fanney and K. O. Lund (eds.), *Solar Engineering 1989,* pp. 97–102. New York: ASME.

Jensen, L. B. 1949. *Meat and Meat Foods.* New York: Ronald Press.

Jewell, W. J., and G. R. Morris. 1974. The economic and technical feasibility of methane generation from agricultural waste. In R. J. Catania (ed.), *Uses of Agricultural Wastes: Food, Fuel, Fertilizer,* pp. 132–164. Regina, Canada: University of Regina.

Jewell, W. J., H. R. Davis, W. W. Gunkel, D. J. Lathwell, J. H. Martin, Jr., T. R. McCarty, G. R. Morris, D. R. Price, and D. W. Williams. 1977. *Bioconversion of Agricultural Wastes for Pollution Control and Energy Conservation.* Division of Solar Energy, ERDA. Springfield, VA: National Technical Information Service.

Jiler, H. 1972. *Commodity Yearbook.* New York: Commodity Research Bureau.

Jones, D. A. 1966. On the polymorphism of cyanogenesis in Lotus corniculatus. Selection by animals. *Canadian Journal of Genetics Cytology* 8: 556–567.

———. 1979. Chemical defense: primary or secondary function? *American Nature* 113: 445–451.

Jordan, W. R. 1983. Whole plant response to water deficits: an overview. In H. M. Taylor, W. R. Jordan, and T. R. Sinclair (eds.), *Limitations to Efficient Water Use in Crop Production,* pp. 289–318. Madison, WI: American Society of Agronomy, Crop Science Society of America, and Soil Science Society of America.

Kahn, A. M., 1986. *Acid Rain Reign of Controversy.* Golden, CO: Fulcrum Inc.

Kane, S., J. Reilly, M. R. LeBlanc, and J. Hrubovcak. 1989. Ethanol's role: An economic assessment. *Agribusiness* 5: 505–522.

Kates, R. W., R. S. Chen, T. E. Downing, J. X. Kasperson, E. Messer, and S. R. Millman. 1989. *The Hunger Report: Update 1989.* Providence, RI: Alan Shawn Feinstein World Hunger Program, Brown University.

Kaupang, B. M. 1983. *Assessment of Distributed Wind-Power Systems.* New York: Electrical Utility Systems. EPRI Report AP2882.

Kedziora, A., J. Olejnik, and J. Kapuchinski. 1989. Impact of landscape structure on heat and water balance. *International Association for Ecology* 17: 1–17.

Kellet, J. 1990. The environmental impacts of wind energy developments. *Town Planning Review* 61: 139–154.

Kendall, H. W., 1991. The failure of nuclear power. In M. Shubik (ed.), *Risk, Organizations, and Society*, pp. 163–217. Boston: Kluwer Academic Publishers.

Kendall, H. W., and D. Pimentel. 1994. Constraints on the expansion of the global food supply. *Ambio* 23: 198–205.

Kennedy, T., J. Finnell, and D. Kumor. 1991. Considering environmental costs in energy planning: alternative approaches and implementation. In T. R. Mancini, K. Watanabe and D. E. Klett (eds.), *Solar Engineering 1991*, pp. 145–150. New York: ASME.

Kerr, R. A., 1992. New assaults seen on earth's ozone shield. *Science* 255: 797–798.

Ketcheson, J. 1977. Conservation tillage in eastern Canada. *Journal of Soil and Water Conservation*, 32: 57–60.

Ketcheson, J. W., and J. J. Onderdonk. 1973. Effect of corn stover on phosphorus in run-off from nontilled soil. *Agronomy Journal* 65: 69–71.

Kevan, D. K. McE. 1962. *Soil Animals*. New York: Philosophical Library.

Keyfitz, N. 1976. World resources and the world middle class. *Scientific American* 235: 28–35.

Keyfitz, N. 1984. Impact of trends in resources, environment and development on demographic prospects. In *Population, Resources, Environment and Development*, pp. 97–124. New York: United Nations.

Khoshoo, T. N. 1986. *Environmental Priorities in India and Sustainable Development*. New Delhi: Indian Science Congress Association.

———. 1987. Personal communication. New Delhi: Tata Energy Research Institute.

Kidd, C., and D. Pimentel (eds.) 1992. *Integrated Resource Management: Agroforestry for Development*. San Diego: Academic Press.

Kitazawa, Y., and T. Kitazawa. 1980. Influence of application of a fungicide, an insecticide, and compost upon soil biotic community. In D. L. Dindal (ed.), *Soil Biology as Related to Land Use Practices*, pp. 94–99. Washington, D.C.: Office of Pesticide and Toxic Substances, EPA.

Klausner, S. D., P. J. Zwerman, and D. F. Ellis. 1974. Surface runoff losses of soluble nitrogen and phosphorus under two systems of soil management. *Journal of Environmental Quality* 3: 42–46.

Klippstein, R. N. 1979. *The True Cost of Home Food Preservation*. Cornell University Information Bulletin No. 158. Ithaca, NY: Cornell University.

Klock, G. O. 1982. Some soil erosion effects on forest soil productivity. In *Determinants of Soil Loss Tolerance*, pp. 53–66. American Society of Agronomy Special Publication No. 45, Soil Science Society of America. Madison, WI: American Society of Agronomy.

Knutson, L. 1989. On the diversity of nature and the nature of diversity. *Bulletin of the Entomological Society of America* 35 (4): 7–11.

Kohl, W. L. 1990. *Methanol as an Alternative Fuel Choice: An Assessment.* Washington, D.C.: The Johns Hopkins Foreign Policy Institute.

Koppleman, L. E., and D. S. Davies. 1987. *Strategies and Recommendations for Revitalizing the Hard Clam Fisheries in Suffolk County.* Hamppauge, NY: Suffolk County Planning Department.

Kotamraju, P. 1986. *Subsistence Economics and Ecological Irreversibilities: The Case of Subsistence Fuels in India.* Duluth, MN: School of Business and Economics, University of Minnesota.

Krebs, C. J. 1985. *Ecology: The Experimental Analysis of Distribution and Abundance.* New York: Harper & Row, Publishers.

Krischik, V. A., and R. F. Denno. 1983. Individual, population, and geographic patterns of plant defense. In R. F. Denno and M. S. McClure (eds.), *Variable Plants and Herbivores in Natural and Managed Systems*, pp. 463–512. New York: Academic Press.

Kuby, W., R. Markoja, and S. Nackford. 1984. *Testing and Evaluation of On-farm Alcohol Production Facilities.* Cincinnati, OH: Acurex Corporation, Industrial Environmental Research Laboratory, Office of Research and Development, U.S. EPA.

Kurian, G. T. 1995. *Encyclopedia of the Third World.* Fourth ed. New York: Facts on File, Inc.

La Rovere, E. L. 1985. A south-south assault on the food/energy problem. *Ceres* 18 (1): 25–28.

Lal, R. 1976. 1981. In R. Lal and E. W. Russell (eds.), *Tropical Agricultural Hydrology.* New York: John Wiley and Sons.

———. 1983. Erosion-caused productivity decline in soils of the humid tropics. *Soil Taxonomy News* 5: 4–5, 18.

———. 1984. Mechanized tillage systems effects on soil erosion from an alfisol in watersheds cropped to maize. *Soil & Tillage Research* 4: 349–360.

Lal, R., and B. A. Stewart (eds). 1990. *Soil Degradation. Advances in Soil Science. Vol. 11.* New York: Springer-Verlag.

Lal, R., and F. J. Pierce (eds). 1991. *Soil Management for Sustainability.* Ankeny, IA: Soil and Water Conservation Society.

Laluce, C. 1991. Current aspects of fuel ethanol production in Brazil. *Critical Review of Biotechnology* 11: 149–161.

Lamarre, L. 1992. A growth market for wind power. *EPRI Journal* (December): 6–15.

Lamb, R., and S. Milas. 1983. Soil erosion, real cause of Ethiopian famine. *Environmental Conservation* 10: 157–159.

Lanly, J. P. 1982. *Tropical Forest Resources.* Rome: Food and Agriculture Organization of the United Nations.

Larson, D. L., and D. D. Fangmeier. 1977. *Energy Use in Management.* New York: Pergamon Press.

Lawrence, K. A. 1979. *A Review of the Environmental Effects and Benefits of Selected Solar Energy Technologies.* Golden, CO: Solar Energy Research Institute, Department of Energy.

Lawrence, M. F. 1990. Economics of fuel methanol: asking the right question. In W. L. Kohl (ed.), *Methanol as an Alternative Fuel Choice: An Assessment,* pp. 259–276. Washington, D.C.: The Johns Hopkins Foreign Policy Institute.

Lawton, J. H., and S. McNeil. 1979. Between the devil and the deep blue sea: One problem of being a herbivore. In R. M. Anderson, B. D. Turner, and L. R. Taylor (eds.), *Population Dynamics,* pp. 223–244. Oxford: Blackwell.

Laycock, G. 1986. *The Alien Animals.* New York: Natural History Press.

Leach, G. 1976. *Energy and Food Production.* Guildford, Surrey, UK: IPC Science and Technology Press Ltd.

———. 1988. Residential energy in the third world. *Annual Review of Energy* 13: 47–65.

Lee, L. K. 1984. Land use and soil loss: a 1982 update. *Journal of Soil and Water Conservation* 39: 226–228.

Lee, N. E. 1955. *Travel and Transport Through the Ages.* Cambridge, UK: Cambridge University Press.

Lee, R. B. 1969. !Kung Bushman subsistence an input-output analysis. In A. P. Vayda (ed.), *Environment and Cultural Behavior: Ecological Studies in Cultural Anthropology,* pp. 47–79. Garden City, NY: Natural History Press.

Lee, R. B., and I. DeVore. 1976. *Kalahari Hunter-Gathers.* Cambridge: Harvard University Press.

Lemckert, A., and J. J. Campos. 1981. *Produccion y consumo de Lena en las Fincas Pequenas de Costa Rica.* Turrialba, Costa Rica: Centro Agronomico Tropical de Investigacion y Ensenanza (CATIE).

Leonard, D. E. 1974. Recent developments in ecology and control of the gypsy moth. *Annual Review of Entomology* 19: 197–229.

Leonard, J. N. 1973. *The First Farmers.* (The Emergence of Man Series). New York: Time-Life Books.

Levin, D. A. 1976. The chemical defenses of plants to pathogens and herbivores. *Review of Ecology and Systematics* 7: 121–159.

Levin, S., and D. Pimentel. 1981. Selection of intermediate rates of increase in parasite-host systems. *American Naturalist* 117: 308–315.

Lewis, C. W. 1976. Fuel production from biomass. Report No. 7, Systems Analysis Research Unit, Energy Studies Unit. University of Strathclyde, Glasgow.

Lewis, O. 1951. *Life in a Mexican Village: Tepostlan Restudied.* Urbana: University of Illinois Press.

Leyton, L. 1983. Crop water use: principles and some considerations for agroforestry. In P. A. Huxley (ed.), *Plant Research and Agroforestry*, pp. 379–400. Nairobi, Kenya: International Council for Research in Agroforestry.

Lieth, H., and R. H. Whittaker (eds.) 1975. *Primary Productivity of the Biosphere*. New York: Springer Verlag.

Lin, E.I.H., R. L. French, M. J. Singer, Y. C. Wu, J. C. McMurrin, R. H. Barbieri, A. L. Walton, S. C. Jones, M. G. Hurick, N. Levine, and P. H. Richter. 1982. *Regional Applicability and Potential of Salt-Gradient Solar Ponds in the United States*. JPL Publication 82–10 ed. Detailed Report. Report prepared for U.S. Department of Energy by Jet Propulsion Laboratory. Pasadena, CA: California Institute of Technology.

Linden, H. R. 1980. *1980 Assessment of the U.S. and World Energy Situation and Outlook*. Chicago: Gas Research Institute.

Lipfert, F. W., R. G. Malone, M. L. Dawn, N. R. Mendell, and C. C. Young. 1988. *Statisical Study of the Macroepidemiology of Air Pollution and Total Mortality*. Washington, D.C.: U.S. Department of Energy, Report No. BNL 52122.

Litovitz, T. L., B. F. Schmitz, and K. M. Bailey. 1990. 1989 Annual report of the American Association of Poison Control Centers National Data Collection System. *American Journal of Emergency Medicine* 8: 394–442.

Loftness, R. L. 1984. *Energy Handbook* (2nd ed.). New York: Van Nostrad Reinhold Co.

Lowe, M., 1991. Rethinking urban transport. In L. R. Brown et al. (eds.), *State of the World 1991*. Washington, D.C.: Worldwatch Institute.

Lucas, R. E., J. B. Holtman, and L. J. Connor. 1977. Soil carbon dynamics and cropping practices. In W. Lockeretz (ed.), *Agriculture and Energy*, pp. 333–351. New York: Academic Press.

Lugo, A. E. 1988. Estimating reductions in the diversity of tropical forest species. In E. O. Wilson (ed.), *Biodiversity*, pp. 58–70. Washington, D.C.: National Academy of Sciences.

Lynd, L. R. 1990. Large-scale fuel ethanol from lignocellulose. *Applied Biochemistry and Biotechnology* 24/25: 695–717.

Lynd, L. R., J. H. Cushman, R. J. Nichols, and C. E. Wyman. 1991. Fuel ethanol from cellulose biomass. *Science* 251: 1318–1323.

Mabbutt, J. A. 1989. Impacts of carbon dioxide warming on climate and man in the semi-arid tropics. *Climatic Change* 15: 191–221.

Machlis, G. E., and D. L. Tichnell. 1985. *The State of the World's Parks*. Boulder, CO: Westview Press.

Mack, J. 1971. *Catfish Farming Handbook*. San Angelo, TX: Educator Books.

MacKenzie, J. J., R. C. Dower, and D.T.D. Chen. 1992. *The Going Rate: What it Really Costs to Drive*. Washington, D.C.: World Resources Institute.

Maeda, Y., and M. Kai. 1991. Recent progress in pervaporation membranes for water/ethanol separation. In R.V.M. Huang (ed.), *Pervaporation Membrane Separation Processes,* pp. 391–435. Amsterdam: Elsevier.

Malthus, T. R. 1926. *First Essay on Population, 1798.* London: Macmillan & Co., Ltd.

Mangelsdorf, P. C. 1966. Genetic potentials for increasing yields of food crops and animals. In *Prospects of the World Food Supply.* Washington, D.C.: Symposium Proceedings of the National Academy of Sciences.

Mannering, J. V. 1984. Conservation tillage to maintain soil productivity and improve water quality. Agronomy Guide (Tillage) AY–222. Cooperative Extension Service, Purdue University, West Lafayette, IN.

Mannering, J., and C. R. Fenster. 1977. *Vegetative water erosion for agricultural areas.* St. Joseph, MI: ASAE.

Margetts, A. R. 1974. Modern development of fishing gear. In F. R. H. Jones. (ed.), *Sea Fisheries Research,* pp. 243–260. New York: John Wiley & Sons.

Marshall, L. J. 1976. *The !Kung of Nyae Nyae.* Cambridge: Harvard University Press.

Marston, E. H., 1975. *The Dynamic Environment: Water, Transportation, and Energy.* Lexington, MA: Xeros College Publications.

Martin, J. P., E. V. Abbott, and C. C. Hughes. 1961. *Sugar-cane Diseases of the World.* Amsterdam: Elsevier.

Matare, H. F. 1989. *Energy: Fact and Future.* Boca Raton, FL: CRC Press.

Matherne, R. 1990. *Testimony of Concerned Shrimpers of America.* Washington, D.C.: Fisheries and Wildlife Conservation and the Environment Subcommittee of the House of Representative Merchant Marine and Fisheries Committee, U.S. Congress. May 1, 1990.

Maugh, T. H. 1982. Solar with a grain of salt. *Science* 216: 213–214.

May, R. M. 1988. How many species are there on earth? *Science* 241: 1441–1449.

McCashion, J. D., and R. M. Rice. 1983. Erosion on logging roads in northwestern California: how much is avoidable? *Journal of Forestry* 81: 23–26.

McGoodwin J. R. 1990. *Crisis in the World's Fisheries.* Stanford, CA: Stanford University Press.

McKey, D. 1974. Adaptive patterns in alkaloid physiology. *American Naturalist* 108: 305–320.

McNeil, S., and J. H. Lawton. 1970. Annual production and respiration in animal populations. *Nature (London)* 225: 472–474.

Meade, G. P., and J.C.P. Chen. 1977. *Cane Sugar Handbook.* New York: John Wiley & Sons.

Meadows, D. H., D. L. Meadows, and J. Randers. 1992. *Beyond the Limits.* Post Mills, VT: Chelsea Green.

Medsker, L. 1982. *Side Effects of Renewable Energy Sources.* Environmental Policy Research Department Report No. 15. New York: National Audubon Society.

Meeks, F., and J. Drummond. 1991. Nuclear power can be environmentally safe. In C. P. Cozic and M. Polesetsky (eds.), *Energy Alternatives,* pp. 46–52. San Diego: Greenhaven Press.

Megahan, W. F. 1972. Logging, erosion, sedimentation—are they dirty words? *Journal of Forestry* 70: 403–407.

———. 1975. Sedimentation in relation to logging activities in the mountains of central Idaho. In *Present and Prospective Technology for Predicting Sediment Yields and Sources,* pp. 74–82. Proceedings of Sediment-Yield Workshop, USDA, Sedimentation Laboratory, Oxford, Mississippi, November 28–30, 1972. USDA Agricultural Research Service, ARS-S-40.

Melody, I. 1991. Solar cooling research for hot, humid climates. *Solar Today* 5: 23–24.

Metcalf, R. L., and R. L. Metcalf. 1993. *Destructive and Useful Insects: Their Habits and Control.* Fifth ed. New York: McGraw-Hill, Inc.

Mierzwa, T., and H. Hiemstra. 1981. Federal programs affecting agricultural land availability. In M. F. Brewer (ed.), *Agricultural Land Availability: Papers on the Supply and Demand for Agricultural Lands in the United States,* pp. 347–387. Washington, D.C.: Government Printing Office.

Mihlmester, P. E., J. B. Thomasian, and M. R. Riches. 1980. Environmental and health safety issues. In W. C. Dickinson and P. N. Cheremisinoff (eds). *Solar Energy Technology Handbook.* New York: Marcel Dekker, Inc.

Miller, W. E. and R. F. Schmalz. 1990. Detection and mitigation of indoor radon. In S. K. Majundar, R. F. Schmalz and E. W. Miller (eds.), *Environmental Radon: Occurrence, Control and Health Hazards,* pp. 144–156. Phillipsburg, NJ: Typehouse of Easton.

Ministerio de Minas e Energia (MME). 1987. Ava liacao do Programa Nacional do A'lcool. Comissao Nacional de Energia, Ministe'rio de Minas e Energia, Brasilia.

Ministry of Food, Agriculture Community Development and Cooperation (MFACDCGI). 1966. *Farm Management in India.* New Dehli: Directorate of Economy and Statistics, Department of Agriculture, Government of India.

Mishra, R. K. (ed.) 1986. *India Toward the 1990s.* New Delhi: Patriot Publishers.

Mitchell, C., and C. J. Cleveland. 1993. Resource scarcity, energy use and environmental impact: a case study of the New Bedford, Massachusetts, USA, fisheries. *Environmental Management* 17: 305–317.

Moldenhauer, W. C., W. G. Lovely, N. P. Swanson, and H. D. Currence. 1971. Effects of row grades and tillage systems on soil and water losses. *Journal of Soil and Water Conservation* 26: 193–195.

Molofsky, J., C.A.S. Hall, and N. Myers. 1986. *A Comparison of Tropical Forest Surveys.* Washington, D.C.: U.S. Department of Energy, CO_2 Research Division.

Montalembert, M. R. de, and J. Clement. 1983. Fuelwood supplies in the developing countries. Forestry Paper No. 42. Rome: Food and Agriculture Organization.

Moore, T. 1992. High hopes for high-power solar. *EPRI Journal* December: 16–25.

Moreira, J. R., and J. Goldemberg. 1981. Alcohol—its use, energy and economics— A Brazilian outlook. *Resource Management and Optimization* 1: 231–279.

Moreira, J. R., and G. E. Serra. 1985. The Brazilian National Alcohol Program— Incentives and Subsidies. International Institute of Environment and Development.

Morris, H. M. 1922. The insect and other invertebrate fauna of arable land at Rothamsted. *Annals of Applied Biology* 9: 283–305.

Morris, S. C. 1981. *Health effects of residential wood fuel use.* Upton, NY: Brookhaven National Laboratory.

Mukanski, J., and S. Strauss. 1992. Non-Burn Electric Generation: How Today's Options Stack Up. *Power* July: 15–20.

Murkowski, F. 1991. America needs Alaska's oil. *N.Y. Times,* April 1: 17.

Murugaboopathi, C., M. Tomita, E. Yamaji, and S. Koide. 1991. Prospect of large-size paddy field using direct seeding supported by surface irrigation system. *Trans. ASAE* 34 (5): 2040–2046.

Musgrave, G. W., and O. R. Neal. 1937. *Transactions of the American Geophysical Union* 18: 349.

Myers, N. 1983. *A Wealth of Wild Species.* Boulder, CO: Westview Press.

———. 1986a. Forestland farming in western Amazonia: stable and sustainable. *Forest Ecology and Management* 15: 81–93.

———. 1986b. Environmental repercussions of deforestation in the Himalayas. *Journal of World Forest Resource Management* 2: 63–72.

———. 1989. *Deforestation Rates in Tropical Forests and their Climatic Implications.* London: Friends of the Earth Report.

———. 1990. Mass extinctions: What can the past tell us about the present and future? *Global and Planetary Change* 2: 82.

———. 1992. Tropical forests: the policy challenge. *The Environmentalist* 12(1): 15–27.

Narayana, D.V.V., and R. Babu. 1983. Estimation of soil erosion in India. *Journal of Irrigation and Drainage Engineering* 109: 419–434.

Nastari, P. M. 1983. The role of sugar cane in Brazil's history and economy. Ph.D. thesis, Iowa State University, Ames, IA.

National Academy of Sciences (NAS). 1971. *Rapid Population Growth.* Washington, D.C.: National Academy of Sciences.

————. 1975a. *Agricultural Productivity Efficiency.* Washington, D.C.: National Academy of Science.

————. 1975b. *Population and Food: Crucial Issues.* Washington, D.C.: National Academy of Sciences.

————. 1977. *World Food and Nutrition Study.* Washington, D.C.: National Academy of Sciences.

————. 1980. *Firewood crops: shrubs and tree species for energy production.* Washington, D.C.: National Academy Press.

————. 1981. *Feeding Value of Ethanol Production By-Products.* Washington, D.C.: National Academy of Sciences.

————. 1982. *Impact of Emerging Agricultural Trends on Fish and Wildlife Habitat.* Washington, D.C.: National Academy Press.

————. 1984. *Casuarinas: Nitrogen-Fixing Trees for Adverse Sites.* Washington, D.C.: National Academy of Sciences.

————. 1989a. *Alternative Agriculture.* Washington, D.C.: National Academy of Sciences.

————. 1989b. *Irrigation-Induced Water Quality Problems.* Washington, D.C.: National Academy of Sciences.

————. 1989c. *Recommended Dietary Allowances.* Washington, D.C.: National Academy of Sciences.

————. 1991. *Malaria Prevention and Control.* Washington, D.C.: National Academy of Sciences.

National Advisory Panel (NAP). 1987. *Fuel Ethanol Cost-effectiveness Study.* Final Report. Washington, D.C.: National Advisory Panel on Cost-effectiveness of Fuel Ethanol Production.

National Oceanic and Atmospheric Administration (NOAA). 1991. *Fisheries of the United States 1990.* Washington, D.C.: U.S. Government Printing Office.

————. 1992. *Status of Fishery Resources off the Northeastern United States for 1992.* Technical Memorandum NMFS-F/NEC–95. Washington, D.C.: U.S. Department of Commerce.

Neal, H. A., and J. R. Schubel. 1987. *Solid Waste Management and the Environment.* Englewood Cliffs, NJ: Prentice Hall, Inc.

Nef, J. V. 1977. An early energy crisis and its consequences. *Scientific American* 237: 140–151.

NES. 1991. *National Energy Strategy: Powerful Ideas for America.* Washington, D.C.: U.S. Government Printing Office.

Newman, P.W.G., and J. R. Kenworthy. 1989. *Cities and Automobile Dependence: A Sourcebook.* Brookfield, VT: Gower Technical.

Nichols, J. O. 1961. *The Gypsy Moth in Pennsylvania—Its History and Eradication.* Harrisburg, PA: Pennsylvania Department of Agriculture Miscellaneous Bulletin 4404.

Nielsen, E. G., and L. K. Lee. 1987. *The Magnitude and Costs of Groundwater Contamination from Agricultural Chemicals. A National Perspective.* ERS Staff Report, AGES 870318. Washington, D.C.: U.S. Department of Agriculture.

Odum, E. P. 1971. *Fundamentals of Ecology.* Philadelphia: W.B. Saunders Co.

———. 1978. *Fundamentals of Ecology.* New York: Saunders.

Office of Technology Assessment (OTA). 1978. *Applications of Solar Technology to Today's Energy Needs.* Washington, D.C.: U.S. Congress Office of Technology Assessment.

———. 1980a. *Land Use and Environmental Impacts of Decentralized Solar Energy Use.* Washington, D.C.: U.S. Congress Office of Technology Assessment.

———. 1980b. *Energy from Biological Processes, Vols. 1 and 2.* Washington, D.C.: U.S. Congress Office of Technology Assessment.

———. 1982. *Impacts of Technology on U.S. Cropland and Rangeland Productivity.* Washington, D.C.: U.S. Congress Office of Technology Assessment.

———. 1983. *Water-Related Technologies for Sustainable Agriculture in U.S. Arid/Semi-arid Lands.* Washington, D.C.: U.S. Congress Office of Technology Assessment.

———. 1984. *Technologies to Sustain Tropical Forest Resources.* OTA-F–214. Washington, D.C.: U.S. Congress Office of Technology Assessment.

———. 1989. *Facing America's Trash—What Next for Municipal Solid Waste.* Washington, D.C.: U.S. Congress Office of Technology Assessment.

———. 1990. *Replacing Gasoline: Alternative Fuels for Light-duty Vehicles.* Washington, D.C.: U.S. Congress Office of Technology Assessment.

———. 1991a. *Energy in Developing Countries.* Washington, D.C.: U.S. Congress Office of Technology Assessment.

———. 1991b. *Improving Automobile Fuel Economy: New Standards, New Approaches.* Washington, D.C.: U.S. Congress Office of Technology Assessment.

———. 1991c. *Expanding Energy Supplies in Developing Countries Raises Problems.* Washington, D.C.: U.S. Congress Office of Technology Assessment.

———. 1992a. *Fueling Development: Energy Technologies for Developing Countries.* Washington, D.C.: U.S. Congress Office of Technology Assessment.

———. 1992b. *Building Energy Efficiency.* Washington, D.C.: U.S. Congress Office of Technology Assessment.

Ogden, J. M., and R. H. Williams. 1989. *Solar Hydrogen: Moving Beyond Fossil Fuels.* Washington, D.C.: World Resources Institute.

O'Keefe, P. 1983. The causes, consequences and remedies of soil erosion in Kenya. *Ambio* 12: 302–305.

O'Keefe, P., and P. Raskin. 1985. Fuelwood in Kenya: crisis and opportunity. *Ambio* 14: 220–224.

O'Keefe, P., P. Raskin, and S. Bernow (eds.). 1984. *Energy and Development in Kenya: Opportunities and Constraints*. Beijer Institute, Royal Swedish Academy of Sciences, Scandinavian Institute of African Studies. Energy, Environment and Development in Africa. Stockholm, Uppsala.

Olah-Zsupos, A., and B. Helmeczi. 1987. The effect of soil conditioners on soil microorganisms. In J. Szegi (ed.), *Soil Biology and Conservation of the Biosphere*, pp. 829–837. Proceedings of the 9th International Symposium. Budapest: Akademiai Kiado.

Opler, P. A. 1974. *Biology, Ecology, and Host Specificity of Microlepidoptera Associated with* Quercus agrifolia (Fagacceae). Berkeley: University of California Press.

Organization for Economic Cooperation and Development (OECD). 1984. *Biomass for Energy: Economic and Policy Issues*. Paris: OECD.

———. 1988. *Environmental Impacts of Renewable Energy*. Paris: OECD.

Ortmaier, E. 1981. The production of ethanol from sugarcane: Brazil's experiment for a partial solution to the energy problem. *Quarterly Journal of International Agriculture* 20: 265–278.

Oschwald, W. R., and J. C. Siemens. 1976. Soil erosion after soybeans. In L. D. Hill (ed.), *World Soybean Research. Proceedings of the World Soybean Research Conference, 1975*. Danville, IL: The Interstate Printers and Publishers, Inc.

Osuji, G. E. 1984. The gullies of Imo. *Journal of Soil and Water Conservation* 39: 246–247.

Packard, A. S. 1890. *Insects Injurious to Forest and Shade Trees*. Washington, D.C.: USDA.

Pankhurst, C. E., and J. I. Sprent. 1975. Effects of water stress on the respiratory and nitrogen-fixing activity of soybean root nodules. *Journal of Experimental Botany* 26: 287–304.

Paoletti, M. G. 1988. Soil invertebrates in cultivated and uncultivated soils in Northeastern Italy. *Estratto da Redia* 71: 501–563.

Paoletti, M. G., M. R. Favretto, S. Ragusa, and R. Z. Strassen. 1989a. Animal and plant interactions in the agroecosystems: The case of the woodland remnants in Northeastern Italy. *Ecology International Bulletin* 17: 79–91.

Paoletti, M. G., B. R. Stinner, and G. G. Lorenzoni. 1989b. Agricultural Ecology and the Environment. *Agriculture, Ecosystems & Environment* 27: (1–4).

Paoletti, M. G., D. Pimentel, B. R. Stinner, and D. Stinner. 1992. Agroecosystem biodiversity: matching production and conservation biology. In M. G. Paoletti and D. Pimentel (eds.), *Biotic Diversity in Agroecosystems*, pp. 3–23. Amsterdam: Elsevier.

Pate, J., 1991. Press Release. Newswire, Washington, D.C.

Pathak, M. D. 1975. Utilization of insect-plant interactions in pest control. In D. Pimentel (ed.), *Insects, Science and Society*, pp. 121–148. New York: Academic Press.

Patric, J. H. 1976. Soil erosion in the eastern forest. *Journal of Forestry* 74: 671–677.

———. 1980. Effect of wood products harvest on forest soil and water relations. *Journal of Environmental Quality* 9: 73–80.

Patric, J. H., J. O. Evans, and J. D. Helvey. 1984. Summary of sediment yield data from forested land in the United States. *Journal of Forestry* 82: 101–104.

Patton, W. P., and R. D. Lacewell. 1977. Outlook for Energy and Implications for Irrigated Agriculture. *Texas A&M University, Water Resources Institute Technical Report No. 87*. College Station, TX: Texas A&M University.

Pendleton, S., 1991. U.S. security, way of life hang on stable oil flow. *The Christian Science Monitor* 6.

Pereira, A. 1983. Employment implications of ethanol production in Brazil. *International Labour Review* 122: 111–127.

Peschka, W. 1987. The status of handling and storage techniques for liquid hydrogen in motor vehicles. *International Journal of Hydrogen Energy* 12: 753–764.

Petersen, B., M. J. Kelly, B. Poe, B. Weaver, and L. Hargan. 1982. Mites and Collembola from adjacent overgrazed and ungrazed pastures in Jackson County, Illinois. *Transactions of the Illinois State Academy of Science* 75: 193–199.

Phillipson, J. 1966. *Ecological Energetics*. London: Arnold.

Pillay, T.V.R. 1990. *Aquaculture Principles and Practices*. Oxford, UK: Fishing New Books.

Pimentel, D. 1961. Animal population regulation by the genetic feedback mechanism. *American Nature*, 95: 65–79.

———. 1968. Population regulation and genetic feedback. *Science* 159: 1432–1437.

———. 1974. Energy use in world food production. *Environmental Biology* 74 (1).

———. 1976. Crisi energetica e agricoltura. In *Enciclopedia della Scienza e della Tecnica*, pp. 251–266. Milan: Mondadori.

———. 1977a. Ecological basis of insect pest, pathogen and weed problems. In J. M. Cherrett and G. R. Sagar (eds.), *The Origins of Pest, Parasite, Disease and Weed Problems*, pp. 3–31. Oxford: Blackwell.

———. 1977b. Biomass energy conversion: ecological, economic, and social constraints. Final Report for the Energy Research Analysis Division, National Science Foundation, Washington, D.C.

——— (ed.). 1980. *Handbook of Energy Utilization in Agriculture*. Boca Raton, FL: CRC Press.

———. 1988. Herbivore population feeding pressure on plant host: feedback evolution and host conservation. *Oikos* 53: 289–302.

————. 1989. Agriculture and ecotechnology. In W. J. Mitsch and S. E. Jorgensen (eds.), *Ecological Engineering: An Introduction to Ecotechnology*, pp. 103–125. New York: John Wiley & Sons.

————. 1990. Environmental and social implications of waste in U.S. agriculture and food sectors. *Journal of Agricultural Ethics* 3: 5–20.

———— (ed.). 1991a. *Handbook of Pest Management in Agriculture*. 3 volumes. Boca Raton, FL: CRC Press.

————. 1991b. Ethanol fuels: energy security, economics, and the environment. *Journal of Agricultural and Environmental Ethics* 4: 1–13.

————. 1991c. Diversification of biological control strategies in agriculture. *Crop Protection* 10: 243–253.

————. 1992. Competition for land: development, food, and fuel. In M. A. Kuliasha, A. Zucker, and K. J. Ballew (eds.), *Technologies for a Greenhouse-Constrained Society*, pp. 325–348. Boca Raton, FL: Lewis Publishers.

———— (ed.). 1993. *World Soil Erosion and Conservation*. Cambridge, UK: Cambridge University Press.

Pimentel, D., and N. Beyer. 1976. Energy inputs in Indian agriculture. Unpublished data at Cornell University, Ithaca, NY.

Pimentel, D. and M. Burgess. 1980. Energy inputs in corn production. In D. Pimentel (ed.), *Handbook of Energy Utilization in Agriculture*, pp. 67–84. Boca Raton, FL: CRC Press.

Pimentel, D., and C. W. Hall (eds.). 1989. *Food and Natural Resources*. San Diego: Academic Press.

Pimentel, D., and L. Levitan. 1986. Pesticides: amounts applied and amounts reaching pests. *BioScience*, 36: 86–91.

Pimentel, D., and M. Pimentel. 1979. *Food, Energy and Society*. London: Edward Arnold.

Pimentel, D., and A. Warneke. 1989. Ecological effects of manure, sewage sludge and other organic wastes on arthropod populations. *Agricultural Zoology Reviews* 3: 1–30.

Pimentel, D., and Dazhong Wen. 1990. Technological changes in energy use in U.S. agricultural production. In C. R. Carrol, J. H. Vandermeer and P. M. Rosset (eds.), *Agroecology*, pp. 147–164. New York: McGraw Hill.

Pimentel, D., L. E. Hurd, A. C. Bellotti, M. J. Forester, I. N. Oka, O. D. Sholes, and R. J. Whitman. 1973. Food production and the energy crisis. *Science* 182: 443–449.

Pimentel, D., S. A. Levin, and A. B. Soans. 1975a. On the evolution of energy balance in exploiter-victim systems. *Ecology* 56: 381–390.

Pimentel, D., W. Dritchillo, J. Krummel, and J. Kutzman. 1975b. Energy and land constraints in food-protein production. *Science* 190: 754–761.

Pimentel, D. et al., 1975c. Potential for energy conservation in agricultural production. Report (#40) prepared by the Council for Agricultural Science and Technology for the U.S. Senate Committee of Agriculture and Forestry, Ames, Iowa.

Pimentel, D., E. C. Terhune, E. C. Dyson-Hudson, S. Rochereau, R. Samis, E. Smith, D. Denman, D. Reifschneider, and M. Shepard. 1976. Land degradation: Effects on food and energy resources. *Science* 194: 149–155.

Pimentel, D., D. Nafus, W. Vergara, D. Papaj, L. Jaconetta, W. Wulfe, L. Olsvig, K. Frech, M. Loye, and E. Mendoza. 1978. Biological solar energy conversion and U.S. energy policy. *BioScience* 28: 376–382.

Pimentel, D., P. A. Oltenacu, M. C. Nesheim, J. Krummel, M. S. Allen, and S. Chick. 1980a. The potential for grass-fed livestock: resource constraints. *Science* 207: 843–848.

Pimentel, D., E. Garnick, A. Berkowitz, S. Jacobson, S. Napolitano, P. Black, S. Valdes-Cogliano, B. Vinzant, E. Hudes and S. Littman. 1980b. Environmental quality and natural biota. *BioScience* 30: 750–755.

Pimentel, D., M. A. Moran, S. Fast, G. Weber, R. Bukantis, L. Balliett, P. Boveng, C. Cleveland, S. Hindman, and M. Young. 1981. Biomass energy from crop and forest residues. *Science* 212: 1110–1115.

Pimentel, D., C. Fried, L. Olson, S. Schmidt, K. Wagner-Johnson, A. Westman, A. M. Whelan, K. Foglia, P. Poole, T. Klein, R. Sobin, and A. Bochner. 1983a. Biomass energy: environmental and social costs. Environmental Biology Report 83–2, Cornell University, Ithaca, NY.

Pimentel, D., S. Fast, D. Gallahan, and M. A. Moran. 1983b. The energetic and environmental aspects of utilizing crop and forest residues for biomass energy. Final Report for U.S. Department of Energy, Washington, D.C.

Pimentel, D., L. Levitan, J. Heinze, M. Loehr, W. Naegeli, J. Bakker, J. Eder, B. Modelski, and M. Morrow. 1984a. Solar energy, land and biota. *SunWorld* 8: 70–73, 93–95.

Pimentel, D., C. Fried, L. Olson, S. Schmidt, K. Wagner-Johnson, A. Westman, A. Whelan, K. Foglia, P. Poole, T. Klein, R. Sobin, and A. Bochner. 1984b. Environmental and social costs of biomass energy. *BioScience* 34: 89–94.

Pimentel, D., W. Jackson, M. Bender, and W. Pickett. 1986a. Perennial grains: an ecology of new crops. *Interdisciplinary Science Review* 11: 42–49.

Pimentel, D., D. Wen, S. Eigenbrode, H. Lang, D. Emerson, and M. Karasik. 1986b. Deforestation: Interdependency of fuelwood and agriculture. *Oikos* 46: 404–412.

Pimentel, D., J. Allen, A. Beers, L. Guinand, R. Linder, P. McLaughlin, B. Meer, D. Musonda, D. Perdue, S. Poisson, S. Siebert, K. Stoner, R. Salazar, and A. Hawkins. 1987. World agriculture and soil erosion. *BioScience* 37: 277–283.

Pimentel, D., A. F. Warneke, W. S. Teel, K. A. Schwab, N. J. Simcox, D. M. Ebert, K. D. Baenisch, and M. R. Aaron. 1988. Food versus biomass fuel: socioeconomic and environmental impacts in the United States, Brazil, India, and Kenya. *Advances in Food Research* 32: 185–238.

Pimentel, D., L. E. Armstrong, C. A. Flass, F. W. Hopf, R. B. Landy, and M. H. Pimentel. 1989. Interdependence of food and natural resources. In D. Pimentel and C. W. Hall (eds.), *Food and Natural Resources*, pp. 31–48. San Diego: Academic Press.

Pimentel, D., L. McLaughlin, A. Zepp, B. Lakitan, T. Kraus, P. Kleinman, F. Vancini, W. J. Roach, E. Graap, W. S. Keeton, and G. Selig. 1991. Environmental and economic impacts of reducing U.S. agricultural pesticide use. In D. Pimentel (ed.), *Handbook of Pest Management in Agriculture*, Vol. I, pp. 679–718. Boca Raton, FL: CRC Press.

Pimentel, D., U. Stachow, D. A. Takacs, H. W. Brubaker, A. R. Dumas, J. J. Meaney, J. O'Neil, D. E. Onsi, and D. B. Corzilius. 1992a. Conserving biological diversity in agricultural/forestry systems. *BioScience* 42: 354–362.

Pimentel, D., N. Brown, F. Vecchio, V. La Capra, S. Hausman, O. Lee, A. Diaz, J. Williams, S. Cooper, and E. Newburger. 1992b. Ethical issues concerning potential global climate change on food production. *Journal of Agricultural and Environmental Ethics* 5: 113–146.

Pimentel, D., U. Stachow, D. A. Takacs, H. W. Brubaker, A. R. Dumas, J. J. Meaney, J. O'Neil, D. E. Onsi, and D. B. Corzilius. 1992c. Biological diversity in agricultural/forestry systems. Environmental Biology Report 92–1. Cornell University, Ithaca, NY.

Pimentel, D., H. Acquay, M. Biltonen, P. Rice, M. Silva, J. Nelson, V. Lipner, S. Giordano, A. Horowitz, and M. D'Amore. 1992d. Environmental and economic costs of pesticide use. *BioScience* 42: 750–760.

Pimentel, D., J. Allen, A. Beers, L. Guinand, A. Hawkins, R. Linder, P. McLaughlin, B. Meer, D. Musonda, D. Perdue, S. Poisson, R. Salazar, S. Sieber, and K. Stoner. 1993a. Soil erosion and agricultural productivity. In D. Pimentel (ed.), *World Soil Erosion and Conservation*, pp. 277–292. Cambridge: Cambridge University Press.

Pimentel, D., C. Kirby, and A. Shroff. 1993b. The relationship between "cosmetic" standards for foods and pesticide use. In D. Pimentel and H. Lehman (eds.), *The Pesticide Question: Environment, Economics, and Ethics*, pp. 85–105. New York: Chapman and Hall.

Pimentel, D., M. Herdendorf, S. Eisenfeld, L. Olander, M. Carroquino, C. Corson, J. McDade, Y. Chung, W. Cannon, J. Roberts, L. Bluman, and J. Gregg. 1994a. Achieving a secure energy future: environmental and economic issues. *Ecological Economics* 9 (3): 201–219.

Pimentel, D., Harman, R., Pacenza, M., Pecarsky, J. and Pimentel, M. 1994b. Natural resources and an optimum U.S. and world population. *Population and Environment* 15 (5): 347–369.

Pimentel, D., C. Harvey, P. Resosudarmo, K. Sinclair, D. Kurz, M. McNair, S. Crist, L. Sphpritz, L. Fitton, R. Saffouri, and R. Blair. 1995. Environmental and economic costs of soil erosion and conservation benefits. *Science* 267: 1117–1123.

Pimentel, D., J. Houser, E. Preiss, O. White, H. Fang, L. Mesnick, T. Barsky, S. Tariche, J. Schreck, and S. Alpert. 1996. Water resources: Agriculture, the environment, and society. *BioScience* (in press).

Pluijm, T. van der. 1982. Energy versus food? Implications of macro-economic adjustments on land-use patterns: the ethanol programme in Brazil. *Boletin de Estudios Latinoamericanos y del Caribe* 33: 85–106.

Podgwaite, J. D., and R. W. Campbell. 1972. The disease complex of the gypsy moth. II. Aerobic bacterial pathogens. *Journal of Invertebrate Pathology* 20: 303–308.

Political and Economic Planning (PEP). 1955. *World Population and Resources.* London: Political and Economic Planning.

Population Crisis Committee (PCC). 1989. *Population.* Washington, D.C.: Population Crisis Committee.

———. 1990. *Population.* Washington, D.C.: Population Crisis Committee.

Population Reference Bureau (PRB). 1977. *1977 World population data sheet.* Washington, D.C.: PRB, Inc.

———. 1983. *1983 World Population Data Sheet.* Washington, D.C.: PRB, Inc.

———. 1990. *1990 World Population Data Sheet.* Washington, D.C.: PRB, Inc.

———. 1991. *1991 World Population Data Sheet.* Washington, D.C.: PRB, Inc.

———. 1993. *1993 World Population Data Sheet.* Washington, D.C.: PRB, Inc.

———. 1995. *World Population Data Sheet.* Washington, D.C.: PRB, Inc.

Postel, S. 1989. *Water for Agriculture: Facing the Limits.* Worldwatch Paper No. 93. Washington, D.C.: Worldwatch Institute.

Power, A. G. 1989. Agricultural policies and the environment: The case of Costa Rica. Committee on US–Latin American Relations, Cornell University, Ithaca, NY. *CUSLAR Newsletter,* October 10–17.

Power, J. F., and R. I. Papendick. 1985. Organic sources of nutrients. In O. P. Engelstad (ed.), *Fertilizer Technology and Use,* pp. 503–520. Madison, WI: Soil Science Society of America.

Pradhan, S. 1971. Revolution in pest control. *World Science News* 8: 41–47.

Prescott-Allen, R., and C. Prescott-Allen. 1986. *The First Resource.* New Haven, CT: Yale University Press.

Price, P. W. 1975. *Evolutionary Strategies of Parasitic Insects and Mites.* New York: Plenum.

————. 1988. An overview of organismal interactions in ecosystems in evolutionary and ecological time. *Agriculture Ecosystems and. Environment.* 24: 369–377.

Price, P. W., C. E. Bouton, P. Gross, B. A. McPheron, J. N. Thompson, and A. Weis. 1980. Interactions among three trophic levels: Influence of plants on interactions between insect herbivores and natural enemies. *Annual Review of Ecology and. Systematics* 11: 41–65.

PSAC. 1965. *Restoring the Quality of Our Environment.* Report of the Environmental Pollution Panel, November. Washington, D.C.: President's Science Advisory Committee.

————. 1967. *The World Food Problem.* Washington, D.C.: President's Science Advisory Committee.

Purvis, G., and J. P. Curry. 1984. The influence of weeds and farmyard manure on the activity of Carabidae and other ground-dwelling arthropods in a sugar beet crop. *Journal of Applied Ecology* 21: 271–283.

Putnam, J. J., and J. E. Allshouse. 1991. Food Consumption, Prices, and Expenditures, 1968–89. *ERS Statistical Bulletin* No. 825. Washington, D.C.: US Department of Agriculture.

Pyke, M. 1970. *Man and Food.* New York: McGraw-Hill.

Rachie, K. O. 1983. Intercropping tree legumes with annual crops. In P. A. Huxley (ed.), *Plant Research and Agroforestry,* pp. 103–116. Nairobi: ICRAF.

Rader, N., 1989. Power surge. In J. Naar (ed.), *Design for a Liveable Planet.* New York: Harper and Row, pp. iv–1.

Rand, M., and A. Clarke. 1990. The environmental and community impacts of wind energy in the U.K. *Wind Engineering* 14: 319–330.

Randrianarijaona, P. 1983. The erosion of Madagascar. *Ambio* 12: 308–311.

Rappaport, R. A. 1968. *Pigs for the Ancestors: Ritual in the Ecology of a New Guinea People.* New Haven: Yale University Press.

————. 1971. The flow of energy in an agricultural society. *Scientific American* 225: 116–132.

Rat von Sachverstandigen für Umweltfragen (RSU). 1985. *Umweltprobleme der Landwirtschaft.* Kohlhammer, Stuttgart, Germany.

Raw, F. 1967. Arthropoda (except Acari and Collembola). In: A. Burges and F. Raw (Eds.), *Soil Biology,* pp. 323–362. London: Academic Press.

Rawitscher, M., and J. Mayer 1977. Nutritional outputs and energy inputs in seafoods. *Science* 198: 261–264.

Reddy, A.K.N., and J. Goldemberg. 1991. Energy for the developing world. In J. Piel (ed.), *Energy for Planet Earth,* pp. 59–71. W. H. Freeman and Co., New York.

Register, W. D., and L. M. Sonneburg. 1973. The vegetarian diet. *Journal of the American Dietetic Association* 62: 253.

Reid, W. V., and K. R. Miller. 1989. *Keeping Options Alive: The Scientific Basis for Conserving Biodiversity.* Washington, D.C.: World Resources Institute.

Reifsnyder, W. E., and H. W. Lull. 1965. Radiant energy in relation to forests. Technical Bulletin No. 1344. Washington, D.C.: U.S. Department of Agriculture, Forest Service.

Reitz, H. J. 1980. Energy use in U.S. citrus production and harvesting. In D. Pimentel (ed.), *Handbook of Energy Utilization in Agriculture,* pp. 285–289. Boca Raton, FL: CRC Press.

Repetto, R. 1990. Deforestation in the tropics. *Scientific American* 262 : 36–42.

Repetto, R. C., and M. Gillis. 1988. *Public Policies and the Misuse of Forest Resources.* Cambridge, UK: Cambridge University Press.

Revelle, R. 1986. Personal communication. University of California at San Diego, La Jolla, CA.

Rhoades, D. F. 1985. Offensive-defensive interactions between herbivores and plants: Their relevance in herbivore population dynamics and ecological theory. *American Naturalist* 125: 205–238.

Ricaud, R. 1980. Energy input and output for sugarcane in Louisiana. In D. Pimentel (ed.), *Handbook of Energy Utilization in Agriculture,* pp. 135–136. Boca Raton, FL: CRC Press.

Rice, R. M., J. S. Rothacher, and W. F. Megahan. 1972. Erosional consequences of timber harvesting: an appraisal. In *Proceedings of the National Symposium on Watersheds in Transition,* pp. 321–329. Fort Collins, CO: American Water Resources Association.

Richards, B.N. 1974. *Introduction to the Soil Ecosystem.* New York: Longman.

Richter, G. 1983. Aspects and problems of soil erosion hazard in the EEC countries. In A. G. Pendergast (ed.), *CEC Soil Erosion and Conservation Symposium Proceedings,* pp. 9–18. Florence, Italy: Commission of the European Communities.

Ricklefs, R. E. 1987. Community diversity: relative role of local and regional processes. *Science* 235: 167–171.

Risser, J. 1981. A renewed threat of soil erosion: it's worse than the Dust Bowl. *Smithsonian* 11: 120–122, 124, 126–130.

Ritschard, R. L., and K. Tsao. 1978. *Energy and Water Use in Irrigated Agriculture During Drought Conditions.* Berkeley, CA: Lawrence Berkeley Lab., University of California.

Roberts, E. B., and R. M. Hagan. 1975. *Energy Requirements of Alternatives in Water Supply, Use and Conservation: A Preliminary Report.* Davis, CA: University of California, Department of Land, Air and Water Resources.

———. 1977. *Energy Requirements of Alternatives in Water Supply, Use, and Water Quality Control in California.* Final Report, Lawrence Livermore Labs, Water

Science and Engineering Section. Davis, CA: University of California, Department of Land, Air and Water Resources.

Robinson, W. E., R. Nowogrodzki, and R. A. Morse. 1989. The value of honey bees as pollinators of U.S. crops. *American Bee Journal* 129: 477–487.

Rochereau, S. 1976. Energy analysis and coastal shelf resource management; nuclear power generation vs. seafood protein production in the Northeast region of the U.S. Ph.D. thesis. Cornell University, Ithaca, NY.

Rochereau, S., and D. Pimentel 1978. Energy tradeoffs between Northeast fishery production and coastal power reactors. *Journal of Energy* 3: 545–589.

Rogers, M., J. Hoelslor, and K. DeGrant. 1991. *Environmental Cost Factors and Utility Decision Making for PV Systems.* 22nd IEEE Photovoltaics specialists Conference 1991. Los Angeles, CA: IEEE.

Römkens, M.J.M., D. W. Nelson, and J. V. Mannering. 1973. Nitrogen and phosphorus composition of surface runoff as affected by tillage method. *Journal of Environmental Quality* 2: 292–295.

Rose, D. J., and M. M. Miller. 1983. *Global Energy Futures and CO_2 Induced Climate Change.* Cambridge, MA: MIT Report. Division of Policy Research and Analysis, NSF.

Rosen, L. and R. Glasser. 1992. *Climate Change and Energy Policy.* New York: American Institute of Physics.

Rosen, M. A., and D. S. Scott. 1988. Energy and energy analyses of the cogenerational potential for fuel cell systems. In T. N. Veziiroglu and A. N. Prosenko, (eds.), *Hydro Energy Progress VII: Proceedings 7th World Energy Conference, Moscow 1988,* pp. 1523–1531. New York: Pergamon Press.

Rosenthal, G. A. 1986. The chemical defenses of higher plants. *Scientific American* 254 : 76–81.

Royal Swedish Academy of Sciences (RSAS). 1975. *Energy Uses.* Presented at Energy Conference, Aspenasgarden, October 27–31. Stockholm, Sweden: Royal Swedish Academy of Sciences.

Russell, B. 1961. *An Outline of Philosophy.* Cleveland: World Publishing.

Rutger, J. N., and W. R. Grant. 1980. Energy use in rice production. In D. Pimentel (ed.), *Handbook of Energy Utilization in Agriculture,* pp. 93–98. Boca Raton, FL: CRC Press.

Ruthenberg, H. 1968. *Smallholder Farming Development in Tanzania.* M‚nchen, Germany: Weltforum Verlag M‚nchen.

———. 1971. *Farming Systems in the Tropics.* Oxford: Clarendon Press.

Safley, L. H., D. W. Nelson, and P. W. Westermann. 1983. Conserving manurial nitrogen. *Transactions of the ASAE* 26: 1166–1170.

Sahlins, M. 1972. *Stone Age Economics.* Chicago: Aldine-Atherton.

Sailer, R. I. 1983. History of insect introductions. In C. L. Wilson and C. L. Graham (eds.), *Exotic Plant Pests and North American Agriculture*, pp. 15–38. New York: Academic Press.

Samples, K. C. 1983. An economic appraisal of sail-assisted commercial fishing vessels in Hawaiian waters. *Marine Fisheries Review* 45: 50–55.

Sanchez-Sierra, G., and A. Umana-Quesada. 1984. Quantitative analysis of the role of biomass within energy consumption in Latin America. *Biomass* 4: 21–41.

Sargent, S. L. 1981. Solar Ponds: Status of the Technology and National Program. Presentation Summaries Solar Thermal Energy Systems Research and Advance Development Program Review. Oakland: Solar Energy Research Institute Publications.

Satchell, M. 1992. The rape of the oceans. *U.S. News and World Report* (June 22): 64–75.

Sauer, E. L., and H.C.M. Case. 1954. Soil conservation pays off. Results of ten years of conservation farming in Illinois. *University of Illinois Agricultural Experiment Station Bulletin* 575.

Schaefer, H., and G. Hagedorn. 1992. Hidden energy and correlated environmental characteristics of PV power generation. *Renewable Energy* 2: 159–166.

Schaffer, H. C., L. E. Barger, and H. E. Kumpf. 1989. The driftnet fishery in the Fort Pierce–Port Salerno area off southeast Florida. *Marine Fisheries Review* 51: 44–49.

Schipper, L., 1991. Energy saving in the U.S. and other wealthy countries: Can the momentum be maintained? In J. W. Tester, D. O. Wood, and N. A. Ferrari (eds.), *Energy and the Environment in the 21st Century:* Proceedings of the Conference Held at the Massachusetts Institute of Technology in Cambridge, MA, March 26–28, 1990. Cambridge, MA: The MIT Press.

Schneider, S. H. 1989. *Global Warming: Entering the Greenhouse Century*. San Francisco: Sierra Club Books.

Schroder, H. 1985. Nitrogen losses from Danish agriculture—Trends and consequences. *Agriculture Ecosystems and Environments* 14: 279–289.

Schultz, J. C. 1983a. Habitat selection and foraging tactics of caterpillars in heterogenous trees. In R. F. Denno and M. S. McClure (eds.), *Variable Plants and Herbivores in Natural and Managed Systems*, pp. 61–90. New York: Academic Press.

———. 1983b. Impact of variable plant defensive chemistry on susceptibility of insects to natural enemies. In P. Hedin (ed.), *Plant Resistance to Insects*, pp. 37–54. Washington, D.C.: American Chemical Society.

Schuman, G. E., R. G. Spomer, and R. F. Piest. 1973. Phosphorus losses from four agricultural watersheds on Missouri Valley loess. *Soil Science Society of America Proceedings* 37: 424–427.

Schurr, S. M., J. Darmstadter, H. Perry, W. Ramsay and M. Russell. 1979. *Energy in America's Future: The Choices Before Us.* A Study Prepared for RFF National Energy Strategies. Baltimore: Johns Hopkins University.

Scott, T. W. 1985. Personal communication. Department of Agronomy, Cornell University, Ithaca, NY.

Scott, W. G. 1982. Energy and fish harvesting. In *Proceedings of the Fishing Industry Energy Conservation Conference,* pp. 1–34. New York: Society of Naval Architects and Marine Engineers.

Segal, A., J. Manisterski, G. Fishbeck, and I. Wahl. 1980. How plant populations defend themselves in natural ecosystems. In J. G. Horsfall and E. B. Cowling (eds.), *Plant Disease,* pp. 75–102. New York: Academic Press.

Service, R. 1962. *Primitive Social Organization.* New York: Random House.

Shah, M. M., G. Fischer, G. M. Higgins, A. H. Kassam, and L. Naiken. 1985. *People, Land and Food Production-Potentials in the Developing World.* Laxenburg, Austria: International Institute for Applied Systems Analysis.

Shang, Y. C. 1992. Penaeid markets and economics. In A. W. Fast and L. J. Lester (eds.), *Marine Shrimp Culture: Principles and Practices,* pp. 589–604. Amsterdam: Elsevier.

Shannon, M. C. 1984. Breeding, selection, and the genetics of salt tolerance. In R. C. Staples and G. H. Toenniessen (eds.), *Salinity Tolerance in Plants,* pp. 231–254. New York: John Wiley & Sons.

Shapouri, H., J. A. Duffield, and M. S. Graboski. 1995. *Estimating the Net Energy Balance of Corn Ethanol.* Washington, D. C.: USDA, Agricultural Economic Report No. 721.

Sharma, A. 1987. *Resources and Human Well-Being: Inputs from Science and Technology.* Calcutta: Indian Science Congress Association.

Sheinkopf, K., 1991. PV potential. *Independent Energy* 21: 80–83.

———. 1989. Passive cooling. In D. A. Andrejko (ed.), *Assessment of Solar Energy Technologies.* Boulder, CO: ASES.

Siemens, J. C., and W. R. Oschwald. 1978. Corn-soybean tillage systems: erosion control, effects on crop production, costs. *Transactions of the American Society of Agricultural Engineers,* 21: 293–302.

Sillman, S., and P. J. Samson. 1990. Impact of methanol-fueled vehicles on rural and urban ozone concentrations during a region-wide ozone episode in the midwest. In W. L. Kohl (ed.), *Methanol as an Alternative Fuel Choice: An Assessment,* pp. 121–137. Washington, D.C.: Johns Hopkins Foreign Policy Institute.

Silva, J.R.C., M. A. Coelho, E.G.S. Moreira, and P.R.O. Neto. 1985. Efeitos da erosao na produtividade de dois solos da classe la tossolo vermelho-amarelo. *Cien. Agron. Fortaleza* 16: 55–63.

Singh, R. P. 1986. Energy accounting of food processing operations. In R. P. Singh (ed.), *Energy in Food Processing*, pp. 19–68. Amsterdam: Elsevier.

Sinha, C. S. 1992. Renewable energy programmes in India: A brief review of experience and prospects. *Natural Resources Forum* 16: 305–314.

Skinrood, A. C., and P. E. Skvarna. 1986. Three years of test and operation at Solar One. In M. Becker (ed.), *Solar Thermal Receiver Systems*, pp. 105–122. Berlin: Springer-Verlag.

Slesser, M., and C. Lewis. 1979. *Biological Energy Resources*. New York: Halsted Press.

Slobodkin, L. B. 1960. Ecological energy relationships at the population level. *American Naturalist* 94: 213–236.

Sloggert, G. 1985. *Energy and U.S. Agriculture: Irrigation Pumping 1974–1983*. Washington, D.C.: Agricultural Economics, USDA.

Smerdon, E. T. 1974. *Energy Conservation Practices in Irrigated Agriculture*. Denver: Sprinkler Irrigation Association Annual Technical Conference.

Smil, V. 1984. On energy and land. *American Scientist* 72 : 15–21.

Smith, D. D. 1946. The effect of contour planting on crop yield and erosion losses in Missouri. *Journal of the American Society of Agronomy* 38: 810–819.

Smith, D. R. 1987. The wind farms of the Altamont Pass area. *Annual Review of Energy* 12: 145–183.

Smith, D. R., and M. A. Ilyin. 1991. Wind and solar energy, costs and value. In American Society of Mechanical Engineers 10th Annual Wind Energy Symposium, pp. 29–32.

Smith, F. A. 1991. *Transportation in America: statistical analysis of transportation in the United States*. Waldorf, MD: Eno Transportation Foundation, Inc.

Smith, J. W. 1991. The Atlantic and Gulf menhaden purse seine fisheries: Origins, forecasting. *Marine Fisheries Review* 53 (4): 20–41.

Smith, K. R., A. L. Aggarwal, and R. M. Dave. 1983. Air pollution and rural biomass fuels in developing countries: A pilot study in India and implications for research and policy. *Atmospheric Environment* 17 : 2343–2362.

Snyder, D. P. 1976. Field crops costs and returns from farm cost accounts. *Agricultural Economic Research Report* 25 (1976). Ithaca, NY: Cornell University Agricultural Experiment Station.

———. 1977. Cost of production—update for 1976—on muck onions, potatoes, sweet corn, dry beans, apples. *Agricultural Economic Research Report,* 11 (1977). Ithaca, NY: Cornell University, Agricultural Experiment Station.

Soileau, J. M., B. F. Hajek, and J. T. Touchton. 1990. Soil erosion and deposition evidence in a small watershed using Cesium-137. *Soil Science Society of America Journal* 54: 1712–1719.

Sourie, J.-C., and L. Killen. 1986. *Biomass: Recent Economic Studies.* London and New York: Elsevier Applied Science Publishers.

Soussan, J. 1988. Energy and the environment: How poor people cope. In *Primary Resources and Energy in the Third World*, pp. 58–80. London: Routledge.

Southgate, D. 1990. The causes of land degradation along "spontaneously" expanding agricultural frontiers in the third world. *Land Economics* 66: 93–101.

Southwood, T.R.E., V. C. Moran, and C.E.J. Kennedy. 1982. The richness, abundance and biomass of the arthropod communities. *Journal of Animal Ecology.* 51: 635–649.

Sparks Commodities. 1990. *Impacts of the Richardson Amendment to H.R. 3030 on the U.S. Agricultural Sector.* McLean, VA: Sparks Commodities, Inc., Washington Division.

Spewak, P. C. 1988. Analyzing the effect of economic policy on solar markets. In R. E. Wesdt and F. Kreith (eds.), *Economic Analysis of Solar Thermal Energy Systems*, pp. 167–204. Cambridge, MA: MIT Press.

Spomer, R. G., R. F. Piest, and H. G. Heinemann. Soil and water conservation with western Iowa tillage systems. *Transactions of the American Society of Agricultural Engineers*, 19: 108–112.

Spurr, S. H. 1982. Energy Policy in Perspective—Solutions, Problems, and Prospects: Proceedings of a Symposium. Lyndon B. Johnson School of Public Affairs, University of Texas, Austin.

Stadelman, R. 1940. Maize cultivation in northwestern Guatemala. In *Contributions to American Anthropology and History, No. 33.* Carnegie Institute of Washington, Publication 523, pp. 83–263.

Stafford, D.A. 1983. Methane from farm wastes and energy recovery. In D. L. Wise (ed.), *Fuel Gas Developments*, pp. 1–17. Boca Raton, FL: CRC Press.

Stanford, G. 1977. *Energy Conservation.* Cedar Hill, TX: Agro-City Inc.

Stanford Research Institute. 1972. *Patterns of Energy Consumption in the United States.* Stanford, CA: Stanford Research Institute.

Stanhill, G. 1979. *Efficiency of Water, Solar Energy and Fossil Fuel Use in Crop Production.* Bet Dagan, Israel: The Volcani Center, Agricultural Research Organization, Report No. 134-E.

Starr, C., M. F. Searl, and S. Alpert. 1992. Energy sources: a realistic outlook. *Science* 256: 981–987.

Steele, A. 1991. An environmental impact assessment of the proposal to build a wind farm at Langdon Common in the North Pennines, U.K. *The Environmentalist* 11: 195–212.

Steinhart, C., and J. Steinhart. 1974. *Energy Sources, Use and Role in Human Affairs.* North Scituate, MA: Duxbury Press.

Stephenson, R. M. 1981. *Living with Tomorrow. A Factual Look at America's Resources.* New York: John Wiley & Sons.

Stoddard, F. S. 1991. California windfarms: an update for the 90s. In *Wind Energy Conversion 1991* (Proceedings of the 13th British Wind Association Conference on Wind Energy and the Environment), pp. 25–31. London: Mechanical Engineering Publications LDT.

Strong, D. R. 1974. Rapid asymptotic species accumulation in phytophagous insect communities: the pests of cacao. *Science* 185: 1064–1066.

———. 1979. Biogeographic dynamics of insect-host plant communities. *Annual Review of Entomology* 24: 89–119.

Strong, D. R., E. D. McCoy, and J. D. Rey. 1977. Time and number of herbivore species: the pests of sugarcane. *Ecology* 58: 167–175.

Stuckey, D., and C. Juma. 1985. Power alcohol in Kenya and Zimbabwe: A case study in the transfer of a renewable energy technology. UNCTAD/TT/61, UNCTAD secretariat.

Successful Farming. 1983. 19,000 lb of milk and 850 kwh of electricity, pp. D2–4, December.

Sugden, A. M., and G. F. Rands. 1990. The ecology of temperate cereal fields. *Trends in Ecological Evolution* 5: 205–206.

Sullivan, K. 1981. Overfishing and the new Law of the Sea. *OECD Observer* 129 (July 1991): 16–19.

Swank, W. T., and J. E. Douglass. 1977. Nutrient budgets for undisturbed and manipulated hardwood forest ecosystems in the mountains of North Carolina. In D. L. Correll (ed.), *Watershed Research in Eastern North America. A workshop to compare results,* pp. 343–363. Vol. I, February 28–March 3. Edgewater, MD: Smithsonian Institution, Chesapeake Bay Center for Environmental Studies.

Swanston, D. N., and C. T. Dyrness. 1973. Managing steep land. *Journal of Forestry* 71: 264–269.

Sweeney, J. L. 1990. Production costs for alternative liquid transportation fuels. In W. L. Kohl (ed.), *Methanol as an Alternative Fuel Choice,* pp. 295–324. Washington, D.C.: Johns Hopkins Foreign Policy Institute.

Szekely, F. 1982. Environmental impact of large hydroelectric projects on tropical countries. *Water Supply and Management* 6 (3): 233–242.

Szluha, A. T., J. M. Loar, R. R. Turner, and S. G. Hildebrand. 1979. An analysis of environmental impacts of water level fluctuations in reservoirs at hydroelectric sites. In *Waterpower* (Conference Proceedings, Oct. 1–3 by U.S. Army Corps of Engineers and U.S. Dept. of Energy), pp. 498–503. Washington, D.C.: Government Printing Office.

Tabor, H. Z., and B Doran. 1990. The Beith Ha'arva 5MWe solar pond power plant (SPPP)—Progress Report. *Solar Energy* 45: 247–253.

Tandon, B. N., K. Ramachandran, M. P. Sharma, and V. K. Vinayak. 1972. Nutritional survey in rural population in Kumaon Hill area, North India. *American Journal of Clinical Nutrition* 25: 432–436.

Teel, W. 1984. *A Pocket Directory of Trees and Seeds in Kenya*. Nairobi: KENGO.

———. 1987. Personal communication. Department of Natural Resources, Cornell University, Ithaca, NY.

Terborgh, J. W. 1988. The big things that run the world: a sequel to E.O. Wilson. *Conservation Biology* 2: 402–403.

Terhune, E. 1977. Energy use in crop production: vegetables. In R. A. Fazzolare and C. B. Smith (eds.), *Energy Use Management*, pp. 769–778. New York: Pergamon.

Thor, C., and E. Kirkendall. 1982. *Energy Conservation*. Manhattan, KS: Extension Engineering, Kansas State University.

Thurston, H. D. 1969. Tropical agriculture. A key to the world food crises. *BioScience* 19: 29–34.

Timmer, C. P., J. E. Austin, and G. Esteva. 1987. SAM, energy, and structural change in the agricultural sector. In J. E. Austin and G. Esteva (eds.), *Food Policy in Mexico:The Search for Self-Sufficiency*, pp. 260–297. Ithaca, NY: Cornell University Press.

Tolba, M. K. 1989. Our biological heritage under siege. *BioScience* 39: 725–728.

Townsend, R. E. 1985. An economic evaluation of restricted entry in Maine's soft shell clam industry. *North American Journal of Fisheries Management* 5: 57–64.

———. 1990. Entry restrictions in the fishery: a survey of the evidence. *Land Economics* 66: 359–378.

Tracey, T. R., C. E. Tyner, and E. R. Weber. 1989. Potential of advanced design solar central receiver power systems. In A. H. Fanney and K. O. Lund (eds.), *Solar Engineering 1989*, pp. 83–88. New York: ASME.

Troeh, F. R., J. A. Hobbs, and R. L. Donahue. 1991. *Soil and Water Conservation*. 2nd ed. Englewood Cliffs, NJ: Printice Hall.

Troeh, F. R., and L. M. Thompson. 1993. *Soils and Soil Fertility*. Fourth ed. New York: McGraw-Hill.

Twidell, J. 1987. *A Guide to Small Wind Energy Conversion Systems*. Cambridge: Cambridge University Press.

Union of Concerned Scientists (UCS). 1991. *America's Energy Choices: Investing in a strong Economy and a Clean Environment*. Cambridge, MA: UCS.

United Nations (UN). 1976. *Statistical Yearbook*, Vol. 30. New York: United Nations.

———. 1982. *Statistical Yearbook, 1980* (Vol. 33). New York: United Nations.

———. 1986. *Energy Balance and Electricity Profiles 1984*. New York: United Nations.

United Nations Environment Programme (UNEP). 1981. *Environment and Development in Africa.* Prepared by Environmental Development Action in the Third World (ENDA). Oxford: Pergamon Press.

————. 1985. *Energy Supply Demand in Rural Areas in Developing Countries.* Report of the Executive Director. Nairobi: UNEP.

————. 1991. *Freshwater Pollution. Global Environment Monitoring System.* Nairobi: UNEP.

United Nations Fund for Population Activities (UNFPA). 1991. Population and the Environment: The Challenges Ahead. New York: UNFPA.

U.S. Bureau of the Census (USBC). 1975. *Statistical Abstract of the United States 1975.* Washington, D.C.: U.S. Government Printing Office.

————. 1976. *Statistical Abstract of the United States 1976.* Washington, D.C.: U.S. Government Printing Office.

————. 1982. *Statistical Abstract of the United States 1982.* Washington, D.C.: U.S. Government Printing Office.

————. 1989. *Statistical Abstract of the United States 1989.* Washington, D.C.: U.S. Government Printing Office.

————. 1990. *Statistical Abstract of the United States 1990.* Washington, D.C.: U.S. Government Printing Office.

————. 1991. *Statistical Abstract of the United States 1991.* Washington, D.C.: U.S. Government Printing Office.

————. 1992a. *Statistical Abstract of the United States 1992.* Washington, D.C.: U.S. Government Printing Office.

————. 1992b. *Current Population Reports.* January edition. Washington, D.C.: USBC.

————. 1994. *Statistical Abstract of the United States 1993.* Washington, D.C.: U.S. Bureau of the Census. Washington, D.C.: U.S. Government Printing Office.

U.S. Congress (USC). 1990. National Energy Strategy: Hearing Before the Subcommittee on Oversight and Investigations of the Committee on Energy and Commerce. U.S. Congress, House of Representatives, Washington, D.C.

————. 1991. National Energy Strategy (Part I & II): Hearings before the Committee on Science, Space, and Technology. 102 Congress, 1st Session, Feb 26 and 28, 1991. U.S. Congress, U.S. House of Representatives, Washington, D.C.

U.S. Department of Agriculture (USDA). 1969. *A national program of research for bees and other pollinating insects and insects affecting man.* USDA, State Universities and Land Grant Colleges, Washington, D.C.

————. 1974. Fertilizer situation. *Economic Research Service, Report No. FS–4.* Washington, D.C.: U.S. Department of Agriculture.

———. 1975. *Agricultural Statistics 1975.* Washington, D.C.: U.S. Government Printing Office.

———. 1976. *Agricultural Statistics 1976.* Washington, D.C.: U.S. Government Printing Office.

———. 1977. *Firm Enterprise Data System.* Stillwater, OK: USDA, ERS, and Oklahoma State University Department of Agricultural Economics.

———. 1980. *America's Soil and Water: Conditions and Trends.* USDA Soil Conservation Service. Washington, D.C.: U.S. Government Printing Office.

———. 1981. Is Excess Irrigation Dribbling Away Profits? *Farmline* (Economic Statistics Service, USDA) 2: 10–11.

———. 1985. *Agricultural Statistics 1985.* Washington, D.C.: U.S. Government Printing Office.

———. 1986. *Fuel Ethanol and Agriculture: An Economic Assessment.* Agricultural Economic Report No. 562. Washington, D.C.: U.S. Department of Agriculture.

———. 1989a. *Agricultural Statistics 1989.* Washington, D.C.: U.S. Government Printing Office.

———. 1989b. *Economics of Ethanol Production in the United States.* USDA-AER–607. Washington, D.C.: U.S. Department of Agriculture.

———. 1989c. *The Second RCA Appraisal. Soil, Water, and Related Resources on Nonfederal Land in the United States. Analysis of Conditions and Trends.* Washington, D.C.: U.S. Department of Agriculture.

———. 1990. *Agricultural Statistics.* Washington, D.C.: Government Printing Office.

———. 1991a. *Agricultural Resources: Cropland, Water, and Conservation Situation and Outlook Report.* Economic Research Service, AR–23. Washington, D.C.: U.S. Department of Agriculture.

———. 1991b. *Agricultural Statistics 1991.* Washington, D.C.: Government Printing Office.

———. 1993. *Agricultural Statistics.* Washington, D.C.: Government Printing Office.

———. 1994. *Summary Report 1992 National Resources Inventory.* Washington, D.C.: Soil Conservation Service, USDA.

USDA-ARS and EPA-ORD. 1976. Control of Water Pollution from Cropland. EPA Report No. EPA–600/2–75–0266, ARS Report No. ARS-H–5–2. 2 vols. Washington, D.C.: U.S. Government Printing Office.

U.S. Department of Commerce (USDC). 1974. *Basic Economic Indicators:Atlantic and Pacific Groundfish.* U.S. Department of Commerce, Natitional Atmospheric and Oceanic Administration, National Marine Fisheries Service, Current Fish. Stat. No. 6271.

U.S. Department of the Interior (USDI). 1982. *Manual of Stream Channelization Impacts on Fish and Wildlife.* U.S. Department of Interior, Fish and Wildlife Service. Biological Services Program. July 1982.

U.S. Forest Service (USFS). 1977. Generalized erosion and sediment rates for disturbed and undisturbed forest land in the Northeast. U.S. Forest Service, USDA.

UWIG. 1992. *America Takes Stock of a Vast Energy Resource.* Golden, CO: Electric Power Research Institute.

Van Doren, D. M., W. C. Moldenhauer, and G. B. Triplett. 1984. Influence of long-term tillage and crop rotation on water erosion. *Soil Scientists Society of America Journal* 48: 636–640.

Van Harmelen, T., and G. Bakena. 1991. *Data Collection on Renewable Energy for EC CO2-Reduction Study.* Petten: Netherlands Energy Research Foundation ECN.

Vanderholm, D. H. 1975. Nutrient losses from livestock waste during storage, treatment and handling. In *Managing Livestock Waste*, pp. 282–285. St. Joseph, MI: American Society of Agricultural Engineers.

Vant-Hull, L. L. 1992. Solar thermal receivers: current status and future promise. *American Solar Energy Society* 7: 13–16.

Vergara, W., F. Welsch, and D. Serviansky. 1977. Utilization of food processing wastes. Unpublished data. Department of Food Science, Cornell University, Ithaca, NY.

Veziroglu, T. N., and F. Barbir. 1992. Hydrogen: the wonder fuel. *International Journal of Hydrogen Energy* 17: 391–404.

Vietmeyer, N. D. 1986. Lesser-known plants of potential use in agriculture and forestry. *Science* 232: 1379–1384.

Vitousek, P., P. R. Ehrlich, A. H. Ehrlich, and P. A. Matson. 1986. Human appropriation of the products of photosynthesis. *BioScience* 36: 368–373.

Voigt, C. 1984. Material and energy requirements of solar hydrogen plants. *International Journal of Hydrogen Energy* 9: 491–500.

Waggoner, P. E. 1984. Agriculture and Carbon Dioxide. *American Scientist,* 72: 179–184.

Walker, C., and R. M. Hunt. 1973. An analysis of costs for tomato production on rockdale soils of South Florida. *Economic Report* 45.

Walls, M. A., A. J., Krupnick, and M. A. Toman. 1989. *Ethanol Fuel and Non-market Benefits: Is a Subsidy Justified?* Discussion Paper ENR89–07. Washington, D.C.: Energy and Natural Resources Division, Resources for the Future.

Walsh, M. R. 1983. *An Assessment of Hydroelectric Power Potential in the United States.* Fort Belvoir, VA: Institute for Water Resources.

Walter, H. 1985. *Vegetation of the Earth and Ecological Systems of the Geo-biosphere.* New York: Springer-Verlag.

Ward, L. K., and K. H. Lakhani. 1977. The conservation of juniper: the fauna of food-plant island sites in southern England. *Journal of Applied Ecology* 14: 121–135.

Warner, J. L. 1991. Consumer guide to energy saving windows. *Solar Today* 5: 10–14.

Waters, J. R. 1991. Restricted access methods of management: Toward more effective regulation of fishing effort. *Marine Review* 53: 1–10.

Weaver, S. H. 1980. Energy use in the production of oats. In D. Pimentel (ed.), *Handbook of Energy Utilization in Agriculture*, pp. 85–92. Boca Raton, FL: CRC Press.

Webb, M., and J. Jacobsen. 1982. *U.S. Carrying Capacity. An Introduction.* Washington, D.C.: Carrying Capacity Network.

Weber, M. 1987. Federal marine fisheries management. In R. DiSilvestri (ed.), *Audubon Wildlife Report 1987*, pp. 131–145. San Diego: Academic Press.

Wen, Dazhong, and D. Pimentel. 1984. Energy inputs in agricultural systems of China. *Agriculture, Ecosystems, and Environment* 11: 29–35.

Wen, Dazhong, 1993. Soil erosion and conservation in China. In D. Pimentel (ed.), *World Soil Erosion and Conservation*. Cambridge: University of Cambridge Press.

West, R. E., and F. Kreith. 1988. *Economic Analysis of Solar Thermal Energy Systems.* Cambridge, MA: MIT Press.

Western, D. 1989. Conservation without parks: Wildlife in rural lanscape. In D. Western and M. C. Pearl (eds.), *Conservation for the Twenty-First Century*, pp. 158–165. New York: Oxford University Press.

Western, D., and M. C. Pearl. (eds.) 1989. *Conservation for the Twenty-First Century.* New York: Oxford University Press.

Westman, W. E. 1990. Managing for biodiversity. *BioScience* 40: 26–33.

Westoby, M., and R. T. Kase. 1974. Catfish farming and its economic feasibility in New York state. Unpublished manuscript, Ithaca, NY.

Westoby, M., J. Krummel, W. Dritschillo, and D. Pimentel. 1979. Direct and indirect use of land, labor, and fossil fuels by some animal production systems. *Environmental Biology Report 79–1*. Ithaca, NY: Cornell University.

Weston, R. F. 1987. *Particulate Emission from Residential Wood Combustion.* Washington, D.C.: U.S. Department of Energy.

Whipple, C. 1990. Historical trends in energy risk comparisons. *Journal of Energy Engineering*, 116: 163–177.

White, L. A. 1943. Energy and the evolution of culture. *American Anthropologist* 45: 355–354.

Whittaker, R. H., and G. E. Likens. 1975. The biosphere and man. In H. Lieth and R. H. Whittaker (eds.), *Primary Productivity of the Biosphere*, pp. 305–328. New York: Springer-Verlag.

Whittaker, R. H., and P. P. Feeny. 1970. Allelochemicals: Chemical interactions between species. *Science* 171: 757–770.

Wiggins, S. L. 1981. The economics of soil conservation in the Acelhuate River Basin, El Salvador. In R.P.C. Morgan (ed.), *Soil Conservation: Problems and Prospects*, pp. 399–415. Chichester: John Wiley & Sons.

Wijewardene, R. and P. Waidyanatha. 1984. Systems, techniques and tools. Conservation farming for small farmers in the humid tropics. Department of Agriculture, Sri-Lanka and the Commonwealth Consultative Group on Agriculture for the Asia-Pacific Region.

Williams, T. A., D. R. Brown, J. A. Dirks, K. K. Humphreys, and J. L. La Marche. 1990. Potential impacts of CO2 emission standards on the economics of central receiver power systems. In J. T. Beard and M. A. Ebadian (eds.), *Solar Engineering 1990*, pp. 1–6. New York: ASME.

Wilson, E. O. 1987. The little things that run the world. *Conservation Biology* 1: 344–346.

———— (ed.). 1988a. *Biodiversity*. Washington, D.C.: National Academy Press.

————. 1988b. The diversity of life. In H.J. DeBlij (ed.), *Earth '88: Changing Geographic Perspectives*, pp. 68–81. Washington, D.C.: National Geographic Society.

Winter, C. J. 1986. Hydrogen energy—Expected engineering break-throughs. In T. N. Veziroglu, N. Getoff and P. Weinzierl (eds.), *Hydrogen Energy Progress VI*, pp. 9–29. New York: Pergamon Press.

————. 1991. High temperature solar energy utilization after 15 years R&D: kick-off for the third generation technologies. In *Solar Energy Materials* 24: 26–39. Amsterdam: North Holland.

Winter, C. J., W. Meineke, and A. Neumann. 1991. Solar thermal power plants: No need for energy raw material—only conversion technologies pose environmental questions. In M. E. Arden, S.M.A. Burley, and M. Coleman (eds.), *1991 Solar World Congress*, pp. 1981–1986. Oxford: Pergamon Press.

Winter, C. J., and J. Nitsch. 1988. *Hydrogen as an Energy Carrier: Technologies, Systems, and Economy*. Berlin: Verlag.

Wischmeier, W. H. and Mannering, J. V. 1965. Effect of organic matter content of the soil on infiltration. *Journal of Soil and Water Conservation* 20: 150–152.

Wittwer, V., W. Platzer, and M. Rommell. 1991. Transparent insulation: an innovative European technology holds promise as one route to more efficient solar buildings and collectors. *Solar Today* 5: 20–22.

Wiviott, D. J., and S. B. Mathews. 1975. Energy efficiency comparison between the Washington and Japanese otter trawl fisheries of the Northeast Pacific. *Marine Fisheries Review* 37 (4): 21–24.

Woodwell, G. M., J. E. Hobbie, R. A. Houghton, J. M. Melillo, B. Moore, B. J. Peterson, and G. R. Shaver. 1983. Global deforestation: contribution to atmospheric carbon dioxide. *Science* 222: 1081–1086.

World Development Report 1995. Published for the World Bank. New York: Oxford University Press.

World Health Organization/United Nations Environment Programme. 1989. *Public Health Impact of Pesticides Used in Agriculture.* Geneva: WHO/UNEP

World Resources Institute (WRI). 1990. *World Resources: A Guide to the Global Environment.* New York: Oxford University Press.

———. 1991. *World Resources 1990–1991.* New York: Oxford University Press.

———. 1992. *World Resources 1992–1993.* New York: Oxford University Press.

———. 1994. *World Resources 1994–1995.* Washington, D.C.: World Resources Institute.

World Tables 1995. Published for the World Bank. Baltimore: Johns Hopkins University Press.

Worldwatch Institute. 1989. *State of the World.* Washington, D.C.: Worldwatch Institute.

———. 1992a. *State of the World 1992.* Washington, D.C.: Worldwatch Institute.

———. 1992b. *Vital Signs.* Washington, D.C.: Worldwatch Institute.

———. 1993. *State of the World 1993.* Washington, D.C.: Worldwatch Institute.

Wright, D. H. 1983. Species-energy theory: an extension of species-area theory. *Oikos* 41: 496–506.

———. 1990. Human impacts on energy flow through natural ecosystems, and replications for species endangerment. *Ambio* 19: 189–194.

Wright, L. L. 1990. *Role of New Wood Energy Crops in Mitigation of Fossil CO2 Emissions.* Conference on Biomass for Utility Applications, Tampa, FL. U.S. Department of Energy, Report No. CONF-p0103667 (NTIS No. DE 91012543).

Wyman, C. E., and N. D. Hinman. 1990. Ethanol: fundamentals of production from renewable feedstocks and use as a transportation fuel. *Applied Biochemestry and Biotechnology* 24/25: 735–753.

Yeager, R., and N. N. Miller. 1986. *Wildlife, Wild Death: Land Use and Survival in Eastern Africa.* Albany, NY: State University of New York Press.

Yoho, N. S. 1980. Forest management and sediment production in the South—a review. *Southern Journal of Applied Forestry* 4: 27–35.

Zachar, D. 1982. *Soil Erosion.* New York: Elsevier Scientific.

Zangrando, F., and D. H. Johnson. 1985. *Review of SERI Solar Pond Work.* Golden, CO: Solar Energy Research Institiute.

Zeuner, F. E. 1963. *A History of Domesticated Animals.* New York: Harper and Row.

Zweibel, K. 1993. Thin-film photovoltaic cells. *American Scientist* 81: 362–369.

INDEX